*Marriage,
the Family,
and Personal
Fulfillment*

Prentice-Hall, Inc., Englewood Cliffs, New Jersey 07632

Marriage, the Family, and Personal Fulfillment

THIRD EDITION

DAVID A. SCHULZ

University of Delaware

STANLEY F. RODGERS

Library of Congress Cataloging in Publication Data

Schulz, David A. [date]
  Marriage, the family, and personal fulfillment.

  Bibliography: p.
  Includes index.
  1. Marriage—United States. 2. Family—United
States. 3. Interpersonal relations. 4. Self-
actualization (Psychology) I. Rodgers, Stanley F.,
[date].   II. Title.
HQ728.S363 1985   306.8'0973   84-11651
ISBN 0-13-559402-2

Marriage, the Family, and Personal Fulfillment
THIRD EDITION
David A. Schulz and Stanley F. Rodgers

Editorial/production supervision: *Edith Riker*
Interior design: *Judith Winthrop and Edith Riker*
Manufacturing buyer: *John Hall*
Photo research: *Anita Duncan*
Cover design: *Christine Gering-Wolf*
Cover photograph: *L.D. Gordon, Image Bank*

Printed in the United States of America

10 9 8 7 6 5 4 3 2 1

ISBN 0-13-559402-2 01

Prentice-Hall International, Inc., *London*
Prentice-Hall of Australia Pty. Limited, *Sydney*
Editora Prentice-Hall do Brasil, Ltda., *Rio de Janeiro*
Prentice-Hall Canada Inc., *Toronto*
Prentice-Hall of India Private Limited, *New Delhi*
Prentice-Hall of Japan, Inc., *Tokyo*
Prentice-Hall of Southeast Asia Pte. Ltd., *Singapore*
Whitehall Books Limited, *Wellington, New Zealand*

CHAPTER OPENING QUOTATIONS and PHOTO CREDITS

1. 1 Corinthians 13:1–2   Ken Karp

2. Excerpted from *Becoming Partners: Marriage and Its Alternatives*, p. 220, by Carl Rogers, Copyright © 1972 by Carl Rogers. Used with permission of Delacorte Press. Edward Lettau, Photo Researchers, Inc.

3. Michael Montaigne, *Essays*, Bk. II, Ch. 1.   Yvonne Freund, Photo Researchers, Inc.

4. Abraham Maslow, *The Farther Reaches of Human Nature* (New York: The Viking Press, 1971), p. 242.   Teri Leigh Stratford

5. Anonymous   Joseph Szabo, Photo Reserachers, Inc.

6. Socrates; James Hillman, *The Myth of Analysis* (New York: Harper & Row, 1970) Bob Combs, Photo Reserachers, Inc.

7. Herant Katchadourian and Donald T. Lunde, *Fundamentals of Human Sexuality* (New York: Holt, Rinehart & Winston, Inc., 1972), p. 23. Copyright © 1972 by Holt, Rinehart & Winston, Inc. Reprinted by permission.   Erika Stone, Photo Researchers, Inc.

8. SEICUS, *Sexuality and Man* (New York: Charles Scribner's Sons, 1970), p. 44. Ed Lettau, Photo Researchers, Inc.

9. Martin Buber, *Between Man and Man* (Boston Beacon Press, 1955). Ken Karp

10. Mary Calderone   Fredrik D. Bodin, Stock, Boston

11. Reprinted by permission of William Morrow & Co., Inc. from *Coming of Age in Samoa*, p. 105, by Margaret Mead. Copyright © 1928, 1955, 1961 by Margaret Mead. The Bettmann Archive, Inc.

12. R.A. Nicholson, *Rumi* (London: Allen & Unwin, Ltd., 1950), pp. 122–23. Reprinted by permission.   Susan Rosenberg, Photo Researchers, Inc.

13. Benjamin Spock, "Women and Children: Male Chauvinist Spock Recants—Almost," in Louise K. Howe, ed., *The Future of the Family* (New York: Simon and Schuster, 1972), p. 155. Copyright © 1971 by Benjamin Spock. Reprinted by permission of the Robert Lescher Literary Agency, New York.   Erika Stone, Photo Researchers, Inc.

14. Erik Erikson, *Childhood and Society* (New York: W. W. Norton, 1963), p. 405. Reprinted by permission. Maggie Kuhn, "Liberating Aging," *New Age*, Feb. 1979, p. 34.   Hella Hammid, Photo Researchers, Inc.

15. Michael Phillips, *The Seven Laws of money* (New York: Random House, 1975). Teri Leigh Stratford

16. Nicholas von Hoffman, commentary in *The Washington Post*, June 5, 1970. Copyright © *The Washington Post*. Reprinted by permission.   Bruce Roberts, Photo Researchers, Inc.

17. Nathaniel Hawthorne, *The Blythedale Romance, The Scarlet Letter*.   Michael Kagen, Monkmeyer Press

18. Suzanne Keller, "Does the Family Have a Future?" *Journal of Comparative Family Studies*, Spring, 1971, p. 14.   Berthomier, Photo Researchers, Inc.

Contents

4 *Conflict and Cooperation in Partnerships* 63

5 *Dating, Hanging Around, and Hanging Out* 91

Preface

Daniel Yankelovich claims that we are rediscovering commitment and defining new rules for it as we close out this century. If this is so, and we believe that it is, it is in no small measure the result of the experimentation in alternative lifestyles that has been going on over the past three decades. This experimentation is not as much in the news today as it was when we published the first edition of this text. Communes and multiple marriages are still with us. Some, such as *The Farm* in Tennessee, are flourishing. Mormons still practice polygamy in Utah illegally. Swingers make the newspapers from time to time, such as, for example, their recent effort to hold a convention in an Ohio motel. The singles population continues to grow. Even more unusual lifestyles are a part of everyday life. But more fundamentally, less than 7 percent of all American families are what we once regarded as "traditional"—ones in which *he* works, *she* takes care of the home and children, and *they* live together in a sexually exclusive monogamous union for life. We have become more of a culturally pluralistic society in spite of our discomfort about this.

The recession of the late 1970s, the lingering sense of economic insecurity, the uncertain character of the international scene, and the increasing divorce rate all make us aware of the value of intimate partnerships. The discovery that none of these partnerships can last unless the couple is willing to work at their partnership makes it apparent that there are costs in maintaining them.

In the third edition, we have reduced the material on communes and multiple marriages and added a new chapter on love in order to accommodate the love research that is beginning to accumulate in the social sciences. We have taken a different approach to such matters as that delightful lovestyle of the middle ages, amour. We have looked again at the works of Abraham Maslow and found new insights on "Being love" that we did not appreciate before. We still find him well worth defending against his critics. In previous editions, we have talked about women's liberation. In this edition, we talk a bit about men's liberation. According to some observers, men will not be truly liberated until they discover the source of energy and decisiveness that lies within them and must be approached through an excursion through the dark side of their nature. This dark side is often discovered through compassion—the willingness to suffer with another. It is more often portrayed in myth and folk tale than in social science, which does not yet have the term as a part of its vocabulary.

Whatever the form of the partnership, we attempt to focus on an assessment of its quality in order to better describe the apparent risks, costs, and benefits likely to be experienced by those willing to live in such a way.

I am grateful to the reviewers for their valuable comments: Richard A. Hanson, North Dakota State University; Patrick C. McKenry, the Ohio State University; and Duane W. Smith, Dutchess Community College.

Though I speak with the tongues of men and of angels, and have not love, I am become as sounding brass, or a tinkling cymbal. And though I have the gift of prophecy, and understand all mysteries, and all knowledge, and though I have all faith, so that I could remove mountains, and have not love, I am nothing.

—St. Paul

*Marriage,
the Family,
and Personal
Fulfillment*

Introduction

Loving **partnerships** do not just happen; they must be developed consciously.[1] Couples who have been married for many years often tell us that it takes a lot of work to keep a marriage going. Young people who are just getting married often say that they intend to make their partnership flexible enough to meet their personal needs even though such flexibility may change their whole idea of what marriage ought to be like. Such couples are taking an experimental approach to marriage.

Whatever the cultural climate, whatever the age, marriage has always been a venture into the unknown for the young couple about to form such a partnership. Whatever society prescribes as an ideal for their marriage, whatever concept of marriage they may have acquired through observation of their parents or other couples, their marriage is something unique, if only in that they are two unique individuals. Whether their marriage works, whether they can change it to meet their evolving needs, whether they can work out a mutually satisfying and fulfilling partnership—these are never predetermined. Marriage, therefore, is always an adventure, whether it is entered into with awareness or simply accepted as a "natural" thing to do.

No book about marriage can eliminate the unknowns from such an adventure. Regardless of what we know from the experience of others about getting married or forming partnerships, such knowledge cannot simply be applied to particular cases the way general principles of, say, geometry or physics can be applied to specific instances. Knowledge may help us reduce the uncertainty of forming partnerships, but it can never eliminate it. Accordingly, this book is not intended to provide a set of guidelines about how to form loving, intimate partnerships—although some guidelines are given from time to time. It is intended to increase your knowledge of some of the issues involved so that however you feel about getting married—or not getting married—you may shape your own partnerships with greater awareness. In the last analysis, the "how to do it" of partnerships can be worked out only in the context of a developing partnership.

ON LOVING AND BEING LOVED

Love is impossible to define adequately. St Paul's famous remarks about love do not tell us what it is so much as they tell us how important it is. And the importance of love is something we all know about, even if sometimes by virtue of the fact that we have experienced so little of it. Nevertheless, even without defining what it is, we can say something about what it means to love and be loved.

Love Is Intimate Self-Disclosure

Part of what is commonly meant when we say that love is a very personal thing is that it involves the intimate disclosure of a unique self. In intimate partnerships our personal idiosyncracies are very important in determining whether or not the partnership develops fruitfully.

A growing partnership is one in which this self-disclosure can take place at ever-deepening levels of self-awareness. The nakedness of lovers is symbolic of their history of self-disclosure. We need not assume that this nakedness demands the type of complete self-disclosure in which there can be no secrets. We need merely assume that in a loving partnership the partners feel able to reveal much more of themselves than they normally do. They feel free to "be themselves" with each other.

A growing partnership is one in which self disclosure can take place at ever deepening levels of self-awareness (Laimute E. Druskis)

Love and Personal Fulfillment

Personal growth and self-actualization are important dimensions of loving partnerships. As we conceive of them, partnerships have lost their vitality, if not their love, when such growth and self-actualization do not occur. To say this is to expect a great deal of partnerships such as marriage, for in our Western tradition we have not always expected marriage to play a significant role in the personal growth of those who participate in it. Indeed, many people contend that it is expecting too much of marriage or any other form of partnership.

When two people grow in a partnership, isn't it just as likely that they will grow apart and "fall out of love" as that they will grow together in increasing love? We all know of partnerships in which the partners grew apart because one partner developed faster than the other. This happens to couples before marriage as well as after, and even to unmarried partners. What are we to do about this?

A common response is to dismiss the importance of personal growth on the ground that a partnership should be a "team effort" and that self-actualization and personal growth are essentially selfish goals. Maybe it really isn't important that marriages retain the vitality that brought the partners together in the first place. Maybe the joys of growth and self-disclosure ought to be short-lived. After twenty-five years, perhaps it's a good thing for the partners in a marriage to settle for comfort and convenience rather than going through the perpetual adjustments that are needed when a relationship is growing. Growth, whenever it occurs, does not come about without struggle, and it often brings pain.

This is a very difficult matter indeed. Life would be a lot simpler if people could grow to greater self-actualization—if they could realize more and more of what they are capable of becoming—and at the same time find that their partnership was deepening and growing as a result. But this is not always possible.

It is a matter of fundamental values to assert that the personal growth of partners should not be sacrificed for the sake of keeping them together. This can be seen as a matter to be considered when one is entering into partnerships such as marriage, as well as a rule of thumb to be applied—but not necessarily always followed—when it looks as if the partners have to choose between their own personal fulfillment and a partnership.

Love Requires Relationship

At the same time we also know that love, even in self-actualizing people, is not strictly a personal matter. We cannot love unless we have experienced love.[2] The experience of **love** is fundamentally the awareness of being acceptable, worthy, and valuable as a person. At the level of relationship, it is a feeling of being in touch with others and potentially with all things in the universe. We commonly understand such feelings in terms of our relationship with others. The Greek word **storge** denotes the basic affection on which all other loves are thought to depend. Parents, relatives, and friends are common sources of storgic love, but storge is a component of all persisting loving partnerships.

There are quite different understandings of the nature of loving, however. Religious teachers throughout history, for example, have held that the most fundamental experience of love comes not from relations with other people, but from an inward experience of Being itself.[3] Such an experience has been described as bliss, enlightenment, mystery, or light. Within Christianity, the term **agape** is used to denote the love of God for human beings. It is a Christian contention that we are obligated to love others—indeed, that we can be commanded to love others because we have been loved by God.

Our present Western understanding of love, however, is more strongly sociopsychological. Whatever self-love we have acquired depends on our having been loved by others. Our parents, friends, and lovers have significantly shaped, if not totally determined, our capacity to love. Thus, our experience of having been loved provides us with prescriptions as to how we should go about our own loving. It is not possible for us to grow and develop unless our basic human need for love and acceptance has been met adequately.[4]

To most people, love means caring for others, looking after them, seeing to their well-being, "for richer, for poorer, in sickness and in health, . . . till death us do part."[5] People often assume that because caring is very much related to the amount of time spent with those we care for, the longer the relationship, the more caring there will be and the more loving. Thus, they ask: "Isn't it important that marriage be for life?" "Must not any partnership last a long time for it to become a deep and meaningful experience?" "After all, what do people know about love who have not had the responsibility of caring for another person over the years?" Indeed, caring is a significant part of what we mean by "working" at a marriage, and it is an important part of any intimate partnership. For this reason, this book has a lot to say about loving in partnerships. But such a conception of caring for others must be balanced by an awareness that the members of a partnership also must work toward their own self-actualization. Caring for one's partner is only half of the relationship, for it is also important to care for and nurture into being one's own creative, growing self.

Love and Suffering—Compassion

Our exploration of alternatives and our struggle to find more satisfying life styles has certainly not been in vain. One of the most valuable aspects of this searching thus far has been the recognition that any partnership requires commitment and effort if it is to grow and develop. We are discovering—some would say rediscovering—why this must be so. The process of self-actualization is neither an activity that can be carried on alone, nor one that is the result of some effortless unfolding of the human potential. Our experience once again tells us that it is unavoidably an interpersonal matter strongly affected by social and environmental factors. It is difficult, if not impossible, to be healthy in a sick society.

The old phrase "growing pains" takes on new meaning as we apply it to adults as well as children and see that a necessary part of every life is the provision of meaning for this pain. It could be said that we are coming to understand something about the positive value of suffering and developing a greater capacity for compassion.[6]

MARRIAGE IN AMERICA

In America, marriage is the social institution designated to harness the energy of an intimate partnership for the benefit of society as well as that of the marital partners. Marriage is always a social contract, although the social functions it fulfills are more prominent in some societies than in our own.[7] This is partly because we think of a marriage, ideally, as initiated and maintained simply for the benefit of two people who love each other. In our society, when two adults who are able to support themselves "fall in love," they are expected to get married.

High Expectations

Judging from statistics, marriage is a very popular partnership. In America today 67.8 percent of the men and 62.4 percent of the women between the ages of 18 and 75 are married.[8] These figures, however, are about 8 percent lower than they were in 1970. Because marriage is a social institution that has been around a long time, we have some widely accepted understandings about what it ought to be like. Most Americans see marriage as the deepest, most vital partnership in a person's life. We tend to look to it for an experience of growth and vitality that we hope will be richly rewarding to both husband and wife. These high expectations of marriage derive from the traditions of romanticism, Western Christian teachings about monogamy, concern for the preservation of private property, and our high regard for personal freedom.

But while we may be in some ways expecting greater things of marriage than we have in the past, we also are willing (or forced) to settle for much less. Study after study sadly concludes that marriage today is a quite

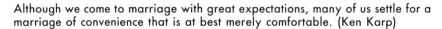

Although we come to marriage with great expectations, many of us settle for a marriage of convenience that is at best merely comfortable. (Ken Karp)

colorless affair. These studies suggest that many couples have settled for marriages of convenience that are at best merely comfortable because they have become routinized and demand little of the partners. If our understanding of what is happening is correct, more and more young people are forming an unfavorable image of marriage. On college campuses women talk of not marrying at all because of their distaste for domestic roles. Young men and women are deferring marriage longer and longer.

Our impersonal society generates a high level of loneliness. Part of our apparent eagerness to eventually marry, therefore, may be seen not as a desire to marry, but as an attempt to escape from the loneliness and impersonality of our society. Americans thus tend to come to marriage with high expectations and great needs at a time when the institution of marriage is being subjected to enormous social pressures that make it difficult for people to realize their expectations.

Particularly hard hit are romantic young people who fall in love and marry, only to wake up and discover that "the honeymoon is over." Their response to this realization will shape the future of their marriage. They can pretend that it is not in fact over, simulate happiness, and live a long time without acknowledging the lack of a deep, intimate partnership. They can cease to expect very much of their marriage and settle for a more or less comfortable routine characterized by lifelessness rather than vitality. They can persist in peaceful coexistence "for the sake of the children" or because there is nothing better in sight. Another alternative, however, is to face their disillusionment and fashion new expectations. Inherent in this alternative is a demand that the couple utilize the skills of creative encounter—which are not easy to acquire in our society—and, perhaps, that they consider a totally new kind of partnership.

In any event, part of the satisfaction to be derived from any of these alternatives results from the expectations that have been realized. The higher the expectation, the greater the difficulty of realizing it. High expectations are easier to hold when it is not necessary to face the problems of living together. This issue is resolved only in part by college students who choose to live together before marriage.

Very few societies expect marriage to depend so heavily on the personal choice and skills of the partners. In many societies, marriages are arranged. In such societies, couples are not expected to be in love before they get married—though they may come to love each other after they have been married for a number of years. Marriage, in these societies, is primarily a social contract uniting kinship groups. The couple are expected to work out a reasonable way of managing their household, raising their children, and fulfilling their other social obligations. But in all these endeavors they are greatly assisted by their kin. In contrast, we expect marriage not only to meet many social needs (such as the bearing and raising of children and the establishment of a fundamental economic partnership that is the major consumer unit in our economy), but also to fulfill most of the personal needs of the partners. Furthermore, the partners are expected to work these matters out as best they can with comparatively little assistance from others. Thus, our romantic young couple faced with the decision to marry or not marry must make that decision largely alone. They are then expected to realize a much higher set of expectations in regard to what this marriage will accomplish for them than is true in most societies—also largely on their own.

If the couple should decide to have children—as most do in our society—they are likely to experience further difficulties. In the view of some experts on the family, parenthood has been romanticized even more than marriage in our culture. Children are idealized as natural assets, and the considerable impact they have on the partnership is often ignored or minimized in discussions of the subject. Although parenthood can mean a fuller life, prospective parents are seldom warned that children may sap the energy and attention of the marital partners, who are more fully responsible for their upbringing in our culture than is true in most societies.

Two results of our placing high and unrealistic expectations on partnerships such as marriage while those partnerships are being subjected to enormous social stress are the increasing divorce rate and the search for new kinds of partnership that demand new and different life styles. Thus, the understanding of what a marriage ought to be like is changing for many people.

Marriage Is Changing

Only a minority of American families are traditional in the sense that they are composed of a husband who is the sole breadwinner and a wife who is homemaker and childrearer. Some might say that economic necessity has produced a different division of labor, though not yet a just one. The percentage of adults who remain single continues to increase, and as the population ages, married couples find more and more time in their marriage that is not devoted to children. A small but still increasing percentage of couples never intend to raise children, and those that do agree that two is the ideal number. There are, in fact, many ways to define an acceptable partnership in the United States, and many of these ways are nonmarital. The sense of excitement and adventure that characterized the exploration of alternative lifestyles seems to have passed. An impressionistic sampling of media coverage and journal articles about marriage and family life in the United States suggests that there is widespread recognition that every partnership has its problems and that none are capable of bringing about the golden age of intimacy that only a few years ago seemed to be just around the corner.

As a political issue, "the family" has attracted considerable attention. The most vocal ideology asserts that our problems are fundamentally moral ones that can be properly addressed only after we give up our exploration of alternatives and follow the Bible's guidance on marriage and family life. Even some humanists are attacking the vision of self-actualization (or personal fulfillment) because, they contend, it has produced a "culture of narcissism" in an age of permissiveness. It is a time of taking stock as well as of knee-jerk reaction.[9] But however much the vision of alternative life styles may be dimmed or tarnished, it is evident that we remain convinced of the value of a number of "new rules" for America. The majority of Americans no longer disapprove of married women working, or of men or women remaining single. Premarital sex is no longer condemned by the majority, nor is the notion of husband and wife taking separate vacations. The importance attached to work as the central element in life, has declined dramatically, yet most men and women state that they would continue working even if they did not have to. There is a notable increase in a "hungering for community."

Marriage as a Socially Constructed Reality

One of the characteristics of lovers is a tendency to withdraw in order to be alone. We smile at their need for privacy when they gaze into each other's eyes, imagine their joy in getting to know one another, and sometimes say that they are "off in their own little world." Peter Berger and Hansfried Kellner underscore the importance of this common remark. They contend

> The plausibility and stability of the world, as socially defined, is dependent upon the strengths and continuity of significant relationships in which conversation about the world can be continually carried on. . . . . Marriage thus posits a new reality. The individual's relationship with this new reality, however, is a dialectical one—he acts upon it, in collusion with the marriage partner, and it acts back upon both him and the partner, welding together their reality.[10]

We have some awareness of how words take on meaning in an intimate relationship, though most of it may seem trivial. Nicknames such as "slats" or "sink" are given by friends in their efforts to distinguish us from all others. Terms of endearment such as "sweets" or "sweatheart" have particular meanings for particular relationships, though they have public meaning as well. Sometimes lovers play with each other by assigning names to each other's genitals, thus enabling them to carry on "private" conversations in public without others catching on. In a more subtle sense, however, the very common word "love" means something different to each couple because their experience of loving and caring for each other is unique. The sum total of their affection, concern, and commitment as manifested in their caring behavior for each other over the years gives meaning to the word—the most important meaning the word may have in their lives. When love is used for the first time in a relationship that has very little history, we have good reason to question what it might mean.

Finally, when a partnership of long duration ends, a large part of the pain and suffering experienced derives from the fact that this intimate taken-for-granted-world has been radically changed. The meaning of all that is true, good, and beautiful can no longer be shared, and it may be that the event ending the partnership was such (for example, betrayal) that the whole significance and value of this world is called into question.

Three Ways of Knowing about Marriage

Without wanting to imply that marriage is the only viable long-term partnership, let us consider how it is possible to know about it.

Convention. This partnership is a very ancient one. Within the Jewish tradition, marriage has existed for nearly four thousand years. Christian marriage has been around at least since the time of Augustine (about 1,600 years). Within the Eastern religions, the ceremony is much older. Conventional marriages change, but the distinctive aspects of this way of knowing about marriage is that we tend to accept the form we are familiar with as authoritative. Marriage, most persons who call themselves Christians would say, is a lifelong commitment between a man and a woman to live together "in sickness and in health" as helpmates who can be trusted to be there for each other. A lot of other expectations associated with conventional Christian marriage are not as widely considered to be essential—the generation of children, sexual exclusivity, the traditional division of labor between husband and wife which binds the former to the job and the latter to the home, and the elaborate set of social expectations about what it means to be a good wife or a good husband. The essence of Christian marriage, however, is commitment. The model for significance of this commitment is in the New Testament—in the understanding of the love and compassion of Jesus, whom the disciples called the Christ.

All conventional views of marriage are supported by myth, ritual, and symbols that establish the significance of this partnership within a particular tradition. Christian marriage, for example, is supported by the story of Adam and Eve, the Marriage Feast at Cana, and the teachings of St Paul, as well as the image of the Christ and the teachings of the Christian churches. There are two very different ways in which we can look at these myths and symbols.

They can be thought of as literal statements about marriage that must be accepted as universal truths, even though we know that such truths were revealed through one particular tradition. Marriage, in this way of looking at things, is an ethnic idea.[11] People who think about marriage in this way tend to believe that their conventional way of defining what it is or ought to be is the only true way of doing so. Such an attitude is difficult to change because the sense of security of the individual is invested in a particular convention. So when women demand a different division of labor and greater equality in the home, for example, they are told that the Bible says they must "obey" their husbands, whom Jesus had made head of the household to rule over them. Other ways of working out a marriage are threatening—especially if those who find other ways satisfying are apparently happy and prospering.

Another way of looking at marriage within a conventional framework, however, is to consider the myths, rituals, and symbols that give it meaning to be "ways" or "paths" that point toward the truth.[12] "Heaven is like a mountain top—there are many ways to reach it." In this way of looking at marriage, commitment may be expressed in different forms at different times. Marriage is an elementary idea that takes on new meaning in new situations. Its significance grows and develops. Thus marriage can accommodate divorce, the intention not to have children, and a redefinition of what it means to be a good husband or wife and still be an expression of commitment that is enriched by the traditional meanings associated with it. Those who think of marriage in this way are not as frightened by others who live differently, nor need they look down upon them as inferior human beings because they live in polygamous marriages or experiment in radically different forms of marriage such as the complex marriage practiced by the Oneida community in the nineteenth century.[13]

Marriage, in this approach, is not a divinely ordained form, ritual, or sacrament that cannot be altered because its sacredness lies in its particular expression. It is an experience of love and acceptance that has been conveyed through these forms—and the people who cherish them—and can be expressed in different forms in the future. When held as "ways," images and symbols invite associations and elaborations. They help us synthesize experience in the creation of meaningful worlds. When held as ethnic ideas, they exclude variation and function more like concepts that are more properly the product of enquiry.

Enquiry. In contrast to knowing about marriage through convention as ethnic idea or way, philosophical and scientific analysis tends to produce concepts that are useful because they exclude extraneous considerations. What is often sought in analysis is a concept or model that adequately defines what marriage is and that can yield hypotheses that can be used to test if this is so or not. The dictionary of anthropology defines marriage as

> The established institution for starting a family. Both monogamous and polygamous marriage is found. There is often an exchange of economic goods in a marriage, and involved is a legal, physical, and moral union between a man a woman, continuing through the raising of their children. Marriage regulates relations between the sexes, and helps establish the child's relation to the community. It is usually associated with a ceremony; magical, religious, social or civil, which formalizes the group's approval. In marriage, the children produced by the women are usually accepted as the legitimate offspring of the married couple.[14]

The effort here has been to define at such an abstract level that the definition can be applied to all known forms of marriage, and yet we can see right away that childless marriages are excluded from this definition, as are marriages between persons of the same gender. This definition might well capture the essential aspects of marriage in the ethnographic record, but clearly it does not encompass all known cases. Conceptual analysis seeks to generalize not on the basis of an assumed shared experience or meaning, but on the basis of a precisely defined concept that is testable. Those who favor the definitional approach tend to want to exclude exceptions in order to preserve the elegance of their definition, and might decide that a partnership between two persons of the same gender could not—should not—be called a marriage because such a partnership does violence to the accumulated evidence of what marriage has been in the past.

One of the problems in the scientific analysis of marriage is that some analysts want to say they are using concepts when in fact they are really using symbols. They want to claim precision when what is in fact compelling about their approach is its symbolic overtones. Much of the intensity of the recent debate over the nuclear family crisis resulted from the fact that the nuclear family is more of a symbol—in the West best expressed as the Holy Family—than a concept. Ironically, its symbolic value as a "building block" of society is probably greater than its utility as a scientific concept.

Personal Experience. The third, and often presumed infallible, way of knowing about marriage is through personal experience. One of the nice things about writing about marriage and the family is that most of us know about at least one marriage—our own or our parent's—intimately. If we have never been married, however, we do not know about marriage in the same way that two people who have been married know about it. Our parents' marriage may or may not be well understood by us, but in any case, it is not known through our own experience—it is known about.

Drawing upon one's own personal experience in partnerships other than marriage in order to anticipate what it will be like to be married is useful, but risky. What seems most real to us may not hold up when conditions change. If we want to generalize dogmatically from our own experience, we are likely to be blind to hazards in new partnerships.

On the other hand, what is produced from personal experience is "my story," which I ought to tell and ought to compare with the story of others. In good storytelling, one is free to decide if the story holds true in one's own case or not without offending the storyteller or feeling obliged to agree with the details of his tale. One generalizes as an artist might on the basis of the intensity of conviction and expression and invites others to see if they can. Those who are interested in studying about marriage often want to exclude their personal stories from their analysis. This has some utility in certain circumstances, but it is also important for an analyst to make use of personal experience in evaluating scientific studies of those institutions of which he or she has some personal knowledge. When the analysis does not ring true for you and you have experienced what is being analyzed, it is just

Most of us know about marriage through our own personal experience or that of our parents, but to infer on the basis of this experience alone what it will be like in a new partnership is a risky business. (Laimute E. Druskis)

as likely that the analysis is at fault as it is that your experience is unique. As a matter of course, students should evaluate all analysis of marriage on the basis of their own personal experience as well as other research efforts.

SUMMARY

We cannot love others if we do not love ourselves, and we are not able to love ourselves unless we have been loved. In condensed form, these seem to be the lessons learned from our experience of loving. Americans expect marriage to satisfy much more of the partners' need for love and acceptance than members of most societies typically expect. When we talk about marriage as a self-actualizing partnership, we are expecting even more; indeed, we may be expecting too much. Without doubt, marriage in its traditional form cannot meet these expectations for everyone, given the tremendous needs we bring to it and the enormous stress social forces place on it. At the moment both the marriage rate and the remarriage rate are declining, though the large majority of adults are married. Many people seem to be experimenting with modifications of traditional marriage, and a few are intentionally experimenting with alternative kinds of partnerships and quite different life styles. Whatever kinds of partnerships we develop, we must struggle to achieve some satisfactory balance between the needs of others and our need for personal fulfillment. Rather than seeing these changes in norms and behavior as symptoms of a "crisis," we choose to view them as having at least the potential for leading to creative alternative forms of partnership.

Marriage and what we expect of it are certainly changing, perhaps at a faster pace today than in the past. Precisely because it is changing, marriage can continue to offer the possibility for growth and development in a changing world. It is not likely that a return to pre-World War II norms and life styles—even if this were possible—would help us avoid the conflict and solve the problem of lack of intimacy and community. Greater cultural civility, greater tolerance for alternative life styles in others will help us discover new ways of living together in intimate partnerships. It can also help restore vitality to old life styles that are chosen intentionally rather than simply lived up to because society expects people to live up to them.

We can know about partnerships such as marriage in three distinctly different ways: We can know them through a tradition and accept the tradition as absolutely true or as a way to a deeper truth; we can know about them through scientific study seeking to discover general laws about them; and we can know about them through personal experience. All three should be used in evaluating how we choose to live in partnerships.

NOTES

1. The term *partnership* is used in this book to mean any human relationship in which there is a shared understanding of what is at stake in the relationship.

2. Useful books on the subject of love include Elaine Hatfield and G. William Walser, *A New Look at Love* (Reading, Mass.: Addison-Wesley, 1981); John Alan Lee, *The Colors of Love*, (Don Mills, Ont.: New Press, 1976); Rollo May, *Love and Will* (New York: Dell, 1969); Erich Fromm, *The Art of Loving* (New York: Bantam Books, 1970); C. S. Lewis, *The Four Loves* (New York: Harcourt, Brace, Jovanovich, Inc., 1960), and Paul Tillich, *Love, Power, and Justice* (New York: Oxford University Press, 1954).

3. Marvelous accounts of this inward encounter are provided in Philip Kapleu (ed.), *Three Pillars of Zen* (Boston: Beacon Press, 1965); and David Steindel-Rast, "The Monk in Us," in Michael Katz et al., *Earth's Answer* (New York: Harper & Row, 1977).

4. Abraham Maslow, *Toward a Psychology of Being*, 2nd ed. (New York: Van Nostrand Reinhold, 1968), p. 25; see also his *Motivation and Personality*, 2nd ed. (New York: Harper & Row, 1970).

5. *The Book of Common Prayer* (New York: Oxford University Press, 1952), p. 302.

6. James Hillman, *The Myth of Analysis* (New York: Harper & Row, 1972).

7. It is probably true that few societies place as much emphasis as ours on the personal choice of a couple who declare that they are "in love." See William Stephen's assessment in *The Family in Cross Cultural Perspective* (New York: Holt, Rinehart and Winston, 1963), pp. 190–207. Ralph Linton observes that

"most societies look upon marriage as a legal contract either between the individuals involved or between their respective families." Ralph Linton, *The Study of Man* (Englewood Cliffs, N.J.: Prentice-Hall, 1936), p. 177.

8. See, for example, the problems in managing privacy described in Paul Rosenblatt and Linda G. Budd, "Territoriality and Privacy in Married and Unmarried Cohabiting Couples," *Journal of Social Psychology*, 97 (1975): 67–76. See also chap. 5, pp. 100–104.

9. See Jerry Falwell, *Listen America* (New York: Bantam Books, 1981), and Christopher Lash, *The Culture of Narcissism* (New York: Norton, 1979).

10. Peter Berger and Hansfried Kellner, "Marriage as a Socially Constructed Reality," in Ruth Coser (ed.), *The Function of the Family*, 2nd ed. (New York: St Martin's, 1981), pp. 159, 165.

11. Joseph Campbell, *The Mask of God*, Vol. 4: *Creative Mythology* (New York: Penguin Books, 1977), p. 563ff.

12. Ibid., p. 564.

13. See the account in Maren Carden Lockwood, *Oneida: From Community to Corporation* (Baltimore: The Johns Hopkins University Press, 1973).

14. Charles Winick, *The Dictionary of Anthropology* (New York: New American Library, 1965).

I want to add that the concept of partnerships—married or not—as a vast and promising laboratory has been forced on me by my learnings from [my case studies]. I did not start with this idea at all. I tried to choose reasonably representative people. They did not—and do not—seem to me to be unusual couples or unusual persons, except for their surprising willingness to tell of their life as it is. Only gradually did I see that there is an enormous, exploring experiment going on all about us. What will be our stance toward it?

—Carl Rogers

2 on Becoming Partners

Although it is sometimes useful to talk about a monogamous instinct or the pair bonding that can be discerned in many species, the forming of partnership is a distinctly human adventure.[1] In our use of the word, a **partnership** is formed when two or more people come to recognize that they share common expectations about what each is to get out of a relationship. There is some form of a contract—written or unwritten—that is mutually acceptable. It may be that a couple decide to accept the conventional understanding of engagement and marriage, with its implications for what it means to be a good husband or a good wife taken for granted. Or they may spend a great deal of time thinking about what they want to get out of their partnership and may even draw up a special marriage contract in which they state very explicitly what they expect of each other. Partnerships may be entered into before or after marriage and may or may not include a married couple. The form of the partnership is not as important, in our view, as the process by which it is entered into and maintained.

In contrast to partnerships, relationships imply no implicit or explicit mutual understanding of what each expects of the other. Each may have her or his own agenda, but in a relationship they have not yet been able to share their expectations. Two people in a relationship may nevertheless know how to behave toward each other because they share the same or a similar culture. It is possible for a couple to marry and not develop a partnership simply because they have not *mutually agreed* to follow convention. They have simply followed it.

One of the most important functions of a partnership, we contend, is to help the partners become more fully what they can become—to self-actualize, in Abraham Maslow's words.[2] In spite of recent criticism, self-actualization should not be understood as selfish egotism or a new narcissism.[3] Although self-actualization can be corrupted to mean a moral obligation to meet any and all of one's personal needs, this is a gross misunderstanding.[4] Self-actualization is achieved, in Maslow's view, only after a person has received sufficient security, love, and acceptance from others, and has built up to an adequate measure of self-esteem as a result. Furthermore, an individual who has self-actualized will be inclined to offer the distinctive contributions that only she or he can make to others. Such people give out of the abundance of their being even though they may have very little material wealth. In this century, Mahatma Gandhi gave us a particularly powerful example of such self-actualization.

In this chapter, we will describe several significant issues relating to the process of becoming partners and suggest what is at stake in each. Since there are many ways of coping with these issues of everyday life, it follows that functional, vital, enriching partnerships may assume many forms—but not any and every form; some partnerships, for example, can be destructive.[5] In the discussion of these issues, we will provide a normative perspective that can help us compare the apparent costs, benefits, and risks of a variety of partnerships. Such a perspective can help us look more thoughtfully at what is going on between the partners in their struggle for self-actualization rather than concentrating on the form or structure their partnership might take. Perhaps we can achieve some insights into creating our own partnerships as a result.

BASIC HUMAN NEEDS

Self-actualization, according to Maslow, cannot occur until certain basic needs—which he calls deprivation needs—are met. The question of whether or not there *are* **basic human needs** is a subject of continuing debate in the

Belonging and acceptance are essential to human development just as food, air, and water are essential but on another level. (Will McIntyre, Photo Researchers, Inc.)

social sciences.[6] Obviously, food, air, water, shelter, and sex are essential for the survival of the individual and the species. These needs may be considered "basic" in the sense that they are common to all human beings.

Are there other basic human needs? Some social scientists contend that there are not, for they feel that human needs are shaped more by culture than by human nature.[7] For example, we often hear it said that a young child needs a certain amount of privacy—"a room of his or her own"—to grow into a healthy adult. In our society, with its emphasis on self-reliance, this may well be true. In other societies with different priorities, however, hundreds of millions of children have grown to be normal, healthy adults even though the idea of privacy for young people was unheard of. In other words, there may be a need for privacy in contemporary American culture, but this is not a basic human need. It is a need only in a specific sociocultural context. Then too, even though everyone must eat food in order to live, what is considered food and the ways in which it is procured, prepared, and eaten vary enormously from one culture to another.

Nevertheless, a number of social scientists have revived the notions of human nature and basic human needs. Human nature requires more than mere survival for its full development, they reason, so there must be needs that are higher than the simple biological needs and yet still qualify as basic human needs in that they are shared by all people regardless of culture. Abraham Maslow is one of those who hold this view.

As Maslow sees it, human beings have many needs in addition to the elementary biological needs. The most productive way of thinking of these needs is to imagine them arranged in a hierarchial order. The lower ones must be satisfied adequately before the higher ones can be realized, but all of them are important for full human development.[8] Maslow divides his hierarchy of needs into five levels:

1. self-actualization
2. self-respect and self-esteem
3. belongingness, love, and acceptance
4. safety and security
5. physiological

Why should these needs be arranged in a hierarchy? Because thinking about them in this way seems to more adequately describe the diversity in human capabilities and permits us to think of growth as a satisfying of progressively "higher" needs. Maslow was very interested in studying health in human beings, not illness. He wanted to describe what inspired people, rather than drove them. He believed that people who were meeting their needs to self-actualize were fuller, more complete, and healthier human beings—but in the process he redefined our conception of health. This notion of self-actualization is unacceptable to some social scientists because they believe it is highly biased in terms of upper-middle-class values. We will return to this point in a later section.

Physiological Needs

Who would argue that we cannot survive without adequate food, air, and water? It seems evident that these physiological needs are basic. The only argument at this level of gratification is what should rightly be considered as a biological or physiolgical need. Is sex, for example, a physiological need the same way that food or air is? It seems to be if we consider the needs of the human species—but is it a physiological need for an individual? If it is, it is certainly much more "flexible" than the others. Individuals vary greatly in their need of it and the same individual varies greatly in his or her need over the life cycle. So, is sex a physiological need or not?

Safety and Security

Our existence as living organisms depends on our satisfying the physiological needs for food, water, air, sex, and so on. Above these needs Maslow defines another very fundamental level of need which he labels "safety & security needs." Our well-being, indeed survival, depends on our success in obtaining sufficient shelter, clothing, and defense. Modern industrialized society has more than provided for these needs for most people. Yet even in the most affluent countries there are large numbers of desperately poor people who are still struggling to meet their needs for safety and security.

Because most Americans do not have to spend a great deal of their energy meeting these needs, they are able to turn a good deal of their attention to higher-level needs. People who are reasonably confident that they will be able to provide clothing and lodging for themselves and their families can more readily attend to satisfying their need to be accepted, their need for self-esteem, and their need to earn the respect of their peers.

The poor, however, are constantly preoccupied with the struggle to satisfy lower-level needs. Repeated frustration, continued deprivation of essentials, the sense of hopelessness and powerlessness associated with poverty go a long way toward making a person feel worthless, just as wealth and social status contribute to the feeling of self-respect, of "being somebody."

It takes a considerable amount of courage to be poor and still retain a positive attitude toward one's inner self. Because the higher-level needs are so intimately related to the ability to form and preserve successful human partnerships, it is no wonder that partnerships are difficult to maintain among those whose lower-level needs are not satisfied fully. Thus, marriages tend to break up more frequently among lower-class people than among those who are better off.[9] The continuing blows to the sense of self-esteem are but one of many factors that make it difficult to develop and maintain partnerships in the midst of poverty. In general, we must have a sense of repeated gratification and an expectation of continued reward before we are able to maintain a positive attitude toward ourselves. We must achieve an adequate sense of protection and security before we can risk growth in interpersonal relationships.

Belonging, Love, and Acceptance

The need for **belonging, love,** and **acceptance** cannot be met adequately until the need for safety and security has been satisfied. Our need for belonging, love, and acceptance derives from our nature as social creatures; it is what brings us into the human community. We achieve a sense of belonging by participating in a common way of life that includes at least a common language, a more or less common view of the world, and a more or less established social structure.

In the normal course of development, acceptance or belongingness is first discovered in the context of family life. In most families, affection and love are less contingent on an individual's accomplishments than is generally the case in society at large. This is especially true in advanced industrial societies, which value achievement and performance on the job. People who do not do the "right" things, are not adequately productive, or do not sufficiently conform to the expectations of others in such societies are quickly made to feel left out. Indeed, sociological studies of our society suggest that large numbers of people do in fact feel left out.[10]

Today the problems of belonging, love, and acceptance are compounded by the rapid rate of change in our society. Traditions are upset before the generation that formed them has died. New techniques, new faces, new expectations are the very stuff of our lives, making it increasingly difficult for modern men and women to feel that they "belong" to a community that is changing almost from day to day.[11] Less than 100 years ago a young person learned the values of his or her parents and then moved easily into the adult community. Today the values of one's parents may seem archaic to one's peers. Countless thousands of young men and women are caught in a conflict between the values of the two groups. They belong fully to neither, yet feel pulled toward each.

One of the tenderest tales of the life of C. G. Jung concerns his treatment of a young girl from a tiny village in Switzerland who had been sent to him by the village doctor because of an ailment he could not treat.[12] Jung soon discovered that she lived in a village that was enthusiastically striving to become modern and in its zeal ridiculed all the simple beliefs and customs that were natural to the girl. Jung sat with her for a few days, danced, sang songs with her, and listened to her stories with so much interest that soon she was delighted to tell him her stories. Soon she was well again, and he sent her back home. The doctor couldn't believe the recovery he saw, and when Jung said it was the result of just talking, listening, singing, and dancing with her, the doctor refused to believe it. But the girl never regressed. She had received sufficient acceptance from Jung to continue her development.

In a complex, rapidly changing, pluralistic society like ours, one must choose carefully among the values, ideals, and ideas one encounters. It is unlikely that anyone can manage to develop a consistent, wholly integrated world view that adequately encompasses our cultural heritage. Because each day we find many people who differ from us in their basic values and commitments, who hold different truths to be self-evident, the development of a consistent and satisfying set of values and beliefs becomes a difficult task. Yet it is a necessary task, for the things we value and the way we look at ourselves and our world determine, to a considerable extent, what we are able to see around us, how we feel about ourselves, and what we will do with our time and talents.

Self-Respect and Self-Esteem

There are two components to esteem needs: (1) a desire for competence, mastery, and a sense of adequacy in the face of the problems of life; (2) the desire for reputation or prestige. Ideally, one's reputation is based on one's achievement, but in fact there is usually a discrepancy between the two. It is particularly risky for an individual to take the praise of others more seriously than his or her own assessment of achievement, or to base one's sense of competence on one's reputation.

Obviously, the need for belongingness, love, and acceptance and the need for self-esteem and self-respect are intertwined in complex ways. In the first place, it is virtually impossible to develop a healthy sense of one's own worth without the aid, especially in one's formative years, of some powerful supportive institution such as a family or a group of peers. For example, the young girl who does not feel fully accepted by her parents because they wanted a boy often finds it extremely difficult to develop a high sense of her own worth as an adult. Similarly, the child of either sex who for some reason is rejected by peers in childhood may well suffer in adulthood from a low sense of self-esteem. This is why Maslow ranks belongingness lower on his hierarchy than self-esteem—the feeling of belonging, of being loved and accepted, is a prerequisite for the sense of self-esteem and self-respect.

Ideally, one's feelings of acceptance and belongingness and one's feelings of self-esteem and self-respect should be complementary, but in many cases they tend to become reciprocal. Many individuals seek to reinforce their sense of belongingness instead of moving on to develop a sense of their own value. These compulsive "joiners" let the group's acceptance of

Before we can develop adequate self-esteem we must feel that we are loved and that we truly belong to a community. (Maureen Fennelli, Photo Researchers, Inc.)

them replace their own acceptance of themselves. Conversely, compulsive "individualists" are people who can feel secure in their sense of themselves only when they oppose the group. Both of these extreme types represent unhealthy adjustments; the one sacrifices self-respect for the security that comes from being accepted, while the other is cut off from the community in order to preserve self-respect. Neither type can enjoy the secure sense of self-esteem that derives from a true sense of belongingness, of being loved and accepted.

Self-Actualization

In Maslow's hierarchy, all the previously discussed needs are categorized as "deprivation needs," meaning essentially that they are experienced as an absence within us.[13] When we are hungry, we need food in order to be full. When we feel rejected, we need acceptance from others and a sense of well-being in order to feel fully ourselves again. We even measure our sense of self-esteem by the world's standards—the things our culture values. As a result, all these things can be used to control us. Just as the behaviorist deprives rats of food in order to motivate them with cheese to learn how to solve the riddle of the maze, so others can motivate us by withholding those things that can fill our deprivation needs. More positively, these needs are more essential to the construction and maintenance of any society than police forces or armies. As a behaviorist who began his career seeking how to understand and control aggression through experimentation with animals, Maslow well understood the salience of such needs in our lives, and he in no sense belittled them.

However, he wanted to look at what was distinctively human and healthy and so he began to speak about the characteristics of Being. Self-actualization is a Being need. It is experienced as something positive, and its fulfillment is more like an unfolding of something within than a response to a reward from without. The gratification of this need enables us to participate consciously in the transformation of our society. In common speech we recognize something of this characteristic in those whom we say are "ahead of their time."

In describing self-actualization, Maslow uses words like "self-fulfillment, emotional maturity, individuation, productiveness, authenticity, full humanness."[14] For Maslow, these are indicators of health or wholeness in the human being which has previously been defined in the medical profession as the absence of symptoms.[15] Self-actualization is more than mere potential, it is a capacity in all of us. It has a dynamism all its own. Jung believed, for example, that the process of individuation was energized by the archetypes of the collective unconscious which are manifested in the dreams of individuals and also in the myths, rituals, and symbols of a culture.[16] It is therefore both a transpersonal process and a personal undertaking. Both Maslow and Jung believed that relatively few people realized this capacity in their everyday lives.

If we are born in poverty we have a harder time just meeting our deprivation needs than if we were born with greater resources. Andrew Buchannan, a 55-year-old black man in an urban ghetto, reflects on his life:

> I haven't done any good to my estimation. Some say I have, and I can see a few things. I hear people talk. They talk my talk. And I see some people using my ideas, so I feel in this way I've done a little good. But to me this is not what I would have liked to achieve, not to achieve what you call greatness, but something that would be outstanding and become institutionalized is what I would like to establish. When I could do something like this then I would think I have done something to my own satisfaction. . . . I would like to do this kind of thing for the benefit of the community . . . something that the community can use for years as long as the community exists. They can use particular programs because it's good and lasting. Way down in somebody's heart they would say "Old man Buchannan done that." I would be proud. This to me is like going to heaven. This to me means you had a good spirit.

The need to belong is so strong that many of us stifle our need to self-actualize in conforming to the wishes of others. Most of us think that we have "arrived" when we have achieved an adequate reputation or prestige or wealth. If we should feel dissatisfied even then, it is easier to discredit this discontent than it is to see it as a yearning to express something within us.

Society cannot directly reward our striving to self-actualize. We may become more productive as a result of striving to realize our potential, but the productivity is a by-product. Even though others may praise our creativity and resourcefulness, the praise cannot directly confirm our effort to self-actualize if for no other reason than this striving may well be expressed on other occasions in ways that society would disapprove. The truly creative artist often leads a bohemian life, but the mere leading of such a life cannot produce the creative artist.

Furthermore, it is incorrect to think of the self-actualizing person as necessarily happier than others, if we mean by happiness, the absence of anguish and suffering. The pursuit of the pleasure principle will not lead to self-actualization. In fact, the inner turmoil of the self-actualizing person is very likely to be more intense than that of a person content to meet merely the deprivation needs. The biographies of great people clearly show this. The joy of realizing one's potential is surrounded by suffering, but suffering itself is no guarantee of self-authentication. It can equally well express illness.

It would seem, therefore, that this inner force, this urge to self-actualize is very evasive. Is it an inner voice that tells us what to do? Is it conscience? Is it an inner conviction of being on the right path, or an awareness of loss after one has left it? Maslow spent a great deal of time trying to describe the observable characteristics of persons whom he regarded as self-actualizing but a great deal of his attention was also directed to the inner experience which he called Being love. He thought we were most aware of Being love in peak experiences.

This book assumes that we all have had such peak experiences—though we may not be very aware of them or value them very much. This experience of harmony and atunement may not tell us anything specific about what to do with our lives, but it does motivate by filling us with the experience of love. The more we become aware of the experience and nourish it in our lives, the more we can follow Augustine's advice and "do as we please" because in the light of such experience what we will be pleased to do will, in most cases, be ennobling, enriching, and growth enhancing for all concerned. There is no guarantee of this, but rather a strong likelihood, we believe. We, therefore, will devote an entire chapter to the experience of love.

In contrast to Maslow's focus on self-actualization as a prime characteristic of healthy people, most of social science research has been focused on illness. Even religious traditions tend to look at sinfulness and estrangement more than gracefulness and atunement. Both are a part of our experience. When we think about the millions of human beings who died in this century as a result of deliberate policies of genocide and the many millions more that died in the wars, it is tempting to declare these pictures descriptively accurate.[17] Some analysts believe that our failure to realize our human potential is a major source of guilt within us all.[18] Andrew Buchannan seems to have expressed this aspect of our experience very well. Others, such as R. D. Laing, are convinced that society has encouraged us to become less and less aware and appreciative of the world around us, rather than more and more fully aware of it. "What we call 'normal' is a product of repression, denial, splitting, projection, introjection, and other forms of destructive action on experience. It is tragically estranged from the structure of being."[19]

If what is considered normal is so tragically estranged from our true being, then it is easy to see why becoming what we really are is so difficult. Virtually everything and everyone around us invites us to settle for so much less. It costs a great deal to be true to ourselves. However, inner being or true self is not a location inside of us; it is a way of experiencing the world and a source of psychic energy that is not bounded by our skins.[20] In ancient times the process of becoming what we are—of realizing our potential—was called "soul making."[21] It was never a completely solitary undertaking. We simply cannot be our true selves without others.[22] "The world and it's humanity is the vale of soul making."[23] We think that Abraham Maslow would be in fundamental agreement with these insights when he speaks of self-actualization.

Many people have found Maslow's works exciting and some have written about self-actualization as if it were a simple unfolding of a potential. Others have thought of it as the simple pursuit of the pleasure principle. It can even be understood as an endorsement of upper-middle-class lifestyles, ". . . the idea that the higher achievement of genuine self-actualization presupposes our ascension through various stages of economic well being is a   peculiarly self-congratulatory philosophy for a materialistic age.[24] Christopher Lasch declares that people today, ". . . cultivate more vivid experiences, seek to beat sluggish flesh to life, attempt to revive jaded appetites," while inwardly they are ". . . plagued by anxiety, depression, vague discontents [and a] sense of inner emptiness. . ."[25] Lasch believes that we have become too concerned with self and have lost our commitment to others.[26]

These criticisms may or may not be so of our age, but if they are, we would argue, it is not because of the effort to self-actualize, but rather because of a misunderstanding of what this means. As far as we are concerned in this book, the predominant trends have historically been to sacrifice the individual's drive toward self-actualization in the formation of conventional partnerships. This has been especially true in terms of the expectations of conventional marriage.

Social institutions such as marriage often tend to work against and frustrate the development of the inner self. It is no accident that our social institutions work in this way, for in important respects they were designed to do so. Modern society has been shaped to a considerable extent by the Judeo-Christian tradition, a tradition that is profoundly ambivalent about the nature of our inner self. On the one hand, the creation of human beings is recorded in the Bible in such a way as to affirm their goodness: They were created after the image of God to have dominion over the earth.[27] On the other hand, the dramatic story of the Fall overshadows this essential goodness for many Christians.[28] The doctrine of original sin emphasizes human depravity in such a way that the net effect seems to be an excessive concentration on wickedness rather than an affirmation of goodness. As a result it becomes difficult for us to talk about ourselves in a positive way without feeling either guilty or self-righteous. To be sure, there is another way of looking at the doctrine of the Fall. It can be seen as the occasion of our becoming human. It can be read as the myth of our "falling" into existence— a story about the birth of our awareness of ourselves and others and the complexity of making choices in finite freedom. But in point of fact this view has been far from dominant in Christian thinking, which has tended largely toward the negative interpretation. Consequently, most of the institutions we have created have been based on the assumption that we are essentially bad and therefore must be rigidly controlled if we are to be civilized. If we have begun to ignore others in our partnerships and make little of our commitments, we believe it is a result of our laziness and ignorance rather than a response to our true inner selves and the experience of love within us.

A PROFILE OF PARTNERSHIP

The preceding discussion of basic human needs has led us to observe that we become human in the human community. When we find love, acceptance, and a sense of belongingness, we enter the human community as social creatures. Therefore, we can now talk of human partnerships. The focus in this book is on marriage, a particular kind of partnership. What we have to say here, however, can be applied to other kinds of partnership as well. Marriage is much more highly institutionalized than other forms of partnership. There is a relatively fixed set of social expectations about what behavior is appropriate in marriage and what society and the marital partners should expect to get out of it. The following profile describes a set of personal expectations that many of us bring to partnerships such as marriage.

Intimacy

Intimacy involves touching and being touched in both a physical and a psychological sense. An intimate partnership is one in which both partners can be open to each other. To be open is to be able to share feelings, both good and bad—particularly about ourselves—to be able to "let our hair down" and reveal who we really are as far as we are able to understand ourselves. We cannot do this in a relationship unless we are confident of being accepted by our partner. Intimacy with someone who rejects you is a painful experience. The extent to which we can expect our partner to accept things we would hide from others determines the degree of intimacy present in the relationship.

Intimacy depends to a large extent on trust. In William Golding's novel *Lord of the Flies*, a group of young boys is marooned on a deserted island. Two of them meet for the first time on the beach, and after they have talked for a while one of them confesses to the other first making him promise never to tell anyone, that back home his nickname was "Piggy." A few minutes later other boys arrive and the new friend soon betrays the confidence by calling his companion Piggy. Everyone has had painful or embarrassing experiences of this nature, and as a result we learn that it is best to be open and intimate only gradually, as our trust in our partner grows. It may be true that people can fall in love "at first sight" and that intimacy can be achieved by two people who are virtually strangers, but more commonly intimacy is a result of a gradual process in which the partners learn to trust each other enough to open up and learn to be more open as they find that their trust is justified.

Commitment

A minimal definition of **commitment** involves the simple acceptance of socially defined roles. Thus, someone might say, "I am really committed to being a good wife (or husband or fiance), meaning that he or she subscribes to the socially accepted expectations that are appropriate to these roles. This often can be done without reflecting or thinking about the unique quality of one's interactions with others in these relationships. For example, I can be a "good husband" without asking whether my being a good husband really meets the needs of my wife or provides us with opportunities for growth or development. Many marriages have ended with, say, the wife wretchedly unhappy while the husband explains to one of his friends, "Look, it wasn't my fault. What did she expect? I was a good husband. If that wasn't good enough for her, you can't blame me." Commitment to the role of being a good husband can sometimes be a way of avoiding a more intimate encounter with one's wife.

Carl Rogers offers a more creative way of defining commitment. As Rogers sees it, commitment should be directed to the partners and not to some set of social expectations or roles: "We commit ourselves to working together on the changing process of our present relationship because that relationship is currently enriching our love and our life and we wish it to grow.[29]

Commitment in this sense places a high value on a voluntary partnership that is personally satisfying. This redefinition is clearly in line with the change that has taken place in our common normative definition of a marriage contract. Most people under 35 no longer think of marriage as a sacrament of the church that can never be terminated or as a social contract that must be fulfilled in spite of personal lack of fulfillment. They tend to think of it as a voluntary contract in which the needs of the spouses should receive primary consideration.

Such an understanding of commitment is on the one hand creative and on the other risky. We are committing ourselves to interaction in a process that is continually changing and whose outcome cannot be guaranteed. What is more, if we commit ourselves to another person in this way, we take personal responsibility for working out a partnership without the supports we typically rely on in other areas of life. That is, we deny ourselves the luxury of being able to say, "It wasn't my fault; don't blame me." We can find evidence of commitment in deep, "heavy" encounters or in simple, ongoing personal exchanges. Indeed, we are not fully human without commitment. It is the essential element behind the traditional notion that partners have to work at their marriage if they want to be fulfilled in it.

Dependability

Dependability is a much-abused concept. Too often, when people say that a husband is dependable they mean merely that he has a good and steady income and doesn't stay out drinking all night. Dependability in a wife often means no more than that she is sexually faithful and puts dinner on the table every night.

Dependability in a partnership should mean more than this. It is the sense that one knows in what circumstances and in what ways the other person can be counted upon. This does not imply that our partner will always do what we expect; it merely means that we know each other well enough so that there will not be needless disruption of the communication process.

Another way of describing dependability is in terms of something that we feel as "presence." Presence is simply the capacity to convey to another person that one is "there," listening and attentive. Presence, then, is the feeling that one can be depended upon to be there in the dialog rather than drifting along thinking about other things.

Vitality

A **vital partnership** is one that is intrinsically rewarding and satisfying to the partners. They enjoy each other, not merely the things they do together. Vitality conjures up words like *joy, spontaneity, freedom, humor, surprise.* It suggests that routines have been transcended, that we have, for the moment, done something new.

We do not ordinarily associate vitality with dependable relationships because dependability suggests routine, whereas vitality suggests spontaneity. But this need not be so. Partnerships become routinized when dependability becomes an end in itself. Conversely, vitality as an end in itself tends to disrupt lasting relationships because of its constant emphasis on the new and the different. The proper balance is like a good jazz musician improvising on a song. The spontaneity of improvisation provides the vitality within the context of the basic melodic and harmonic structure of the song. When Miles Davis plays "Moonlight in Vermont," it's never the same thing twice but it's always "Moonlight in Vermont." Such a combination of vitality and dependability is possible in a partnership, too.

Vitality, in the context of a lasting partnership, presupposes an acknowledgement of the many facets of our personalities. It rejoices in the fact that we are not merely the aspects of ourselves that are called forth by our daily routine, but far more besides. Vitality is experienced in a partnership when the partners have the capacity to call forth something new in each other and to reveal something new in themselves. For most of us, vitality is associated with our emotions because we are trained to control our emotions more than other aspects of ourselves. When we experience emotions we feel alive and vital, especially when this experience also brings us a sense of being closer to others. The process of self-actualization often is an experience of vitality.

Separateness and Togetherness

When you enter a partnership, it is important that you preserve your own uniqueness. It should not be expected that you give up being yourself in order to melt into your partner.

The issue of **separateness** and **togetherness** most frequently focuses on expectations about what is to be shared in the relationship and what is not. The emphasis on togetherness that was so characteristic of people's expectations of marriage in the 1950s stressed sharing as much as possible. Indeed, judging from the magazines of the day a couple had a bad marriage if she didn't develop a passion for football and he didn't cultivate an interest in gardening. To the apostles of togetherness, it was better for a couple to do nothing at all than to do things separately.

One of the major tasks of any partnership is the mutual determination of how much separateness and how much togetherness is desired. (Teri Leigh Stratford)

Trying to fulfill these expectations very often leads to unhappy compromises, one partner feeling that for the sake of the marriage she must give up what she really wants to do while the other feels obliged to participate in activities that don't interest him. Such a marriage can get to be little more than an encumbrance. Thus, one 55-year-old unmarried man, who has a son, remarks:

> Marriage is simply an institutional arrangement for the immature—for people who can't stand the strain of regulating their lives themselves—who need laws and public opinion and the Church to tell them what to do and what not to do. So I'm all for marriage for the country and for most people, but not for me . . . To do my best work I need to be unencumbered—and even with the most ideal marriage I've seen, there is a lot of simple encumbrance.[30]

Any relationship must have "psychological space" in it. Some of us need more such space than others, and some of us are more afraid of it than others; but all of us must work out a satisfactory solution to the problem of how much autonomy and how much togetherness we are going to experience in each relationship. Much of our success in doing this depends on our capacity to accept our differing needs for autonomy and togetherness.

Self-Disclosure

The hazards of a developing relationship derive from the fact that in a given situation it is sometimes impossible to determine the intention of the other from the cues provided. The partner may not be aware of his or her true intentions, may be intentionally and skillfully deceiving, or may in fact be open and aboveboard. **Self-disclosure** usually takes place incrementally, in proportion to the amount of trust the relationship has established. We enter into various types of partnerships partly to reduce this uncertainty. Intimacy points to the experience of openness. Self-disclosure points to the increasing capacity to share what we know or feel, to allow others to penetrate more deeply as we develop more fully. Without self-disclosure at some depth, there is little intimacy; but on the other hand even an intimate relationship is not a confessional in which it is a sin to keep any secrets.

Few of these dimensions of a vital partnership would be possible without love. Love—as basic affection, passionate desire, shared friendship, and an accepted obligation to always acknowledge the partner as a person—will be present in different mixtures in all enduring partnerships.

Compassion

Ordinarily we think of compassion as a characteristic of an individual, but its essential meaning links it to partnerships. To be compassionate means to suffer with someone, and partnerships of any intensity or duration demand suffering. Why is this so? Isn't love supposed to conquer all, overcome all suffering and pain and enable two people to live together in perfect harmony? Such is the light side of love. Compassion opens us to its dark side.

Partnerships in which both partners (or just one) are growing and realizing more and more of what they are capable of becoming are continuously stressed by the tendency to grow apart. Partnerships in which there is little growth and development on the part of each partner are stressed by the pressure to self-actualize that each feels inside but is unable to realize.

It is extraordinarily difficult to empathize with anyone who is suffering, particularly when one is struggling to deny the pain in one's own life. Given the nature of things, it may be that the capacity to bear the pain of another is punished rather than rewarded—the partner in pain too proud or too angry to permit such graciousness at this time. Developing compassion in a partnership is extremely risky and extraordinarily necessary. The idea that we may not be able to change things and our appropriate response is to endure the situation runs counter to our inclination to experiment and try out new types of partnerships, and it certainly undermines our confidence in a rational world in which we will be able to work things out if we just have the right information or try harder. It is simply not clear in many situations what is expected of us and what we are able to do—much less what we **should** do. A great compassion for all living things produced the well-known prayer, "Lord, grant me the strength to change those things that I can change, the courage to endure those that I cannot change, and the wisdom to know the difference."

COSTS AND BENEFITS

On the preceding pages we have discussed some of the needs and expectations that we bring to partnerships. They may be conscious or unconscious; they may be only partly fulfilled in any one of our relationships. But all of them are important issues for vital, self-actualizing partnerships. These dimensions are in tension with each other. For example, sometimes we have to pay a price for achieving dependability by losing touch with the possibility of spontaneous vitality. Similarly, in striving for separateness we may lose the opportunity for intimate discovery of another person. In self-disclosure we may offend our partner and lose a sense of intimacy. But if we cannot risk self-disclosure we cannot grow in our partnerships, and self-actualization will become more problematic.

Some of these ingredients of partnerships are more likely to develop over time than others. We can describe a brief encounter as a vital or even an intimate affair, but we normally do not think of it as involving much of a commitment. Love at first sight would not be recognized as such if the couple who fell in love at first sight had not continued their relationship. The emotions they experienced in the single encounter are likely to be given some other label than love if it turns out that that encounter was not the first of many.

Finally, these ingredients of relationships are valued differently by each of us. In general, most of us would say that a valuable relationship should be dependable, vital, intimate, and committed, and should involve a considerable degree of togetherness. However, the precise weight we give to each of these elements will vary, and the extent to which we are willing to trade one for the other will differ. For some of us, dependability will be the most important aspect of a relationship; for others, it will be vitality or intimacy. In fact, most people value these ingredients differently in different relationships, wishing to be intimate with some people and not with others.

Any choice of one thing has within it the possibility of losing another. In this, as in any situation, there is always a cost and a risk as well as a benefit. By **benefit** we mean the realization of something we desire, value, or need. **Cost** refers to what we have to pay in order to get what we desire, value, or need. **Risk** takes place when there is no apparent relationship between the costs and the benefits. Indeed, all choices are made with some degree of risk. The choice to enter into and maintain a relationship is no different from other choices in this regard. Because it is easy to miscalculate the benefits and the costs of entering into a relationship, the risks in human interaction are greater than in most other choices. Creative partnerships require risk taking to a greater extent than less creative ones.

SUMMARY

We have begun our discussion of marriage by noting that a partnership means a lot more than a casual date or an affair. Partners have an understanding or "contract" between them as to what they each expect to get out of their partnership. Marriage is a partnership in which there is a long, complex history of expectations that can be either accepted at face value or modified to better express a particular couple's desires. Some partnerships may have nothing to do with marriage. However, in creative partnerships a primary ingredient is the expectation of self-actualization.

Abraham Maslow describes self-actualization as the highest of our basic human needs. It can be achieved only after the lower (or deprivation) needs have been met reasonably well. Men and women must be able to find safety and security, feel belonging, love, and acceptance, and achieve a reasonable degree of self-esteem before they can give themselves to the process of self-actualization. It is not possible to self-actualize without the love and concern of others and the expectation that one will give at least as much as one receives. Self-actualization is not a new form of egotism or narcissism.

Marriage—and other types of partnership—should be assessed in terms of the extent to which what goes on between the partners encourages self-actualization. By looking at the dimensions of intimacy, commitment, dependability and vitality, separateness and togetherness, and self-disclosure, and compassion, we focus on the process of the partnership rather than on its form.

The profile of partnership sketched in this chapter describes some of the personal expectations we associate with self-actualizing partnerships. We will look at a number of different forms of partnership in this book. Self-actualization can occur in most of them, but there are different costs, risks, and benefits in each.

NOTES

1. Two well-known animals that commonly pair for life are wolves and Canada geese. Others, such as baboons, buffalo, and rats, pair with several females and attempt to establish dominance over a band or herd of females and lesser males. Lower forms of life manifest a variety of types of relationships. It is unrealistic to try to establish the "natural" character of lifelong monogamy by inference from animal behavior. Whatever tendency to pair with a single partner the human species may have acquired from its evolutionary history, it is clear that culture and personal inclinations can and often do establish divergent patterns.

2. Self-actualization is best discussed in the second edition of Maslow's *Motivation and Personality* (New York: Harper & Row, 1970), pp. 149–203. See also Abraham Maslow, *Toward a Psychology of Being*, 2nd ed. (New York: Van Nostrand Reinhold, 1968), pp. 97ff, and *The Farthest Reaches of Human Nature* (New York: Viking Press, 1971), pp. 41–56.

3. Christopher Lasch, *The Culture of Narcissism* (New York: Norton, 1979).

4. Daniel Yankelovich, *New Rules: Searching for Self-Fulfillment in a World Turned Upside Down* (New York: Bantam, 1982), pp. 231–40.

5. The evaluation of the destructiveness of partnerships—particularly those that are radically different from ones that we are familiar with—should be made with caution. By destructive we mean primarily those that do not enhance self-actualization. However, in the course of an individual's life a destructive relationship in this sense may be beneficial in the long run in that it helps establish more clearly than a less destructive partnership what the possibilities for growth might be.

6. Gerhard Lenski provides a discussion of this debate in *Power and Privilege* (New York: Basic Books, 1966), pp. 25–31; another is found in Amitai Etzioni, *The Active Society* (New York: Basic Books, 1968), pp. 622–30. Another approach to describing the distinctively human is found in E. F. Schumacher, *Guide to the Perplexed* (New York: Harper & Row, 1977), pp. 101–21, 15–27. Psychologists sometimes do the same thing when talking about instinctual groups. Jung distinguishes hunger, sexuality, the drive to activity, reflection, and a creative instinct. These are comparable to the instincts listed by the animal behaviorist Konrad Lorenz: feeding, reproduction, aggression, and flight. Since Lorenz was concerned with animal behavior, he did not include a creative instinct.

7. Human nature is both a normative and a descriptive concept. To use it simply as one or the other is to reduce the experience of the human enterprise that is directly available to each of us. Human nature need not be conceived of as a static set of attributes. It can be pictured as a unique set of processes that create distinctively human forms. While Robert Ornstein does not use the term *human nature* in the following works, he edits a major magazine called

Human Nature and seems to understand human consciousness in a similar fashion. Robert E. Ornstein, *The Psychology of Consciousness*, 2nd ed. (New York: Harcourt Brace Jovanovich, 1977); *The Nature of Human Consciousness* (San Francisco: W. H. Freeman, 1973). See also Abraham H. Maslow, *The Psychology of Science* (Chicago: Henry Regnery, 1969), and Schumacher, pp. 101–21.

8. Maslow, *Toward a Psychology of Being*, p. 155.

9. The effects of deprivation on partnerships such as marriage are illustrated in such works as Lee Rainwater, "Crucible of Identity," *Dadaelus*, Winter 1965, pp. 172–216; Joyce Ann Ladner, *Tomorrow's Tomorrow* (Garden City, N.Y.: Doubleday, 1971); and David A. Schulz, *Coming Up Black: Patterns of Ghetto Socialization* (Englewood Cliffs, N.J.: Prentice-Hall, 1969).

10. See especially the collection of studies in Eric Josephson and Mary Josephson, *Man Alone* (New York: Dell, 1962); Philip Slater, *The Pursuit of Loneliness: American Culture at the Breaking Point* (Boston: Beacon Press, 1970); Jules Henry, *Culture Against Man* (New York: Random House, 1963); Erich Fromm, *The Art of Loving* (New York: Bantam Books, 1970).

11. The effect of rapid social change on human relationships is described particularly well in Warren G. Bennis and Philip E. Slater, *The Temporary Society* (New York: Harper & Row, 1968); and Alvin Toffler, *Future Shock* (New York: Bantam Books, 1970); and *The Third Wave* (New York: Bantam, 1981).

12. Laurens van der Post, *Jung and the Story of Our Time* (New York: Random House, 1975), p. 57.

13. Maslow's hierarchy is a normative model of human development derived from a vast amount of inquiry into human behavior. Maslow did not expect that every individual would progress through the levels of his hierarchy in the same way or with the same indications of having passed through. The hierarchy, nevertheless, reflects human experience roughly in that we all know that when we are hungry, food dominates our awareness so much that it is difficult to think of anything else until our hunger is satisfied. If we are poor, the search for food must occupy more of our time and attention than if we are rich and can have someone cook for us. So also, if we have not received sufficient confirmation of our worth from others, it is difficult—but not impossible—for us to affirm our own. What is most important in this notion of hierarchy is that the gratification of lower needs encourages the higher needs to emerge. Gratification plays a role in human motivation in another way. Those whose lower needs have been gratified are more able to tolerate their later deprivation. Finally, this is but a small part of Maslow's theory of motivation. There is also a hierarchy of cognitive needs (the need to know must be gratified before the need to understand) and an undeveloped esthetic category.

14. Maslow, *Toward a Psychology of Being*, p. 197.

15. Maslow's work has contributed a great deal to the holistic health movement. See David Sorel (ed.), *Ways of Health: Holistic Approaches to Ancient and Contemporary Medicine* (New York: Harcourt Brace Jovanovich, 1979).

16. For a clear, concise exposition of basic Jungian psychology see Jolande Jacobi, *The Psychology of C. G. Jung* (New Haven, Conn.: Yale University Press, 1951).

17. R. D. Laing, *The Politics of Experience* (New York: Ballantine Books, 1978), p. 28; Irving Louis Horowitz, *Taking Lives: Genocide and State Power*, 3rd ed. (augmented) (New Brunswick, N.J.: Transaction Books, 1982).

18. Fromm, *Escape from Freedom*.

19. Laing, New York: pp. 26-27.

20. Hillman, *The Myth of Analysis* (New York: Harper & Row, 1970).

21. Maslow called self-actualization "instinctoid," and Jung at times spoke of a "creative instinct."

22. *Collected Works of C. G. Jung*, trans. R. F. C. Hull (Princeton, N.J.: Princeton University Press), Vol. XVI, para. 44.

23. Hillman, p. 25.

24. Yankelovich, pp. 232–33.

25. Lasch, pp. 11, 13.

26. A graphic account of the withdrawal from politics of those associated with the human potential movement or the "New Age" is found in Michael Rossman, *New Age Blues: On the Politics of Consciousness* (New York: Dutton, 1979).

27. Genesis 1:26.

28. Genesis 2:7–3:24.

29. Excerpted from the book *Becoming Partners: Marriage and Its Alternatives* by Carl R. Rogers. Copyright © 1972 by Carl R. Rogers. Reprinted by permission of Delacorte Press. Pp. 92–99.

30. Arlene Skolnick and Jerome Skolnick, *The Family in Transition* (Boston: Little, Brown, 1968), p. 158.

Whoever will look narrowly into his own bosom, will hardly find himself twice in the same condition. I give to my soul sometimes one face and sometimes another, according to the side I turn her to. If I speak variously of myself it is because I consider myself variously; all the contrarieties are there to be found in one corner or another; after one fashion or another; bashful, insolent; chaste, lustful; prating, silent; laborious, delicate; ingenious, heavy; melancholic, pleasant; lying, true; knowing, ignorant; liberal, covetous, and prodigal: I find all this in myself, more or less, according as I turn myself about; and whoever will sift himself to the bottom, will find in himself and even in his own judgement this volubility and discordance.

—Montaigne

3 on *Communication* and *Confirmation*

Often the partnerships that we have entered into seem to be little more than habits and rituals that go on with little awareness and even less choice on our part. We live out the patterns, the ruts or routines of our everyday existence, simply because we have "always" done so or because that is "the way we are." There is a certain comfort in this apparent stability. Indeed, we like to think of ourselves and others as having personalities or identities that are relatively constant so that we believe we know who we are and how we stand with others. Without these regularities in our lives, it is probable that the anxiety and uncertainty of having to choose how we shall live each moment would be too much to bear.

But as we become more aware of ourselves and our world, things do become much more uncertain. Every person is a rich reservoir of different and often contradictory traits. In the midst of such variety the desire actively to fashion our own lives is likely to be overshadowed by the fear that we do not know what we are doing and will make the wrong choice. The evidence of the social sciences suggests that most of us live mostly on the basis of habit and convention, in part out of fear of making the wrong choice. Freedom is something that everyone wants and everyone flees.[1] Few people have the courage of Montaigne to face the complexities of self-awareness continuously.[2]

Nevertheless, this chapter is about the hope in all partnerships that partners can cope with their fears and uncertainties and take an active role in shaping their common life in such a way as to further the growth of both partners. Self-actualization describes the growth of human beings from the point of view of an individual; confirmation describes this process from the point of view of partnerships. Confirmation is the capacity to "call forth" another person. In this chapter we will look first at what confirmation means in specific cases and then consider some of the skills that seem to be helpful in realizing this capacity.

CONFIRMATION

The philosopher-theologian Martin Buber writes of **confirmation** that

> the basis of man's life with man is twofold and it is one—the wish of every man to be confirmed as what he is, even as what he can become, by men; and the innate capacity in man to confirm his fellow man in this way. That this capacity lies so immeasurably fallow constitutes the real weakness and questionableness of the human race; actual humanity exists only where this capacity unfolds.[3]

Whether we realize it or not, the longing for confirmation in this sense is perhaps the greatest expectation we bring to loving partnerships. Why, then, do we give it so little attention that it lies, as Buber says, "fallow"?

One answer is, quite simply, that nobody ever told us that we really can help others realize their human potential. We have been told, of course, that we can help our children develop their skills by providing them with the best teachers and equipment, with the time and encouragement they need if they are to succeed in a competitive society. But nobody ever told us that we could or should do anything in particular to help our children self-actualize.

Furthermore, if we think at all about helping another person realize his or her potential, we tend to think of it as a process that entails greater costs than benefits for ourselves. This is because we are not really thinking about this question in Buber's terms; rather, we are thinking merely in terms of the acquisition of skills. Thus, when we deal with the situation of a wife who wants to develop her professional career, we tend to think first of the costs in terms of the services and attention she will be unable to give her family, and we assess the benefits in terms of the added income she will be able to provide. But how do we assess the benefits that might derive from her greater authenticity as a person? It is easy to imagine that she might benefit by being happier and more fulfilled, but our normal way of analyzing this situation all too often leaves out such factors. Thus, we are likely to conclude that the husband who helps his wife in a case like this is an altruistic benefactor rather than a partner in a joint process of growth.

Obviously, the power and capacity for confirmation are greater in an ongoing partnership than in a relationship of short duration, but this does not mean that we cannot find and give confirmation and support even in short-term or nonintimate relationships. Confirmation depends on moments of touching deeply, regardless of who does the touching. The following example illustrates some of the dimensions of confirmation:

> Jim is a vice president of Continental Packaging Corporation. He has made a radical suggestion to improve sales and production that will involve a major shakeup in the fiscal status of the company and a reassignment of personnel. The plan is basically acceptable and is desired by the majority of the board, but because of the radical shift it entails, the board is leery and anxious. Jim has reason to believe that the board meeting he is about to attend will be explosive and that he will be challenged at every turn. As he prepares to leave his office for the meeting, his secretary touches him on the arm and says, "You'll make it. I know it. The plan is great. Good luck!"

Although this seems like a simple exchange, Jim reported later that these words and the touch on the arm allowed him to go through this grueling experience with much more self-confidence. As Jim thought about it, he saw in this exchange a power of confirmation that goes much beyond what appears on the surface. He heard an expression of genuine concern for himself, a concern that revealed a knowledge of his inner self he had not expected. His secretary not only had confidence in his plan, but also seemed to know just what he was thinking at that moment, and her words said more than just her opinion of the plan. They said that she was with him just then. Although in the past he had felt that women could not share his feelings about his job, in this instance he believed she had done so. He reported that this had been a truly supportive experience.

The exchange between Jim and his secretary is an example of confirmation. What is important in this event is an attentiveness that carries within it care, concern, and a genuine knowledge of the other person and what he was experiencing. The encounter contained an insight, a support, and a warmth that transcended what Jim thought of as the normally defined masculine and feminine roles. The secretary called forth Jim's confidence by affirming a side of him that he was aware of but needed to have affirmed by another person.

Confirmation depends on moments of touching deeply, regardless of who does the touching. (Irene Springer)

Confirmation may involve calling forth a side of the partner that the partner did not previously recognize in herself or himself. Sometimes this can result in a very dramatic change in self-image and behavior, as Irene, the subject of one of Carl Rogers's case studies, discovered. Joe, the man with whom she was living, had the capacity to confirm in Irene aspects of her personality that had not been awakened in her previous partnerships:

> Joe came into my life, and he's a man who has always been loved, knows it, accepts it without question, and I still feel in awe of that. He knows he has worth—that's something that is never questioned—and yet at the same time, he could look at me, who had an almost exact opposite opinion of myself, and not be bothered by that, or be put aside by that, and not encourage it either. He never confirmed my negative feelings about myself. He would hear them and accept them, and then, in his own way, say that they were kind of nonsense. "I realize you feel that way, but that's not the way you are."
> And I began to try to look at myself. It was as if, just maybe, the way he sees me is closer to the way I am than the way I see me, and I began to sort of try that on a little bit.[4]

Joe's ability to accept Irene's negative feelings without confirming them, while at the same time presenting to her another image of herself that was more positive and self-fulfilling, lies at the basis of many growing partnerships in which the partners help each other experience growth and self-actualization. In Irene's case, because she had been deeply troubled by self-doubt, such growth was experienced as a kind of therapy. Joe enabled her to realize much more of her potential through his sensitive confirmation.

Whether because of or in spite of its importance, confirmation is not an easy thing to engage in. This is particularly true when we are involved in a relationship with someone who is quite different from us. People differ from one another in values or world view, in physical stamina, in sex drive, in gregariousness, and in a host of other ways. Because of these differences, we aspire to different things, handle ourselves and the world around us in different ways, and place differing values on our relationships. In growing partnerships—that is, partnerships in which each partner is becoming more self-actualized—differences have a positive value because an important part of growth lies in discovering the uniqueness of others.

Unfortunately, however, people tend not to like to discover significant differences between themselves and others, particularly those with whom they enter into partnerships. These differences tend to create a feeling of loneliness (because one feels that the partner cannot possibly understand) and invite comparison ("My way is better"), and thus are likely to generate tension. It is easier to confirm in one's partner what is discoverable in oneself. Instead of confirming what is unique in one's partner, there is a tendency to try to disconfirm it, to discourage the partner from developing the sides of himself or herself that are different.

In *Sanity, Madness, and the Family*, psychologists R. D. Laing and A. Esterson describe a patient, Claire, whose mother felt threatened by any apparent differences between Claire's views and her own. Far from confirming Claire's own existence as an autonomous individual with feelings and thoughts of her own, her mother met every sign of Claire's difference from herself with some form of repudiation.

A constantly repeated sequence

Laing and Esterson write:

is that Claire makes a statement, and her mother invalidates it by saying:

(i) she does not really mean what she says, or
(ii) she is saying this because she is ill, or
(iii) she cannot remember or know what she feels or felt, or
(iv) she is not justified in saying this.[5]

In Claire's case, the result of these repeated disconfirmations of her thoughts and feelings was intense insecurity about her own autonomous existence as a unique individual with ideas and opinions of her own.

Although most people do not carry their intolerance for difference as far as Claire's mother did, the tendency to refuse confirmation to our partners when they differ from us is a common one, and it is one that we should try to eliminate as much as possible. Every disconfirmation of our partner's assertions of his or her uniqueness thwarts the development of the individual and in fact is an obstacle to the growth of the partnership.

There can be a real joy in discovering that one's partner is a unique and different person. Indeed, a large part of the excitement of courtship lies in two people's discovering each other—both their similarities and their differences. This exciting process of revelation and discovery can be continued in an ongoing partnership if we do not let ourselves forget that both parties are richly varied individuals with complex mixture of feelings, meanings, and values. If we continue to meet signs of difference by accepting them honestly, by confirming our partner's unique individuality, the relationship is free to change and grow, and the process of discovery can continue indefinitely.

Confirmation is an objective that cannot be realized without some sensitivity and skill in communication. Clear communication is contingent on being clear about what it is that one wants to communicate and on possessing sufficient skill to do so. Getting in touch with others depends in part on getting in touch with ourselves.

GETTING IN TOUCH WITH OURSELVES

It has been said that the degree to which we are capable of knowing another person is directly related to the degree to which we know ourselves. The more I know about myself and my own feelings, the more receptive I can be when another person reveals something about herself or himself. For example, if in the quietness of my own existence I have known, tasted, and experienced loneliness, I can recognize loneliness when another hints of it.

The problem is that in many cases we do not know what is going on inside ourselves. To some extent this is unavoidable, for we do not want to be self-involved, so constantly preoccupied with taking our own mental temperature that we lose sight of other things. Inevitably, therefore, we must fall short of a full understanding of ourselves, and there will always be thoughts that we think without knowing why and feelings that we feel without acknowledging them to ourselves. For most people, though, the danger is not one of too much self-involvement but one of too little. To a considerable extent this problem results from the way we are trained, for we are all taught as we grow up that certain emotions and feelings are bad or wrong. If not at home then at school, and probably in both places, children learn that it is "wrong" to express anger and hostility. We learn to hide these emotions in many cases even from ourselves. Consider the following story:

> Marge spent the afternoon with an old boyfriend from her college days while her husband Bill stayed home and babysat with their children. When she got home, Bill greeted her curtly and quickly took off for his office.

It has been said that the degree to which we are capable of knowing another person is directly related to the degree to which we know ourselves. (Ken Karp)

Later that evening Marge, sensing a certain coolness in his behavior, asked if anything was wrong. "Not a thing, honey. Did you have a good time this afternoon?" Bill answered.

"Yes, we did, but why didn't you ask when I got home?"

"I was in a hurry and I had other things on my mind," Bill said.

Marge felt that he wasn't telling her the whole story. "Are you angry about something?" she asked.

"No, but you know that I do have a lot to do at the office and you were a little late."

"But you said that you thought that it would be great for me to go and now you are angry," Marge protested. "I don't understand."

"I am not angry!"

Bill himself doesn't understand. He behaves from a level of feelings that are real for him, but he doesn't know what those feelings are, and as a result he has lost control of his feelings and has also lost the ability to communicate with Marge. Later he confessed to a counselor that he was indeed angry, that he really had nothing to do at the office, and that what he was mad about was the fact that his wife had had a good time while he had stayed home and struggled with the children. Because he was unaware of how he really felt when he first confronted Marge, Bill confused her and they were unable to resolve the conflict. Bill did not know he was angry because for him anger was an inappropriate emotion in this situation.

In a sense he was right, His anger *was* inappropriate. But dealing with an inappropriate emotion by hiding it from oneself usually serves only to make things worse. Consider what would have happened if Bill had acknowledged what he was feeling. If Bill had said, "Yes, I'm angry. I had to stay home all afternoon while you went out and enjoyed yourself," the situation would have been out in the open and the two of them could have talked about it. Perhaps Marge would have pointed out that she often helped him out in similar ways. In the end, if they were open and candid with each other, Bill might well have come to realize that indeed he had been angry but there was in fact "nothing to be angry about." Inappropriate emotions often dissipate when we recognize their inappropriateness, but we can't do this until we have recognized the emotion.

The Visceral Quality of Feelings

The feelings, thoughts, and emotions that fill our inner world are very important to us. We are these things and more, and not to share them is to isolate ourselves from others and from ourselves. Making believe they do not exist leads to disaster. When we no longer know how we truly feel about the world and ourselves, we no longer know ourselves and we confuse others. The poet T.S. Eliot used the phrase "hollow men" to describe people who are cut off from their own inner natures. When hollow men are angry they do not know that they are angry, and of course they do not know why they are angry.

Getting in touch with ourselves is a tantalizing task. We know that emotions are real in a way that ideas are not, for we can feel them if we let ourselves. Although there are powerful forces in our culture telling us to "control our emotions," we all have experienced intense moments when we could "taste" the authenticity of our feelings. Perhaps this accounts for why we are attracted toward our inner feelings and at the same time are threatened by them. Yet however frightening the prospect may be, the possibility of savoring these feelings is an exciting one.

Just as the possibility for confirmation very often lies fallow within us, so also the ability to get in touch with our inner selves often eludes us. If it is true, as we observed earlier, that getting in touch with others is a function of getting in touch with ourselves, it is no less true that getting in touch with ourselves is in important ways a function of getting in touch with others. We discover ourselves in interaction as well as in reflection. But because interaction with others has so many variables, it seems at first glance to be a most difficult arena for self-discovery.

In a society that is oriented toward activity, emphasizes big events, and is continually in search of fun and excitement, the inner life is easy to neglect. A life that is full of activity is frequently mistaken for one that is full of purpose. In such a society it is doubly important to spend some time alone—not just to analyze our thoughts and feelings, but fully to experience our lives. Part of the attraction of Eastern practices such as tai-chi and yoga is their capacity to help us experience ourselves fully here and now. Experiencing one's feelings and emotions is quite different from analyzing them or worrying about them. It involves accepting those feelings and emotions for what they are without believing they have to be expressed in order to be experienced. Such awareness can also lead to more socially appropriate ways of expressing feelings.

The Imaginal Mind

So much of our everyday life is based on an attentiveness to practical concerns and so much of modern education attempts to define the practical in rational ways that we have neglected most of our being at our great peril.[6] In spite of the fact that our modern society gives little explicit recognition of their value, myths, poetry, folktales, fables, and the arts are capable of evoking parts of ourselves that go unrecognized. Rather than being mere flights of the imagination, they are sources of psychic energy and power that we can tap.[7] Often we resist doing so because the images are dark and violent and unrestrained by the conventions of everyday life.

The poet Robert Bly is convinced that the myths and images of folktales have a great deal to say to modern people.[8] In his travels about the country, Bly notes that the men in his audiences are warm, friendly, ecologically aware, and hard workers for peace. They have come to accept women's need for equality and in their practical everyday partnerships have practiced equality. But, Bly feels, they are strangely de-energized. They lack decisiveness and a sense of personal meaning. He believes this is so because in large measure they have not been able to face the dark side of their own nature because they confuse it with its distorted expression in the macho male. Many of these men are living with strong, assertive women.

To try and help them engage their deep and dark "inner" natures, Bly makes use of folktales and mythology. For example, he tells the story of Iron Hans from the Grimm's fairy tales.[9] Iron Hans is a large, rust-colored man covered with nothing but long, shaggy hair from head to foot. He was found at the bottom of a lake (after a series of misadventures in which a number of men disappeared in its vicinity) by the king's men. Through a number of trials, Iron Hans is set free by the king's young son and in gratitude helps the boy become a man. The story develops the theme that in order to become whole, it is necessary to be in touch with one's dark side—but not, however, to become it.

A similar theme is developed in the Swedish folktale of the horrible Linnworm.[10] In this story, a king and queen who wished dearly for a long time to have children at last do. The queen first delivers a dark, slimy Linnworm, which the midwife quickly throws out the window, not wishing to disturb the queen, who is still in labor. The queen then gives birth to a lovely fair-haired, blue-eyed boy. All goes well in the kingdom until it is time for the young prince to marry. When he sets out to find his bride, he is confronted by an enormous Linnworm who bellows, "Older brothers marry first." The quest to find a bride for the Linnworm provides the occasion for a young woman of the provinces (after several prospective brides had failed and paid the price of failure with their lives) to transform the horrible Linnworm into a handsome, dark-haired prince.

The theme of the story is that a true marriage cannot take place until one has gotten in touch with one's dark side. Myths and folktales from all over the world tell us that if we do not do this, the things we repress will besiege us from the edge of the woods at night and rage along the border of our awareness by day.[11] We will live in perpetual fear and uncertainty until we face them and come to understand what we have to fear. It is interesting that the dark side of women is better known than the dark side of men—probably because it has been a justification for men persecuting women throughout the ages. The image, of course, is the witch, who in spite of her terrible reputation is also known to have healing powers as well as destructive ones in most traditions.

Congruence

Carl Rogers uses the term **congruence** to describe successful functioning in both modes of our being—that is, both as private individuals and as members of partnerships with other human beings. For Rogers, a person is congruent who is aware of his or her feelings and is able to communicate them accurately to another person. A person who is congruent creates the sense of authenticity and presence that encourages another to respond authentically. Thus, the concept of congruence bridges the gap between getting in touch with ourselves and getting in touch with others. As Rogers sees it, congruence is the basis of good, healthy partner relationships, which depend on self-awareness and open communication.

GETTING IN TOUCH WITH OTHERS: MODES

"Words, words, words," Hamlet complained, well aware that we rely on words to communicate our feelings and that often they are inadequate for this task. Their inadequacy arises both from our inability to use them with complete accuracy and from the inadequacies of language itself. In addition to being symbols with common meanings that are universally accepted within a language community, words have more or less private meanings arising out of the experiences we associate with them. Because each of us has a unique history or biography, the words we use tend to have unique meanings for us, for similar reasons, for those listening to us. These private meanings generally do not interfere with the transaction of everyday affairs, but they can be quite troublesome when we try to use words to say

A person who is congruent creates the sense of authenticity and presence that encourages another to respond authentically. (Ken Karp)

something important about who we are or how we feel about another person.

One of the more obvious problems with language is the fact that the same words mean different things to different people. This is true on both the private level and the social level. Indeed, it may well be that if a class of 15 or 20 students were to discuss the role of arguments in family life, no two of them would be talking about the same thing; for one an argument would be a healthy airing of differences, while for another it might be a deadly battle of wills that should be avoided at all costs, and for a third it might mean fist fights that never-the-less, helped clear the air and pave the way for reconciliation.

In addition to the different meanings words have on the private level, there are also socially determined differences. On this level, the associations I have with certain words are shared by others in my social group but not by people in different groups. For example, words like *rich*, *poor*, and even *work* obviously mean different things to people in different social classes; words like *masculine* and *feminine* undoubtedly mean different things to men and women; words like *liberal*, *radical*, and *conservative* mean different things to people with different political outlooks. A mother might tell her friends that the young man her daughter is going out with is "a nice boy," but perhaps the daughter wouldn't understand those words in the same way or, if she understood them, might use other words entirely.

Perhaps even more important than the fact that words have different meanings to different individuals and groups is the fact that, even when such communication problems do not exist, language is often inadequate to convey our deepest emotions. We all have had the experience of wanting to say something and not knowing how. Indeed, it is often the tenderest, warmest, most human emotions that are most difficult to express in words. Greeting card companies thrive on the fact that people find it so difficult to say things like "I care about you and am really sorry to hear that you are sick" that they must fall back in desperation on prefabricated expressions of emotions like concern, love, and gratitude.

Because of these inadequacies of language, intimate, caring partnerships tend to develop their own language in which common words have very private meanings. Consider the following telephone conversation:

Caller: Hello, Beth, am I disturbing you?
Beth: Oh no, we were in the meadow. [Giggles]
Caller: The meadow?
Beth: We were getting up.

Over the years of their marriage Beth and her husband had come to call their bed "the meadow." Once the association between "bed" and "meadow" is made, however, even an outsider can understand the warm and carefree feelings that they must have associated with their lovemaking. Through the use of one word of their private language, Beth and her husband can convey to each other a rich heritage of experience that is uniquely theirs. This private language enables them to express easily a wide range of feelings and emotions and to recall events in which they have been able to move closer to one another in the past.

Most of us have used words this way to some extent. Friends develop a common language. Groups of people who live together for any length of time tend to develop a set of words to express important aspects of their lives together. For most of us, the type of relationship commonly known as courtship consists partly of developing a private vocabulary.

Of course, many people are not particularly verbal in their behavior. These people may not invent words or radically change the meanings of common words; instead, they may rely on nonverbal signs and gestures to supplement their associations with common words like "I love you." For most people, in fact, the language of relationship goes far beyond words. It involves the whole being. We communicate by our tone of voice, by our facial expression, by the use of our eyes. Our whole body is a medium of communication. If we are congruent—that is, if we know how we think and feel about ourselves and our world and can express this to others—the signals we give off are apt to be clear. If we are not in touch with ourselves or cannot bring ourselves to express what we feel, then we are likely to confuse others when we try to communicate, as in this simple example:

"It's good to see you," he said with his eyes glued steadfastly to the floor.

Here the lack of eye contact seems to contradict what is said. We wonder whether the speaker is just shy or whether he really is not very pleased to see us. Even such a simple discrepancy can hinder our ability to understand what is being communicated. We have to wait for further information to be sure just what is being "said." All of us give off discrepant signals like this from time to time. But when such behavior becomes a persistent aspect of a partnership, the partnership itself may be unable to grow and develop.

Making Contact

To communicate with another person is to make contact with him or her. In intimate partnerships, actual physical touching is an important part of the way the couple communicate, but in a sense any two people who try to communicate with each other are trying to touch.

Most Americans do not look into another person's eyes when talking. We tend to reserve eye contact for intimate relationships and to limit its use in public interaction. Nevertheless, our eyes can readily convey our feelings even in public contexts. This is why people who want to conceal something about themselves sometimes wear dark glasses. They intuitively sense the communication potential of the eyes, and they are right: Our eyes are part of our equipment for communicating that we all too often ignore.[12]

Touching is also an important part of any complete communication process—so important that psychologist Bruno Bettelheim claims that "the ability to experience touch as pleasant must precede any human relationship."[13] Again, Americans as a people tend to minimize their use of touch in communication. As Sydney Jourard observed, "in Paris the average couple come into physical contact 110 times during an hour (and they were just having a conversation); in San Juan, Puerto Rico, couples patted, tickled, and caressed each other 180 times during the same interval; but the typical London couple never touched at all, and Americans patted each other once or twice in an hour's conversation."[14]

Touching another person on the arm or shoulder conveys warmth, just as withdrawal from touch conveys distaste. Most people respond positively to being touched, although a substantial number of individuals typically find touching unpleasant or threatening.

To a large extent the use of touch as a means of communication is governed by socially accepted conventions. Among Americans, touching is considered inappropriate in casual social situations and therefore tends to be confined to intimate and sexual behavior. This is unfortunate, because it produces a vicious circle that severely inhibits our communication resources. The more touching is seen as exclusively a sexual mode of communication, the more rigorously it is avoided by people who are not on intimate terms with each other; and the more it is avoided, the more exclusively sexual it becomes.

In our society, a man who habitually did such things as reaching across a table to put his hand on a woman's hand or forearm to get her attention or in response to something she said would run the risk of having her think he was making sexual advances. Indeed, inhibitions about touching are not confined to relations between the sexes; in other societies, for instance, it is not at all unusual for men to embrace and touch each other. In America, however, such contact is largely forbidden, for our predisposition to see touching as sexual immediately makes us suspect that any touching between members of the same sex must be homosexual. We have, however, all seen football players patting, slapping, and hugging their teammates, and many of us are familiar with the sight of two prizefighters embracing in the center of the ring after the final bell as a way of communicating without words the feelings of respect and closeness their intense struggle has generated.

One cannot help feeling, when one sees such demonstrations, a bit sorry that we are not free to make greater use of this means of communication. Of course, it would not be reasonable to advise anyone simply to ignore the social conventions of his or her culture and engage freely in types of touching that our society disapproves of, for the result probably would not be an increase in communication. Because of the socially conditioned responses of the person being touched, excessive departure from the norms in this area might well end in misunderstanding. But this doesn't mean that we can't make small and gradual changes in our attitudes toward touching and being touched. Any effort to be a bit more free, a bit less inhibited, in our use of touch is bound to have beneficial effects on our ability to communicate with other people with whom we come into contact. It is possible for us to broaden our communications repertory, even though we live in a society that tends to be relatively restrictive in this regard.

Body Language

We communicate with others in many ways. Just as we are often unaware of the richness within ourselves, so also we are unaware of the richness of interpersonal communication. The subtleties of our communication cover a wide range that includes not only our use of words, eye contact, and touching, but also a whole gamut of almost imperceptible things that we "say" with our bodies. Indeed, a few years ago a widely read book was devoted to the subject of "body language"; here we will confine ourselves to suggesting some of the potential of this communications resource.

Undoubtedly, we are all aware that a person's posture often betrays feelings that are not expressed in words. The position of someone's body as she or he sits in a chair and listens to someone else speaking readily betrays interest or noninterest. By the same token, it is difficult to say convincingly that you are not tired when your whole body betrays the fact that you are.

These two examples make it clear that body language is not something we can use or not use as we choose. We are using it all the time, whether we know it or not. Thus, if our communication is to be as full as possible, it is important for us to realize what we are saying with our bodies. Consider the following incident.

Your roommate says, "I've got to meet my date in about ten minutes and I don't know what time the movie starts. Do me a favor and call the theater." You don't really want to do it—you're reading and don't want to be interrupted; your roommate should have taken care of these things without depending on you—but on the other hand you don't think it would be right to refuse. So you decide to do it, but unconsciously you want your roommate to know how you feel. You say "Okay," but you get up very slowly from your chair, as if it's a real problem for you to move, and slouch over to the telephone.

Your roommate sees the way you are moving and gets the point. Perhaps she says, "Oh, don't bother. You don't feel like doing it and it'll only take me a minute. I'll do it myself." Or perhaps she merely makes a mental note that she owes you a favor. In any case, the discrepancy between the way your body acted and what you said communicated a complex message: that you would do this thing but that you didn't really like doing it. There's nothing wrong with such a discrepancy in this case, for the two parts of the communication accurately conveyed the two things you were thinking and feeling.

Problems might arise, however, when one does not pay attention to one's body language, so that one is out of touch with one's own feelings. We probably all have been in situations like the one just described, and at some time or another we may have reacted by not being open about our communications. The following dialog might result in such a situation:

Betty:	Do me a favor and call the theater.
Suzanne:	Okay. [Moves laboriously toward the phone]
Betty:	Oh, never mind. You don't want to do it, so I'll do it myself.
Suzanne:	I *said* I'll do it.
Betty:	I know, but you don't feel like it, and it's no trouble for me.
Suzanne:	I didn't say I didn't feel like it, I *said* I'd do it.

The result is a kind of double bind. Betty correctly interprets Suzanne's reluctance to make the call and drops her request. But Suzanne, who probably feels that it is wrong not to want to do this favor and therefore refuses to admit that she feels that way, denies having communicated what her body language clearly says and then gets annoyed with Betty for responding to it. The result is one of those little squabbles that almost invariably result from a failure to communicate. Both parties are made unnecessarily uncomfortable.

Our bodies, in short, are almost always communicating our feelings to other people. A large part of this communication is unconscious, but it is important that we try to make ourselves aware of as much of it as possible. Only in this way can we get in touch with our own feelings and be aware of the messages we are sending to other people.

GETTING IN TOUCH WITH OTHERS: MEANS

In the context of this chapter, communication with others is a means of helping others (and ourselves) become more authentic, more fully that which we are capable of being. The various modes of communicating with others offer us the possibility of touching each other deeply. The extent to which we feel comfortable using these modes is a measure of the extent to which we have come to grips with our own inner feelings and have tasted our own authenticity.

Attentiveness

One of the marks of authenticity in a person is his or her ability to be attentive to others. Attentiveness means a whole range of things, and perhaps the best way to clarify what we mean by the term is to recall some instances in which we have felt another person being attentive to us. The attentive waiter notices a slight movement of the hand toward the empty coffee cup and fills it almost before the diner has become aware of his own wishes. The host who is there with an ashtray when you light a cigarette is being attentive. Of course, the fact that we expect people in these roles to be attentive does not diminish our feeling of pleasant surprise when they are.

One of the factors that tend to make a person attentive is awareness of what the relationship means to him or her. The host, for example, is attentive to his guests for a number of reasons having to do with such things as his regard for them as friends and associates, his conception of himself in the socially determined role as host, and so forth; the waiter is attentive because his relationship to his customers can mean financial reward if it is a pleasant one and because he may take pride in his role in the relationship. That is to say, both the host and the waiter are eager to succeed in their roles, and their attentiveness is a result of the amount of meaningfulness they attach to the relationships in which they act out these roles.

The same is true of the roles of husband, wife, lover, parent, or friend. All relationships have some value to us, or we would not be in them. Unfortunately, sometimes we either are not aware of or cannot acknowledge our real stake in a particular relationship. Whenever this happens, the result is likely to be a failure of attentiveness on our part. When our relationship with a particular person doesn't matter to us, we do not *attend* to what he or she is saying. Consider the following dialog:

Sally: Gosh, I had a great time in New York yesterday.
Ben: Yeah, New York is great. I went to New York two weeks ago.
Sally: I spent two hours at the Guggenheim Museum. What a fantastic place!
Ben: Yeah, well I went to the Museum of Modern Art. They have some really beautiful things there. Like . . .
Sally: I particularly liked David Smith's sculpture.
Ben: Oh, sure, Smith is good, but you should have seen . . .

Ben is obviously more interested in telling his story than in hearing what Sally has to say. Although she initiated the conversation, he never picks up on what she is saying in such a way as to encourage her to say more. Instead, he uses each of her observations as though its only purpose is to provide him with an opportunity to tell his thoughts and experiences.

This is a fairly typical kind of conversation. It could take place between casual acquaintances or a married couple. Whatever the level of intimacy in the relationship, this kind of conversation can be damaging. If Ben and Sally are just strangers striking up a conversation, they are missing the possibility of a good conversation and are likely to end up knowing as little about each other as when they began talking. If they are in the process of developing a lasting relationship their chances are not very good, because Ben is signaling Sally that he doesn't really care about her thoughts and feelings. He may say he cares about her, but his inattentiveness indicates otherwise. And if this kind of conversation is a persistent feature of a long-term partnership such as marriage, then it is clear that the partnership has lost an important part of its capacity to grow.

Of course, we should recognize that any particular example of inattentiveness may not be decisive for the relationship as a whole. It is perfectly normal for there to be areas in a person's life that simply are not very interesting to his or her partner. Imagine for a moment that Ben is an art major while Sally is majoring in economics. He is going through a stage in which he is trying to get his bearings in the world of art, so when she brings up the subject it is an occasion for him to talk about his thoughts on art, which for the time being are far more important to him than her thoughts. The point is that husbands and wives often notice that their partners are inattentive in certain areas, and it does their partnership no harm. But when inattentiveness spreads beyond certain well-defined, limited areas to characterize the partnership as a whole, it is safe to say that the partnership has become one in which the partners do not relate.

One of the things that makes us attentive is a genuine interest in others. This means having some appreciation for another person simply as a person, and also some recognition of the value of that person's experience. It involves a recognition that we enjoy being with other people and an acceptance of the possibility that we can learn from them.

Inquisitiveness

Inquisitiveness or interest does not mean simply that Ben should listen to Sally tell her story. It involves his recognizing in her story the things that are of value to her and the possibility of pursuing them because they may also be of interest to him. This, in effect, changes the conversation from one in which the partners are simply exchanging information to a conversation that may have intrinsic value for both because both are really "turned on" by what is happening.

Learning to Transfer Skills

There are no easy ways of teaching people the skills involved in being an attentive and inquisitive partner. On the other hand, many of us already have these skills but do not readily transfer them to our intimate partnerships. For example, a good salesman must be an attentive and inquisitive listener. In his job he has developed the capacity to intervene creatively in conversations. If he didn't have these skills, he wouldn't be a good salesman. But even though he has skills and knowledge about developing relationships, he frequently fails to utilize them in his personal life. It may not dawn on him that if he listened to his wife as attentively as he listens to prospective buyers, there would be payoffs in terms of their personal relationship as surely as there are payoffs in his business dealings.

All of us need to become more aware of the fact that it is appropriate to use such highly prized skills in our intimate partnerships. Of course, the skills of the salesman need some adjustment when they are applied to personal partnerships. The aim should be cooperation rather than manipulation, and the growth of the partnership must be more important than the advancement of one member's personal objectives. Sensitivity plays an important role here. Increased awareness of the expressed and unexpressed needs of each partner helps redirect the skills that are used on the job simply to sell a product.

A Sense of History

In any partnership, what our partner is telling us must be heard in the context of a history of past self-disclosure. This history bears directly on our response in the present because it provides us with another means by which we can infer what is most valuable to our partner. If a couple has a relatively full history of self-disclosure in which they have been able to give of themselves in their relationship, they can build on this in the present. Conversely, if they have been unable to give much of themselves in the past, they must clear up the ambiguities in their communication before they can progress.

For example, suppose a woman has for years had a vague feeling that her role as a wife and homemaker is not fully satisfying and that she would like to resume her education or find some sort of work in which she can find satisfaction. Every once in a while she mentions these aspirations to her husband, but he refuses to confirm them. He doesn't say that she must not do any such thing, but he generally gives her no encouragement and brushes her remarks aside with a casual statement such as, "Well, I don't see any need for it, but if that's what you want to do, go ahead."

Receiving no encouragement, she puts her desires to one side. Finally, however, she reaches the point at which she decides that having some sort of career outside the home is of considerable importance to her. She enrolls in courses at a local university, but her husband treats her new career as a student lightly. Because he was not attentive to what she was saying all these years, he cannot imagine that it is important to her and he tends to regard her studies as little more than a way to "get out of the house" for a few afternoons a week. Even when she tells him this is not the case he is skeptical because, from where he stands after years of inattentiveness, her decision looks like a spur-of-the-moment notion. Had he been listening to what she was saying all along, he could have saved her years of frustration and, what is more, could now be sharing, as an interested and confirming partner, in her new experiences.

Long-term partnerships such as marriage require constant attention if they are to continue to provide for the developing needs of the partners. This is especially true if the partners are attempting to live a distinctly unconventional life style. We have previously discussed some of the characteristics of good partnerships and said that these are not necessarily related to a specific kind of partnership. However, while we cannot specify the *form* of a good partnership, it is possible to provide some guidelines about the processes that seem to contribute to the growth of partnerships. Carl Robers has provided a set of four such guidelines in the conclusion to his *Becoming Partners*. We should:

1. Redefine the nature of our commitment to one another, focusing on what is happening between us rather than on the "oughts" that we have been taught about how partners should behave toward one another. Rogers says:

   "We commit ourselves to working together on the changing process of our present relationship because that relationship is currently enriching our love and our life, and we wish it to grow."[15]

   The emphasis here is on the partnership itself, which is maintained because it is personally fulfilling to the partners.

2. Keep the channel of communication open, Rogers says.

   "I will risk myself by endeavoring to communicate any persisting feeling, positive or negative, to my partner—to the full depth that I understand it in myself—as a living, present part of me. Then I will risk further by trying to understand, with all the emphasis I can bring to bear, his or her response, whether it is accusatory and critical or sharing and self-revealing."[16]

As we have seen in this chapter, the communication of feelings is critical to vital relationships. Rogers points out that it is particularly important to communicate persisting feelings because these are the ones that are likely to tell us what parts of our relationship are working well and what parts need adjustment.

3. "We will live by our own choices, the deepest organismic sensings of which we are capable, but we will not be shaped by the wishes, the rules, the roles which others are all too eager to thrust upon us."[17] This guideline is also known as *role transcendence*, meaning that it is possible for individuals to transcend socially prescribed roles and in that transcendence discover more authenticity as persons. Open communication is especially important in this area.

4. Try to keep in touch with your inner self. Rogers believes that it is only through deep awareness of our inner natures that we can find authenticity or self-actualization and that only by becoming more authentic ourselves can we participate fully in a growing partnership.

SUMMARY

As we come to know ourselves better, we recognize the contradictory elements in our lives, our mixed motivations, and the varied tapestry of our emotions and feelings. Most of us flee from such self-awareness and seek security in comfortable routines, rituals, and roles. It is tempting to want conventional partnerships because we think we know what we are supposed to do in such partnerships.

While self-actualization focuses on the process of growth from the point of view of an individual seeking to achieve greater authenticity, confirmation is an important aspect of partnership. In vital, growing partnerships each partner selectively affirms the positive aspects of the other. Positive personal traits that were recognized previously may be confirmed, those that were not may be identified. In such a way partners help each other grow.

A number of communication skills are necessary if confirmation is to occur. Among the most important of these are attentiveness, inquisitiveness, and the ability to transfer skills learned in other contexts to the partnership.

It is not possible to get in touch with others if one is out of touch with oneself. *Congruence* is the term Carl Rogers uses to denote a clear relation between a person's perception of his or her inner feelings and the ability to communicate effectively and appropriately. Words are by no means adequate to convey the richness of what we experience in partnerships. Nevertheless, the private language of lovers often enriches a partnership because the words used quickly call forth the intimate warmth and affection of a history of self-disclosure. In our communication with others, furthermore, our body language, touch, eye contact, and presence often speak louder than words.

NOTES

1. Erich Fromm, *Escape from Freedom* (New York: Avon, 1964); R. D. Laing, *The Divided Self* (Baltimore: Penquin Books, 1969); Philip Slater, *Earthwalk* (Garden City, N.Y.: Doubleday, 1974), pp. 37–66.

2. Michel Eyguem de Montaigne, *The Essays* (1588), bk. II, chaps. 1, 2,; bk. III, chap. 13.

3. Martin Buber, *To Hallow This Life* (New York: Harper & Row, 1958), pp. 24–25.

4. Excerpted from the book *Becoming Partners: Marriage and Its Alternatives* by Carl R. Rogers. Copyright © 1972 by Carl R. Rogers, Reprinted by permission of Delacorte Press.

5. R. D. Laing and A. Esterson, *Sanity, Madness, and the Family*. Vol. I, *Families of Schizophrenics* (New York: Basic Books, 1965), p. 74.

6. A good documentation of this assertion is to be found in the works of Robert E. Ornstein, *The Psychology of Consciousness*, 2nd ed. (New York: Harcourt Brace Jovanovich, 1977), and Kenneth Peletier, *Toward a Science of Consciousness* (New York: Delta, 1978). A more popular treatment is to be found in Bob Samples, *The Metaphoric Mind* (Reading, Mass.: Addison-Wesley, 1978).

7. The theory, as noted in Chapter 2, derives from the depth psychology of C. G. Jung. An interesting exposition is found in Joseph Campbell, *Myths to Live By* (New York: Bantam Books, 1982).

8. Keith Thompson, "What Men Really Want: New Age Interview with Robert Bly," *New Age*, May 1982, pp. 30ff. See also Robert Bly, *Of Solitude and Silence* (Boston: Beacon Press, 1982).

9. *The Complete Grimm's Fairy Tales*, introduction by Padraic Colum, commentary by Joseph Campbell (New York: Pantheon, 1972), pp. 612–19.

10.

11. Marvelous accounts of the less well known African folktales are found in Laurens Van der Post, *Patterns of Renewal*, PendleHill Phamphlet No. 121; and in his *The Heart of the Hunter* (New York: William Morrow, 1961).

12. Leonard Zunin, *Contact: The First Four Minutes* (Los Angeles: Nash, 1972), pp. 74–88.

13. Quoted in ibid., p. 84.

14. Quoted in ibid., p. 85.

15. Rogers, p. 201.

16. Ibid., p. 204.

17. Ibid., p. 206.

There is no Garden of Eden, there is no Paradise, there is no heaven except for a passing moment or two. Whatever satisfactions are given to human beings it is inconceivable that they should be perfectly content with these.

—Abraham Maslow

4 *Conflict and Cooperation in Partnerships*

Thus far we have not discussed the role of **conflict** in partnerships. If a purpose of a vital, creative partnership is the self-actualization of the partners and if confirmation is one process by which this takes place, then creative management of conflict can be another such process. Part of our problem in acknowledging the role of conflict in an intimate partnership is that we want to believe that happy, growing partnerships ought to be without conflict. We are conditioned to think in terms of consensus or conflict. Either the partners are in agreement on all fundamental issues (or can readily reach such an agreement), or they are in conflict. We assume that partners who agree with each other are more likely to be happy, and we fear that those who do not will break up.

But there is a third possibility: We can cooperate with one another. In growing partnerships, when the partners grow apart they can acknowledge their differences and continue to cooperate. They can manage their disagreements creatively and grow as a result. We are more familiar with the need to cooperate with business associates or classmates with whom we disagree and in whom we have invested little of ourselves. But there is an art to managing conflict in an intimate partnership in which we have invested a great deal of ourselves. It is part of what traditional wisdom means by "working" at a marriage. **Cooperation** in intimate partnerships such as marriage requires a loving commitment to the partner and a degree of self-regard. Otherwise, it is likely to amount to little more than a mutual adjustment between two fearful strangers or a simple business transaction in which the partnership stays together, but its vitality withers.

Conflict must not be confused with **violence.** Violence is never appropriate to an intimate partnership—though it may occur—whereas conflict is inevitable. Controlling aggression or assertiveness so that conflict does not erupt into violence involves cooperation. Simply "letting it all hang out" is not an adequate way of managing conflict or violence. The more violence is expressed, the more it tends to be expressed in subsequent conflicts. Violence feeds on itself. Cooperation and the management of conflict and disagreement assume respect for the partner, an underlying love that values the partner whatever the disagreement or difference might be. To close one's eyes to disagreement and conflict in intimate partnerships, to pretend that a happy marriage is one that is conflict-free, and to withdraw from any disagreement is to retard the growth of a partnership.

In this chapter we will explore some of the dimensions of conflict as it occurs in intimate partnerships. The dynamics of conflict will be examined, with the initial focus on some of the major sources of conflict. We will then turn to a discussion of the creative aspects of conflict management and cooperation. A growing, vital partnership cannot afford to be dominated by conflict, nor can it survive in the sterile atmosphere of conflict-free intimacy. Conflict is thus both unavoidable and necessary, and couples can learn to cooperate in managing it effectively.

SOURCES OF CONFLICT

Conflict can arise from sources within an individual, from out of the relationships between two or more individuals, or from the environment.[1]

Intrapersonal Sources

It is a common experience that when we are tired, we tend to be irritable. Fatigue can be brought about by heavy work, worry, or unresolved psychological conflicts. It can also be precipitated by physiological factors that may have a genetic origin, such as a tendency toward low blood sugar. Some forms of mental distress also precipitate conflict as a form of acting out. One of the most difficult aspects of dealing with conflict that arises from within us is that we may not at first recognize its source and assume that others are responsible for our foul mood. Being sensitive to the mood of one's partner involves recognizing when it is not a good time to discuss sensitive issues or bring up difficult problems.

Defensiveness. Defensive behavior generally is directed not toward satisfying a need, but rather toward alleviating the tension and self-deprecation associated with failure to meet the need in question. In this sense defense-oriented behavior differs from what we may call reality-oriented behavior in that it is aimed at achieving some substitute goal that will reduce tension rather than at overcoming the barrier to attainment of the primary goal. Among the most common defense mechanisms are withdrawal, conversion of tension into physical illness, substitution, rationalization, excessive sleeping, and fantasizing.

In *Communes U.S.A.*, Dick Fairfield reports a dramatic form of withdrawal. One of the members of Harrad West was so torn by the tensions in the group that he hid in a closet for several days.[2] His behavior was, of course, an extreme version of a type of defense that we all use from time to time. When you avoid calling a friend because you lost the book you borrowed from him, you are using withdrawal as a defense. So is the young man who avoids sexual conflict with his girlfriend by scheduling all their dates so that they are never alone together until he has to take her home.

Rationalization is probably the most commonly used defense mechanism. A student who attributes her failure to bias on the part of teachers is engaging in a rather transparent form of rationalization. There is an old adage that advises, "When confronted with failure, redefine success." In some cases, this may be sound advice. If you always wanted to be a jockey but didn't stop growing until you were six feet three inches tall, you would be well advised to revise your goals. The trouble with the adage is that it is difficult to tell whether you have tried hard enough before redefining success. If the slightest obstacle leads you to abandon your objectives, you are not being realistic so much as engaging in a form of rationalization.

One of the main reasons why people engage in defense-oriented behavior is because reality, when it is especially unpleasant, threatens their image of themselves. If an important part of your self-image is your belief that you are a great lover, you may respond to sexual problems in your partnership with such strategies as avoiding sexual situations or attributing the problem to your partner. Similarly, the man who shouts at his wife, "I am not shouting!" when she tells him to stop shouting and be reasonable probably does so because he is trying to preserve his image of himself as a reasonable man who handles conflict in a reasonable way.

These strategies, of course, do not solve the problem at hand; all they can do is save you the pain of recognizing that your own image of yourself does not correspond to reality. If you have a sexual problem, you cannot begin to deal with it until you admit to yourself that you are not an accomplished lover; the angry husband cannot contribute to a resolution of the situation that has made him angry until he acknowledges his anger.

What is more, the problem with defense-oriented strategies is not merely the fact that they fail to contribute to a resolution of the conflict. Often, in fact, they intensify conflict. The woman who refuses to speak to her husband when he comes home late not only does nothing to avoid a repetition of the incident, but also provides a new source of tension between them. The man who avoids confronting his sexual problem by avoiding intimate situations is adding to his marital difficulties by making his wife feel rejected. Defensiveness, in short, is not only an inadequate means of coping with conflict, but also an important source of conflict in its own right.

Differences in Background and Outlook. Differences in background and outlook between the partners are a rich storehouse of potential problems. Here such factors as differences in social class, economic position, family structure, religion, and race may come into play.

Such differences are far more significant in our modern, highly mobile society than they used to be. Until quite recently, the range of people available for mate selection tended to be quite narrow. It was not at all uncommon to marry the boy or girl next door. If for no other reason than lack of geographic mobility, an individual's acquaintances were likely to be found within a very narrow territory. This made it more probable that

Differences in background and outlook between partners are a rich source of conflict. (Susan Rosenberg, Photo Researchers, Inc.)

one's mate would share many of one's own socially determined attitudes and beliefs.

Today all this is changed. Especially in urban settings, public schools draw their students from a wide variety of backgrounds, and colleges intensify this trend. The people you meet in your college classes come from just about every segment of our society and, indeed, from all over the country. Sociologically speaking, the range of potential mates is much wider than was formerly the case, and with this change comes an increase in the likelihood that any partnership you form will contain greater divergence in background and outlook.[3]

We do not mean to suggest that it would be wiser or safer to limit yourself to partners who share your background. On the contrary, differences in background and outlook can contribute immensely to the growth potential of a partnership, for there are few things more helpful in opening a person's mind to new experience than an intimate association with someone whose view of the world differs markedly. We might almost speculate that there may be something seriously wrong with anyone who failed to grow and develop in such a situation. On the other hand, it would be unrealistic to imagine that major differences in world view do not produce significant problems that partners must confront.

A marriage in which, say, the husband is the son of a corporation vice president and the wife is the daughter of an assembly line worker is going to have problems that would not have arisen if the two partners had each married individuals whose backgrounds were more like their own.[4] These problems are going to include not only obvious differences in attitudes toward money, but also differences in feelings about entertaining friends, leisure activities, personal habits, domestic roles, and even sexual preferences. Each of these differences is a potential source of conflict, just as each is a potential source of growth. It is, to use a popular term, a liberating experience to learn that the way you, your family, and your friends have always done things is not the only way of doing things. As you learn this you find that you have more options, a richer variety of responses to a given situation. But it can also be a painful process, for the discovery of new options can be profoundly unsettling, inasmuch as it forces you to give up the comfortable assumption that your way is the only one.

Another type of conflict involving differing outlooks arises from what sociologists call *discontinuity of role conditioning*. Adult roles in our society are discontinuous from childhood roles. That is to say, the role of mother is not at all like that of daughter; the role of father is not at all like that of son. A man who wants his partner to treat him the way his mother used to treat him is likely to have a troubled partnership. Nor is it reasonable for him to want to treat his partner as though she were his mother. Yet when two people form an intimate partnership, especially for the first time, they have little or no experience in the new roles they are expected to fulfill. To a certain extent, the wife may expect her husband to relate to her in many of the ways in which her father related to her, just as the husband may expect his wife to "mother" him to some degree. Fortunately, this sort of conflict tends to diminish as the partners "grow up" and learn both what is expected of them in their new roles and what they can reasonably expect from their partners. Of course, if one or both of the partners does not grow up in the relationship, destructive conflict is likely.

Eros and Chaos

Perhaps the most difficult aspect of conflict for us to understand is that it arises in intimate partnerships because love requires it. This is not a social scientific observation, nor a common interpretation of everyday life. It is an insight most carefully preserved in mythology and interpreted in some theologies. In some of the accounts of Greek mythology, Eros forever seeks to re-create the conditions of its birth. "Eros will attempt again and again to create those dark nights and confusions which are its nest. It renews itself in affective attacks, jealousies, fulminations, and turmoils. It thrives close to the dragon."[5] Most of us find it difficult to associate love with destruction as well as creativity. This is one of the reasons that we find Eros such a difficult love style.

Yet these dark images of love abound in mythology and point to a shallowness in our present understanding. Martin Luther was deeply troubled by the violence of his age, perhaps the more so because he saw in much of it "God's strange love." Given our cultural proclivity, a close association between love, conflict, and destruction is strange indeed. What could it mean?

In previous chapters we have spoken a great deal about self-actualization. This dynamic process can be understood as love's continuing effort to become manifest. It is expressed socially as various love styles.[6] The German philosopher Frederick Neitzsche called the process "the will to power." His interpretation clearly suggests that self-actualization is not an easy unfolding of an inner potential; it is a constant struggle with the chaos monster or the dragon of nonbeing. This theme is well represented in the creation stories of the world's mythology. It is also beautifully depicted in the adventures of the Knights of the Round Table and their quest for the Holy Grail. From this perspective, the work of self-actualization (or soul making) is in constant danger of incompletion. We can avoid the call to become. We can end the unbearable pressure we sometimes feel to realize ourselves in suicide, or accommodate it in psychosis. Life demands a courageous affirmation, a great love, from all of us if we are going to become fully human.

But individuals differ in their capacity to self-actualize—to choose life in the face of death. According to the Existentialists, they differ in their power of being. This fact alone can account for much of the conflict in human relationships. The theologian Paul Tillich writes:

Life . . . in a human individual transcends itself. It runs ahead and it encounters life in another human individual which also pushes forward, or which withdraws, or which stands and resists. In each case another constellation of powers is the result. One draws another power into oneself and is either strengthened or weakened by it. One throws the foreign power of being out or assimilates it completely. One transforms the resisting powers, or one adapts oneself to them. One is absorbed by them and loses one's own power of being, one grows together with them and increases their and one's own power of being. These processes are going on in every moment of life, in all relations of all beings.[7]

Existential theology may seem a bit abstract because the level of analysis is unfamiliar. Nevertheless, we can appreciate such conflict perhaps in our own struggle for participation and recognition. An excellent example is the constant conflict between brothers and sisters struggling for recognition from their parents and intent upon establishing a pecking order that will clearly declare who is most powerful. Nothing is so nonsensical to someone not involved in the power struggle. Take the matter of watching television on the color television in the family room rather than on the black and white set in the bedroom. To a disinterested observer, it seems incredible that the slight difference in pleasure obtainable from color television could precipitate a major brawl between siblings, but such conflict can be observed in almost any family in which there are two or more children (and two or more television sets). A part of what is at stake in such confrontations is a power struggle. Even the establishment of a relatively stable pecking order does not eliminate the conflict; it merely transforms its character to a more covert mode of expression.

In the best of all possible worlds, perhaps, the inherent conflict between self-actualizing individuals with different powers of being would be resolved in such a manner as to give each her or his due—that is to say, to give greater social recognition to those with greater power of being. The social roles and institutions thus established would be an expression of justice by one understanding of it, and coercion in such partnerships would be unnecessary. In the imperfect world in which we live, however, the power of being in another—or in ourselves—is not clearly perceived and is imperfectly recognized in social roles. **Power**, therefore, is most often expressed in human society as the ability to impose one's will on another in spite of the other's opposition.[8]

From this perspective, conflict in intimate groups is inevitable, particularly if the groups are composed of individuals with a great capacity to self-actualize. But to argue for the necessity of conflict in intimate partnerships is not to argue for its expression in any and every way. It is rather to stress the importance of conflict management and to further suggest the inherent difficulty of the undertaking in intimate partnerships, since love itself requires it.

Since each of us has grown up in a somewhat different environment and has experienced life from a unique perspective, we differ in our capacity to tolerate stress and manage conflict. We have different needs, some of which may be difficult for our partners to meet, and impossible for us to resolve alone. Because our parents failed to show enough care and consideration for us when we were growing up, it may be difficult for us to love our children as parents. All these factors and many more create conditions for conflict in intimate partnerships.

Interpersonal Sources

The personal and interpersonal often intertwine, but we can point to sources of conflict that seem to arise out of the partnership itself rather than out of the particular traits of the partners.

Misunderstood Agreements. Marriage means different things to each of us. We are just beginning to document some of these meanings.[9] Because of the difficulty of communicating our personal needs, the changing circumstances of our lives, and our changing understanding of what is desirable in a partnership, the implicit or explicit contract we negotiate must be renegotiated from time to time. Where once we thought we had an agreement, it may later appear that we did not mutually understand what was at stake or what was important to ourselves or our partners.

Little squabbles over sexual behavior, managing money, or dealing with in-laws may originate in a divergent understanding of what the partnership should be like. If the partnership is supposed to be one in which there is no disagreement or conflict, then any disagreement or conflict is seen as threatening. If the partnership is supposed to be one in which the partners are allowed maximum freedom and privacy in which to do their own thing, then efforts by one partner to do things with the other may threaten the partnership. If the partnership is one in which things are to be worked out together as much as possible, then the efforts of one or both partners to do their own thing may be disruptive.

It is possible to have such conflict and not recognize it because the effort to settle the squabble obscures the basic misunderstanding. "What we expect from each other," therefore, ought to be a continuing element in the conversation and concerns of partners—especially those who are attempting to grow within their partnership. It is possible to avoid the whole matter of renegotiation on the assumption that "actions speak louder than words." As long as the partner does not object to what is done in a partnership, some people may contend there is no need to be concerned. But this tactic is likely to put off the inevitable day of confrontation and increase the likelihood that conflict will destroy the partnership.

Inadequate Feedback. The term **feedback** is used by sociologists to describe the signals given off by our environment (personal or impersonal) in response to our behavior.[10] We can use this feedback to adjust or modify our behavior. Sometimes this adjustment takes place consciously, as when an associate tells you you look good in bright-colored clothes and you take this response into account the next time you are shopping for something to wear. Sometimes it occurs unconsciously. For example, if you are a salesperson who tends to "come on strong" with your customers, you may instinctively adopt a softer approach with customers who seem unresponsive to your usual method, without even realizing that you are doing so. Problems tend to arise when people are unaware, either consciously and unconsciously, of the feedback they are receiving and when the feedback they are receiving is not adequate to allow them to assess the situation and make the proper adjustments.

When we think of feedback a number of examples from the nonpersonal environment come readily to mind. Thermostats and computers are well-known devices that employ feedback; when you tune an engine or a musical instrument, the sound you hear after each adjustment is the feedback that tells you what to do next. But feedback in human interaction is much more complicated because so much more is involved. In the first place, the environment gives off many cues, not just a single stimulus such as, in the case of the thermostat, a change in the amount of heat. We are able to respond to many stimuli simultaneously, although we may not be consciously aware of all of them. Furthermore, behavior is not a set of discrete acts but a process. Thus, it is sometimes difficult, if not impossible, to relate the feedback we are receiving to a specific act. Finally, before we can use the feedback we receive, we must interpret it in terms of our own capacities and self-image. Our interaction with our environment is a complex process, with many messages being communicated in many directions at the same time. Consider the following incident, which occurred in a training group:

Don:	John, it seems to me that every time Eric tries to say something, you interrupt him.
John:	Oh, I don't think that's true.
Eric:	I think you do.
Sue:	I don't think John interrupts Eric. I feel that every time Eric makes a contribution, John seems to add to and build upon what Eric said. Don't you feel that way, Eric?
Eric:	No! Sue, you always seem to be supporting John. As far as you're concerned, John can do nothing wrong in this group.
Mary:	I agree with Don. I think John does interrupt Eric, and I'm annoyed that Sue always stands up for John.

This is a classic example of a lot of feedback being given in a group setting. John, of course, is getting conflicting feedback about his behavior in this group. There is a discrepancy between the signals he is getting from Don, Eric, and Mary and the signals he is getting from Sue. How is he to evaluate what he hears? What is he to make of this discrepancy? What changes should he make in his behavior as a result? Can he assume that Don, Eric, and Mary must be right simply because they constitute the majority of the group? Probably not. The point is that in real-life situations responding to the feedback you receive from your environment is not an easy task because the feedback is often complex and even contradictory. What is more, as can be seen in the preceding example, the other members of the group also are getting feedback about their behavior. The communication of feedback is a complicated, ongoing process.

Members of partnerships can grow only if they receive adequate feedback. The feedback you give and receive can be classified in a number of ways. It may be divergent or convergent. **Divergent feedback** tells us that our behavior is not bringing us a result that we desire; **convergent feedback** tells us that our behavior is appropriate to our objectives. In a partnership or a marriage divergent feedback moves the partners away from one another and engenders frustration. A sensible response to divergent feedback would be to make an attempt to clarify the issues so that appropriate adjustments of behavior become possible. Often, however, people respond to divergent feedback by pouting, becoming miffed and angry, and by trying to make their partner feel uncomfortable too. There is a tendency to answer divergent feedback with more divergent feedback, so that the spiral of disengagement accelerates. Often a "cooling-off" period is necessary before this pattern can be broken. Sometimes the partners may push each other away for weeks or months, perhaps even ending the partnership.

Feedback can also be classed as limited or free, immediate or delayed. In the nonpersonal world of inanimate objects, feedback is typically free and immediate. In the world of interpersonal relations, it is typically limited and delayed. Because feedback in partnerships is likely to be limited and delayed in many situations, and because it is almost always ambiguous (inasmuch as it reflects a multitude of needs), couples must work hard to interpret correctly the feedback they receive from their partners and to reduce the ambiguity in the feedback they give off. If they cannot do this, their partnership is in for a lot of trouble. Conflict is inevitable and inevitably will be destructive.

One reason why feedback is important is that the feedback a person receives has a lot to do with the formation and maintenance of her or his self-image. Our conception of who we are is derived from the feedback we have received throughout our life—particularly the early portion of it. Convergent feedback makes us feel comfortable, adequate, and at ease with ourselves. Indeed, a person who has benefited from consistent convergent feedback in one area of life may feel relaxed and competent in many other areas.

Just as convergent feedback is an essential part of the process by which the self-image is maintained, so divergent feedback is essential for modifying the self-image. Because we are always to some extent a mystery to ourselves, we are constantly listening to others to find out who we are. Statements or behaviors that make emphatic judgments about us are not easily dismissed. This is a common experience in training sessions. Kurt Back reports having had conversations with two of five men who were on special assignment during the first year of the National Training Laboratory in Bethel, Maine. As part of the assignment, they received intensive divergent feedback and criticism. Both reported the pain of the experience ten years later and vowed never again to expose themselves so openly to the criticism of others.[11]

The destructive potential of divergent feedback has important implications for intimate partnerships. In a partnership we are likely to be open enough to lower many of the normal defenses, and in this sense we are most vulnerable in our most intimate relationship. When our partner attacks us at this deep level, we tend to see this as disloyalty and betrayal, for it is very difficult to withstand attacks that are directed against one's self-image at a very deep level.

On the other hand, the fact that partners can and should reinforce each other's self-image presupposes a willingness on their part to accept the differences between them. If one partner lacks this willingness, the other may feel pressured to change. Unfortunately, there is a common tendency to limit the convergent feedback we give in areas in which we are not aware of differences and, when we cannot confirm a partner, to feel that this is somehow the partner's "fault." In fact, however, the areas in which convergent feedback and confirmation are not possible may well be those in which the other has the greatest potential for growth.

For example, imagine a situation in which a wife was overly dependent on her husband's judgment in most of the major decisions that confronted her. As she grows less dependent, however, her husband may find himself incapable of supporting and confirming her new-found independence. The feedback she gets from him may be mostly negative. What is progress and growth from her point of view may be threatening to his self-image, and conflict may result. However, the conflict may accelerate her growth toward independence, and the negative feedback he receives from her may open his eyes to the fact that his image of himself as a decisive man does not have to depend on her indecisiveness. This example reminds us once again that conflict is an integral part of any relationship and that it can be a life-giving and growth-enhancing force.

Frustration. Frustration, which often manifests itself in feelings of depression, anger, or indifference, derives from our inability to realize our objectives, to meet our needs or expectations. When we cannot live into our self-image or fulfill our dreams, frustration is a likely response. Often it is difficult for a person to identify the sources of his or her frustration. Although sexual frustration readily comes to mind as an example, it is by no means the only or even the major source of frustration in partnerships. Inability to get work done around the house, job presures that are carried over to the partnership, the unmatched needs and expectations of the partners—all can be sources of frustration.

One possible response to frustration is aggression. When things do not go the way we expect them to, we often give vent to an angry outburst at the supposed culprit. Frustration can also be turned inward, so that the frustrated person feels deeply depressed, often without knowing why. A third response to frustration is projection, an unconscious process in which responsibility for the frustrating situation is "projected" onto another person. Thus, for example, a man who is frustrated by the inefficiency of his staff may project his anger onto his wife, scolding her for not having dinner ready on time. The wife is thus unwittingly brought into the conflict generated by the frustrations of the job. If it is not clear to the husband or the wife that his real reason for scolding her is his anger at his staff, they are likely to get involved in a fight that seemingly has no purpose.

No one reacts to frustration the same way all the time. Each of us can probably call to mind examples in our own behavior of all three ways of responding to frustration. Nevertheless, most people tend to favor one type of response over the others, so that it can be identified as their typical way of handling frustrating situations. The fact that this is so can be of some help to one's partner. If you are able to recognize that some of your partner's behaviors are his or her usual response to frustration, you may be able to cope with the situation far better than you could if you took the response at face value. There is, of course, no reason why a wife should be expected to tolerate outbursts of anger directed at her simply because she knows that something that happened at work has upset her husband. But she will be able to deal with the situation in a far more appropriate way if she recognizes its real source. As long as she misunderstands the situation, her response to his anger is likely to be merely defensive—perhaps consisting of trying to explain why dinner was late—but once she understands the real cause of his anger she can take the offensive, attempting to show him the root of the problem.

It is not uncommon to find that couples who know each other well have learned to tell when what they are fighting about is "really" what they are fighting about and when it is not. This knowledge can be of tremendous help because it makes it easier to keep conflict in perspective. The partners know when real issues are at stake and respond accordingly; they also know when an apparent conflict is simply a result of the fact that one of the partners is responding to frustration by "letting off steam," and they don't let this sort of inessential conflict get out of hand. As we will see when we discuss learning how to fight, an important part of the successful management of conflict involves knowing what is worth fighting over and what isn't. Partners who do not know this are likely to find their relationship degenerating.

TROUBLE SPOTS

No one can predict in advance what areas will prove troublesome in an intimate partnership. Each pair of partners is unique, and one couple may slide blissfully through areas in which others bog down in squabbling and contention. The following discussion, therefore, attempts merely to describe in an approximate way the places where couples most frequently run into difficulties. Our assumption is that before we can begin to discuss conflict in general terms, it is useful to have some idea of the specific types of conflict that commonly arise.

We have chosen—somewhat arbitrarily, to be sure—three areas for preliminary examination. These are sex, money, and in-laws. It is not our intention to tell you how to avoid conflict in these areas. Rather, by raising the question of why conflict arises so easily in these areas we hope to come to some understanding of the dynamics of conflict in intimate partnerships—what kinds of things cause it, what kinds of effects it has. Then we can move on to a more general discussion of the sources of conflict and its creative and destructive aspects.

Sex

Sexual relations not only are the most intimate aspect of an intimate partnership, but are probably also, for a great many people, the most potentially troublesome. Nor is it difficult to see why this should be so. Whatever the sexual feelings, desires, attitudes, and behaviors of oneself and one's partner, it is important to realize that they have developed over a lifetime and are not likely to change overnight. While some partners may come to their marriage or partnership relatively well matched in terms of these feelings and attitudes, others may be so mismatched and "incompatible" that a great deal of patience is needed for them to achieve a mutually satisfying sexual relationship.

It is commonly thought that sexual incompatibility is a result of a mismatch in sexual drive.[12] Usually we assume that the man wants sex more often than the woman. However, it is becoming increasingly apparent that different needs for sexual intimacy are not determined by biology alone. They reflect a host of subtle social conditionings that can be unlearned only with patience and cooperation. Furthermore, part of the problem of so-called sexual incompatibility derives from the fact that so much of a couple's understanding of what sex is is focused on sexual intercourse.

If one or both partners believe that good, healthy, mature, delightful sex is limited to sexual intercourse in the man-on-top position, then not only will the couple miss out on a great deal of noncoital pleasure, but the alternatives for fulfilling each other's sexual needs are greatly reduced. A full understanding of sex in its broadest context and willingness to try a wider variety of techniques can virtually eliminate the problem of sexual incompatibility.

But given our traditional attitudes toward sex, this is not an easy thing to accomplish. Indeed, such an effort may be particularly difficult for some couples. Research suggests that there are two different basic attitudes toward sex. **Erotophiles** are individuals who can be said to have a love for the erotic. **Erotophobes,** on the other hand, have a basic fear of it.[13] Erotophiles are more willing to experiment and prepare for sexual experiences. Erotophobes are more likely to be troubled by thinking about sex and much less likely to prepare for sexual encounters. One very serious consequence of this lack of preparation is that erotophobes are much less likely to make adequate use of contraceptives. Their fear of the erotic prohibits them from thinking about such matters, but it does not completely remove their sexual desires. The fear of sex also makes it difficult for this type of person to discuss sexual differences with a partner and thus makes it more difficult to work out such differences. There is no guarantee that both members of a developing partnership will have the same attitude toward sex.

Finally, in his analysis of different love styles, Lee concludes that sex plays an extremely important role in the love style that he calls Eros.[14] The erotic lover wants to get into bed as quickly as possible in order to find out whether the beloved fulfills his or her ideal. For erotic lovers, carnal knowledge is a very important dimension of knowing another person. On the other hand, stoic lovers know each other for a long time and rely on basic affection much more than on erotic infatuation to maintain their partnership. While the courtship process might reduce the probability that an erotic lover and a stoic lover would end up trying to maintain an enduring partnership, it does not guarantee it. Many partnerships are entered into with little or no advance preparation, and then the differences implied by these two love styles has to be handled during the partnership. Such differences in sexual desire need not destroy a growing partnership. However, coping with the conflict that is necessary to overcome or live with such differences can demand a great deal of cooperation from the partners.

Think for a moment about what your "ideal" sexual partner would be like. If sex is to be an important aspect of the communication process in your partnership, your partner undoubtedly would be a person with complex and varied sexual tastes that match your own complex and varied feelings. Sometimes you want your physical intimacies to communicate the tender, loving, and gentle aspects of your relationship; at other times your lovemaking will be more passionate.

From this it follows that your "ideal" sexual partner will be someone who is capable of expressing through sex all the things you want expressed. This is where the snag comes in, because unless your partner is a sexual robot whom you can program to be tender when you want tenderness, passionate when you want passion, seductive when you want to be seduced, submissive when you want to be dominant, and dominant when you want to be submissive, you undoubtedly are going to find that your needs and desires are not always met the way you want them to be met. Precisely because sex is such a complex part of any intimate relationship, even an "ideally" matched couple is not going to find that their desires are perfectly synchronized throughout their relationship.

Unless you, your partner, and your partnership become static, you will never outgrow the need to sit down and discuss your feelings, desires, attitudes, and behaviors. As Richard Klemer observed in *Marriage and Family Relations*, "For the great majority of young marrieds, though, the sex adjustment process itself is both necessary and rewarding. After all, there is no other adjustment in which just trying can be so satisfying and so love enriching."[15]

Money

Except among a handful of inordinately rich people, money is a subject that is likely to be associated with some form of conflict in most partnerships. Let us confine ourselves here to a few general observations about the nature of money conflicts in a partnership.

Money is what economists call a scarce resource; but the desires of you and your partner for things that cost money are not scarce. In a sense the whole problem is no more complex than this one sentence. Even wealthy people must make decisions about how to spend their money, and these decisions must be shaped by some hierarchy of priorities. In some families the choice is between lamb chops for dinner and staying home or macaroni and cheese for dinner and going to a movie; in others a decision must be made about whether to get a new television set or to have the dents taken out of the car; and in still others it is a matter of choosing between the yacht that sleeps 12 or that lovely old 14-room house in Bucks County.

Money is a common trouble spot in partnerships. (Teri Leigh Stratford)

Except among the fabulously rich, lines have to be drawn somewhere, and the drawing of these lines is a task that most partners will have some trouble negotiating.

Money conflicts provide an excellent example of the fact that mutual awareness of each other's habits and attitudes is probably the most effective factor in reducing conflict of all sorts. In any new partnership there is a tendency for the partners to look askance at the way their mate spends money simply because the mate's habits are unfamiliar. A young wife, for example, may be shocked when her husband spends $600 for stereo equipment. She has to admit that they can afford the expense, but to her $600 is a lot of money to throw away on something trivial. It seems that way to her because music wasn't as important to her parents as it was to her husband; her father once spent $50 for a portable phonograph, but that was the extent of his spending in this area. On the other hand, her father drove a car as big as a houseboat and traded it in every two years. So if her husband had announced that he wanted to invest $8000 in an automobile, she probably wouldn't have batted an eyelash; but when he lays out a fraction of that for his stereo system, she complains about his financial irresponsibility. In time, though, she will learn that it is not a matter of responsibility; it is simply that her husband has priorities that are different from those with which she is familiar.

Conflict over money management can arise as a result of several common issues. The monthly, if not daily, effort to pay the bills is one such issue. While most couples' income is usually quite fixed within a particular year, their wants continue to expand. Few are completely satisfied with their income. Indeed, one of the bitter ironies of recent research is that the higher the income of a family, the more additional income the family thinks is necessary in order to have an adequate income.[16]

A second money issue is likely to produce conflict in intimate partnerships. Regardless of how much income a couple has, it is necessary to allocate it, to spend it for some things and not for others. What to spend money on can be a tremendous source of conflict, particularly when there is little explicit agreement on common goals. This problem is not limited to marriage partnerships. With more and more couples living together without a marriage contract, the issue of money management takes on new significance. The recent court case involving Lee Marvin and his companion of eight years, Michele Triola Marvin, raised, but did not settle, the matter of the rights of unmarried persons in the economic resources of their partner. It is easy in principle but difficult in practice to live with someone and not tend to merge economic resources. Without a marriage contract, these merged resources are sometimes difficult to recover in the event of a breakup.

A third money issue is really a catchall. Perhaps the biggest problem in the management of money is the fact that what is involved is not always economics. There is a great deal of entertainment and satisfaction to be found in playing the stock market, for example. If you are playing the market for pleasure and your partner expects you to be turning in the bucks on a regular schedule or thinks that you can't afford to engage in such playfulness, there is likely to be trouble. Money promises to give status and power, benefits that are quite independent from economic benefits. Making the decisions about how income should be earned or spent, therefore, is rarely simply a matter of making wise economic choices about the allocation of dollars. The fact that money management is a frequent source of conflict is poignantly illustrated by the fact that 99 percent of the runaway husbands traced by the Tracer Company of America had left home because of their inability to manage the sizable family funds available to them.[17]

Of course, familiarity does not entirely eliminate conflict in this area. In a sense, each change in a couple's financial situation—the birth of a baby, a significant increase in his or her salary, the added income when she starts working again once the children are all in school—presents a new situation that they must learn to handle afresh. But if the partners have had conflicts over these matters before, if they have learned to tell each other what they think and to listen to what the other has to say, and if each has learned to respect the other's judgment and to have confidence in his or her own judgment, then conflict over money matters can take the form of clear presentation of grievances, a fair assessment of the situation by both individuals, and a sensible resolution.

In-Laws

Jokes about mothers-in-law are about as old as the institution of marriage, and it is only because of the sexual biases of our society, which tend to make the female partner in a marriage and her female parent frequent targets for humor, that jokes about fathers-in-law aren't as common. We joke about in-laws for a very simple reason: They make us nervous. While we have pretty clear expectations about what it means to be a good husband or a good wife, we do not know with anything like the same assurance what it means to be a good in-law. Some societies go to great lengths to define precisely how one should behave with every conceivable in-law.[18] Ours does not. This means in practice that an in-law is someone we should feel close to somehow—especially if the in-law is a parent-in-law—but we are not quite sure how to express this closeness. It is a very rare mother- or father-in-law who can fully accept being treated like a parent, and a very rare person who is able to treat them as such. Because formal rules regulating how we ought to relate to our in-laws are largely absent in our society, we are freer to define these relationships as we would like them.

Some of our problems with in-laws result from our failure to resolve conflict with our parents. For some individuals, for example, marriage promises to be a way out of a conflict-ridden home. But such a marriage seldom resolves old issues and often creates new conflict with in-laws.

Relationships with in-laws may be sought for the purposes of (1) extending a fundamentally happy family life over a larger portion of the life cycle, (2) providing love that has not been found at home, (3) providing social status of financial support, or (4) confirming the fact that all parents are cold and rejecting. "Conflict arises when the partner seeks but does not find what he needs, either because the in-laws are unwilling or unable to meet the need or because the method of expressing the need unwittingly alienates them.[19] Any effort to work out old conflicts with parents through relationships with in-laws is likely to produce conflict between the marriage partners as well.

Cohabiting couples face the additional question of whether to let both sets of parents "in" on their arrangement. If the parents are not likely to meet each other, it is not necessary that either or both sets be informed. But in a situation in which there is likely to be some interchange between the in-laws and some contact with the couple, it is difficult to avoid letting them in. And of course, it is likely that the inlaws have different attitudes toward such behavior—another potential source of conflict.[20]

A lot of conflict involving in-laws boils down to a matter of simple jealousy. Before marriage, your parents and siblings are your family; after marriage, your spouse is your family. In most cases this change isn't traumatic; rather, it is a subtle shifting of loyalties that may go almost unnoticed but is nonetheless real. It is not easy to assess just what this change entails, but it is probably safe to generalize and say that for most people becoming married is a gradual process. In a marriage your primary commitments are to each other and to your partnership, but these commitments are not formed overnight. While they are developing, it would not be unusual to experience some doubts about whether your mate really is fully committed to you and, conversely, about whether you are fully committed to your mate. Often these doubts center on your in-laws, who are the chief rivals for the loyalty you expect. "Why do we have to go over to your parents' house so often?" a young wife may complain. "Don't tell me your sister's coming to visit again. Don't you two get enough of each other?" a new husband may lament. "Can't you find someone else to go shopping with besides your mother?" "If you think Consolidated Asbestos is a good investment, go ahead and buy it. I don't see why you have to ask your father's advice." All these are statements of mates' jealousy of their partners' involvement with their families. But if you are or have ever been married, you probably have had the experience of heading home with your spouse after a visit to your parents' house and saying or feeling something like, "You know, it's funny, but while we were sitting there in the living room this afternoon it suddenly struck me that I don't live there any more."

What we are saying, in short, is that people's relations to their parents are highly complex. And one's relations with one's partner are every bit as complex—probably more so. Put the two sets of relationships together and you have six people who are connected with each other in an extremely intricate web of emotions.

THE CREATIVE DIMENSIONS OF CONFLICT

Conflict that is creative—or at least has the potential for being so—is conflict that recognizes the personhood of the partner. This means essentially that neither partner in the conflict attempts to reduce the other to the status of a nonperson through labeling or abusive language or denial; rather, each partner sees the other as a "worthy adversary" with ideas, dreams, and thoughts that are valid and must be taken into account. It takes an intense openness to appreciate and respect the ideas of another person when they are in direct conflict with our own, but this is in fact the only way in which conflict can be creative. Only equals are worthy adversaries.

If equals engage in conflict, and if their communication is significant, what emerges is a complicated process that enables each to define and clarify—both for himself and herself and for the other—the issue on which the conflict is focused. This does not mean that the contestants simply accept any statement their partner may make, but it does mean that they take advantage of the intensity of the debate, with its defining and redefining of the issues, so that the conflict provides an opportunity to deepen their understanding of what is at stake.

If the issues are drawn with clarity, the conflict almost inevitably serves to broaden the base of contact between the partners. Things that would have been simply accepted or rejected had there been no conflict are explored, examined, and defended. Thus intimacy is facilitated.

Respecting Feelings

One of the major sources of conflict in intimate relationships is the fact that two partners are likely to have quite different feelings about some things. The conflict thus serves to bring these different feelings into the open, but in many cases it will not do anything to change them. You may be tempted to assume that this means conflict is pointless. If a husband and wife have different feelings about something, argue about it and still have different feelings, what, you may well ask, is gained from the conflict?

To answer these questions, we must first understand that changing your partner's attitudes and feeling should not be the primary goal of conflict. A person feels what he or she feels, and being told (or telling yourself) that it is wrong to feel that way doesn't do much to change it. The feelings remain, and added to them is a sense of guilt for feeling that way in the first place. If either partner were to be pressured into renouncing his or her feelings as a result of conflict, that partner would be surrendering an authentic part of himself or herself. (On the other hand, we do not mean to suggest that people do not sometimes genuinely learn, as a result of conflict, that their feelings were wrong. Most people have had the experience of getting into an argument with someone and admitting in the course of the conflict,

"You know, you're right; I don't know why I let myself get so worked up about that. I guess I wasn't thinking straight; I just got carried away.")

If we cannot reasonably expect one of the partners to renounce his or her feelings, what does the conflict accomplish? If we recognize that conflict often arises from the fact that an ongoing relationship has numerous goals that sometimes are mutually exclusive, we can see that conflict can help bridge this gap as long as each partner realizes that it is important to respect the other's feelings. If the two of them simply denounce each other for being selfish, they will only make the situation worse. But if as a result of the conflict they come to a fuller appreciation of each other's feelings, they will be better able to navigate the difficult periods in their relationship. The important thing is not to make conflicts go away. It is to appreciate and respect each other's feelings so that you and your partner can approach your problems as something you are struggling with together rather than as something that is driving you apart.

Avoiding Win–Lose Battles

An old adage says that how you play the game is more important than whether you win or lose. It is probably safe to say that in our competitive society not many people take this adage seriously; it seems old-fashioned, naive, and unrealistic. Twentieth-century America is unmistakably a meritocracy in which "nothing succeeds like success"; in such a society it matters quite a bit whether you win or lose. How you play the game also matters, but perhaps not quite as much.

One could argue at great length about whether the American success ethic, with its emphasis on winning, is good or bad, healthy or unhealthy. We are going to avoid the temptation to take a side in this argument. Instead, we will simply point out that in most situations of conflict between intimate partners, who wins and who loses is not very important. Regardless of how you feel about the importance of winning in business, sports, or life in general, an intimate partnership simply is not a competitive situation.

Conflict situations in which one partner can win only at the expense of the other's loss tend to be destructive for both parties. When conflict in a partnership is conducted on the winner-take-all principle, there is little possibility that the conflict will produce mutual growth, for one partner can "grow" only at the expense of the other. In a **win–lose** situation someone is always going to get hurt, regardless of how socially acceptable or appropriate the loss may be.

Unless there is something seriously wrong with your partnership, you probably do not engage in conflict with your partner in order to score points. Rather, you come into conflict when one or both of you feel that something is wrong that must be corrected. Usually, too, the aggrieved party feels that his or her partner is responsible for the situation. If the tele-

In partnerships it is very important to avoid trying to win the argument. (Richard Hutchings, Photo Researchers, Inc.)

vision isn't working right the situation needs correcting, but it is not an occasion for conflict. But if the television isn't working and you think your partner should have fixed it—that is, if you hold your partner responsible for the problem—then it is a situation that could lead to conflict. But your point in initiating the conflict was not to force the other party to confess, "I was wrong, you were right"; it was to get the television fixed, that is, to do something about the problem that caused the conflict in the first place.

Often it is unfair to take a win–lose approach to conflict. In many partnerships the individuals are not equally matched in their ability to fight. Often the woman is at a disadvantage for the simple reason that our society tends to encourage aggressiveness in males and discourage it in females. In many partnerships, therefore, the husband will find that if he pushes a fight far enough and hard enough his wife will surrender. This discovery can be the undoing of a partnership, for there is no denying that winning is a tempting prospect.

Closely related to the win–lose approach to conflict is the type of conflict that arises out of competition between the partners. Some people are highly competitive; they try to turn almost any kind of activity into a competitive game. Such people may carry this tendency over into their partnership. They compete with their partners for other people's attention, or they compete with each other to see who can do more chores or who can manage the affairs of the partnership better. This sort of behavior can easily become a source of endless conflict, and it quickly degenerates into a continuous win–lose battle. When you compete with someone else, you are attempting to demonstrate that you are better than that person. This also means that you are attempting to demonstrate that the other person is "worse" than you. Insofar as this is the case, competition is a denial of your partner's personhood. The fact that our society places a high premium on competition on the job, in school, and in the marketplace indicates that this is one area in which the interpersonal skills rewarded by our society may in fact be destructive to interpersonal relationships.[21]

Of course, it is easy enough to advise people to avoid win–lose confrontations, but it is not so easy to follow this advice in the heat of conflict. Creative conflict involves accepting the anger and hostility in oneself and in one's partner as real and legitimate. But feelings can be accepted and experienced without being acted upon either by letting it all hang out in a violent fistfight or by spewing out an uncontrolled avalanche of abusive language intended to exterminate one's partner. The ability to allow the partner to "save face" even in the heat of an argument is a skill that can be learned. It takes time and patience and, we think, begins with cultivating the ability to accept feelings that we commonly find unacceptable.

Learning to Fight

The Intimate Enemy, by George Bach and Peter Wyden, describes the repertory of skills that are necessary for creative fighting in partnerships.[22] Their book is highly recommended for anyone who wishes to explore further this fascinating and important aspect of intimate relationships. It should be read along with Suzanne K. Steinmetz and Murray A. Strauss's *Violence in the Family*, which demonstrates, on the basis of a study of 385 couples, that certain kinds of verbal "ventilation" of aggressive feelings can be quite destructive.[23] Because the subject is too complex to be dealt with fully here, we will confine ourselves to a few basic observations.

For some people, learning to fight means starting with the fundamentals of self-defense. That is to say, some people come to a partnership without having learned how to stand up for themselves. It may be that in their parents' home conflict was always hidden from the children; or it may be that the parent who was the young person's role model was chronically submissive in any conflict. Whatever the reason, you cannot realistically expect your partner to be able to see things from your point of view if you are not able to defend that point of view.

For other people, learning to fight means learning to fight fair. Boxing and wrestling have sets of rules that dictate what is fair and what is unfair; even war is subject to internationally accepted standards. Unfortunately, no one has yet codified the laws that govern intimate conflict. Nevertheless, it is important that couples work out their own standards. What these are will vary from one couple to the next, but it is not hard to figure out the sort of thing that would constitute a "low blow" in any partnership.

The important thing to bear in mind when fighting with your partner is to keep the conflict in perspective. You want to drive home your points, but you don't want to inflict permanent damage. Suppose a husband and wife have gotten into an argument about sex; she initiated it by complaining to him that he is in too much of a hurry. After a few minutes of quiet discussion the situation escalated into an argument. For the first ten minutes it was kept within bounds. Then he hit her with a low blow, angrily shouting, "Don't blame me for the fact that you're terrible in bed! I had plenty of women before we were married and I never got any complaints." Or suppose a husband and wife have gotten into an argument about how much she spends on clothes, food, or anything else. Tempers flare over whether or not she budgets carefully enough, but then she floors him with a rabbit punch, ending the fight by saying, "If you made a decent living we wouldn't be having this problem. I'm sorry if I haven't adjusted to the fact that you'll never amount to anything!"

Finally, learning to fight means learning when to stop. For many people this isn't a problem; indeed, their most passionate moments of closeness may come after their bitterest fights. Such couples, however, are probably far more rare than the folklore about marriage would have us believe. In real life calling off a fight is a difficult art to master. In part this is because the desire to win dies hard, and it is not easy to recognize when you have made your feelings clear to your partner and your partner has made his or her feelings clear to you. One couple we know of hit upon a deceptively simple strategy for stopping fights. One partner—we won't say which—would say, "If I was wrong, which I tend to doubt, I'm sorry." And the other would say, "And if I was wrong, which I tend to doubt, I'm sorry."

The strategy worked because it provided a convenient way out of the conflict when both parties recognized that there was nothing to be gained by pursuing it. This formula isn't magic, though. Even after the couple in question discovered the formula, they still pushed some of their fights too far simply because neither partner was willing to invoke it. There is, in fact, no strategy that can guarantee you and your partner will be able to stop your conflicts before they become counterproductive, but experienced couples generally find that it helps to work out some mutually intelligible signal for letting your partner know when you think it is time for a truce.[24]

Leveling

Psychologist Carl Rogers claims that one of the keys to a successful relationship is a commitment by both partners to expressing any persistent feeling about the partnership that they may have. This also entails a commitment to listen to the partner's reaction. In short, the partners promise to **level** with each other.

Leveling is difficult to do because of the natural fear of hurting or offending one's partner or of being hurt or offended by his or her response. When we are afraid to level with our partner, we tend to run away from a potential fight. Sometimes this is an appropriate reaction to a looming conflict, but it should not be allowed to become a habitual response to tension. It is generally a good idea to postpone a fight in order to avoid engaging in conflict in an unsuitable setting, but if a couple makes these postponements permanent, they are not leveling with each other. Although no conflict may be apparent, the reality is that communication has broken down.

SUMMARY

In this chapter we have explored some of the dimensions of conflict in intimate relations. We have seen that it can be either a creative or a destructive force in partnerships. Conflict is a necessary ingredient if an intimate partnership is to grow and develop. Acceptance and recognition of conflict are the first steps toward its creative use. As long as conflict is seen as a means to an end—the growth and development of each partner—it can be a creative mode of communication.

When conflict becomes an end in itself, however, it is usually destructive. When it becomes a win–lose proposition for the partners, it tends to create a situation in which one partner gains at the other's expense. By losing, a partner can suffer a diminution of his or her personhood that is not easy to regain.

We have explored five major sources of conflict: misunderstood agreement, defensiveness, differences in background and outlook, inadequate feedback, and frustration. In addition, we have looked at some of the most common trouble spots in intimate partnerships: sexual relations, money, and relations with in-laws.

Conflict can be creative when it respects the personhood of the partner. It can provide an occasion for honest and open interpersonal communication that allows a couple to express feelings and clarify and define the issues in their partnership. Thus, it can contribute to the freedom and autonomy of the individual partners. Conflict is necessary to the growth of partnerships. Violence rarely, if ever, leads to productive outcomes in intimate partnerships.

NOTES

1. John F. Crosby, *Illusion and Disillusion: The Self in Love and Marriage* (Belmont, Calif.: Wadsworth, 1973); H. L. Rausch et al., *Communication, Conflict and Marriage* (San Francisco: Jossey-Bass, 1974)
2. Richard Fairfield, *Communes U.S.A.: A Personal Tour* (Baltimore: Penguin Books, 1972), p. 300.
3. See, for example, the following studies that support an assimilation model in some select cases: Steven Martin Cohen, "Socioeconomic Determinants of

Inter-ethnic Marriage and Friendship," *Social Forces*, 55 (June 1977): 997–1010; John N. Tinker, "Intermarriage and Ethnic Boundaries: The Japanese American Case," *Journal of Social Issues*, 29, 2 (1973): 49–65; and Thomas P. Monahan, "Some Dimensions of Interreligious Marriage in Indiana, 1962–67," *Social Forces*, 52 (December 1973): 195–203.

4. Stephen R. Jorgenson, "Social Class Heterogamy Status Striving and Perception of Marital Conflict, a Partial Replication of Pearlin's Contingency Hypothesis," *Journal of Marriage and the Family* (November 1977): 653–61. Jorgensen contends that marital conflict for wives who value status striving is greatest for those who marry below their status. The greatest conflict for those who do not value status is reported by those who marry above their own status. See also L. I. Pearlin, "Status Inequality and Stress in Marriage," *American Sociological Review*, (June 1940): 344–57.

5. James Hillman, *The Myth of Analysis* (New York: Harper Row, 1972), p. 99.

6. John Alan Lee, *The Colors of Love* (Don Mills, Ont.: New Harper Press, 1976).

7. Paul Tillich, *Love, Power and Justice* (New York: Oxford University Press, 1954), p. 42.

8. This is, of course, the Weberian definition of power and is often used in the social sciences. In everyday life this expression of power is often apparent in spanking children. A high percentage of American families use physical punishment to discipline children. Susan Steinmetz, "Violence Between Family Members," *Marriage and Family Review*, 1 (May–June, 1978): 50. Violence tends to beget violence in the next generation. R. J. Gelles, "Violence in the Family: A Review of the Research in the Seventies," *Journal of Marriage and the Family*, 42 (November 1980): 873–85.

9. See, for example, Joseph Harry, "Evolving Sources of Happiness for Men Over the Life Cycle," *Journal of Marriage and the Family* (May 1976): 289–96.

10. Verbal and nonverbal communication processes are aspects of environmental feedback. We would also prefer to limit the discussion of communication processes to dyadic relationships and use the term *feedback* to cover cases of multiple messages coming from multiple sources. In an intimate one-to-one situation, feedback and communication tend to merge. Note, finally, that confirmation can be conceived of as a special case of convergent feedback. For a good work book on communication skills, see Sherod Miller, Elam W. Nunnally, and Daniel B. Wackman, *Talking Together* (Minneapolis: Interpersonal Communications Program, 1979).

11. Kurt Back, *Beyond Words* (New York: Russell Sage Foundation, 1972), pp. 52–53.

12. The importance of a sex drive is emphasized in psychoanalysis and minimized in the works of such researchers as John Gagnon.

13. Donn Bryne, "A Pregnant Pause in the Sexual Revolution," *Psychology Today*, July 1977, pp. 67ff.

14. Lee, *The Colors of Love.*

15. Richard Klemer, *Marriage and Family Relationships* (New York: Harper & Row, 1970).

16. Lee Rainwater, "Work, Well Being and Family Life." Paper prepared for Secretary's Committee on Work in America, HEW, June 1972, pp. 4–7.

17. Carlton Smith and Richard Putnam Pratt, *The Time-Life Book of Family Finance* (New York: Time-Life Books, 1969).

18. Typically, these societies are unilinear societies in which descent, inheritance, and succession to office are traced through either the mother's side or the father's side of the family. For a detailed description of how kinship controls

interpersonal behavior in such societies, see William N. Stephens, *The Family in Cross-Cultural Perspective* (New York: Holt, Rinehart and Winston, 1963).

19. Arthur L. Landen, "The Place of In-Laws in Marital Relationships," *Social Case Work* (October 1975): 488.

20. Most cohabitors believe their parents would disapprove of their cohabitating. See, for example, Donald W. Bower and Victor A. Christopherson, "University Student Cohabitation: A Regional Comparison of Selected Attitudes and Behaviors," *Journal of Marriage and the Family* (August 1977): 477–52.

21. See particularly the critique of the antipersonal and anti-intimate society in Jules Henry, *Culture Against Man* (New York: Random House, 1965), and Erich Fromm, *The Art of Loving* (New York: Bantam Books, 1970).

22. George R. Bach and Peter Wyden, *The Intimate Enemy: How to Fight Fair in Love and Marriage* (New York: William Morrow, 1969). See also the more analytic chapter, "Mental Conflict or a Positive Force," in John Scanzoni, *Sexual Bargaining* (Englewood Cliffs, N.J.: Prentice-Hall, 1972) pp. 61–103.

23. Suzanne K. Steinmetz and Murray A. Strauss, *Violence in the Family* (New York: Dodd, Mead, 1974). See also Murray A. Strauss, "Leveling, Civility, and Violence in the Family," *Journal of Marriage and the Family*, (February 1974): 13–29. In this article Strauss examines the factual basis for therapy and family advice urging "leveling in the sense of giving free expression to aggressive feelings" in a study of 385 couples. "The study tested the hypothesis that verbal aggression is a substitute for physical aggression." His conclusion was that the hypothesis was wrong; he found that partnerships with more verbal aggression also had more physical aggression. The results were particularly pronounced for working-class couples. Conceptual and methodological issues are discussed further in Bruce Glick and Steven Jay Gross, "Marital Interaction and Marital Conflict: A Critical Evaluation of Current Research Strategies," *Journal of Marriage and the Family* (August, 1975): 505–11; and Murray A. Strauss, "Measuring Intra Family Conflict and Violence: The Conflict Tactics (CT) Scales, *Journal of Marriage and the Family*, (February 1979): 75–85.

24. An analysis of the process of communication in conflict situations is provided in John Guttman, Howard Markmann, and Cliff Notarius, "The Topography of Marital Conflict: A Sequential Analysis of Verbal and Non-Verbal Behavior," *Journal of Marriage and the Family* (August 1977): 461–77.

Dating, Hanging Around, and Hanging Out

The best divorce is the one you get before you are married.

—Anonymous

5 Dating, Hanging Around, and Hanging Out

Dating in the United States has undergone a number of changes in the ninety or so years since it has become recognized as an acceptable way for young people to get to know one another. What until late in the nineteenth century was a closely supervised activity in which parents played a very direct role has become a largely informal matter of getting together with one's friends and working out one's own partnerships. In the 1980s a young girl will smile at her mother's account of dating when she was a teenager. Drive-in movies, rock concerts, school-sponsored weekends open to both men and women all point to the immense changes in the circumstances under which high school dating occurs.

Dating in highschool serves a number of important functions in a young person's life: It is fun, it provides an opportunity to try on adult notions of masculinity and femininity, it provides a context within which to develop social skills, overcome loneliness, and experience sexual intimacy. It remains one means by which a future mate may be discovered. College provides an even richer context for getting to know others in a variety of living arrangements that can best meet an individual's needs. You can live in a gender-segregated dorm, or live together off campus if you have the means and the inclination.

In this chapter we will look at the process of becoming partners in our society and consider how getting to know a person of the opposite gender may or may not lead to marriage. One of the less studied aspects of this process is how we learn to break off partnerships that just don't seem right.

DATING PATTERNS

For a considerable number of young people, the term *date* is dated. As normally defined, a **date** is a *prearranged* meeting to go somewhere or do something. Movie, party, coke, and study dates are common examples. The emphasis is on the couple. Even though a couple may double-date or go to a movie or a party with a group of friends, they are still doing whatever they are doing primarily with each other. Historically, dating began as a first step in the long and often interrupted process of finding a partner in marriage. It owes much of its character to a romantic notion that two people should get married because they are in love with each other, not because society or their parents say that they should.[1] Marriage may be far from the minds of a young couple setting out on their first date. Both individuals may date often before finding someone they love and want to marry. Nevertheless, the mutual understanding of what they are doing as "a date" sets their activity apart and associates it with a socially accepted way of meeting a person of the opposite sex.

Anthropologist Margaret Mead points out a number of distinctive characteristics of the traditional dating pattern as it appears in our society: (1) A young man does not have to be introduced to a young woman by a member of her family. (2) The couple do not have to be chaperoned. (3) Beyond the time of the date itself, there is no obligation on the part of either the male or the female to continue the relationship. (4) Elders do not plan the date; it is planned by the young people themselves. (5) Sexual intimacies are expected rather than forbidden, but the degree of such intimacy is dependent on a number of variables, including the socially announced state of the relationship.[2]

This dating pattern emerged in the United States along with the increasing popularity of the public high school (which did not segregate students by gender as private schools tended to do) and the automobile

The automobile has significantly influenced American courtship patterns. (Arthur Tress, Photo Researchers, Inc.)

(which permitted courtship to take place in relative privacy outside of the parlor).[3] Public school enrollment exceeded private school enrollment around the turn of the century, and the automobile became a popular means of transportation shortly thereafter.

Prior to the 1920s, American courtship patterns reflected to some extent the desire of parents to see that their daughters were chaperoned so that their value in marriage would not be reduced by loss of their virginity. In the 1920s women not only won the right to vote, but also established a considerable degree of social independence. The "flapper" was a symbol of this ideal. Women could also file for divorce, and many did. Women went to work in large numbers, not only providing themselves with an independent source of income but also putting themselves in much closer contact with men outside the home. Dating emerged as a further measure of this independence, and was in keeping with the romantic emphasis on falling in love. The popularization of the views on human sexuality developed by Sigmund Freud turned Freudianism into a proclamation of the "naturalness" of the sex drive (even infants had it) and an endorsement of greater sexual experimentation (after all, repression was bad). What is more, the development of increasingly effective contraception reduced some of the risk involved in such experimentation. Thus, young people were given more time to spend together, more options as to how they should spend that time, and a changing perspective on sexuality. The result was the dating pattern that emerged in the 1920s and has continued to evolve and change ever since.

Most American boys and girls date.[4] Dating begins at about the age of 14 for both boys and girls. Boys and girls from happy homes tend to begin dating somewhat earlier—perhaps at the age of 12—whereas young people from "broken" or unhappy homes do not typically begin to date until they are 16. In any event, dating does not last long. It typically ends at about the age of 20 or 21.

When a boy and a girl date, they may experience a relationship that progresses in a clearly discernible way. Over time we have come to give names to the stages of this development. The terminology is quite faddish and may well vary from place to place around the country. Nevertheless, one group of students defined the following sequence. In *casual dating* the purpose is to get to know each other and the level of sexual activity is most commonly a goodnight kiss. *Steady dating* involves going out with one person more than with others, but with no agreement that the couple must only date each other. Necking is permissable. Going steady is an elaboration of the courtship process which was initiated shortly before World War II. It is a stage in which both individuals may feel free to initiate the date, a great deal of time is spent with each other, and heavy petting is permitted. There is an expectation of an exclusive partnership. There may be a gift to publicly establish this stage in this developing partnership. There may be also an extreme form of going steady called "engaged to be engaged," in which the couple talk about marriage and educational goals and may "go all the way" in their sexual relationship. *Engagement* is primarily a period of preparation for marriage in which professionals are consulted and specific plans for marriage are made.[5]

Not all these stages are recognized in all parts of the country, but the assumption that a sex code of some sort is linked to a more or less explicitly acknowledged state in a relationship remains fairly constant. The specific strictures dictated by the sex code vary greatly, so that one finds different norms prevailing in different parts of the country, in different social classes, and even in different "sets" or cliques within the same school. Generally, young people know what the guidelines are for each stage in a relationship in their particular community of peers. This knowledge serves to ease some of the pressure on individual decision making.

Dating and Courtship Today

Since the 1960s there have been further developments in the dating and courtship patterns of American teenagers: increased opportunities for informal contact between college men and women, the acceptance of a variety of codes to govern sexual conduct, and a deemphasis on the formal request to arrange a date. Being half of a couple is becoming less of a prerequisite for engaging in extracurricular social activity. You may come out of a party or a movie with a girlfriend or boyfriend, but it is not necessary to have a girlfriend or boyfriend in order to go to a party or a movie. In other words, with this type of arrangement social occasions provide the context in which couples may form, whereas in traditional dating two people who may not in any meaningful sense constitute a couple are expected to agree to act like a couple for the purpose of entering the social context.

The availability in many communities of different sets with different norms makes it possible to some extent for a young person to choose a group of peers who subscribe to a sexual ethic with which he or she can be comfortable. Especially in large urban or suburban high schools and colleges, it is possible for the young man or woman who is sexually adventurous to find a social milieu in which his or her preferences will not lead to being stigmatized as promiscuous. Conversely, the young person who wants to take her or his sexual development more slowly often can find a congenial set of peers who will not insist that reluctance to engage in sexual activity is a symptom of frigidity, impotence, or even latent homosexuality.

In a sense, the emergence of different groups with markedly different sexual standards is nothing new. The parents of any college-age person today probably can remember that there was a clearly identifiable "fast set" in the high school or college they attended. What seems to be new, however, is the extent to which such differences are coming to be seen as differences in taste or life style rather than as moral differences. Instead of there being one standard ethic with clearly delineated deviations on both sides, there seems to be a genuine plurality of ethics, none of which can be clearly identified as dominant.

Sexual Codes

It has been suggested that there are at least four major codes governing the sexual behavior of college students in the United States: (1) abstinence from premarital coitus; (2) a permissive norm that does not specify the character of relationships in which sexual intercourse is permissible; (3) a **permissiveness-with-affection** norm that asserts that it is permissible for a couple to have sex if they are in love; and (4) a **double standard** in which it is permissible for the man to experience sexual intercourse outside of marriage, but not for the woman. In 1972 Ira Reiss, the sociologist who proposed these categories, contended that the double standard was the dominant code on the college campus and that permissiveness with affection was the emergent code.[6]

More recent research distinguishes two additional kinds of permissiveness codes. A hedonistic "fun morality" holds that sex is legitimate at any time, with any person, under any circumstances. A second permissiveness code allows for sex without love or advanced romantic relationship, but considers any sexual exploitation of the partner to be immoral.[7] Without specifying that one level is morally better than another, Jurich and Jurich point out that in their study subjects with a low level of cognitive moral development chose abstinence, the double standard, or permissiveness without affection.[8] Those who were defined as having a moderate level of cognitive moral development chose permissiveness with affection, and those with a high level of cognitive moral development chose the nonexploitive permissiveness.

In the first instance those with a low level of cognitive moral development could rely on fairly well-established patterns to guide their sexual behavior. It requires more sophistication to evaluate the level of the partnership as well as the partner before deciding whether or not sexual intercourse is permissible. This kind of evaluation would be necessary under a permissiveness-with-affection code. Finally, in the case of nonexploitive permissiveness, the decision of whether or not to engage in sex must change with the situation as well as the person (and the level of development of the relationship). It may not be moral to engage in sex with a person with whom you have already experienced coitus if the rights of either party are ignored. It requires more effort to engage in moral behavior under the nonexploitive permissiveness norm than it does under any of the other norms.

The double standard was the code governing sexual conduct on campus—and around the nation—well into the 1960s. Although a few studies point to its continued prevalence, most document its demise.[9] Most research now confirms that the dominant sexual code on campus is permissiveness with affection.[10] Furthermore, there is a tendency to evaluate later sexual partnerships more highly than earlier ones as being an expression of "being in love."[11] It appears that the major change in the norms governing sexual behavior outside marriage has been in the direction of finding sexual intercourse acceptable based on the quality of the partnership rather than the formal stage in a courtship process.

Sexual Behavior

Not only have the norms changed over the past two decades, but teenage sexual experience has changed as well. Increasing numbers of teenagers are experiencing a wider range of sexual behaviors at somewhat earlier ages. A recent study of college women found that one-half had experienced sexual intercourse while dating, two-thirds while going steady, and three-fourths while engaged.[12] At one university, a random sample of students (ages 18 to 23) found that 75 percent of the men and 60 percent of the women had experienced intercourse at least once and 60 percent of the men and 56 percent of the women had experienced oral-genital sex. Of those currently going with a partner of the opposite sex, over half were having intercourse on the average of one out of every three times they were together.[13]

THE DEVELOPMENTAL TASKS OF DATING

Dating serves many functions today. It can be a form of recreation, a way to avoid loneliness, a means of gaining status, a way to learn social skills and discover one's personal identity. It enables young people to try on sex roles, find love, experiment with sexuality, and eventually find a mate in some cases. It is such a potentially valuable opportunity for development that it is easy to forget its problems—particularly when expressed in its traditional form.

In our society, preadolescents generally associate with members of their own sex. Indeed, they often have difficulty relating to members of the opposite sex. Dating provides them with an opportunity to overcome some of these difficulties. As interest in the opposite sex increases with the onset of puberty, young people gain experience with members of that sex through dating. The context of dating provides many people with an opportunity to develop the skills necessary for successfully relating to the opposite sex.

Of course, in many cases the opposite is true. For countless young people of both sexes, the dating years are a period of almost unrelieved trauma.[14] It would be easy to assume that dating is a problem only for "unpopular" individuals, but this would be an oversimplification. Consider for a moment what is meant by "popularity" in this context. When we say that a young person is "popular," generally we mean simply that she or he is successful at relating to the opposite sex in dating situations; she or he has the social graces, whatever they are, of a desirable dating partner. The folklore is rich with examples of high school girls and boys who have many friends but few dates. Any young man in college probably can remember a female classmate from his high school days with whom he could enjoy spending an afternoon, who was a stimulating colleague on the school newspaper or in the student government, who was the sort of bright and intelligent person one liked to get together with to prepare for an exam, but whom he would never have dreamed of "asking out." Young women probably can come up with analogous examples among their male classmates.

Clearly, such people were extremely "popular" in all contexts except dating; obviously, then, lack of popularity does not explain why some individuals have trouble with the dating process. But it does explain why the dating years can be so traumatic. The fact is that dating is simply one of many types of social interaction in which young people engage, but it is often mistakenly taken to be the alpha and omega of social competence. We can imagine a boy saying, "Yeah, she's terrific to work with on the yearbook committee, but I wouldn't want to go out with her." We tend to take this as a serious criticism. On the other hand, if he were to say, "Betty's great to take to a movie or a concert or a dance, but if you ever had to spend two afternoons with her trying to work out arrangements for a class picnic you'd never want to do it again," we might tend to assume that he wasn't criticizing her in any fundamental way. That is to say, we take success in one type of interpersonal relationship as a sign of overall popularity and assume that success in other types of relationship doesn't count for much. The fact that even the young people who suffer from the application of such standards may accept the validity of the criteria being used means that dating problems can be far more damaging to the self-image than is really warranted.

In this connection it is important to recognize that dating is a highly artificial social situation. When two young people of the opposite sex spend an afternoon together working on a project, notice that it is past six o'clock and that they are both hungry, adjourn the conference for dinner together, continue it at his house or her house until they are finished, and then spend the rest of the evening together, their social contact flows naturally out of the things they are doing together. Similarly, a group of young people may get together for a pizza after school and then spend the afternoon just "hanging around;" maybe one of them will say, "I feel like seeing that movie that just opened downtown—anyone wanna go?" and an ad hoc group ends up agreeing to see the movie together. This type of social situation also evolves naturally from the larger social context in which the young people operate. But when a young man says to himself, "I gotta get a date for Friday night. Who should I call?" he is attempting to fabricate a social context where none existed before. It is this artificial quality of the dating experience that has led to its decline in recent years.

Many young people get to know each other by hanging out in groups in which it is not important to be part of a couple. (Richard Hutchings, Photo Researchers, Inc.)

Another aspect of the dating process is significant here. For many young people, dating provides occasions for rehearsing conventionally accepted adult masculine and feminine roles. From their earliest days boys have been taught to be aggressive, but they have never before had an opportunity to learn what it means to be dominant over females. Heretofore, it is likely that all the women in their lives—mainly their mothers and teachers—have been dominant over them. The context of dating thus gives the boy an opportunity to develop the socially expected skill of being dominant over the female. He is expected to make the date, to decide where they should go, to initiate whatever sexual advances are to be made. Eventually he may learn to do these things with some style.

Conversely, in the dating process girls learn to be submissive to boys. The skills that they are encouraged to master are the purely passive skills of seduction. That is to say, girls learn not how to initiate social contact but how to get someone else to initiate it (e.g., how to get asked out by the boy you want to go out with, rather than how to ask him out). Similarly, in the sexual relations of the couple the girl is expected to play a passive role. To be sure, she is permitted to encourage sexual experimentation, but only on the condition that her encouragement is manifested in subtle and almost imperceptible ways. She may make herself as sexually alluring as the bounds of propriety permit, but the code dictates that she is not openly to initiate sexual advances. If a couple is to get together sexually, in other words, it is the boy's job to express desire and the girl's job to make herself desirable. The girl who gives evidence of sexual desire runs the risk of being stigmatized as "aggressive"—clearly a gross distortion of the English language, inasmuch as a loving desire for intimate contact with another person is about as far from an act of aggression as it is possible to get.

Paradoxically, there is one area of the dating situation in which the girl is expected to be in control. To the extent that the couple is to refrain from sexual activity, it is the girl who is expected to "draw the line." If sexual play is to begin, it is his job to initiate it; if it is to stop short of consummation, it is her job to call a halt. Inevitably, these norms of sex role behavior lead to conflict between the sexes. For boys especially, the conflict that arises may not necessarily be damaging. A young boy who experiences some success in being the initiator may gain a degree of self-assurance. He also may fail occasionally, and this may lead him to discover that he can live with that too. As long as there is some balance between his success and his failure, he may see this conflict as positive—at least in terms of his development as a self-confident male. On the other hand, many people feel—undoubtedly with some justification—that this sort of sexual contest is damaging to the young men who engage in it insofar as it encourages them to see sex as a competitive game. Even if they emerge from it with their egos intact, they will tend to look on women as friendly adversaries, much as professional athletes regard players on rival teams, but not as partners in a joint endeavor. The use of the slang term *scoring* to describe sexual success indicates how pervasive these attitudes are.

The preceding discussion applies to traditional patterns of dating. As dating has been modified by emergent sexual norms and the influence of group activities of a less formal sort, new patterns have emerged. There is a more spontaneous type of social intercourse and the emphasis on male dominance is much less apparent. When a young girl, for example, can attend a party without having to be invited by a boy, her position with regard to the boys at the party is much more nearly one of equality. Even where traditional dating is still the dominant pattern, it is no longer unheard of for a girl to telephone a boy and ask him for a date. To be sure, girls who ask boys out, like girls who initiate sexual activities, are running the risk of scaring away potential boyfriends, who may tend to see such conduct as threatening to their own conception of their roles. Apparently, a fair number of young women are willing to run this risk, however, and as their numbers increase, the risk should diminish simply because the boys will be forced to adjust to this new balance of power in sexual relationships.

Class Variations in Dating Patterns

The sexual behavior of Americans differs with socioeconomic class. These differences are reflected in differences in dating patterns that appear to be class based.

Because upper-class families have a vested interest in preserving the family fortune, they often attempt to retain a considerable degree of control over the mate selection process by sequestering their homes and sending their children to private schools, clubs, and chaperoned social activities. Upper-class families commonly express concern over who is dating whom, and such expressions of concern can be effective in enforcing the family's norms because of the threat of disinheritance. Another unique characteristic of the social activities of upper-class young people is the great amount of formality and ritual involved, especially as expressed in the "coming out" parties of debutantes. This ritual is the formal announcement of a daughter's introduction to the prescribed social world. Daughters usually "come out" at the age of 18, although ordinarily they have had dating experience prior to that time.

In certain lower-class urban communities, dating has a quite different pattern because it occurs under very different conditions. For example, children may have played with sex from a very early age—and boys may be sexually experienced before adolescence. Girls, too, often engage in sexual intercourse "for fun" when they are still quite young and as a form of exchange when they are older. As Ladner and Hammond report in a study of an urban ghetto, "Girls have been known to engage in sexual intercourse in exchange for a movie date, a ride in a car, food, and other things that will take them out of the family life. The male in turn offers these things because he knows the girl is desirous of them and can offer what he wants in exchange."[15] In such contexts dating generally is not something the family regulates or participates in. Indeed, in a sense it is inappropriate to use the term *dating* to describe heterosexual relationships in this environment, inasmuch as social encounters between the sexes usually are not planned in advance by the boy or the girl. Rather, boys and girls hang around public places and couples may "single out" for part of the evening, but there is no decision to participate in dating.

In middle-class communities, dating often emerges in response to intense expectations on the part of parents and peers. Middle-class mores place a heavy emphasis on the value of the social skills. This is understandable in light of the fact that in many middle-class occupations success depends to a considerable extent on being liked by one's business associates. Popularity thus counts heavily in the middle-class ethic, and as a result parents encourage their children to get early training, through dating, in the social graces necessary for popularity. Fortunately, because middle-class children often have a great range of social activities available to them through school, clubs, churches, and a variety of coeducational interest groups, they are often able to respond positively to the pressure to date early.

The outline presented here of the three major class variants in the dating pattern is, of course, only a crude sketch. A detailed study of the phenomenon would show countless variations between the extremes of intense parental involvement in the dating process and absolute ignorance of the dating behavior of children, between the highly stylized and formal dating situation of a debutante ball and the almost completely unstructured ambience of streetcorner contact. What is more, there is considerable variation in the way different communities—and different families in the same community—subscribe to the norms that we have associated with particular socioeconomic classes. The reader is cautioned, therefore, against taking any of the foregoing description as normative for any particular social class. Our point in offering this description is simply to demonstrate that dating patterns vary considerably and that these variations can be correlated, in at least an approximate way, with the socioeconomic position of the people involved.

Engagement

For many middle-class couples, engagement is the final stage before marriage. It takes on quite a different character from any previous dating because by the time a couple become engaged they have already begun to ask serious questions about each other that can help them determine whether they would make desirable marriage partners. It is a time for self-disclosure and deeper self-knowledge—at least it is supposed to be such a time. It is also the time during which the couple may consult professional marriage counselors, take physical examinations, and make concrete plans for marriage. Engagement involves a great deal more work and self-conscious commitment than any previous stages in the couple's developing relationship. Landis estimates that one-half to two-thirds of all engagements end in marriage.[16]

Because engagement is thought of as a much more binding relationship than any of the other stages, it is not rushed into rapidly. For 54 percent of the couples in one study, engagement came at least nine months after the first date. In the early part of this century, short engagements were encouraged because engagement was primarily a period of preparing for marriage—making wedding arrangements and domestic arrangements for after the wedding—but not a time for testing the relationship. Today marriage counselors often urge couples to seek longer engagements—from six months to two years—so that they have an opportunity to discover each other before marriage. The classic correlation between reports of good marital adjustment and long engagement seems to support their argument. Nevertheless, the extent to which engagement actually functions as a means of testing potential marriage partners remains somewhat questionable, inasmuch as the conditions of engagement are quite different from those of marriage.

Various things need to be cleared up during the engagement period. Some professionals provide a checklist of individual characteristics both partners should complete as a test of their suitability for marriage to each other. Some feel it is important that engaged couples begin to try to answer some of the important questions they will face in marriage, such as whether or not they should have children. Such steps may or may not be beneficial, but they can distract the couple from the real tasks of engagement if they lead them to view marriage as a static situation and to assume that engagement is like marriage. A young couple should not forget that engagement should be a time in which two partners begin to develop their own style of coping with the problems of everyday life. For example, if a neat woman is engaged to a sloppy man, there is potential for trouble. Sometimes a couple become engaged without really realizing that they differ even in such obvious ways. Each person has seen how the other lives, but neither has given any thought to the fact that their blatantly different styles could be a source of conflict when they begin to live together. An engaged couple need to know this kind of thing about each other and should have the capacity to talk about it and enough skill in give and take so that a reasonable resolution can be reached. Engagement, in other words, is the period when the partners should develop their skills and their style of handling basic differences. An engaged couple should be working on what they know about each other with regard to the potentially creative and destructive aspects of their relationship. In short, they need to become adept at communicating their feelings about their partnership.

LIVING TOGETHER

In addition to the traditional dating sequence, from steady dating through engagement to marriage, living together is becoming an increasingly viable alternative environment within which partnerships can develop. It is rather new in our society, not having come into prominence until the 1960s. Precisely because of this newness, it offers considerable possibility for experimentation and flexibility in defining role expectations within the developing relationship. Where this environment is available, it will have its effect on the kinds of choices people make in becoming partners. It shapes the experience they will have and influences the nature of the information they will be able to obtain about each other.

The fact that young unmarried heterosexual couples live together has attracted a good deal of attention in the popular press in recent years. Ever since 1968, when Linda LeClair, a Barnard College sophomore, asserted before the college's Judicial Council that she felt Barnard's regulations governing the living arrangements of single students were unjust, newspapers and magazines have been filled with articles about **cohabiting**.

Living together is an increasingly popular lifestyle that does not seem to be simply an alternative to marriage. (Chester Higgins, Photo Researchers, Inc.)

There are now a number of studies on the subject, and we are beginning to see some of the characteristics of this life style more clearly.

One survey, for example, reports that 71 percent of the men and 43 percent of the women interviewed thought they would like to try "living with" someone.[17] By "living with," these researchers meant "eating, sleeping and socializing at the same residence with someone of the opposite sex." If we accept as a definition of "living together" something like "Two single persons of the opposite sex living together in a common residence," then a rough estimate of the number of college students who have lived with someone of the opposite sex at some time in their college careers is about 30 percent.[18]

Contrary to popular belief, students who live with roommates of the opposite sex do not generally think of themselves as revolutionary. Thus, in a study conducted at Penn State, although a significant number of students who were living together thought that unmarried cohabitation was the most desirable postcollege choice, very few thought they would prefer to live in communes.[19] This finding suggests that cohabiters are not radical experimenters in alternative family styles. They remain strongly attached to the norms of dyadic partnerships and marriage. In many cases, they are not outspoken advocates of innovative life styles. Rather, they seem often to have gradually worked their way into their arrangements, as the following statement by a student at Columbia University suggests:

> "We began studying together," she says. "Then I made his dinner before we studied. Then we came back and I made him coffee. At first, I let him out. Then he let himself out. Then he stayed and I made him coffee in the morning. Then he went shopping for groceries and in a week he was here all the time."[20]

Such an arrangement, it should be clear, is easy to enter into. Unlike marriage, which requires blood tests, licenses, and some sort of ceremony at a minimum, partners who want simply to live together can just move in—and out. In fact, rough estimates suggest that perhaps no more than one-third of the relationships between unmarried couples living together last more than 6 months. At Cornell, the average length seems to be about 4 1/2 months, and many such arrangements apparently last only a few days or weeks.[21]

From these statistics it is easy to jump to the conclusion that such relationships have a high rate of failure. This conclusion would be unjustified, however, for it is based on the erroneous assumption that living together can be judged by the same criteria we use in judging marital stability. Couples often live together without either partner's making the assumption that the relationship is to be permanent; indeed, it is often precisely because they either do not want or do not expect permanence that they refrain from getting married. Thus, the dissolution of their arrangement should not be taken as evidence of a failure in the partnership, which may well have satisfied all the goals both participants set for their relationship.

What kind of person is likely to choose this form of partnership? The answer is far from clear in most details. As far as parentage is concerned, he or she could be anybody's child. There is no evidence at present to suggest that children from "broken" or unhappy homes are more likely to choose this option than children from happy homes. Cohabitors do seem to share a different life style, however. They see themselves as politically liberal, are more likely than the average college student to smoke marijuana, and most often consider themselves agnostic or atheistic.[22] Most cohabitors think their parents do not know about their living arrangement and would disapprove if they knew.[23] While there is some evidence of greater willingness among cohabitors to experiment with alternative life styles, the traditional division of labor between the sexes is still present in cohabiting arrangements.[24]

There is great diversity among cohabiting students with regard to what their partnership means to them:

> "Do you consider yourselves engaged or going steady or . . . ?" a couple at Florida State University in Tallahassee was asked. "We don't consider ourselves anything," the nonmate said. "We've never tried to pin it down." In Iowa City, Iowa, a girl says, "I guess he came and never left." At L.S.U., Dale says brightly that her arrangement with Tom "is the first time I've gone steady."[25]

With such diversity of opinion, it is no wonder that researchers are confused about what "living together" means.[26] The major question most of them raise is, "What does it have to do with marriage?" Is "living together" a more honest form of courtship? Is it an alternative life style that is someday going to replace marriage? The answers to these questions are ambiguous. Most couples, it seems, do not consider their premarital cohabitation to be a trial marriage while they are experiencing it. That is to say, if we define a trial marriage as an arrangement in which two people who intend to marry each other decide to live together in order to assess their compatibility before formalizing the relationship, the evidence seems to indicate that trial marriage is not often the motive for cohabiting. On the other hand, many couples who live together ultimately marry each other, and insofar as they may not have married had they not lived with each other, we can conclude that in retrospect their cohabitation functioned very much like a trial marriage. What is more, most cohabiting partners report that marriage is one of their eventual objectives, although they do not intend to marry the partner with whom they are living. For such people cohabitation is equivalent to trial marriage only in the limited sense that it is a test of how well they can adapt to marriage as an institution—that is, a test of their ability to share living conditions with a partner of the opposite sex.

Sex is not a big issue for most cohabitors, although the Penn State study cited earlier suggests that cohabitors are more likely than the average student to report that they have a "heterosexual relationship of very high quality."[27] But very few will contend that they are living with their mates because of the greater pleasures they can derive from sexual intercourse. Indeed, sexual relations were not mentioned in our definition of "living together" because several researchers contend that many students do not see sex as an essential dimension of their arrangement. There seems to be a wide variation in the kinds of sexual relationship that can be found among cohabiting couples. Some such couples apparently have no sexual relationship at all; their cohabitation is for economic, social, or emotional reasons and explicitly excludes sex. To be sure, nonsexual cohabitation is probably the exception rather than the rule. On this score, about the only thing that can be said is that the data now available do not permit us to generalize with any confidence about the sexual behavior of unmarried cohabiting couples.

MATE SELECTION

In our society, couples are supposed to fall in love before they get married. By world standards, this is an odd assumption. In many societies marriages are arranged and the field of eligible mates is severely restricted by explicit, formal norms. In some traditional societies, such as Japan, love is expected to develop after marriage, not before it. Most of us find it very difficult to understand the young Japanese girl who apparently is satisfied to let her parents choose her mate:

> We girls don't have to worry at all. We know we'll get married. When we are old enough, our parents will find a suitable boy and everything will be arranged. We don't have to go into competition with each other. . . . Besides how would we be able to judge the character of a boy? . . . We are young and inexperienced. Our parents are older and wiser, and they aren't deceived as easily as we would be. I'd far rather have my parents choose for me. It's so important that the man I marry should be the right one. I could so easily make a mistake if I had to find him for myself.[28]

Falling in Love

In our society, falling in love implies freedom of choice in a relatively open marriage market. Theoretically, any two people should be able to marry if they fall in love, but of course we know that this is not the case. To be sure, our social system places very few formal restrictions on the choice of a mate; rather, it tends to rely on informal but quite effective controls to ensure that everyone marries the "right" person. For example, in any given year approximately 4 percent of all blacks who marry, marry whites. Obviously, a much smaller percentage of all whites who marry, marry blacks.[29] Likewise, if we break down religious denominations into the gross categories of Protestant, Catholic, and Jew we discover that most marriages tend to take place within these groups (**endogamy**) rather than between them (**exogamy**). Studies produce varying results, but a 1960 report based on a large sample of 35,000 households indicated that 91 percent of the Protestants, 78 percent of the Catholics, and 93 percent of the Jewish population made **homogamous** choices (choices in which the partners are similar).[30] Sociologist Paul H. Besancency cautions, however, that these figures tend to under represent the actual rate of mixed marriage, inasmuch as many individuals convert to the religion of their spouse in order to have a more harmonious household.[31]

Additional restrictions on mate selection seem to be in effect with regard to age and socioeconomic status. Statistics show that Americans tend to choose mates who are within 2 1/2 years of their own age. In 1976 the average age at first marriage of the bride was 21.3 years and that of the groom 23.8 years.[32] There is also a tendency to marry members of one's own socioeconomic class. Although there is some indication that exogamy is increasing in all these dimensions, the trend in this direction is moving quite slowly. However free we may perceive our choice of mates to be, the fact remains that we are most likely to marry someone from the same ethnic, religious, and class background, someone who is nearly the same age and lives in the same city if not in the same neighborhood.

Bernard Murstein has developed an interesting theory to explain how young people in our culture go about choosing their mates.[33] As he sees it, there are three basic stages in this process. First comes the "stimulus" stage, in which physical attractiveness is of considerable importance, particularly in the open-field setting, where continuing interaction is unlikely to occur as a matter of course.[34] This is followed by a "value" stage wherein couples explore each other's attitudes toward life, politics, religion, sex, and the roles of men and women, as well as their general style of viewing the world. In Murstein's view, the fact that people who are alike in terms of socioeconomic background will tend to have similar values and life styles is one of the major factors leading to endogamous mate selection. This is because endogamous selection increases the likelihood of finding a partner who will support one's own value system. This is important, Murstein points out, because many of the values an individual holds are so personal that their rejection is experienced as a rejection of the individual.

In the final stage, which Murstein calls the "role" stage, the prospective partners experiment in compatibility. At this stage, couples can be said to be making good progress in the courtship process to the extent that they are able to satisfy each other's role expectations.[35]

Of course, the fact that homogamous mate selection offers certain payoffs in terms of increased likelihood of compatible values does not mean that heterogamous choices should not be made. We all know that couples can and do make choices in their selection of a mate that go against social expectations. Couples marry in spite of racial, class, religious, ethnic, and regional differences. It would be naive to deny that such couples must pay a certain price for their choice. They may experience greater stress in their partnership than homogamous couples, and they may find that family, friends, and outsiders are willing to give them less support in coping with their problems than they would give to a homogamous couple. How important these factors are will vary greatly from case to case. On the one hand, it is safe to say that many potentially successful heterogamous marriages have run aground under the constant onslaught of family and peer group pressures. On the other hand, it is no secret that two autonomous individuals with widely different backgrounds can bring to their union a rich diversity in outlooks that helps each of them grow and strengthens their partnership.

Breaking Up

Breakups before marriage are not often studied because they are assumed to be unimportant by most adult researchers, who may have forgotten the pain of their earlier years. Fortunately, one excellent study can help us understand what is happening a bit better. Hill and others discovered, in a two-year study of 103 breakups among college students, that they were rarely mutual and that women were more likely than men to terminate the relationship because they were somewhat more likely to perceive problems in them. The school calendar provided often-used natural breaking points, it being easier to say "I'll see you in the fall" or "While we're apart we ought to date other people" than to say "I don't think we had better see each other again." Women were more likely to differentiate between liking and loving in a relationship, and the researchers conclude that unequal involvement in the relationship is a major factor contributing to its decay.[36] Another study suggests that individuals can be placed on a continuum from those who expect high equity of exchange in their relationship to those who expect low equity. A person who expects high equity will be embarrassed if someone does him or her a favor that cannot be repaid. Such a person is inclined to see love as a series of reciprocal exchanges. A person at the opposite pole would not be at all concerned with such mental bookkeeping. The authors conclude that those who seek high exchange in their relationships make for good friends, whereas couples in which at least one partner does not seek a high level of exchange make the best marital couples.[37]

CONTEXTS FOR COUPLING—PROS AND CONS

Looked at as one social environment in which partnerships can develop, the traditional courtship pattern, from dating to marriage, has some apparent costs as well as some easily recognizable benefits.

Traditional Dating

Three major benefits of dating are as follows:

1. *Respectability*. Because this sequence was the generally accepted way in which heterosexual relationships develop, people who follow this sequence still meet with general social acceptance. They need not hide from anyone to feel guilty about their relationship as long as it conforms to the norm. This respectability thus serves as an affirmation of themselves and their relationship.
2. *Well-defined expectations*. Couples generally know the stage of sexual intimacy that is appropriate to a given stage of their relationship in a given social context. They also have some idea about what is traditionally expected of them as men and women. Most couples know something about how long it should take for them to move through each stage of their relationship. All these things provide standards by which they can evaluate themselves and their relationship.
3. *Greater access to professional advice and consultation*. Because the orientation of the professional world is still largely toward the traditional courtship sequence, a couple following the standard path can more readily turn to professionals if they experience problems that they cannot handle or if they desire advice.

Three of the most significant costs of the traditional approach to developing relationships are the following:

1. *A tendency toward role conformity*. Because the traditional approach provides clearly defined roles, there is a temptation to conform to these role expectations rather than to discover one's own uniqueness—and one's partner's—in a relationship.
2. *Sexual inequality*. The so-called double standard is still the dominant sex code in the traditional courtship environment. The cost to the woman's development as an autonomous individual may be considerable. What is more, as a sex code the double standard entails a built-in tendency toward deception.
3. *The expectation of marriage*. Couples following the traditional path may well feel themselves propelled toward marriage. It is possible that someone who would really like to get out of a developing relationship may find himself or herself unable to get off the train.

Living Together

Because we know so little about living together, it is difficult to assess accurately the costs and benefits of such an experience. Nevertheless, the following generalizations seem appropriate on the basis of what we do know. Three major benefits seem possible.

1. The couple have greater freedom than they would have in the tradi-
    tional dating pattern to set their own role expectations and to define
    the character of their relationship. They can decide whether or not sex
    is to be part of their relationship; they can decide whether or not they
    are going to share most of their expenses; and they can decide whether
    their relationship is to be exclusive or whether they will be free to seek
    sexual partners outside the relationship.
2. Compared to the couple who choose to become engaged and to post-
    pone cohabitation until marriage, unmarried cohabitors enjoy the pos-
    sibility of getting to know each other in a wide variety of situations,
    including the running of a household. They are therefore likely to have
    a much less idealized image of each other than a couple who enters
    marriage without such experience.
3. Compared to engaged couples, couples who cohabit have less compul-
    sion to marry. We reach this conclusion from the fact that the per-
    centage of cohabiting people who choose not to marry their room-
    mates is higher than the percentage of engaged people who choose not
    to marry their fiance or fiancee. This suggests that engagement is a
    much less revocable step toward marriage than cohabitation is. In
    other words, it is easier to end a "living together" arrangement than to
    end an engagement. In either case, of course, there is the possibility of
    hurt feelings.

Three major costs of living together also seem evident on the basis
of our present knowledge:

1. Living together creates the danger of greater exploitation, particularly
    of the woman, than the traditional sequence of engagement and mar-
    riage. This danger arises from the fact that the woman may assume the
    responsibility for keeping house and may give up her job or career in
    order to fulfill this responsibility. Unlike the married woman, how-
    ever, the cohabiting woman has no legal safeguards to protect her in
    case the union dissolves. She thus may find herself with no claim to
    support by her former mate and little chance of earning the living she
    could have earned if she had not interrupted her career to become a
    homemaker. Trost suggests that Swedish law be modified to reduce
    these dangers.[38]
2. To some degree the couple who choose to "live together" may be cut
    off from their parents and some of their old friends. This means that
    they must provide their own authentication of their relationship and
    may not be able to rely on those around them for support. In this con-
    nection, however, it should be noted that morals are changing rapidly
    and that parental acceptance of unmarried cohabitation is far more
    common than it was even a decade ago. Consider the fact that in the
    1940s, when film star Ingrid Bergman bore a child by a man who was
    not her husband, the event was greeted with such vociferous outrage
    that Ms. Bergman was unable to continue her career. A few years ago,
    however, actress Mia Farrow bore twins by a man to whom she was
    not married and the event was reported in the social columns of news-
    papers and magazines with scarcely a twitch of editorial eyebrow; in-
    deed, the birth announcement was often accompanied with a laconic
    note to the effect that "Mr. Previn and Ms. Farrow announce that they
    have no intention to marry at present." Given this social climate, it is
    not at all unheard of for parents to accept the fact that their child is liv-

ing with his or her partner and to treat the partner much as they would a son-in-law or a daughter-in-law. In such circumstances cohabitation becomes, in the eyes of concerned onlookers, a sort of de facto marriage. Nevertheless, although such acceptance is far from unheard of, it is also far from universal—indeed, it is probably still less common than rejection.

3. "Living together" can prematurely narrow the range of the dating experience for some college students. Although the data suggest that in the typical case students who choose cohabitation already have dated about twenty-five individuals and therefore can be said to be fairly experienced in heterosexual relationships at the dating level, some students move in with a partner without having reached this level. Cohabitation thus shuts them off from the widening experience offered by the social life of the college community.

SUMMARY

Dating in the United States developed along with the public high school and the automobile about the turn of the century. Until the 1960s, there were widely accepted stages in a developing relationship from casual dating to engagement that helped to define the acceptable level of sexual intimacy. Since the 1960s, there has been an increase in the opportunity for informal contact between college men and women, an acceptance of a wider range of sexual codes, and a de-emphasis on the formal request to arrange a date. It is not as important to have a partner in order to hang out with the gang as it once was. There are class and regional patterns in dating behavior—even variation within a particular school—and, overall, a greater acceptance of this variety than was true in the 1950s.

Cohabitation has emerged as an alternative to the traditional dating pattern as well. About 30 percent of all college students have cohabited at least once during their college years. There is little evidence that this is an alternative to marriage. It is yet another way of preparing for marriage. Among the formerly married, however, it may provide a permanent alternative for a small number of couples.

Although we believe that love dictates our choice of a mate, research confirms that we tend to fall in love with people who are very much like us as far as religion, education, income, and race and who tend to complement our personality. Murstein's SVR model shows that we are attracted to someone whom we consider physically attractive in the stimulus stage, screen out those who differ too much from us in belief in the value stage, and tend to marry those with whom we can negotiate a mutually acceptable set of role expectations in the role stage.

NOTES

1. Hugo Beigel, "*Romantic Love*," *American Sociological Review*, 16 (June): 326–34; Sandra R. Herman, "Loving Courtship on the Marriage Market: The Ideal and Its Critics, 1871–1911," *American Quarterly*. 1973.

2. Margaret Mead, "The Life Cycle and Its Variations: The Division of Roles," in Daniel Bell, ed., *Toward the Year 2000: Work in Progress* (Boston: Beacon Press, 1969).

3. Theodore Caplow et al., *Middletown Families: Fifty Years of Change and Continuity* (St. Paul: University of Minnesota Press, 1982).

4. Judson T. Landis and Mary G. Landis, *Building a Successful Marriage*, 5th ed. (Englewood Cliffs, N.J.: Prentice Hall, 1973), pp. 34–35; Edward S. Herold, "A Rating Adjustment Scale for College Students," *Social Forces*, 1979, pp. 52–60.

5. Landis and Landis, p. 36.

6. Ira L. Reiss, "How and Why America's Sex Standards Are Changing," in Joanne S. and Jack R. Delora (eds.), *Intimate Life Styles* (Pacific Palisades, Calif.: Goodyear, 1972).

7. Anthony P. Jurich and Julie A. Jurich, "The Effect of Cognitive Moral Development upon the Selection of Premarital Sexual Standards," *Journal of Marriage and the Family* (November 1974): 736–41.

8. L. Kohlberg, "Stage and Sequence: The Cognitive Development Approach to Socialization," in David A. Goslin, ed., *Handbook of Socialization Theory and Research* (Chicago: Rand McNally, 1969), pp. 37–480.

9. M. Z. Ferrell et al., "Maturational and Societal Changes in the Sexual Double-Standard: A Panel Analysis (1967–1971; 1970–1974)," *Journal of Marriage and the Family*, 39 (May 1977): 255–71.

10. E. Walster, G. W. Walster, and J. Traupmann, "Equity and Premarital Sex," *Journal of Personality and Social Psychology*, 36 (January 1978): 82–92.

11. J. Kelley, "Sexual Permissiveness: Evidence for a Theory," *Journal of Marriage and the Family*, 40 (August 1978): 455–68.

12. R. R. Bell and K. Coughey, "Premarital Sex Experience Among College Females, 1958, 1968, 1978," *Family Relations* 29 (July 1980): 155–357.

13. J. D. DeLamater and P. MacCorquodale, *Premarital Sexuality: Attitudes, Relationships, Behavior* (Madison: University of Wisconsin Press, 1979). Karl King, Jack O. Balswick, and Ira E. Robinson, "The Continuing Premarital Sexual Revolution Among College Females," *Journal of Marriage and the Family* (August 1977) found that 73.9 percent of the men and 57.1 percent of the women in his range of college students at a southern university in 1975 had experienced coitus—an 8.8 percent increase for men since 1965 and a 29.4 percent increase for women; J. Richard Udry, Karl E. Bauman, and Naomi M. Morris, "Change in Premarital Coital Experience of Recent Decades of Birth Cohorts of Urban American Women," found particularly significant increases for 15- to 19-year-old women in the 1960s; Arthur M. Verner and Cyrus S. Stewart, "Adolescent Sexual Behavior in Middle America Revisited: 1970–1973," *Journal of Marriage and the Family* (August 1977): 543–48, found that in 1970 by the age of 17, 38 percent of the men and 27 percent of the women had expeirenced coitus. By 1973 these figures had changed to 34 percent for men and 35 percent for women. These investigators also discovered increases in heavy petting and sequential intercourse with more than one partner.

14. See, for example, M. J. Williams, "Personal and Family Problems of High School Youth and Their Bearing upon Family Education Needs," *Social Forces*, 27 (1949): 279–85; Harold T. Christiansen, *Marriage Analysis* (New York: Ronald Press, 1950); and Edward S. Herold, "A Dating Adjustment Scale for College Students," *Social Forces*, 1973, pp. 51–66.

15. Joyce Ladner and Boone Hammond, "Socialization into Sexual Behavior," paper presented in the Society for the Study of Social Problems, San Francisco,

August 1967, pp. 12–13. See also their article in Carlfred Broderick and Jessie Bernard, *The Individual, Sex and Society* (Baltimore: Johns Hopkins, 1969), p. 49.

16. Landis and Landis, pp. 191 ff. When couples were asked why their engagement was broken off, the most common reply (39 percent of the men, 40 percent of the women) was that they "lost interest in the relationship." Although about 10 percent of the students in one study reported that they got over the emotional involvement of engagements by the end of the final date with their former fiancé or fiancée, 30 percent of the women and 46 percent of the men took at least three months to recover.

17. Lura Henze and John W. Hudson, "Personal and Family Characteristics of Cohabiting and Non-Cohabiting College Students," *Journal of Marriage and the Family* (November 1974): 722–27. The authors found that 29 percent of the males and 18 percent of the females were currently cohabiting or had cohabited.

18. Dan. J. Peterman, Carl A. Ridley, and Scott M. Anderson, "Comparison of Cohabiting and Non-Cohabiting College Students," *Journal of Marriage and the Family* (May 1974): 344–45, found that one-third of their sample had reported a period of living together. Donald W. Bower and Victor A. Christopherson, "University Student Cohabitation: A Regional Comparison of Selected Attitudes and Behavior," *Journal of Marriage and the Family* (August 1977): 447–52, found that about one-quarter of their student sample had cohabited at one time. Finally, Richard R. Clayton and Harwin L. Voss, "Shacking Up: Cohabitation in the 1970s," *Journal of Marriage and the Family* (May 1977): 273–83, found on the basis of a nationwide random sample of 2,510 young men that 18 percent had lived with a woman for at least six months but only 5 percent were currently cohabiting. Twenty-nine percent of the blacks and 16 percent of the whites had cohabited.

19. Peterman, p. 351.

20. *Time*, May 1973.

21. See J. L. Lyness et al., "Living Together: An Alternative to Marriage," *Journal of Marriage and the Family*, 1972, pp. 305–11.

22. Henze and Hudson, p. 725.

23. Bower and Christopherson, p. 452.

24. Ibid. Also, Rebecca Stafford, Elaine Backman, and Pamela Dibona, "The Division of Labor Among Cohabiting and Married Couples," *Journal of Marriage and the Family* (February 1977): 43–55.

25. *Time*, May 1973.

26. Bowers and Christopherson found that cohabitors were as likely as noncohabitors to marry but at a somewhat later age and with fewer children, p. 457. Peterson et al. report that cohabitors are more likely to regard their arrangement as a trial marriage when they are in their last year of college. There is a limited commitment to permanency during the early years of college, p. 354. Henze and Hudson report that some members of their sample viewed their arrangement as a trial marriage and some did not. They favor viewing cohabitation as an expanded dimension of the courtship process, p. 726. In a study of Swedish cohabitors Trost concludes that women are more likely than men to view their cohabitation as equivalent to marriage. Jan Trost, "Attitudes Toward and Occurrence of Cohabitation Without Marriage," *Journal of Marriage and the Family* (May 1978): 398.

27. Peterman and Ridley, p. 350.

28. David and Vera Mace, *Marriage East and West* (Garden City, N.Y.: Doubleday, 1960), p. 131.

29. An excellent review of empirical literature on the subject of interracial marriage is found in James D. Bruce and Hyman Rodman, "Black–White Marriages in the United States: A Review of the Empirical Literature," in Irving R. Stuart and Lawrence E. Abt (eds.), *Interracial Marriage: Expectations and Realities* (New York: Grossman, 1973), pp. 147–61. This report notes that a study in Los Angeles showed that only 0.1 percent of all black marriages involved a white partner, while in Hawaii 16.9 percent of all black marriages involved a white partner. These two cases represented the range. In the nation as a whole the percentage of marriages involving one black partner, as a percentage of all marriages, ranged from a low in Michigan of 0.03 percent to a high in Washington, D.C. of 0.77 percent. See Stuart and Abt, p. 151, for a summary table.

30. Paul C. Glick, "Intermarriage and Fertility Patterns Among Persons in Major Religious Groups," *Eugenics Quarterly*, 1 (1960): 31–38; and Robert O. Blood, Jr., *Marriage* (New York: Free Press, 1962), p. 81, shows how this percentage varies for Catholics, depending on the percentage of the population that is Catholic in Canadian provinces. Thus, 2 percent of Quebec's Catholics marry non-Catholics, whereas 46 percent of British Columbia's Catholics do so. Eighty-eight percent of Quebec's population is Catholic, while only 14 percent of British Columbia's is. Thomas D. Monahan's study, "Some Dimensions of Interreligious Marriages in Indiana, 1961–1967," *Social Forces*, December 1973, concludes that Jews are by far the most endogamous of these religious groups.

31. Paul H. Besancency, S.J., *Interfaith Marriages: Who and Why* (New Haven, Conn.: College and University Press, 1970), pp. 48–74.

32. U.S. Bureau of the Census, *Statistical Abstract of the United States: 1977* (Washington, D.C.: U.S. Government Printing Office, 1977), p. 74.

33. Bernard Murstein, "Stimulus—Value—Role: A Theory of Marital Choice," *Journal of Marriage and Family*, 1970, pp. 465–81.

34. Data supporting Murstein's hypothesis regarding the importance of physical attractions are found in such studies as James P. Curran, "Correlates of Physical Attractiveness and Interpersonal Attraction in the Dating Situation," *Social Behavior & Personality*, 1973, pp. 769–72. Curran concluded, however, that personality information is readily available from the first date on.

35. There are several other factors that affect the rate at which a partnership is able to develop in Murstein's model. Among the most important of these is a similarity in sex drive. Couples who have dissimilar sex drives—particularly those in which the woman has a much greater sex drive than the man or in which the man's sexuality involves greater neurosis—will have greater difficulty making good courtship progress than couples whose sex drives are more nearly matched or those whose sex drive dissimilarity is in line with the traditional notions of male dominance. This point is not an argument for male dominance but, rather, an indication of the extent to which this cultural trait has played a role in the socialization of most people before now.

36. Charles T. Hill, Zech Restun, and Letitia Anne Peplau, "Breakups Before Marriage: The End of 103 Affairs," *Journal of Social Issues*, 32 (1976): 147–67.

37. Bernard Murstein, Mary Cerrets, and Marcia G. MacDonald, "A Theory and Investigation of the Effect of Exchange-Orientation in Marriage and Friendship," *Journal of Marriage and the Family* (August 1977): 543–48.

38. Trost, p. 398.

on the Nature and Experience of Love

I say of myself that I am ignorant about all things except the nature of love.

—Socrates

Can anyone live with authenticity unless he believes and trusts in the basic meaningfulness and rightness of the movement of his love?

—James Hillman

6 on the *Nature* and *Experience* of *Love*

Konrad Lorenz, the animal behaviorist, is a lover of the European grey goose. Their great grey wings encircle the pond on his estate all year round, as some always remain behind the flocks that are winging south on their fall migration. In his book *King Solomon's Ring*, Lorenz tells of one of the most satisfying experiences in his life with them.[1] He was intent on discovering how young goslings became paired with one female and one female only and one day decided to conduct an experiment. He waited beside a half-dozen eggs that were just about ready to hatch and made sure that he was the first living thing the goslings saw when they emerged. He took care to crouch down on his haunches so that he was about the same height above

117

the ground as a female grey goose, and he imitated the female's calls. When the goslings broke out of their shells, they identified him as their "mother," to the delight of all the onlookers who saw him wobbling around his yard with a string of grey goslings in tow. He had changed some fundamental beliefs about "maternal instincts" and "pair bonding" that day, and he went on to discover much more about the process he called *imprinting*, but he was more fundamentally interested in understanding love.

Love arises out of our experience of life. Its primary source is not relationships or partnerships: These become possible because there is love. The word points to that which is deepest in ourselves and truest in life, the ground of our being, the center of our lives. The Gospel according to St John says, "God is love." It does not say "Love is god," and thereby the better preserves the essential mystery. Love, according to Jung, cannot be taught nor learned, given nor taken, withheld nor earned. It is discovered through experience. It happens to us.[2]

Words fail us when we talk about love because, even though we can experience it in its fullness, we split it apart when we talk or write about it. What is experienced as an overcoming of opposites, a reuniting of prodigals, a bridging of the abyss of separation and loneliness, is often presented as a paradox. The experience of love so far exceeds the capacity of our images and concepts to express it that it is forever pulling us out of our conventional worlds, forever calling us to know more of it.

We welcome the delights love brings, the exuberance of spirit, the transformation of most ordinary things into wonderous symbols, the passionate desire for the beloved, the sense of harmony with the universe and contentment with our lot in life. Life is radiant in love's springtime. But how can these good things be reconciled with love's darker gifts? Surely love cannot bring hatred, pain, suffering, sorrow, and fear as well?

And what about sex? There are many who say that we do not need to speak of love. The more freely we express ourselves as sexual beings, the more fully we realize our full humanity. Nothing is gained by calling such sexual experience love. Indeed, to do so is to saddle sex with all the inhibitions imposed on it over the past two thousand years by the disciples of love. This chapter will not resolve these issues. It will, however, talk about them in the effort to draw nearer to love.

WHOLE EARTH LOVE

According to one Greek myth, in the beginning the great black winged bird Night (*Nyx*) laid a great egg. From the upper portion of that egg the heavens were formed, and from the lower portion the earth. Love (*eros*) flew forth from the broken egg.[3] Heaven and earth thereafter were drawn together by love and their union produced the Titans. The image of love binding together heaven and earth depicts it as the primal force or energy of the universe. It binds together the fundamental opposites—Sky Father and Earth

The image of love binding together heaven and earth depicts love as the primal energy of the universe. (Royal Archives, Great Britain.)

Mother. Whatever else love is in the world's mythologies, it is a binder, a healer, a bridger of great chasms.

The Story of Gilgamesh

But love is also a destroyer, a refiner's fire for purification. It sets people apart as well as binding them together. In one of the oldest myths ever written, the Babylonian epic of Gilgamesh, the destructive dimension of love is portrayed in the beautiful—and terrible—goddess Ishtar. Ishtar loves the hero of the epic, Gilgamesh, and Gilgamesh spurns her love:

> Thy love is like a door that letteth in the storm. Thy love is like a fortress that falls upon and crushes the warriors within it. The lover of thy youth, Tammuz, even he, was destroyed; destroyed are all the men whom thou has to do with. The creatures who come under thine influence rejoice, but

they rejoice for a while only; the wing of the bird is broken through thee; the lion is destroyed; the horse is driven to death. Thou sayest thou lovests me, Ishtar. Loved by thee I should fare as they have fared. . . .[4]

The goddess is the energy of the seasons of the year and the seasons of life. Her bountiful love comes and goes as the flowers of the field burst forth in the spring and die off in winter. Her seasonal love creates and destroys in endless cycles. Ishtar is enraged by his reply, but Gilgamesh, the proud ruler of the city of Erech, would have a more permanent, less temperamental love.

While Gilgamesh is warring with Ishtar, a hunter leads a temple prostitute into the woods in order to trap a wild man he has caught a glimpse of. The wild man's name is Enkidu. He falls in love with the temple woman at first sight.

> He saw her; she held her arms out to him; she took off her veil. Then Enkidu was astonished. He went towards her, and she took his hand, and she led him away. He came under the spell of the Temple woman's beauty. He would not leave her, but stayed where she stayed at the edge of the forest. On the sixth day he rose up and went away from where she stayed. His heart had become hungry to look upon the wild beasts whose friend he had been. He went towards where companies of gazelles were. The gazelles fled from him.[5]

When the wild beasts smelled the scent of the woman on Enkidu, they fled in fear from an alien presence. His infatuation had cost him the companionship of the beasts. So Enkidu returned to the city with the woman and there met Gilgamesh. They became close. They hunted together, made war together, confided in each other, rejoiced in their stamina and youthful vigor. They loved one another mightily. After a time Gilgamesh put off his royal robes to run wild with Enkidu. But it came to pass that Enkidu died. Gilgamesh looked upon the strange sleep of death and wondered if he too must follow Enkidu in this as well. He fled from such a thought and sought the plant of immortality at the bottom of a great lake where his ancestor, Uta-Napishtim, told him he would find it. Gilgamesh dove to the bottom of the lake, found the plant, and prepared to eat it after the appropriate nine days of waiting. But while he was bathing a serpent came and ate the plant—the whole of it—leaving Gilgamesh nothing. Gilgamesh wept, but the spirit of Enkidu came to him and told him how men fared in the land of the dead and to fear not. Such in barest outline is one of the oldest love stories in recorded history. As a story about beginnings, it is a story about what it means to love in which the dark side of love is not hidden or cast aside.

If one loves the earth and all life upon it—if, indeed the earth becomes for one a single living organism—then the terrible and the beautiful, the demonic and the angelic, are bound together in close encounter, and strife and harmony are found inevitably in every home. Every meal is a meal prepared before the face of adversaries, yet every adversary is a compatriot or a lover unaware. Love may be freely given, but it exacts a cost in that any commitment or choice excludes other options, just as Enkidu cannot be simultaneously a lover of woman and beasts.

Things Fall Apart

We fear to look at the whole of love in large measure because events in the nineteenth century so shattered our images of wholeness. Freud called them our "naive self-love." Intellectuals of that century were disturbed by some of the implications of the theory of evolution. The image of nature that was presented was strongly ambivalent. On the one hand, evolution could be wedded to a notion of progress or even spiritual development. Nature could be envisioned as orderly development, through successive stages perhaps, toward the emergence of *Homo sapiens*. As the crowning touch of such a creative process, the human being could be proud even of animal ancestry and anticipate unprecedented development in the future. This vision of progress was a secularization of the biblical myth of the coming of the kingdom.

On the other hand, the cost of such progress was enormous. Nature seemed indifferent at best to the destruction of millions upon billions of organisms and the extinction of hundreds, perhaps thousands of species that could not adapt to the changing environment. Every ecological niche was a battleground over scarce resources. Ernest Becker observes: "Every organism raises its head above a sea of corpses, smiles into the sun, and pronounces life good."[6] We cannot live save by taking life in some form, and our increasing capacity to do so often makes us proud. But nature appears "blood red with tooth and claw." As human beings, furthermore, we know what the organism presumably does not know—namely, that we will die. We know that there was a time when we were not, and that there will be a time when we will not be. And we are anxious about this. It is not so much death as a termination of life that we fear, Becker argues. It is a death without significance. It is too much for us to bear to believe we have lived a life that has made no difference, that has had little or no significance to anyone, and that we have loved in vain.

Therefore, we have collectively created a social world over and against the world of nature in which we can find comfort. Culture is our immortality vehicle. We know that we must die, but what we believe in can live after us. We can even achieve great recognition through dying for what we believe in, and because we have such an investment in our shared beliefs and values—our culture—we are not only willing to die for them, but to inflict on others who believe differently great pain and suffering. It is not through the struggle to survive that the greatest evil has entered into the world, but rather through our terrible investment in our fragile immortality vehicles. Pain and suffering come into the world because of our investment in the things we love.

It is not possible to avoid creating meaning and value. We certainly cannot live without loving. But what price are we willing to pay for the preservation of these things that we love, and how can we be assisted in their dissolution? In loving partnerships it is possible to create shared worlds of significance and value and also learn how to survive their dissolution. Love is greater than the things we love. It does not eliminate fear, anxiety, and suffering. It overcomes them, and this we can discover the more we become open to the experience of life through our love of it.

But nineteenth-century writers and thinkers present us with a formidable obstacle to such openness. The sudden prudishness that descended upon the Western world in the nineteenth century is well illustrated by the case of the physician Thomas Bowdler. In 1818, Bowdler published a popular version of the works of William Shakespeare in which "those words and expressions are omitted which cannot with propriety be read aloud in a family."[7] He applied his method to Gibbon's history as well, and his name has entered the *Oxford English Dictionary*, in which "to bowdlerize" means "to castrate." In the spirit of Bowdler, love devolved into sentimentality and pornography, statues acquired fig leaves, and polite society lost the capacity to speak openly of human loving.

Love as a Dimension of Being

But whatever our capacity to express love may be, each of us knows of it in the core of our being. In our lives, we make much of this knowledge or little. Drawing near to this love that is "within" all of us is an extraordinarily simple task for some and an extraordinarily difficult one for others. It is probable that most of us become aware of such love in instances of insight—peak experiences or religious experiences. In such moments love engulfs us. We do not take it, accept it, control it, or in any way alter it. It takes us and we can grow from it. We can also cultivate our awareness of it and look forward to its coming.

For some, a particularly powerful experience triggers this new awareness. The astronaut Russel Schweikart writes of the experience of seeing the earth hanging out there in space:

> It is so small and so fragile and such a precious little spot in the universe that you can block it out with your thumb, and you realize that on that small spot, that little blue and white thing, is everything that means anything to you—all of history and music and poetry and art and death and birth and love, tears, joy, games, all of it on that little spot out there that you can cover with your thumb. And you realize from that perspective that you've changed, that there's something new there, that the relationship is no longer what it was.[8]

For others, disciplined effort is required to love the world. The Zen monk works hard at the task of preparation, but the experience of enlightenment is not a direct product of any particular ritual or discipline. When enlightenment comes, it is often described in terms of a great love. Thus a Japanese executive of 47 writes:

> 4 A.M. of the 29th: Ding, dong! The clock chimes. This alone is. This alone is. There's no reasoning here. Surely the world has changed. But in what way? The ancients said the enlightened mind is comparable to a fish swimming. That's exactly how it is—there is no stagnation. I feel no hindrance. Everything flows smoothly, freely. Everything goes naturally. This limitless freedom is beyond all expression. What a wonderful world! Dogen, the great teacher of Buddhism, said: Zen is the wide, all-encompassing gate of compassion. I am so grateful, so grateful.[9]

What is most characteristic of such moments is that they arise out of our being rather than our doing even when we have spent so much time preparing for them. This had led to the practice of withdrawal from the world in religious communities in order to put aside time for the cultivation of such experience. But such communities are very much in touch with the world, and not at all cut off from doing. One of the greatest Western mystics, the fourteenth-century Cistercian Meister Eckart, warned against overindulging in such mystical experiences:

> Supposing, however, that all such [experiences] were really of love, even then it would not be best. We ought to get over amusing ourselves with such raptures for the sake of that better love, and to accomplish through loving service what men most need, spiritually, socially or physically. As I have often said, if a person were in such a rapturous state as St. Paul once entered, and he knew of a sick man who wanted a cup of soup, it would be far better to withdraw from the rapture for love's sake and serve him who is in need.[10]

This monk was not only a mystic, he was also the abbot of a large monestary and a manager of wealth and property. He found love in both withdrawal and engagement.

In a time such as ours, however, it seems that the task has become more complicated. Our society invites our attention to matters (deadlines, work schedules, bank balances) that tend to become ends in themselves rather than means by which to live more fully. We are distracted from life by our very attempts at engagement in it, because what we do in our everyday lives has less and less significance. It casts less and less light on our basic vocation to become a celebrant of life. We therefore would seem in need of a great deal of reflection and withdrawal as well as decisive action.

LOVE RESEARCHED

If the experience of love is as far beyond our images and concepts of it as the preceding discussion has suggested, it follows that in a fundamental sense it is beyond research. It is essentially mysterious. Nevertheless, love is mani-

The fundamental problem we all face is achieving a balance between passionate love and companionate love. (Ken Karp.)

fested in behavior, and we can appreciate it the more we examine the attitudes, emotions, and actions we associate with loving. Love researched is not love explained, it is love approached by another route.

Some Recent Studies

Nevertheless, love has remained beyond the pale of scientific research even while the intimacies of human sexual behavior have been explored in increasing detail. That it should remain so was emphatically endorsed by Senator William Proxmire, who in making his 1975 Golden Fleece Award, declared in his press release attacking an NSF grant to the University of Minnesota for a study of passionate and companionate love:

> I object to this not only because no one—not even the National Science Foundation—can argue that falling in love is a science; not only because I'm sure that even if they spent $84 million or $84 billion they wouldn't get an answer that anyone would believe. I'M ALSO AGAINST IT BECAUSE I DON'T WANT THE ANSWER.
> I believe that 200 million other Americans want to leave some things in life a mystery, and right at the top of things we don't want to know is why a man falls in love with a woman and vice versa. . . .[11]

But genuine mysteries are not vulnerable to scientific analysis—they speak from other dimensions of our being than the material. Fortunately, the work continues and we are beginning to understand some very interesting things about love. For example, there is a growing body of research that supports the general theory of emotion put forth by Stanley Schachter of Columbia University.[12] According to Schacter, there are two fundamental components to the experience of an emotion. The first is a physiological arousal that is characteristic of all intense emotions—a racing heart, heightened breathing, sweating, tensed musculature. The second is the person's subjective labeling of this arousal as anger, fear, love, sexual passion, or whatever. Well and good! The interesting thing is that since at least the time of Ovid, the advice of the experienced lover reflects some remarkable insights. In the *Art of Love*, Ovid noted that an excellent time for a man to arouse passion in a woman was while watching the disembowelment of gladiators in the arena. He was proposing a "fear breeds passion principle" that has been documented in some recent research in Vancouver, British Columbia. Donald Dutton and Arthur P. Aron conducted their experiments on two footbridges that cross the Capilano River.[13] One bridge is a narrow, shaky thread that sways in the wind 230 feet above the stream. The other is a solid structure only 10 feet above it. Near the end of each bridge, an attractive female experimenter approached men who were crossing and asked if they would take part in an experiment on "the effects of exposure to scenic attractions on creative expression." They were asked to write down their associations to a picture she showed them. The men who were stopped on the narrow suspension bridge were more sexually aroused than the men on the solid bridge, which was inferred from the amount of sexual imagery in their associations. An unanticipated by-product that further supported the fear-breeds-passion hypotheses came when it was discovered that the men who crossed on the suspension bridge were more likely to call the researcher afterward "to get more information about the study."

When University of Minnesota researchers recently asked college students what they meant by passionate love, some gave responses that were expected: the joy of loving and being loved, the pleasure of having someone understand you, sexual fulfillment, having fun, and so on.[14] But for some love was more readily associated with pain. It had its moments, no doubt, but more often it was associated with anxiety (would they be loved in return), uncertainty, confusion, and pain. Sometimes a sexual experience may help convince a person that he or she is "in love." One respondent declared that she was surprised to discover she enjoyed having sex with her boyfriend. Until that time, she had been uncertain as to whether or not she was actually in love.

William Kephart, a sociologist at the University of Pennsylvania, asked over a thousand students, "If a boy (girl) had all the qualities you desired, would you marry this person even if you were not in love with him (her)?" Most people said that they would not, but most women refused to respond with an out and out "No." One woman declared: "If a boy had all the other qualities I desired, and I was not in love with him—well, I think I could talk myself into falling in love."[15] In our society, people who are planning to marry for a whole host of different reasons typically come to decide that they are "in love." It seems that the general state of physiological arousal determines if we feel any emotion at all, and a very complex process of labeling defines what specific emotion we are experiencing and whether we consider that emotion to be generally pleasant or painful.

In contrast to popular opinion, several studies indicate that women are not as subject to rule by their emotions as we tend to think. In studies of couples on both coasts, it was discovered that men tend to fall in love quicker than women and that women are more likely to break up the relationship.[16] It is reasoned that perhaps this is so because women are still more dependent upon men than men are upon women. Women therefore must be careful to make the right choice of a mate, whereas men can afford to be more romantic.

Schacter's two-stage theory of emotions fits well with John Gagnon's view that sexual arousal is a function of social scripting rather than physiological instinct or drive.[17] According to Gagnon, the definition of a situation as sexually arousing results from a host of cues that are learned or scripted. A man coming back to his hotel room during a convention and finding a beautiful nude woman on his bed is not automatically aroused. More than likely, he will make inquiries as to why she is there before proceeding further. Script theory is an elaboration of the second stage suggesting why it is that we subjectively perceive certain events (an internal stage of physiological arousal and an external set of social cues) as a specific emotion such as love, passion, joy, fear, or anger.

If we accept the general notion of a two-stage theory of emotion and acknowledge that we learn how to identify certain behaviors and external cues as appropriate to a specific emotion, then we can also ask does it make any difference if we call it love or sex? The primary concern of individuals involved has always been, What is at stake here? Are we going to bed because we enjoy each other's sexual responses and are delighted to be able to play around a bit, but nothing is expected in the long term? Are we "having sex?" Or do we mutually envision a future together that may lead to marriage and further commitments? Are we "in love"? This is a conventional distinction, and while it is very imprecise, it does call attention to a commonly held need to be clear about the nature of our commitments. For simplicity's sake, let us assume that in both cases both partners experience a significant degree of the physiological arousal we commonly call "passion."

Our tradition has been very leery of passion, and it has tried to enforce some very ambivalent attitudes as a result. The most peculiar assumption is that we all know when this physiological arousal is sex and when it is love, and further that we can be reasonably sure that our partner sees things as we do. The evidence is growing that neither assumption is a valid one. In the first instance, we are not naturally informed by our instincts whether what we are experiencing is sex or love. We *define* the physiological arousal as one or the other and we may—or may not—do this mutually. It begins to look as though it can be a glorious part of our creativity to define it clearly one way or the other, but we cannot do this unless we are aware of the experience of love at the center of our being, our basic love style for its expression, and spend some time being clear with our partner about our mutual commitment. Looked at analytically, it seems like an incredibly difficult task. But fortunately analysis is only one component of our understanding of love. We love out of the fullness of our being and the resulting experience is preserved in our whole body, not merely in our mind.

Passionate Love

Elaine Hatfield and associates have offered the following definition of **passionate love:**

> A state of intense absorption in another. Sometimes lovers are those who long for their partners and for complete fulfillment. Sometimes lovers are those who are ecstatic at finally having attained their partners' love, and momentarily complete fulfillment. A state of intense physiological arousal.[18]

They suggest that such a definition includes the fundamental understanding of love from Plato to Freud to a number of modern researchers. They note further that there are several tell-tale signs of love—increased amount of eye contact, diminished distance and increased touching, an inclination to lean toward one another when sitting or standing, and body language that invites exploration. These signs are given off by an individual who experiences internal physiological arousal, and they help establish the fact that there is a mutual interest in one another. They also suggest the probable intensity of this interest. Such signs are useful in mutually establishing an understanding about what is at stake. But they are not infallible signs and are sometimes used to deceive as well as disclose emotion. The only way to be sure about what is at stake is to make every effort to confirm what you infer about your partner's behavior and to be as clear as possible about the signs you are giving.

There is always a risk in trying to establish what is at stake in any commitment. Self-disclosure may produce rejection as well as acceptance, and courtship is by no means an inevitably increasing intimacy. The nature of the commitment itself changes over time. The traditional solution—devised before there were adequate contraceptives and gender and marriage roles were more clearly defined—was to advise against becoming sexually involved beyond heavy petting, until there was at least the socially recognized commitment of engagement and preferably not until marriage. Passionate love is inherently unstable and requires a considerable degree of testing before it is acted upon. But on the other hand, couples are supposed to be passionately in love before they decide to get married. Even today, most couples in our society declare they are "in love" when they marry even if they are marrying for other reasons. After marriage, tradition advises, passionate love will not last. The honeymoon may last longer for one couple than another, but it will end and the routine of married life, the securing of a home and the raising of a family, require a willed commitment beyond the ups and downs of emotion. Couples must work at their marriage if they want it to survive.

Companionate Love

Hatfield and associates distinguish between passionate love—the explosive mixture of emotions fueled by delightful as well as painful experiences—and **companionate love**, a steadier state fueled by delightful experiences but extinguished eventually by painful ones. It is not quite what tradition has considered "working at a marriage" to mean, because of the concession to possible termination, but it is closer to this view of commitment than it is to passionate love. Companionate love starts with a quest for a culturally acceptable mate, but expects a lot more. It is based on liking and a sense of equity rather than passionate longing.

The major departure from traditional notions about "working at a marriage" in the notion of companionate love is the contention that very few people are in fact able to be altruistic in their love relationships. Companionate love is based on a sense of equity in a relationship. Each partner should work to get the few things he or she really wants in a relationship, even though they can never get exactly what they want. Equity theory states that: (1) People are biologically set to seek pleasure and avoid pain. (2) Society is composed of selfish people who must learn to compromise if they are to survive. (3) Most people feel comfortable in a relationship when they feel they are getting exactly what they deserve. (4) Men and women who find that they are in an inequitable relationship strive to restore equity, strive to restore psychological equity, or end the relationship.[19]

Sexuality is very much a part of companionate love, but the sexual satisfaction is not the primary ingredient sustaining the relationship; the sense of equity is.

Achieving a Balance

The fundamental problem we all face in living satisfying lives is to achieve a balance between the two types of loving. Passionate love is excitement and adventure. It is stimulated by a variety of partners and experiences.

Painful experiences may stimulate it as well as delightful ones. It is characteristically of short duration and high intensity. Companionate love thrives on a sense of security and well-being. It demands reciprocity and attentiveness. Painful experience extinguishes it. It is of lower intensity and is much longer lasting. Hatfield and associates contend that we want both experiences and strive to realize them in our lives.

Most material on human sexuality understandably stresses passionate love. In marriage, it is argued, it is possible to rekindle passion in a number of ways through providing an opportunity to experience different sexual techniques and/or partners. Swinging and open marriage are two ways of modifying the marital commitment to include sexual experiences with other partners. Sex manuals offer seemingly endless ways of changing technique. Even the radical right has its answer in books like *The Total Woman*, in which it is asserted that the sexual fire is the wife's responsibility and—contrary to what might be advised by feminists—the happily married woman should learn to submit herself completely to her husband ("obey" as in "love, honor and obey") and his career and strive constantly to make herself seductively attractive in his eyes—cocktails, black panties, mirrors, and the like.[20]

But all this emphasis on passion prevents a more honest recognition of the companionate needs and the role this love plays in our lives. There is no universal answer to what "balance" might mean in a particular couple's case, but the relationship depends on their achieving enough of a balance to meet their particular needs.

FOUR DIMENSIONS OF LOVE

The Chinese call love a many splendored thing. Almost all cultures have more than one word to describe love. We are impoverished in this regard because we try to make one word cover a multitude of feelings, behaviors, and commitments. Let us distinguish four principal kinds of love: affection (storge), friendship (philias), eros, and agape.[21] If Rollo May is correct, a major problem of our sexual liberation is that many have attempted to make sex carry the entire load of their feelings for others. This has resulted in the banalization of sex and the increase in loneliness so characteristic of our age.

Affection

The love that the Greeks called **storge**, which we roughly translate as "affection," is a low-profile love. It is a bond commonly felt between kin, especially between parents and children.

Affection . . . is the humblest love. It gives itself no airs. People can be proud of being "in love," or of friendship. . . . It usually needs absence or bereavement to set us praising those to whom Affection binds us. We take them for granted.[22]

Nevertheless, this is a basic love out of which others spring. Our experiencing this fundamental love gives most of us the first sense of self-confidence, the sense of being loved, that later critically affects how we love others. Affection is often found intermixed with the other kinds of love.

Lee contends that storgic lovers never consciously select a love partner. Storgic love is love without fever or folly. Storgic lovers are likely to treat each other as old friends, even though they may have met as strangers. It is slow-burning, and sexual contact of any extent is likely to develop late in the relationship. The constant emphasis upon sex in the media makes it difficult for storgic lovers to persist in their belief that sex is not all that important in love, but they do.

While affection is the most unassuming form of love, it can become an all-consuming demand, as in the case of the mother who lives for her children or the animal lover who pampers a pet. The distortion of affection is readily observable in the case of the teacher who affectionately nourishes

Affection is a bond commonly felt between kin, especially between parents and children. It gives us the first sense of self-confidence and affects how we love others. (UNICEF photo by Tom Marotta.)

a student toward independent thought and then becomes offended when the student achieves a degree of independence and thinks for himself or herself.

Friendship

Friendship, or philias, is characterized by common interests and is founded on a common devotion to causes. Friends are characterized by their ability to relax in each other's presence because they share more or less the same world view and take the same things for granted. While it is possible to experience an erotic love and a friendship with the same person, nothing is less like a friendship than a love affair. Lovers are always talking to each other about their love affair, but friends rarely say to one another, "you are my best friend." Lovers are normally face-to-face, absorbed in one another. Friends are side-by-side absorbed in a common interest. Erotic love is best expressed between two people, but two is far from the best number of friends. Friendship is the least biological of the natural loves. It is not homosexual or abnormal when friends treat each other affectionately. And yet, because of our often frantic fear of being considered homosexual, we often treat our friends less affectionately than we might otherwise.

Friendship becomes perverse when it creates an in-group that is insensitive to anyone else. Friends share the same jokes, support each other's advance in business, and in many ways define themselves as different from the rest of the world because they care about the same truths. They can be a threat to government when they have the power to assert their exclusiveness. Yet, throughout all ages, little bands of friends have turned their backs on the world and have often transformed it. The snobbish elite from the outside is often a group of friends from the inside.

Eros

The form of love called **eros** is partially expressed when two people feel they have fallen in love. The Greeks thought of it as a passion or fascination for ideal beauty—a search for the one ideal beloved. In our time, however, we have tended to reduce eros to sexual attraction, as shown in our use of the word *erotic*. But it is of the utmost importance that we distinguish between sex and eros. Ruddick and others contend that eros evolves or can evolve out of sexual attraction, but others disagree. C. S. Lewis, for example, sees the process of falling in love somewhat differently. Some people may feel sexually attracted toward another and then go on to fall in love, but Lewis thinks this is not the common case. What is more common is that there is at first a delighted preoccupation with the beloved. A man lusting for sexual satisfaction doesn't want the woman in her totality, but only the pleasure she can provide as an instrument. Eros is not primarily a gratification of desire, a release of tension, or a pursuit of pleasure, although all these elements may be a part of erotic love.

"Eros is a kind of loving motivated by great appreciation of beauty. Of course, the particular bodily forms which each lover considers beautiful vary a good deal."[23] Such a lover may be unable to find a truly suitable partner because of a rigid commitment to a particularly scarce ideal form of beauty. Erotic lovers must frequently compromise or live a life of unfulfilled love.

Because this image of the beloved is idealized, the erotic lover will want to discover as quickly as possible if the real flesh-and-blood partner is what he or she seems. Hence, the rush into bed and the frequent confrontation with disillusionment that gives erotic love its trials and tribulations. One of Lee's erotic lovers remarked, however: "Our sex is good, sometimes its really great, but it was never the thing that held us together. We make love; sex doesn't make us love."[24]

Erotic lovers often have difficulty controlling the sensation of touch. They are powerfully drawn to each other's bodies, and yet mere sexual intimacy soon becomes blunted. Therefore, they are more apt than others to employ fantasy and to enjoy the cultivation of techniques to preserve their delight in the partner's body. Lee contends, in contrast to Lewis, that erotic lovers typically launch into intercourse early in their relationship because they must directly and intensely experience the embodied personality of the beloved. Growth in erotic love is achieved by expanding the base of erotic intimacy and self-disclosure. And yet, how often can you reveal your deepest feelings and ideas without the very act of revelation becoming boring?

Nonjealous erotic lovers, Lee finds, are those who have not been disappointed in their previous loves and whose current erotic needs are fulfilled by the partner. Because the ecstacy of eros cannot be maintained, the continuing problem facing the erotic lover is how to combine eros with the other forms of love, without allowing those other forms to take over. Lee contends that although eros could readily be transformed into others, he found no erotic lover that began loving with another love style.[25]

Sex for the erotic lover is primarily a means of knowing the beloved. But because it is an art that most of us must cultivate in order to be at ease and achieve adequate communication with the beloved, the unskilled or inexperienced erotic lover may be turned off by a potentially compatible partner because of the clumsiness of their lovemaking.

> The rapid disclosure of self, early sexual experience, honesty of emotion, and intensity of feelings all make this a difficult lovestyle. Of course, these qualities also make it the most ecstatic, exilerating, and challenging kind of love for some people.
>
> Your chances of successfully enjoying Eros are substantially reduced when you lack some of the important qualities of self-confidence, self-esteem, and social stability. A would-be erotic lover should first put his own psychological house in order, enjoy his work, surround himself with

good close friends, and have a good relationship with his parents, if possible, before attempting an erotic approach to love.

You might well say, 'If a person has all of these advantages he doesn't need a love anyway,' precisely. The successful erotic lover must not need to be in love. Rather he finds the right person to love and then allows himself to need that person. Eros is not a way of being happy, but of being happier.[26]

The demonic characteristic of eros is not so much to be found in its sensuousness or its sexuality, but rather in its tendency to demand unconditional devotion from the lovers. It is not the idolization of the beloved, nor the idolization of sensual pleasure, but rather the elevation of erotic love to a law in its own right that threatens the greatest danger to the lovers. "The pair can say to one another in an almost sacrificial spirit, it is for love's sake that I have neglected my parents, left my children, cheated my partner, failed my friend at his greatest needs. These reasons in love's law have passed for good."[27]

Agape

Agape is defined as "esteem for the other, the concern for the other's welfare beyond any gain that one can get out of it; disinterested love, typically the love of God for man."[28] The New Testament usage of the word *charity* is really a poor translation of agape, though it retains an element of selfless giving. Agape is gift-love, and it implies an obligation or duty to love whether or not the other is lovable. Lee laments:

Unfortunately, I have yet to interview any respondent involved in even a relatively short-term affiliative love relationship which I could classify without qualification as an example of agape. I have encountered brief agapetic episodes in continuing love relationships.[29]

Altruism, much less agapetic love, has failed to make much of an impression on social science models of human love. There is so little evidence of the existence of such behavior. If we try hard enough, it is always possible to come up with a motive, a vested interest that motivates our behavior. Sexual behavior and human loving are no exceptions. And yet, agape is an answer to the questions posed by the other loves and, paradoxically, we must receive it as a free gift. We cannot actively create it, though we may hunger and thirst after it. Its effectiveness in our lives depends on the extent to which we are open to receive it. Agape, however, is not a substitute for the other loves. It is best to say that it can enrich all of them.[30]

Agape is more akin to the expression of intentionally or will than it is to emotions or sensations. In the Christian view it is commanded, "Thou shalt love the Lord thy God, with all thy heart and all thy soul and all thy mind. This is the first and great commandment, and the second is like unto it, Thou shalt love thy neighbor as thyself." This commanded love is to include all people, enemies as well as friends, the leper as well as the healthy person. Christian theologians do not claim that it is often realized in the lives of human beings. Lewis remarks, "It is dangerous to press upon a man the duty of getting beyond the earthly love when his real difficulty lies in getting so far."[31]

According to Erich Fromm, the lover must love out of duty with care, knowledge, responsibility, and respect. The lover must strive to love rather than to be loved or to become lovable.

> . . . love is exclusively an act of will and commitment, and therefore fundamentally it does not matter who the two persons are. . . . We are all one—yet each one of us is a unique, unduplicable entity. Inasmuch as we are all one we can love everybody in the same way in the sense of brotherly love. But inasmuch as we are all also different, erotic love requires certain specific highly individual differences.[32]

Theologians tell us that we are all one family of brothers and sisters because God is our father. This is a mystical unity, not an apparent one. Our differences seem to divide us more than our similarities unite us. If, however, it is possible to become open to this gift-love, then we can love others out of an abundance of love rather than out of a scarcity.

SUMMARY

Love does not arise out of relationships or partnerships. They are possible because it is. Love happens to us. It pulls us out of our conventional understanding of love and demands that we learn ever anew of it. Love's light side is greatly desired, but its darker gifts are often feared. A part of our problem in experiencing love comes from wanting to control our lives in such a way as to exclude the unexpected and the painful. Yet a life that does not open to love is hardly worth living. The multidimensionality of love is best preserved in myths such as the Gilgamesh Epic and the Grail stories.

Our culture often hinders as much as it helps our efforts to be open to love. Aware of our mortality we have created customs and conventions to survive us. We are even willing to go to war and to die for what we believe in. Thus pain and suffering come into the world because of our strong attachment to the things we love.

It is not possible to live without making some kind of investment in life. It is not possible to live without some sense of meaning. It is not possible to live long without loving. Happily, love is greater than the things we love. It does not eliminate fear, anxiety, and suffering; it overcomes them. The experience of love is essentially the experience of unity-at-oneness with all that is, however much it may be talked about as paradox.

We frequently experience love as a depth dimension in our being, but most often we do not make much of such experience. There is little in our culture to encourage us to do so. Besides this, our little events, such as the wonder at a rainbow in a dewdrop, are so insignificant in comparison to seeing the whole earth from a space ship or to experiencing enlightenment after long months of Zen training.

The love research does not explain love, it merely approaches it from another angle. If we see love as a two-staged phenomenon after Schacter, a physiological arousal common to all intense emotions, and a subtle labeling of the arousal as love, hate, or fear, we are more aware of the intertwining of these emotions in our lives and less surprised by the dark side of love.

Hatfield and associates suggest that in any persisting partnership there is the continuing effort to achieve a balance between passionate love and companionate love. Passionate love is intense, short term, and can be kindled by either pain or pleasure. Companionate love is slow burning, long term, and eventually extinguishable by painful experiences.

A more ancient typology describes four basic forms of love: *Eros* which is based on the intense attraction for a particular beloved and urges us to hop into bed to discover as soon as possible if this person is the ideal in our heads. It is much like Hatfield's passionate love. *Storge*, on the other hand, is the basic affection upon which all other loves depend. It resembles companionate love, but is best expressed in the relationship between parents and their children. *Filias* is the love between friends which from the outside may appear to create an elite and snobbish group. *Agape* is the disinterested altruistic love the Bible declares is characteristic of the love of God toward creation. It is an act of will that can be commanded. Since it depends on the intention of the lover rather than the characteristics of the beloved, all persons can be so loved. Such love, poets, philosophers, and researchers alike declare, is very rare in human behavior.

NOTES

1. Konrad Lorenz, *King Solomon's Ring* (New York: Harper & Row 1976).
2. C. G. Jung, *Modern Man in Search of a Soul* (New York: Harcourt, Brace and World, 1933), p. 226.
3. Padraic Colum, *Myths of the World* (New York: Grosset and Dunlap, 1930), p. 61.
4. Colum, p. 23.
5. Ibid., p. 24.
6. Ernest Becker, *Escape from Evil* (New York: Free Press, 1976).
7. James Hillman, *The Myth of Analysis* (New York: Harper & Row, 1970), p. 135.
8. Russel Schweikart, "The Whole Earth" in Lindesfarne Assoc. (ed.) *Earths Answer: Exploring Planetary Culture at the Lindesfarne Conferences* (New York: Harper & Row, 1979).
9. Phillip Kapleau, *Three Pillars of Zen* (Boston: Beacon Press, 1965), p. 208.
10. *Meister Eckhart: A Modern Translation*, trans. Raymond Bernard Blakney (New York: Harper & Row, 1941), p. 14.

11. Quoted in Elaine Hatfield and G. William Walster, *A New Look at Love* (Reading, Mass.: Addison-Wesley, 1981), p. viii.

12. Stanley Schacter, "The Interaction of Cognitive and Physiological Determinants of Emotional State," in *Advances in Experimental Social Psychology*, vol. 1, ed. L. Berkowitz (New York: Academic Press, 1964) pp. 49–80.

13. Donald Dutton and Arthur P. Aron," Some Evidence for Heightened Sexual Attraction under Conditions of High Anxiety," *Journal of Personal and Social Psychology*, 30 (1974): 510–17.

14. Zick Rubin, "The Love Research," *Human Behavior Magazine* (February 1977), quoted in Arlene Skolnick and Jerome H. Skolnick, *Family in Transition*, 3rd ed. (Boston: Little, Brown, 1980), pp. 279–85.

15. Ibid., p. 281.

16. Charles T. Hill, Zick Rubin, and Letitia Anne Peplau, "Breakups Before Marriage: The End of 103 Affairs," *The Journal of Social Issues*, 32 (1976): 147–68.

17. John H. Gagnon, *Human Sexualities* (Glenview, Ill.: Scott, Foresman, 1977), pp. 78–96.

18. Hatfield and Walster, p. 9.

19. Ibid., p. 135.

20. Marabel Morgan, *The Total Woman* (New York: Pocket Books, 1973). See also H. B. Andelin, *Fascinating Womanhood* (Santa Barbara, Calif.: Pacific Press, 1965); and "J", *The Sensuous Woman* (New York: Dell, 1969).

21. This classification is after C. S. Lewis, *The Four Loves* (New York: Harcourt Brace Jovanovich, 1960). Other typologies of interest include Rollo May's fourfold division of love into sex (lust or libido), Eros, Philia, and Caritas in *Love and Will*, p. 37; and John Alan Lee's characterization of six *Love Styles* (not types of love necessarily) as Eros, Ludus (playful love), and storge as primary love styles and mania (jealous, obsessive, possessive love), pragma (common sense, compatible love) once commonly expressed in arranged marriages, and agape (charitas or gentle unselfish, dutiful love) as secondary love styles. See John Alan Lee, *The Colors of Love* (Don Mills, Ont.: New Harper Press, 1976), pp. 9, 10.

22. Lewis, p. 56.

23. Lee, p. 12. Used by permission of the author.

24. Ibid., p. 36.

25. Ibid., p. 34.

26. Ibid., p. 37.

27. Lewis, p. 157.

28. May, p. 316.

29. Lee, p. 156.

30. See, for example, the discussion in Rustum Roy and Della Roy, *Honest Sex: A Revolutionary Sex Ethic By and For Concerned Christians* (New York: New American Library, 1968), pp. 34–46.

31. Lewis, p. 165.

32. Erich Fromm, *The Art of Loving* (New York: Bantam, 1970), quoted in Lee, p. 159.

the *Biology*
of *Sex*
and
Reproduction

The human body has no other parts as fascinating as the sexual organs. Venerated and vilified, concealed and exhibited, the human genitals have elicited a multitude of varied responses. They have been portrayed in every art form, praised and damned in poetry and prose, mutilated with religious fervor, and amputated in insane frenzy.

—Herant A. Katchadourian
and Donald T. Lunde

7 the *Biology of Sex and Reproduction*

In our discussion thus far, we have talked about loving partnerships in terms of mental and emotional states. We have talked a great deal about the experience of the world and of love at the center of our being. And we have taken for granted some of the most wonderful dimensions of this experience that come about because we have the particular kind of body we have. A university education tends to foster the conviction that we exist almost exclusively above our necks. Sometimes shame and modesty prevent us from exploring below the belt.

A simple, straightforward knowledge of our anatomy is useful for an adequate understanding of human sexuality, and is helpful in making us feel at ease with our selves in intimate partnerships. In this chapter we will cover the rudiments of the biology of sexuality from arousal to childbirth. More details will be provided on contraception and the art of lovemaking in later chapters.

HUMAN ANATOMY

Although it is certainly not necessary to have a detailed understanding of anatomy to perform adequately sexually, some knowledge in this area helps dispel some of the numerous myths and fallacies that surround our understanding of human sexuality.[1] Understanding our bodies helps us feel comfortable with them, and this is an important part of developing good relationships.

External Genitalia

The male and female genitals are **homologous**; that is they develop from the same tissues in the process of the differentiation of the embryo. The penis is the homologue of the clitoris. The scrotum develops from the same embryonic tissue as the major lips, or labia majora, but under a different set of influences. The testes and ovaries were initially undifferentiated gonads, and both retain tissues that are more fully developed in their opposite-sex homologue. While looking at the apparent differences of the sexes, therefore, it is well to remember their less apparent similarities.

Male Anatomy. The reproductive system of the human male is an integrated and complex system of which some parts are housed in the body and some are located outside the body. Naturally, we are more familiar with the external portions of the system. The internal portions are, more often than not, as much a mystery to us as the function of any other highly complex internal organ. Just as we are aware of the ears as external organs but remain largely ignorant of the workings of the inner ear, so the external sexual organs have very obvious sexual significance while the internal "plumbing" that makes them work is more or less a mystery.

The *penis* and the *scrotum* are the external reproductive organs of the male. (The *testes*, which are carried in the scrotum, are not technically considered external organs.) The penis serves not only as the organ of copulation but also as the organ through which the male urinates. The average penis is 3 to 4 inches long when fully relaxed and somewhat more than 6 inches long when erect. Its diameter increases about one-quarter inch in erection. Penises, however, can be considerably smaller or larger than average. The length of the penis bears little relationship to its physiological capacity to stimulate the female in sexual arousal. A wide

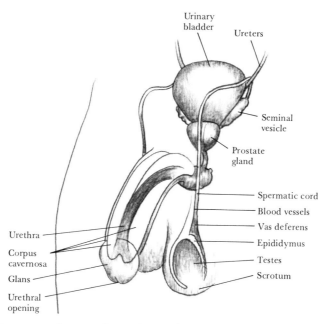

Urinary
bladder

Ureters

Seminal
vesicle

Prostate
gland

Spermatic cord

Blood vessels

Vas deferens

Epididymus

Testes

Scrotum

Urethra

Corpus
cavernosa

Glans

Urethral
opening

FIGURE 7.1 Male genitalia and reproductive system.

penis, however, does seem to be more stimulating than a narrow one. The size of the penis is not significantly related to body size.

The foreskin of the penis, or *prepuce*, has been an object of ritual mutilation ever since the earliest times in recorded human history. Removal of this skin, or *circumcision*, often is performed early in a boy's life for both religious and hygienic reasons. After circumcision *smegma*, a cheesy substance with a distinctive smell secreted by glands in the penis, cannot accumulate under the prepuce. Sociologist Alex Comfort contends that the uncircumcised male can enjoy more erotic pleasure than the circumcised male because of the greater variety of manipulations of the penis that are possible with the prepuce present.[2] But many authorities do not support this contention. On the contrary, they maintain that circumcision, by exposing the sensitive tip of the penis, heightens sexual sensation.

The penis is attached to the pelvis at its root. The body of the penis, the pendulous portion, is made up of three channels. These three separate channels of spongelike tissue are served by a network of blood vessels and nerves. During erection they become engorged with blood, thus creating the characteristic stiffness of the erect penis. The *glans penis* is the smooth round head of the penis. It is the most sensitive part of the penis and contributes greatly to the pleasure of sexual arousal when stimulated. The neck of the penis is also rich with nerve endings, but the shaft itself is relatively insensitive. The *urethra* runs through the middle of the penis. It is the passageway through which urine is emitted. It also serves as a channel for the emission of semen during sexual intercourse.

The scrotum is a sac of skin, darker in color than the rest of the body, that lies directly behind the penis. It is sparsely covered with hair and tiny pimples or sweat glands. It keeps the testes outside the body cavity because the production of sperm will not occur at body temperature. Sperm are continuously being produced in the testes. They are generated in the *seminiferous tubules* of the testes and mature in the *epididymis*. If ejaculation does not occur within 30 to 60 days, the sperm die and are replaced by new ones.

Because a change in temperature of even two to three degrees centigrade will adversely affect sperm production, the scrotum regulates the temperature of the testes by drawing them closer to the body on cold days and allowing them to hang farther from the body on hot days. The fact that sperm production is inhibited by increases in temperature has led to the widely held belief that taking a hot shower before sexual intercourse can serve as a contraceptive technique. Although it is true that a hot shower will kill some sperm, the effect will be negligible as far as contraception is concerned. The hot-shower method may reduce the chances of impregnating the woman by some small fraction of a percent, but any sensible person would have to regard it as a highly unreliable means of contraception.

Female Anatomy. The term used to refer to the external female genitalia is *vulva*. The most visible portion of the female genitalia is the *mons pubis*, the elevation of fatty tissue over the pubic bone. In a woman who has reached puberty, it is normally covered with pubic hair.

The *clitoris* is the female homologue of the penis. It does not hang free from the body, however, and only its upper portion, or *glans clitoris*, is visible. It is one of the few organs of the human body—if not the only one— whose sole purpose is to provide pleasure. Being essentially a bundle of nerve endings, it seems to have no other function. The discovery of the pleasure-providing role of the clitoris and the techniques by which it may be stimulated are essential components of the sexual revolution. Like the penis, the clitoris has suffered ritual mutilation in various societies.

The clitoris is located near the upper joining of the *labia majora*, or major lips. The shaft of the clitoris may be located by tracing the finger upward between the lips until their juncture is reached. The glans is about one inch below this juncture at the joining of the *labia minora*, or minor lips. Typically, the clitoris is a little over an inch in length, including its buried portion, and in diameter it measures about one-quarter inch.

The labia majora are the homologue of the scrotal sac. They cover the minor lips and the clitoris. The appearance of these lips varies; sometimes they are heavy and bulging, sometimes small. They almost always hang together, thus closing the vaginal orifice. In front, the major lips are ridgelike and pronounced, but toward the anus they recede into the surrounding tissue.

The labia minora, like the labia majora, are two vertical folds of skin. But unlike the major lips, which are partially covered with pubic hair

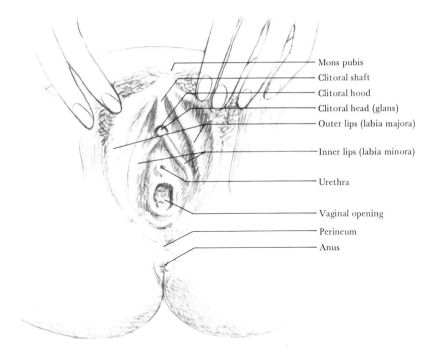

FIGURE 7.2 Female genitalia.

on the outside, the minor lips are pink and hairless. They form the vestibule to the vaginal opening and are very sensitive to the touch. The urethral opening is found above the vaginal orifice and is protected by the labia minora.

The vaginal orifice varies in appearance, depending on the condition of the *hymen*. Much folk custom has been associated with the hymen, or maidenhead, a membrane located inside the vaginal opening. It has traditionally been regarded as the seal of the virgin, under the fallacious assumption that the presence of an unbroken hymen was proof of virginity while its absence was proof of prior sexual intercourse. It is true that the hymen normally remains intact unless it is ruptured by penetration of the vagina. But it is also true that the hymen cna be ruptured in other ways and that it is possible to engage in sexual intercourse without damaging this sturdy membrane. Be that as it may, the fact that the rupture of the hymen is often accompanied by bleeding led to the practice in some countries of displaying the sheets of the wedding night with their bloodstains to signify that the hymen had been broken.

Strictly speaking, the female breasts are not part of the reproductive system inasmuch as they do not play a determinative role in the process of conception. But they are, of course, closely linked to the reproductive system. They undergo changes in size and sensitivity in response to hormonal signals that are part of the menstrual and reproductive cycles.

Lactation, which occurs during pregnancy, is also a hormonally triggered response. What is more, the breasts play an important part in sexual arousal. The nipples are the most sensitive portion of the breast, but this sensitivity is totally unrelated to the size or shape of the breasts.

The Menstrual Cycle

The menstrual cycle in the female is regulated by the hypothalamus—the sexual control center in the brain. The onset of the menses occurs normally between 12 and 16 years of age and, for reasons not well understood, the average age of onset throughout the industrialized world is declining. The cycle begins on the first day of bleeding and averages 28 days in length. The bleeding—or period—commonly lasts five days, with a normal range of three to seven days. About 2 fluid ounces of blood and the inner lining of the uterus is lost.

Ovulation occurs on about the fourteenth day, but this can be affected by stress and health factors. The egg must be impregnated within about one day after ovulation. However, since sperm can live in the Fallopian tubes up to about four days, conception can occur a few days after intercourse. If fertilization has occurred, the egg implants itself in the wall of the uterus. Half of it develops into the placenta, and half into the embryo. The placenta excretes hormones that help prevent another ovulation. If conception has not occurred, the egg passes out of the uterus and the cycle begins again.

HUMAN SEXUAL RESPONSE

The human mind is a sexual organ. We do not commonly think this is so because of our traditional association of sex with reproduction. The feeling that sex is a bodily function and that the mind ought to be "above all that" has led to preoccupation with the genitals and neglect of the imagination. This is also true of the scientific study of sex outside of psychotherapy. But the more human sexuality is considered as a source of pleasure, the more important the mind becomes.

Human beings differ from most animals in that they can be said to be in a general state of readiness for sexual experience throughout most of their lives. Human sexual arousal is, broadly speaking, controlled by both the endocrine system and the nervous system. A sexual control center in the *hypothalamus*, a part of the brain, regulates the *pituitary gland* through the secretion of a specific hormone. Because of the dual role of the hypothalamus, emotional events such as stress can alter the hormonal rythyms of the body (e.g., the menstrual cycle). The basic level of activity in the sexual control center is also largely responsible for the general state of readiness for sex.

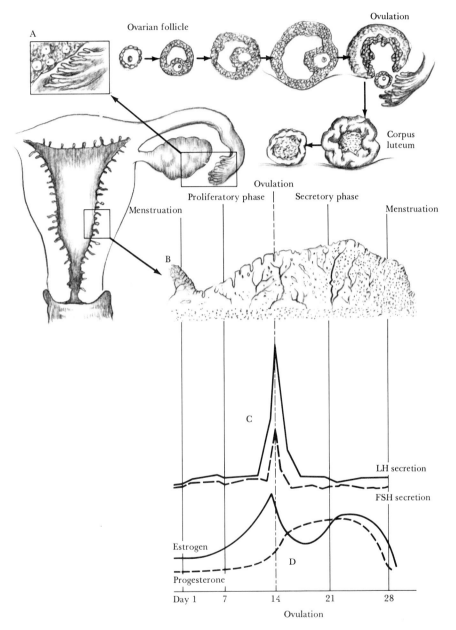

Ovarian follicle

Ovulation

A

Corpus
luteum

Ovulation

Proliferatory phase   Secretory phase

Menstruation   Menstruation

B

C

LH secretion

FSH secretion

Estrogen

D

Progesterone

Day 1   7   14   21   28

Ovulation

FIGURE 7.3 Ovulation and menstruation. (A Book About Birth Control,
Montreal Health Press, Inc.)

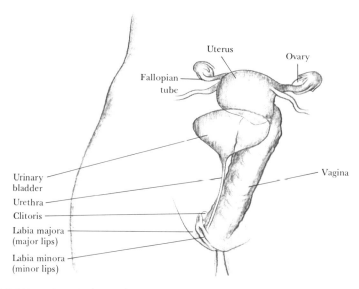

FIGURE 7.4   Female reproductive system.

In general, the sexual control center receives two types of impulses: information about the environment, and the interpretation of this information in terms of an individual's past experience. The sense organs provide much of the former information, while the cerebral cortex of the brain provides the latter. It is sometimes possible for the sensory input to act directly on the hypothalamus without cerebral interference. For example, a male who has not had sex for a long time may experience a buildup of secretions in his prostate gland. These sensations of fullness could then be transmitted as stimulating messages to the sexual control center. In the case of the female, retention of water in the cells of the genitals before menstruation may similarly stimulate the sexual control center.

The cerebral cortex can both inhibit and amplify sexual stimuli. For example, if a person is caught up in the task of paying bills, the cortex sends fewer impulses to the sexual control center. Through fantasy the cortex can initiate and amplify sexual impulses. In the male, the process of erection is begun by the stimulation of an erection control center located in the lower sacral portion of the spine. This erection center can be stimulated by impulses from the brain (the cerebral cortex or the sexual control center or both) or by impulses coming directly from the penis. Thus, the penis of a man whose spine has been damaged in such a way as to prevent messages from the sexual control center from reaching the genitals can nevertheless become erect in response to touch.

In the genitals the signals from the control centers expand the arteries that carry blood to the sexual organs and slightly decrease the size of the veins that carry blood away. The result is an accumulation of blood in these tissues, creating what is called the orgasmic platform in the female and assisting in the production of an erection in the male. In the case of the male, tiny valves controlling the flow of blood into the spongy tissues of the penis are relaxed, allowing blood to enter and thus creating the erection. The clitoris retracts beneath its hood as well as expanding in size in response to stimulation, but it does not have the spongy tissue that creates the erection in the penis.

There has been quite a bit of discussion recently about an area on the anterior wall of the vagina between the posterior side of the pubic bone and the cervix that has been called the *Grafenberg spot*.[3] This area is especially sensitive to stimulation in some women. Its anatomical structure is not well defined at present, and it is not easy to find. It is described as a swelling of variable dimensions that hardens when stimulated. The extent to which this area is developed in the female population is not known, but in those women who can be identified as female ejaculators, its stimulation produces a distinctive, deeper, normally more intense type of orgasm, often associated with the ejaculation of fluid from the urethra. This fluid is believed to come from the Skene's glands, which are considered to be the female homologue of the prostate. The distinctive orgasm produced by the stimulation of this area has revived interest in the notion of the vaginal orgasm.

The model developed in the following section is after Masters and Johnson. However, Helen Kaplan, of Cornell University's Medical Center in New York, has noted that many of her patients never entered the excitement phase at all because a number of psychological problems prevented arousal. She concluded that it is necessary to add another stage at the beginning of this sequence called the "desire stage."[4] Most of us react to sexual stimulation in such a taken-for-granted way that we are not aware of all the factors that contribute to the definition of a situation as arousing. But when psychological problems prevent arousal, we can no longer take the excitement stage for granted.

Sexual Response in the Male

The external genitalia and the breasts of the female have been objects of sexual arousal for the male from time immemorial. In some cultures exposure of the vulva by the female constitutes an invitation to sexual intercourse. In our own tradition there seems to be a preference for covering the sexually stimulating body parts and letting the suggestion of their presence produce the desired erotic effect.

Although there is considerable debate over the matter, it seems that men respond to visual stimuli differently than women do. It is common knowledge that men experience erection in response to visual stimulation, and it is often maintained that women do not commonly manifest such signs of sexual arousal as lubrication of the vagina in response to purely visual phenomena. This difference—if in fact it exists—may well be a result of cultural conditioning rather than of physiological differences in the response mechanisms of the two sexes.

The Excitement Phase. The sources of excitement or arousal need not be specified at this point. Suffice it to say that different men are "turned on" in different ways and that visual stimuli are frequently effective in this regard.[5]

The first obvious response to effective stimulation is erection of the penis, which occurs involuntarily. The penis becomes engorged with blood and achieves varying degrees of stiffness, depending on the state of arousal. One cannot will an erection; one can only relax and remove any distractions that may impede its occurrence. Nor can one will an erection away, although one can, by deliberately distracting oneself, effectively eliminate the source of stimulation from one's perceptual field, after which the erection will subside spontaneously.

Men are capable of maintaining an erection in the excitement stage for many minutes. Various kinds of diversions, such as loud noises, obvious changes in lighting, or conversation on an extraneous subject, may cause partial or total loss of the erection.[6]

During the excitement phase the scrotum contracts and the testes are pulled toward the body cavity. The folds disappear. During prolonged copulation the scrotum may relax without loss of erection.[7]

The Plateau Phase. The plateau phase is reached when the fully erect penis undergoes a slight involuntary enlargement of the cap and a small amount of mucoid fluid is secreted from the *Cowper's gland*, which is located on the urethra just below the prostate gland. This secretion generally is clear or slightly clouded in color. Researchers are not certain of its function. It may serve to lubricate the urethra in preparation for the passage of semen, or it may serve to reduce the acidity of the urethra, which is essential if conception is to occur because sperm cannot survive in an acidic environment. In any case this secretion may contain a small amount of semen, thus making it possible for conception to occur without ejaculation. For this reason the practice of *coitus interruptus*—withdrawing the penis from the vagina before ejaculation—may prove ineffective as a contraceptive technique.

There are no further changes in the scrotum in either the plateau or the orgasmic phase of sexual response. A reddening of the skin (sex flush) occurs infrequently in the plateau stage.

Internally, the testes enlarge to about 1½ times their normal size and are pressed against the body. This pressing of the testes against the body is necessary for orgasm and anticipates its occurrence.

The Orgasmic Phase. *Orgasm* is a highly pleasurable involuntary response to sexual stimulation. In the male it normally lasts for 2 to 10 seconds, after which a period of relaxation (refractory period) ranging from a few minutes to several hours is necessary.

In the male orgasm is experienced as a set of involuntary contractions of the urethra and the muscles around the base of the penis and the anus. These contractions involve the entire length of the urethra and are responsible for the ejaculation of the seminal fluid, which occurs at about 0.8-second intervals for the first three or four contractions. These initial contractions are followed by others at gradually lengthening intervals and with weakening intensity.

Orgasm is normally a very intense physiological response, as is evidenced in the changes in heartbeat, blood pressure, and breathing that occur with orgasm. The heartbeat increases from a norm of about 70 to 80 beats per minute to a high of 110 to 180 beats per minute. Blood pressure may double. Respiratory rates increase from the normal 18 per minute to as high as 40 per minute, although if the orgasm is mild or of short duration there may be no increase in the rate of breathing at all. Many people experience a sense of loss of oxygen and respond by gasping for air or hyperventilating.

The internal organs participate in the orgasmic response. The sperm that have been maturing in the epididymis are forced upward through the *vas deferens* by the contraction of its walls. Before entering the urethra they are enveloped in a milky liquid produced in the *seminal vesicle* and the *prostate gland* to form the *semen*. The passage of the semen through the urethra is furthered by contractions of the urethral walls. These contractions are responsible for the feeling of inevitability that accompanies orgasm.

The ejaculate emerges from the erect penis in a series of spurts. Semen may be ejected from the penis with a force capable of propelling it a distance of three or four feet, or it may simple ooze from the urethra. Once ejected, the sperm will die unless they reach the fallopian tubes of the female, where they typically survive for two or three days. In rare instances they can survive in the fallopian tubes for five days or longer.

The more effective the sexual stimulation, the more completely the entire body is involved in the release of tensions that occurs in orgasm. About 25 percent of the male population in Masters and Johnson's study experienced a well-developed sex flush or reddening of the skin during orgasm.[8]

In the male, orgasm is almost always marked by the ejaculation of semen.[9] Semen is characteristically white. It varies from a thick, almost gelatin-like fluid to a thin, watery substance. The more frequent the ejaculation the thinner the fluid. The amount of semen ejaculated is normally about one teaspoon. McCary estimates that the caloric value of the ejaculate is around 36 calories and concludes that "the evidence is therefore convincing that a normal discharge of semen cannot in any way 'weaken' a man."[10] This evidence contradicts the folk notion that a man must conserve his semen to conserve his strength. The amount of semen in the ejaculation is positively correlated to the pleasure experienced by the male in orgasm, particularly after long periods of abstinence.[11]

The Resolution Phase. Masters and Johnson observe that a basic rule of male response to sexual stimuli is that there is "psychophysiological resistance to sexual stimuli immediately after an ejaculatory experience."[12] This period during which males are unresponsive to sexual stimuli is called the *refractory stage*. Its length varies greatly. Masters and Johnson cites an example of a male subject who was able to "ejaculate three times within ten minutes of the onset of stimulative activity,"[13] but with most men stimulation following within a few minutes after ejaculation will fail to produce a second erection and ejaculation, let along a third. Some men, however, can experience a second orgasm without experiencing complete resolution after the first orgasm.

During the first stage of resolution the penis typically shrinks to about twice its flaccid size. During the second stage it returns to its normal prestimulated size. This stage may be prolonged or shortened, depending on the effectiveness of the sexual stimulation experienced. It is likely to be prolonged if the penis is kept in the vagina and the couple continue to hold each other close and to caress. The penis will rapidly lose its erection in both stages if the couple disengage and the male's attention is directed to nonstimulating activities such as urinating or smoking.

The testes return to normal size during resolution. This may occur rapidly or slowly, depending on the length of the plateau phase.[14] The scrotum loses its tenseness and returns to its prestimulated state.

Sexual Response in the Female

The female, of course, may receive semen from the male without being sexually aroused. She may be penetrated with the assistance of artificial lubricants—or by sheer force, as generally happens in cases of rape—and thus may conceive a child without ever experiencing sexual pleasure. Indeed, in puritanical cultures the female is not expected to enjoy sexual intercourse, and many women do not. However, Masters and Johnson have clearly demonstrated that the female capacity to enjoy sexual stimulation is far greater than that of the male.[15] Women, in fact, are physiologically capable of experiencing a fairly large number of orgasms in rapid succession, whereas men, as we have seen, generally do not experience a second orgasm until a considerable period has elapsed since the first one. Conclusions reached by Kinsey and Freud to the effect that women are not as excitable by sexual stimuli as men and do not have an adequate body image because of supposed "penis envy" have reinforced common folk notions about the sexual inferiority of women. These notions, it is now becoming clear, have absolutely no basis in fact. Indeed, Seymour Fischer contends that "the woman can more easily integrate her body meaningfully into the pattern of her life than can the man. It is the man, rather than the woman, who is more likely to feel insecure from his body and alien from it."

The material presented in Fischer's study, *The Female Orgasm*, clearly indicates that there is no factual basis for regarding women as less sexually secure or able than men. To continue to promulgate ideas about such alleged inferiority would seem to be an expression of antifeminine prejudice.[16]

The Excitement Phase. During the excitement phase the clitoral shaft increases in diameter and length. The major lips of woman who have not had children flatten and separate. The lips of the vulva begin to expose the vaginal opening. In women who have had children there is a thickening of the major lips and a slight opening. The major lips thicken and expand toward the vaginal vault. Within 10 to 30 seconds after effective sexual stimulation, lubrication appears in the vagina and the vaginal vault lengthens and expands.

In both sexes the nipples of the breast become erect and increase in size. The breasts of the female enlarge and develop a pronounced veinous engorgement. A sex flush typically appears first on the abdomen and then spreads to the breasts during the late stage of excitement. The entire uterus elevates at the onset of sexual stimulation. The cervix slowly retracts upward from the vaginal vault.[17]

The production of the egg in the female's ovary and its migration down the fallopian tube ordinarily is unrelated to the presence of sexual stimulation. However, the frequency with which the so-called safe period in the woman's menstrual cycle proves not to be safe at all may well be attributed to the fact that females sometimes ovulate in response to sexual arousal. The ovaries are generally almond-shaped and measure about one and a half inches in length. They normally weigh about .25 oz and are therefore somewhat lighter than the testes. Unlike the male, who must continuously produce new sperm, the female is born with about 400,000 imperfectly developed eggs. The typical pattern of maturation is one in which one egg develops in each ovary in alternate months. However, an ovary may produce two eggs at a time or may produce an egg more than once during a single month if the woman experiences intense sexual stimulation.[18]

The ripened or matured egg breaks the surface of the ovary and, by a process that is not yet known, "seeks" the opening of the fallopian tube. Normally, fertilization by the sperm occurs at the opening of the fallopian tube.

The Plateau Phase. In the plateau phase the clitoris draws back and is positioned directly above the pelvic bone. The labia majora of women who have never given birth to children may become enlarged. In women who have borne children, they continue to become engorged with blood at this phase of arousal. The outer third of the vagina further increases in length and depth, swelling into what Masters and Johnson have called an orgasmic platform. The *Bartholin gland* excretes a mucoid liquid that aids in the lubrication of the vaginal outlet. The major source of lubrication, however, is simple perspiration.

The nipples become further enlarged and distended; breast size increases; and the engorgement of the *areola*—the pigmented area surrounding the nipple—increases. There is further voluntary and involuntary tension in the facial and abdominal musculature.

The uterus becomes fully elevated as the continued retraction of the cervix further increases the sensitivity of the vaginal vault.

The Orgasmic Phase. During orgasm the clitoris and the major and minor lips do not change their structure. Contractions in the vagina occur at about 0.8-second intervals (as in the male pattern) and reoccur from 5 to 12 times. After the first 3 to 6 contractions, the intervals lengthen and the intensity diminishes. The breasts do not undergo any noticeable change. The sex flush parallels the orgasmic experience in about 75 percent of females. There is a momentary loss of voluntary control of muscle groups, and involuntary contractions are experienced.

As the involuntary contractions of the orgasmic platform take place in the vagina, there are also involuntary contractions of the anal sphincter. The female's experience of hyperventilation and increase in blood pressure and heartbeat generally is similar to the pattern experienced by the male. Because orgasmic intensity varies more widely in the female than in the male, a woman may experience heartbeat rates above 180 per minute.

Just as a male's anxiety about his sexual prowess focuses on his ability to achieve and maintain an erection, so the female's centers on her ability to experience orgasm. All women register the physiological responses of orgasm, but many do not experience the sensations that accompany these responses. That is to say, they have orgasms but are inhibited—most often for psychological reasons—from feeling them. The fears and inhibitions men and women bring to their sexual behavior in our society are to a large extent products of cultural conditioning.

The Resolution Phase. Unlike the male, the female does not have a physiologically determined refractory period. She is capable of experiencing another orgasm immediately if stimulation is resumed. If it is not stimulated, the clitoris returns to its normal size and position within 5 to 10 seconds. The major and minor lips return to their normal thickness and midline position within 10 to 15 seconds. The relaxation of the vaginal wall may take as long as 10 to 15 minutes. The cervical orifice remains open for 20 to 30 minutes. There is a rapid diminution of the areolae and an involution of the nipples. The sex flush disappears. Muscle tensions rarely are carried more than 5 to 10 minutes into the resolution phase.

In the resolution phase of the female's sexual response, the appearance of a widespread film of perspiration not related to the degree of physical activity is noticeable. In the male, this sweating reaction, when it occurs, is usually confined to the soles of the feet and the palms of the hands, but in females it is often more pervasive.

As Figure 7.5 indicates, there is considerable similarity in the sex-

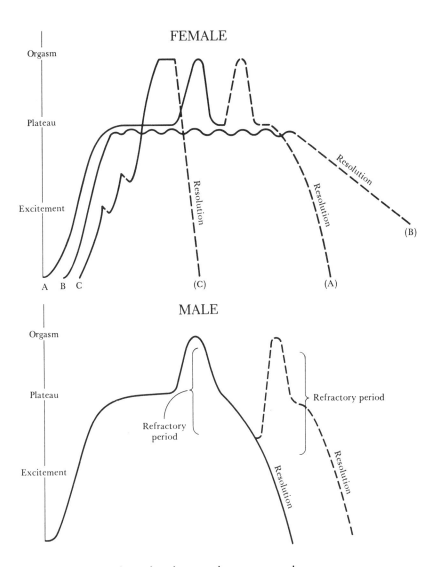

FIGURE 7.5 Female and male sexual response cycles.

ual response cycles of the male and female, especially through the plateau stage. The typical female pattern (A) closely approximates the typical male pattern, except that there is no refractory period, so that a second orgasm can occur within seconds of the first. (Some men also are capable of experiencing a second orgasm within a few seconds if their refractory period is short.) In Figure 7.5 (B) and (C) represent less typical feminine response patterns. In B, the excitement mounts rapidly and immediately bursts into a series of sustained orgasms, which are experienced as one sustained climax. In such cases the resolution phase lasts longer. Pattern C shows more abrupt moments of excitement followed by an intense climax and a rapid resolution.

The Reactions of Older People

We are sexual beings throughout our lives. Indeed, some of us may not fully experience the pleasures of sexual intercourse until we have reached what is commonly regarded as old age.[19] This is an unusual pattern, but one that should cause us to think twice before assuming that older people are asexual. The more common course is to bring the pattern of sexual behavior experienced in middle age into old age.

Most societies that have been studied fully anticipate that people continue to enjoy sexual intercourse with little diminution of pleasure well into old age. Women, in particular, express strong sexual interest in their old age in most societies and relate this strong interest to a lessening of a fear of pregnancy. In about 27 percent of the societies, both men and women reported a lessening of inhibitions in sexual conversation, humor, and gestures. This was truer for women than for men.[20]

What little research there is on the sexual behavior of older people has tended to focus on intercourse to the neglect of masturbation. This is true in part because there is a strong prejudice against masturbation among the elderly in this country. Nevertheless, about a quarter of men and women over 60 masturbate, and Catonia and White[21] suggest that it is one of the few controlled outcomes that older people can count on throughout most of their lives. They found it was more common among those elderly who had a strong sense of inner control and suggest that it functions to help these people maintain a sense of sexual identity, which may increase their chances of finding a satisfying interpersonal relationship.

As with other parts of the body, the process of aging causes changes in the sexual organs. These changes modify, but need not radically alter, sexual performance. Most men and women over 65 are capable of experiencing orgasm, although cultural conditioning often makes them embarrassed about their sexual capacity.

The older male requires a longer time to achieve an erection, regardless of how exciting the sexual stimulation may be. In many instances manual stimulation of the penis is necessary when visual stimulation formerly was sufficient to bring about an erection. In the elderly male the penis typically does not achieve full erection until just before orgasm. If the man should lose his erection during lovemaking, it is more difficult for him to recover it. However, he is usually capable of maintaining an erection longer than in his youth. Ejaculation declines in vigor, and in very old age the semen simply flows from the penis and is not forcefully ejected.

The internal organs may be affected by the aging process. Typically, the scrotum does not change in appearance or structure, but the testes may cease to expand in size during sexual intercourse. The resolution stage is much more abrupt, and the refractory period is likely to last longer. Thus, older men generally do not seek several orgasms in succession, although some are quite capable of doing so.

The aging female undergoes greater physiological changes. After menopause the vaginal walls decrease in thickness and lose their color, texture, and elasticity. Lubrication of the vagina occurs more slowly and is less complete. The swelling of the first third of the vagina associated with the plateau stage becomes less noticeable, but this change is partially compensated for by the increased tightness in the introitus. As with the aging male, the female's orgasmic responses are fewer in number, less intense, and shorter in duration.

The uterus undergoes dramatic changes after menopause. When the reproductive period has passed, the uterus diminishes in size until it is no larger than the cervix. Although neither elevation nor contraction of the uterus occurs in the typical aging female, some women report unpleasant spasms of the uterus that discourage them from engaging in sexual intercourse. This phenomenon, however,. is far from universal; the majority of women, like the majority of men, can continue to enjoy sexual intercourse into old age. The external genitalia also undergo a reduction in size. The minor lips, however, continue to swell upon excitation, and the clitoris remains largely unchanged in its sexual sensitivity even into very old age. The nongenital physiological response to orgasm in old age is generally less intense.

In sum, despite the stereotyped belief that sexual pleasure is reserved for the young, elderly people are in fact quite capable of leading full, rich sex lives.

CONCEPTION AND PREGNANCY

Conception

Fertilization of the egg normally occurs in one of the Fallopian tubes. As the fertilized egg moves down the Fallopian tube, it begins the process of cell division that will eventually produce a full-term fetus. There is little change in the overall mass of the fertilized egg as it moves down the Fallopian tube, but it continues to divide into cells, which form a shell around a liquid core. Between five and seven days after ovulation, the fertilized egg makes its way to the uterine wall and, with the assistance of enzymes that dissolve the lining of the uterus, links itself with the blood supply beneath the tissue. By the tenth to the twelfth day, it becomes firmly attached to the uterine wall and has established a continuing supply of nutrient. There is no overt sign of pregnancy at this time, however, because menstruation is not due to occur for several days.

Pregnancy

The normal term of pregnancy in the human female is 266 days, or approximately 9 calendar months. For convenience this gestation period is conventionally divided into three **trimesters**. These trimesters will be described on the basis of what is happening to the pregnant woman. Those who are interested in fetal development and embryology can find more detailed coverage of these topics in standard textbooks on these subjects.[22]

The First Trimester. One of the first signs of pregnancy is failure to menstruate. Although this is not a reliable sign, it certainly is a sign that most women recognize. The reactions to missing a period will vary, depending upon whether a child is expected or not. A woman may fail to menstruate for many reasons other than pregnancy. Emotional upsets, illnesses, age, conditions associated with nursing a child, and so forth may cause a woman to miss a period. To complicate the matter further, some women can be pregnant but still emit a smaller menstrual flow called spotting. Spotting can be an early sign of miscarriage, but it normally occurs in about 20 percent of all pregnancies and is not necessarily a bad sign.

Other symptoms of pregnancy include enlargement and tenderness of the breasts. The nipples become more sensitive to tactile stimulation. Many women experience "morning sickness"—a general feeling of nausea occurring shortly after getting out of bed—during the first six to eight weeks (four to six weeks after missed period). This can be accompanied by vomiting and aversion to food. Fatigue, drowsiness, and a desire for more sleep very often are signs of pregnancy during this period. There is an increase in the need to urinate because the swelling of the uterus puts pressure on the bladder.

A woman should see a doctor as soon as she suspects that she is pregnant. A doctor can tell her for sure whether or not she is pregnant and can help her take proper care of herself and her baby. Nevertheless, a newly developed pregnancy test has recently been put on the market. It is available in drugstores without a doctor's prescription. The kit contains everything you need in premeasured amounts and costs about $10. The advantages of using this at-home version are privacy and speed. The test is fairly accurate when done about nine days after a missed menstrual period. But whether they are negative or positive, the results should be confirmed by a physician. Another newly developed test, called the beta unit HCG (human chorionic gonadotropin) radio immunoassay, is not yet widely available. It is an extremely accurate test that can detect pregnancy about eight days after ovulation or about five days *before* the first missed period.[23]

Once pregnancy has been established, the most likely date of delivery can in most instances be determined within five days by the use of the following formula: Add one week to the first day of the last menstrual period, subtract three months, then add one year. Sixty percent of all deliveries will occur within five days of the projected date.

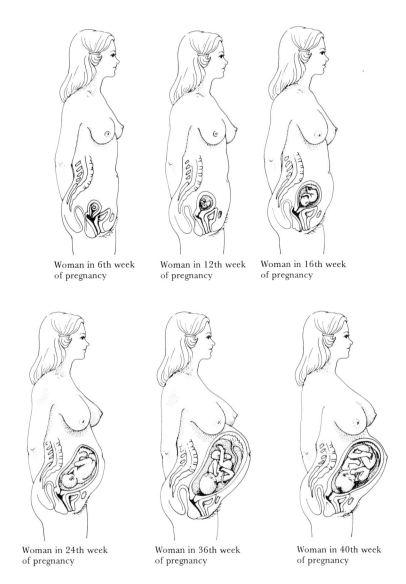

Woman in 6th week
of pregnancy

Woman in 12th week
of pregnancy

Woman in 16th week
of pregnancy

Woman in 24th week
of pregnancy

Woman in 36th week
of pregnancy

Woman in 40th week
of pregnancy

FIGURE 7.6 Development of the fetus by weeks.

In the first trimester there is no reason why pregnancy or the suspicion of pregnancy should inhibit sexual activities. Sex is not likely to harm the developing fetus. There may be some practical considerations, however. Morning sickness may inhibit desire for sexual activity in the early part of the day, just as fatigue and sleepiness may limit such activity in the evening. Because of the physiological changes described earlier, the already tender breasts may become painful during sexual stimulation. Nevertheless, most couples can find mutually satisfactory occasions for continuing sexual relations during pregnancy.

During the first trimester the *placenta* begins to develop. This is the organ through which the growing fetus exchanges nutrients and waste products with the mother. It also serves as the endocrine gland, producing hormones that are essential to the maintenance of pregnancy. Most complications of pregnancy that occur during this period are transmitted through the placenta. Many drugs have been known to have an effect on the development of the embryo; an example is thalidomide, a sedative that was banned in the 1950s after it became known that the drug caused abnormal development of the arms and legs. Regular users of addictive drugs such as heroin and morphine have produced babies who were born with an addiction to the drug. When such children are born, they suffer withdrawal symptoms if they are not given further doses of the drug. Synthetic hormones resembling progesterone, if administered during the first trimester to a woman who shows signs of possible miscarriage, sometimes result in the masculinization of a female fetus. Antihistemines, anticoagulants, large doses of aspirin, vitamins D, B-6, K, and A have also been associated with abnormal fetal development. Diseases such as rubella, or German measles, are quite likely to produce serious disorders in the fetus if the mother contracts them during the early part of the first trimester. As a result many people argue that women who contract German measles during the first two months of their pregnancy should be allowed to have abortions. During the third month of pregnancy the risk that German measles will produce abnormalities in the fetus decreases to 10 percent.

The Second Trimester. By the time the second trimester begins (by the fourth month of pregnancy), it is possible to detect fetal heartbeat and movement. An X ray of the mother's abdomen will show a fetal outline. However, the dangers of radiation limit the use of X rays to extreme situations.

During the second trimester the nausea and drowsiness experienced in the first trimester tend to disappear. Concern about miscarriage should diminish now, and the pregnant woman can continue her normal activities. She will feel the movement of the fetus and notice an increase in her waistline. Her abdomen will begin to protrude.

With decreased nausea, drowsiness, and breast tenderness, sexual intercourse can be enjoyed more fully. Women often report increased interest in sexual activities and greater sexual satisfaction during this period. Indeed, many women report that they find sexual intercourse more satisfying at this time than at any other time in their lives. During sexual stimulation there is a significant increase in vaginal lubrication. Late in the second trimester, however, certain coital positions, (such as man on top), become too tiring or painful for the woman.

At the end of six months the developing fetus weighs about 2 pounds and is about 14 inches long. The fetus moves its arms and legs spontaneously and can open its eyes. If the fetus is delivered at this time, there is a 95 percent chance that it will die.

The Third Trimester. During this period—the seventh to ninth months of pregnancy—the fetus becomes more active. In her swelling abdomen the woman experiences what seems to be perpetual kicking, tossing, and turning, which is sometimes severe enough to keep her awake. During this trimester physicians often become concerned about the weight of their patients. Until fairly recently most physicians considered a weight gain of about 20 pounds to be ideal. Of those 20 pounds, the average infant accounts for about 7.5 at birth.[24] The remaining 12.5 pounds consist of the placenta, the amniotic fluid, the increase in uterine size, the enlargement of the breasts, and fluid and fat accumulated by the mother. However, more recently it has been discovered that a weight gain of 25 to 30 pounds tends to produce somewhat healthier babies. Controlling weight is often difficult

Lamaze groups, such as this one, help both partners to prepare emotionally and physically for childbirth. (Robert Goldstein, Photo Researchers, Inc.)

for the mother, for she may have to struggle against an increase in appetite caused in part by the hormonal changes of pregnancy. Women who gain a lot of excess weight have trouble moving and subject themselves to the possibility of medical complications such as strain on the heart and high blood pressure.

In the third trimester of pregnancy most women are anxious to be delivered. They begin to count the days and wonder about the character of their about-to-be-born infant. What will the baby be like? Will it be a healthy, normal child? They begin to make concrete plans for the nursery and for bringing the baby home.

Although sexual activity need not be discontinued during the third trimester if the woman is in good health, it does tend to decrease during this period. Many woman feel uncomfortable, complaining of backaches and fatigue that tend to decrease their sexual interest. Yet many women are surprised by their responsiveness during late pregnancy. Many people fear that intercourse during the third trimester will induce premature labor, but there is no evidence that this is likely as long as the woman is in good health. Although fear of infecting the fetus leads some physicians to advise their patients to abstain from sexual intercourse during the last four to six weeks of pregnancy, sexual relationships need not be disrupted. Mutual masturbation and other forms of sex play can be enjoyed if the couple so desire.

The fetus continues to mature, and by the seventh month it has developed all of the essential organ systems. A baby prematurely born at the end of the seventh month has a fifty-fifty chance of survival. By this time the fetus normally has assumed the head-down position, with only about 12 percent of all fetuses remaining upright beyond this point. By full term only about 3 percent are still in the upright (breech) position. At birth the average infant weighs 7.5 pounds and is 20 inches long. In inner cities, where medical care is often terribly inadequate, the infant mortality rate is high. It is not uncommon for 40 out of every 1,000 live births to die within the first year of life. Overall, about 95 percent of all full-term babies survive the first year.

About 7 percent of the live births in the United States are premature. Mothers who have high blood pressure, heart disease, or syphilis or are experiencing multiple pregnancy are especially prone to give birth prematurely. In about 50 percent of the cases, the cause of premature delivery is not clear.

Childbirth

As the end of pregnancy approaches, some women, particularly those who have not previously had children, may experience false labor, that is, contractions of the uterus at irregular intervals. These irregular contractions, which resemble the regular contractions of labor, do not signal impending delivery. We do not know what finally initiates labor.

The fetus drops to a lower position in the abdomen three or four weeks before delivery, and the cervix begins to soften and dilate. Just before labor begins, a woman may notice a small, slightly bloody discharge; this discharge represents the plug of mucus that has blocked the cervix. About 10 percent of pregnant women experience a dramatic bursting of water as the fetal membrane breaks and the amniotic fluid escapes. If labor does not ensue within 24 hours, there is risk of infection. The mother should be hospitalized for observation after such a rupture.

Labor. There are three stages of **labor**, which consists of regular contractions of the uterus and dilation of the cervix. The first stage is the longest, and during it the woman, if she is hospitalized, is usually confined to the labor room. Her husband may or may not be present, depending on hospital rules. (If a couple are interested in having the husband present during labor, they should find out about hospital policy beforehand so that they can plan to have the baby delivered in a hospital where the husband is allowed to be present in the labor room.)[25] The contractions that occur during this stage of labor can start at 15-minute intervals and increase to 4- or 5-minute intervals. This stage can last from 8 to 15 hours. It is marked by the beginning of contractions and ends with complete dilation of the cervix to a diameter of about 5 inches.

The second stage of labor may last from a few minutes to a few hours. This stage begins when the cervix is completely dilated and ends when the baby is delivered. At most hopsitals it takes place in the delivery room, which is similar to a surgical operating room. The husband may or may not witness the delivery, depending on local laws, hospital regulations, the discretion of the physician, and the wishes of the couple. (Again, this is an area that the couple would do well to investigate beforehand if they are interested in having the husband present at the delivery.)

In the third stage the placenta and fetal membranes separate from the uterine wall and are discharged as the *afterbirth*. The uterus contracts to a significantly smaller size during this stage, which lasts about an hour. During this time the physician examines the baby and mother carefully and, if the vaginal opening has been torn, it is repaired.

If the baby is too large to be delivered through the mother's pelvis, it is delivered by *Caesarean section*—an operation in which the infant is surgically removed through the abdominal wall.

"Natural childbirth" is a label that is given to several techniques aimed at conditioning the mother to dissociate pain, fear, and tension from the experience of childbirth. The two major techniques are the Lamaze method and the Dick-Read method. The Lamaze method originated in Russia and was popularized by a French physician, Bernard Lamaze. This method is based on Pavlov's conditioned reflex responses. The Dick-Read

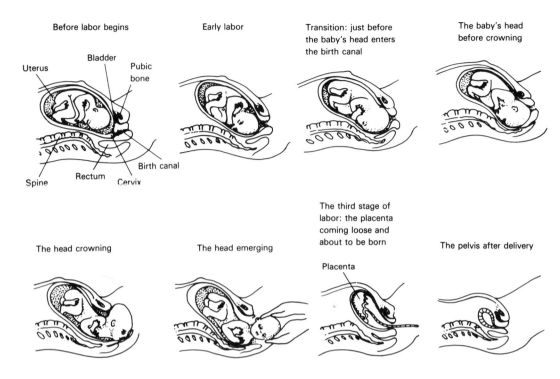

Before labor begins

Uterus
Bladder
Pubic bone

Spine
Rectum
Birth canal
Cervix

Early labor

Transition: just before the baby's head enters the birth canal

The baby's head before crowning

The head crowning

The head emerging

The third stage of labor: the placenta coming loose and about to be born

Placenta

The pelvis after delivery

FIGURE 7.7 Childbirth.

method, introduced by the English physician Grantly Dick-Read in the early 1930s, involves eliminating fear through education about the birth process before delivery.

The Postpartum Period. Today it is common practice for women to return home three to four days after a normal delivery. Bringing a child home can often be a chaotic experience, as the couple must learn the techniques of feeding the child (sometimes at all hours of the day and night), bathing him or her, changing diapers, and countless other details of infant care. What is more, the process can be complicated by an anxious father and a host of curious, well-meaning, but intrusive friends. A new mother experiencing these new pressures may well be fatigued and perhaps will feel "let down." Many women go through a period of depression at this time, experiencing moments of sadness and fits of crying during the first ten days after delivery. This phenomenon is called **postpartum blues**.[26] Husbands are well advised to be prepared for manifestations of these feelings, which they should recognize as a normal and usually transitory phase through which new mothers often pass.

Sexual Activity after Childbirth. There is great variation in the time that elapses before the first menstrual period after childbirth. Mothers who are nursing may go as long as eighteen months before having a period. However, because ovulation can occur while a mother is nursing, and because in any event ovulation occurs before the first period, it is possible for a woman to become pregnant without having experienced her first period after childbirth.

For the most part, physicians advise women to refrain from intercourse during the first six weeks after delivery, although the only medical reason for this advice is the fear of possible infection. Of course, the recommended period of abstinence from vaginal intercourse need not be a period of total abstinence from sexual activity. Manual stimulation of the genitalia, crural intercourse, and other forms of nonvaginal intercourse can safely provide sexual enjoyment for both partners if they so desire. In many cases, however, factors such as fatigue and physical discomfort may decrease the desire for sexual activity.

Infertility

About 10 to 15 percent of all couples in the United States are involuntarily childless. Sometimes their childlessness can be overcome by minor adjustments in their lovemaking techniques or by hormonal treatment. For others the "cure" may involve surgery or extended treatment. For some it is a permanent condition called **sterility**. About 40 percent of infertile marriages are a result of sterility in the male partner. When a couple wish to have a child, a year with no success should alert them to the need to see a physician.

The physician normally will take complete medical histories. Each partner will have a complete physical examination, with particular attention to the reproductive organs. A series of laboratory tests will be made to rule out infections, anemia, and hormonal deficiencies. The husband will be tested more thoroughly in the early stages because male infertility is easier to determine. He will be instructed to provide a complete ejaculation for a sperm count. Such a count should contain between 60 million and 100 million sperm per cubic centimeter, 60 percent of which should be active.[27] In this connection it is important to be clear about the distinction between infertility (or sterility) and low fertility. As the figures just cited indicate, a normal ejaculate contains an immense number of sperm, but only one sperm is needed to fertilize an egg. If a man's ejaculate contains a significantly smaller number of sperm, or if the sperm are significantly less active than normal, the chances of his impregnating a woman are reduced. But fertilization is, of course, possible. Such a man is not sterile, but unless steps are taken to increase the odds in his favor, he may not succeed in impregnating his mate. Various techniques are available for enriching the sperm (increasing the sperm count). Artificial insemination with the husband's sperm is also a possibility when the problem is one of low mobility of the sperm.

If tests of the husband indicate that the failure to conceive cannot be traced to a low sperm count or low sperm activity, the wife will be instructed to keep a temperature chart during her menstrual cycles in order to help determine when and if she ovulates. If it is determined that the female is ovulating and that the male is producing adequate sperm, further tests will be necessary. These tests will focus on the female.

A "Rubin's test" will be performed to see whether the Fallopian tubes are obstructed. This test consists of forcing carbon dioxide into the uterus. If the pressure diminishes, the tubes are clear. If the tubes prove to be open, the cervix is examined. Normally, the mucus of the cervix impedes the progress of the sperm to a considerable degree except during ovulation, when it becomes thinner and more penetrable. Thus, abnormality in the composition and viscosity of this mucus is a possible cause of infertility.[28]

There are many more tests that can be performed to help diagnose the cause of infertility. Considerable assistance can be provided to most couples who seek help in having children. Many can be helped to conceive with a minimum of tests. In a few cases a woman has conceived after she and her husband sought help from a clinic but before anything had been done for them—an indication that the couple's infertility may well have had a psychological cause. About half of the infertile couples who come to clinics can be helped to have children.

Artificial Insemination. In instances in which the wife has been shown to be fertile while her husband has been diagnosed as sterile, the couple may wish to conceive through artificial insemination. This is not a totally successful procedure, but many women have become pregnant by this means and it is now widely available. In artificial insemination the sperm from a fertile male is mechanically inserted into the vagina by a physician at a time when the woman is ovulating. Impregnation takes place in the normal way. Because so many considerations impinge on a decision to use artificial insemination—including religious, legal, moral, psychological, and physiological questions—it is important that any couple considering this approach learn all the dimensions of the problem before reaching a decision.

Many people, especially men, react to the idea of artificial insemination with a spontaneous feeling of aversion. The initial reaction of many husbands is one of repugnance, and they often express the feeling that a child produced by the sperm of an anonymous donor would not really be "their" child. In a sense, of course, this is true, but often husbands who feel this way are quite willing to adopt a child once they are convinced they are sterile—a clear indication that such husbands are not in fact unwilling to accept responsibility for the rearing of children who are not their biological offspring. Perhaps one way to look at artificial insemination is as a sort of semiadoption in which the husband agrees to raise what is, in effect, an adopted child while his wife, who is capable of conception, can enjoy the personal satisfactions that come from carrying and giving birth to a baby.

In many cases artificial insemination is effected with the sperm of the husband. As mentioned previously, this procedure is recommended when either a low sperm count or low sperm mobility makes it extremely unlikely that the woman will conceive by her husband's sperm unless it is "enriched"—that is, concentrated—artificially and delivered directly to the egg it is to fertilize.

Surrogate Mothers. An ancient custom recorded in the Old Testament permitted an infertile wife to appoint another woman, usually a slave, to bear a child for her. Thus Sarah had children for Abraham by means of the concubine Hagar. Recent television coverage was given to a couple who asked a friend to fulfill this ancient role. The husband's sperm was artificially injected into the friend's womb, and she conceived. The marked decline in the number of babies available for adoption because of increasingly effective birth control techniques, increases the need for some such practice. There are now several agencies which will make arrangements for the services of a surrogate mother.

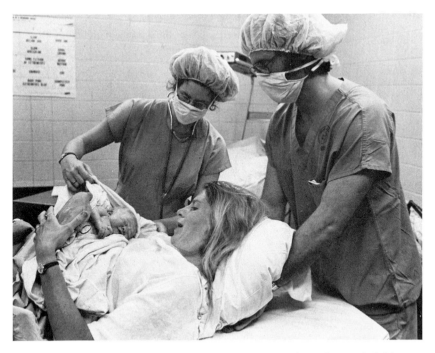

Many doctors now believe that it is important for both mother and child to have close skin contact immediately after birth—a contact that may not be possible in conventional practice. (Suzanne Szasz, Photo Researchers, Inc.)

SUMMARY

Understanding something of the biology of human sexuality can help us feel more at ease with ourselves. This is an important part of developing intimate partnerships such as marriage. In this chapter we have presented the fundamentals of the biology of sex and reproduction, including a brief description of the external genitalia, a discussion of human sexual response, and a short account of conception and pregnancy from the point of view of the pregnant woman. We stand at the threshold of a biological revolution in the extent to which we will be able to control these processes. This revolution should have an enormous impact on the future of intimate partnerships.

Whatever the extent to which our sexual behavior is determined by our biology, the more we understand our biology the more we find it possible to shape that biology after our own desires. In addition, an understanding of the biology of human sexuality can help dispel the numerous myths that have clouded our self-awareness and can help us be more fully open to others.

NOTES

1. For further information on human sexuality, see any of the following texts: Robert Francouer, *Becoming a Sexual Person* (New York: Wiley, 1982); Gilbert D. Nass, Roger W. Libby, and Mary Pat Fisher, *Sexual Choices* (Monterey, Calif.: Wadsworth, 1981); and David A. Schulz, *Human Sexuality* (Englewood Cliffs, N.J.: Prentice-Hall, 1984).

2. Alex Comfort, *The Joy of Sex* (New York: Crown, 1972), p. 67.

3. See E. G. Jr., "Orgasmic Explusions of Women," *The Journal of Sex Research*, 17 (February 1981): 8ff; J. D. Berry and B. Whipple, "Pelvic Muscle Strength of Female Ejaculators: Evidence in Support of a New Theory of Orgasm," *The Journal of Sex Research*, 17 (February 1981): 32; Frank Addiegigo, "Female Ejaculation: A Case Study, "*The Journal of Sex Research*, 17 (February 1981): 13–21.

4. Helen Singer Kaplan, *Disorders of Sexual Desire and Other Concepts and Techniques in Sex Therapy* (New York: Bruner Mazel, 1979).

5. See Schulz, *Human Sexuality*, for a more detailed account of the role of fantasy in sexual arousal.

6. Masters and Johnson, *Human Sexual Response* (Boston: Little Brown, 1966). p. 183.

7. Ibid., p. 205.

8. Ibid., p. 290.

9. Orgasm and ejaculation are not the same in the male, but because of the obvious effect of the latter and its close association, in most instances with intense pleasure it is most often thought that (1) males cannot experience an orgasm without ejaculation and (2) a "proper" orgasm for both men and women is one in which a sharp climax is recorded. Neither conjecture is accurate.

10. Schulz, p. 33.

11. Masters and Johnson, p. 216.

12. Ibid., p. 214.

13. Ibid.

14. Ibid., p. 293.

15. Ibid., p. 65.

16. Seymour Fischer. *The Female Orgasm: Psychology, Physiology, Fantasy* (New York: Basic Books, 1973), p. 393.

17. Masters and Johnson, p. 112.

18. James L. McCary, *Human Sexuality: A Brief Edition* (New York: Van Nostrand Reinhold Co., 1973).

19. Isadore Rubin, *Sexual Life after Sixty* (New York: Basic Books, 1965).

20. Rhonda L. Winn and Miles Newton, "Sexuality in Aging: A Study of 106 Cultures," *Archives of Sexual Behavior*, 4 (August 1982): 283–98.

21. Joseph A. Catonia and Charles B. White, "Sexuality in an Aged Sample: Cognitive Determinants of Masterbation," *Archive of Sexual Behavior*, 4 (June 1982): 237–45.

22. For some excellent textbooks on human embryology, see the following: R. Rugh and L. B. Shettles, *From Conception to Birth* (New York: Harper & Row, 1971); K. L. Moore, *The Developing Human* (Philadelphia: W. B. Saunders, 1973); and H. Tuchmann-Duplessis and P. Haegel, *Illustrated Human Embryology*, trans. L. S. Hurley (New York: Springer Verlag, 1973).

23. Boston Women's Health Book Collective, *Our Bodies, Ourselves*, 2nd ed. (New York: Simon & Schuster, 1976), p. 258).

24. Harold D. Swanson, *Human Reproduction and Social Change* (New York: Oxford University Press, 1974), p. 238.

25. An excellent account of some alternatives to hospitalization is found in *Our Bodies, Ourselves*, p. 272.

26. A. J. George and K. C. Wilson, "Monoxomine Oxicase Activity and the Puerperal Blues Syndrome, *Journal of Psychosomatic Research*, 25 (1981): 409–13; Ian Brockington, "Puerperal Psychosis: Phenomenon and Diagnosis," *Archives of General Psychiatry*, 38(July 1981): 819–823; R. E. Kendell et al., "The Social and Obstetrical Correlates of Psychiatric Admission in the Puerperium," *Psychosomatic Medicine*, 11 (May 1981): 341–50.

27. Lawrence Crawley, James L. Malfetti, Ernest I. Stewart, Jr., and Nini Vas Dias, *Reproduction, Sex and Preparation for Marriage*, 2nd ed. (Englewood Cliffs, N.J.: Prentice-Hall, 1973), p. 218.

28. Ibid., p. 219.

The groups best informed about contraception are not necessarily the most permissive. Boys are not necessarily better informed than girls, Negroes than whites, lower class than upper classes, and yet permissiveness varies considerably among these groups—not always in the same direction of the better informed being the most permissive.

—Seicus

8 *Contraception and Abortion*

The average healthy couple has an estimated 90 percent chance of conceiving a child during the first year of sexual intercourse if they do not take any measures to prevent conception. By choosing a suitable means of birth control and using it intelligently, any couple can ensure that they will have the number of children they want and no more. This permits both greater freedom to enjoy sex and greater responsibility to make sure every child that is born is wanted and every child that is wanted is born.

Birth control is not limited to contraception, although it is frequently assumed that the two terms are synonymous. Birth control is a general term that applies to any method used to prevent the birth of children. **Contraception**, on the other hand, refers only to methods that prevent conception from occurring in the first place. There are four basic techniques of birth control: abstinence, contraception, sterilization, and abortion. Each technique has costs as well as benefits. The decision to control conception by means of a particular technique must take these factors into consideration.

Abstinence is the most difficult form of birth control for most people. However it is a form that is appropriate during certain critical periods of pregnancy and shortly thereafter, as a mutually agreed upon discipline of lovers, and for a few as a lifetime effort. Contraception is appropriate for those people who want to be sexually active, do not wish to have children as a result, and have not yet had the number of children that they want. Sterilization is a virtually irreversible procedure that should be used only after due consideration of all the consequences. It is preferred among many who have the number of children they want. Abortion should be used to terminate an unwanted pregnancy—preferably in the first trimester—but should not be used as a form of contraception. It is unwise to become sexually active, not use contraceptives, and think "I can always have an abortion."

ABSTINENCE

One method of birth control that is socially approved, especially for the unmarried person, is **abstinence**, the self-imposed denial of sexual intercourse. It is very important that sexual experience occur when one is ready and at the level of sexual intimacy that one is prepared to experience. It should not be necessary for anyone to have to defend a lack of experience or to engage in sexual intercourse to prove anything to anyone. Young people may therefore practice abstinence for some time before their first experience of sexual intercourse. Some people—usually those who are very devout—are able to practice abstinence as a form of self-discipline. When it is evident to others that they are loving, caring, concerned human beings, they can provide vivid examples of the myriad ways of loving that need not involve sexual intercourse.

Within marriage, temporary abstinence from sexual intercourse may be necessary during illness, in the later stages of pregnancy, or in the early postpartum period. But abstinence as a regularly practiced means of birth control runs contrary to the sexual urges of most people. Unless it is to have troublesome side effects, the practice of abstinence must be a mutual decision on the part of both partners. If one partner makes such a decision unilaterally, he or she is disregarding the needs of the other. Moreover, abstinence from one form of sexual behavior need not mean abstinence from all sexual behavior. Even in cases in which abstinence from intercourse is necessary or desirable, an imaginative couple may still enjoy sexual outlets such as mutual oral or manual stimulation.

CONTRACEPTION

Techniques to prevent conception are part of the folk wisdom of most peoples. The oldest records on the subject come from Egypt and date from between 1900 and 1100 B.C. The practice of *coitus interruptus* (withdrawal of the penis before orgasm) is thought to be forbidden in the Bible.[1] Early attempts to control fertility frequently involved magic, superstition, and religious beliefs. The methods employed by a culture were related to its knowledge of the reproductive process and its traditional beliefs. The ancient Chinese, for example, believed that a woman would not become pregnant if she remained completely passive during intercourse,[2] the Egyptians are responsible for the oldest known medical prescription for a contraceptive—a vaginal suppository concocted of crocodile dung and honey.[3] Various other unbelievable birth-preventive substances have been advised, including mouse dung, amulets, and induced sneezing. The Greeks believed that oil impeded the movement of sperm and advised inserting an oil-permeated material such as paper into the vagina to cover the cervix.

Ancient peoples are not alone in having folk methods for preventing conception. Even today various folk ideas persist, many of them unsupported by evidence of their effectiveness. For example, some people believe that having intercourse while standing will prevent pregnancy or that if a woman urinates immediately after intercourse she will not become pregnant. We also tend to cloud the issue when we assert that certain periods of the month are "safe."

Modern interest in contraceptive technology has produced a host of contraceptives that vary greatly in terms of effectiveness, cost, and convenience. Some have no side effects; others have many. The choice of a contraceptive depends on many factors in a person's life, not the least of which is his or her motivation for using contraceptives. For example, if a couple already have the number of children they desire, sterilization might be the best option for them. The following is a survey of contraceptive alternatives.

Teenage Contraceptive Use

About half of the teenage population in the United States is sexually active, according to one major study.[4] Sexual activity has increased particularly among women, but there has not been a comparable increase in effective contraceptive use. As a result, there are over a million teenage pregnancies each year, the vast majority of which are unwanted.[5] Over 40 percent of all babies born out of wedlock are born to teenage mothers. Although teenagers are only about 18 percent of the female population, they account for 46 percent of the out of wedlock pregnancies and 31 percent of all abortions.[6]

One nationwide study found that 15 percent of the sexually active teenage females never used contraceptives, 66 percent used them some of the time, and 19 percent used them all of the time.[7] It appears that about half of all teenage females do not use effective contraceptives.[8] It is important to recognize that contraceptive use is not a simple function of knowing about contraceptives; it is also a function of dating patterns, amount of sexual activity, sex guilt, attitudes toward erotica, self-esteem, body image, accessibility of contraceptives, income, and parental attitudes toward premarital intercourse.

People who feel guilty about their sexuality are generally ineffective contraceptive users.[9] Their guilt does not prevent them from engaging in any sexual activity; it prevents them from planning ahead and taking adequate precautions against unwanted pregnancies. Studies have found that teenagers who are not inclined to discuss their sexual behavior with their parents were less likely to use contraceptives effectively.[10] An important factor related to effective contraceptive use is the length of the relationship and the frequency of intercourse.[11] Teenagers who are sexually active in long-term relationships tend to be more effective contraceptive users. Finally, accessibility is an important consideration. One study found that a female college student's satisfaction with the pill is a complex function of the client's perception of her physician's humaneness, the organizational setting where the pill was obtained, her negative attitudes toward the pill, and her experience with side effects. If the attitudes of the staff were thought to be negative, it is less likely that the pill will be used effectively.[12]

Contraceptives Available Without a Prescription

The Condom. Perhaps the most widely used contraceptive in the United States is the *condom*. It is the only mechanical device used by males. It is cheap, easy to use, easy to obtain, easy to dispose of, and effective. The first condoms were made in England in the early eighteenth century from the intestines of sheep. The Philadelphia World's Fair of 1876 introduced the first vulcanized-rubber condom.

A condom is a thin, flexible sheath that fits over the erect penis. It measures about 7½ inches in length. In common language condoms are known as "rubbers," "prophylactics," "French letters," and "skins." The rubber type is the most widely used; an estimated 700 million are sold annually in the United States. They come packaged, rolled and ready for use, sometimes with a small amount of lubricant. There are two major types of condom in use today; plain and reservoir tip. Choosing between them is wholly a matter of personal preference, as both are equally effective.

A condom without a reservoir tip should be unrolled about half an inch before being placed on the erect penis. This half-inch should be firmly squeezed to prevent an air pocket from forming when the rest of the condom is unrolled. If the condom is not lubricated, some lubricant may be applied to increase the ease of insertion into the vagina. Petroleum jellies should not be used as lubricants with a condom. They tend to erode the rubber and can cause mild irritation. Good lubricants are contraceptive foams or jellies. Once intercourse has been completed, the ring end of the comdom should be held tightly around the shaft of the penis as it is withdrawn. The condom should be checked for any obvious leakage. Any indication of condom failure should be followed up by a "morning-after pill" within 72 hours. Such a pill cannot be obtained without a prescription.

A condom can fail if it has a hole in it, breaks during intercourse, slips off, or loses sperm because the man does not retain his erection long enough after ejaculation to allow safe withdrawal of both penis and condom. The use of condoms in combination with spermicidal foam or cream increases their effectiveness. Even when used alone, however, the condom claims an effectiveness rate of 10 to 15 pregnancies per 100 women per year. The condom is also the best contraceptive method currently available for reducing the incidence of sexually transmitted disease. It is also well suited for the "unplanned for" sexual encounters of teenagers in that it can be easily carried at all times—preferably not in a wallet, as body heat reduces its flexibility.

Spermicidal Substances. Readily available in drugstores, spermidical substances are easy to use. They consist of various foams, jellies, creams, and suppositories that kill sperm. Plastic applicators enable a woman to inject the substance into the vagina before intercourse. This must be done at least 10 to 15 minutes before ejaculation, and the substance must be reapplied if intercourse is repeated. It has been noted that the foam type of spermicide (actually a cream packaged in an aerosol can) provides the best distribution within the vagina. Foam has a failure rate of about 3 to 10 pregnancies per 100 women per year when properly used—a somewhat better rate than that reported for creams and jellies.

Another chemical contraceptive is the vaginal suppository, a small, solid cone that melts at 95 °F. These suppositories must be inserted at least 15 minutes before ejaculation. Also available are vaginal tablets, which are supposed to dissolve in the vagina. These tablets may present problems because they are very unstable in damp climates and may need more moisture than is present in the vagina in order to dissolve. Both tablets and suppositories are less effective than foam. They depend a great deal on mixing with natural lubricants and are difficult to disperse properly. The pregnancy rate with suppositories is 5 to 27 pregnancies per 100 women per year; that of tablets is 8 to 27. Part of the reason for these high failure rates is the fact that if ejaculation occurs before the suppositories melt sufficiently to lubricate the vagina, mixing and dispersion of these agents does not occur to an adequate extent. Failure rates for foams, creams, and jellies are in the 20 percent range.

Douches. The term *douching* refers to washing out the vagina immediately after intercourse. It is one of the most ineffective methods of contraception in common use. Indeed, many physicians feel that douching is *less* effective than nothing, inasmuch as the washing fluid, which is not a spermicide, may serve to increase the distribution of the sperm. About the best thing that can be said of the technique is that it is very simple. It requires only a douche bag and tap water, sometimes with the addition of some substance that is believed to make the douche more effective. Some of the common products used in this way include vinegar, lemon juice, soap, and salt. In actuality, these additions add little to the spermicidal qualities of tap water and may, in fact, irritate the vaginal tissues. Since it is possible for sperm to make their way into the cervical canal (beyond the reach of the douche) within one or two minutes after ejaculation, douching is quite limited as a contraceptive method. The failure rate is about 30 to 36 pregnancies per 100 women per year.

Withdrawal. Probably the oldest known method of birth control is withdrawal, technically known as *coitus interruptus*. This method, which is still common throughout the world, requires that the male withdraw his penis from the vagina before he ejaculates. Although many people find this practice satisfactory, others find it very frustrating because the man must withdraw at the crucial moment—or sooner—and must wait a considerable time before engaging in intercourse again. What is more, the secretion of the Cowper's gland, which is given off prior to ejaculation, may contain a few sperm and therefore can impregnate the woman. The withdrawal method has a failure rate of from 8 to 40 pregnancies per 100 women per year. Cultural variations in lovemaking styles make this technique more effective among some ethnic groups than others.

Rhythm. The rhythm method is the only contraceptive technique endorsed by the Roman Catholic Church. It requires that a couple engage in periodic abstinence from sexual intercourse during what is presumed to be the woman's fertile period. This method is unreliable, however, particularly in women whose menstrual cycles are irregular. Only about 30 percent of all women have sufficiently regular menstrual cycles to permit reasonable pinpointing of the "safe" period. Add to this the fact that some women ovulate in response to sexual stimulation, and the whole procedure becomes even more unreliable.

A more sophisticated variant of the rhythm method is based on the fact that a woman's temperature changes during her menstrual cycle. To use this method, the woman must take her temperature every morning immediately before arising and before eating, drinking, or smoking. One of the major problems with this method is that many women have no marked or consistent temperature changes during the menstrual cycle. What is more, colds or sore throats may throw off the temperature chart. Both the rhythm and temperature methods have a medium pregnancy rate of 14 to 35 per 100 women per year.

Contraceptives Available Only with a Prescription

Prior to the introduction of the birth control pill and the intrauterine device (IUD), the diaphragm and the cervial cap were the most commonly used contraceptives. These mechanical devices, designed for use by the woman, operate by covering the cervix, thus preventing entry of the sperm into the uterus.

The Diaphragm. The *diaphragm* is thin, dome-shaped rubber cup attached to a flexible, rubber-covered metal ring about 3 inches in diameter. The diaphragm must be fitted by a physician; if it is not the correct size and shape for a particular woman, it will be ineffective. Before a woman can be fitted for a diaphragm, the hymen must be broken. After childbirth a woman should not resume use of the diaphragm she was using before she decided to become pregnant. Because changes in the size or shape of her cervix may cause it to be ineffective, she should be fitted with a new one. If it is inserted properly, the diaphragm should not interfere with the conduct or pleasure of sexual intercourse.

A common error is the mistaken assumption that a diaphragm itself is an adequate means of contraception. The diaphragm must be used with a contraceptive cream or jelly whose purpose is to kill sperm. The spermicidal cream or jelly has the added benefit of providing lubrication. In order to ensure that the jelly is effective, the diaphragm should be inserted no more than 4 to 6 hours before intercourse. If a woman does not know in advance that she is going to have intercourse, she will have to stop during lovemaking to insert the diaphragm. (Unwillingness to interrupt sex play to insert a diaphragm is one common reason for failure of the diaphragm method.) After intercourse the diaphragm should remain in place for at least 6 hours, although it may be left in for as long as 24. The diaphragm should then be removed and washed, and additional jelly should be applied before reinsertion.

The diaphragm-plus-spermicide method fails, for any of a number of reasons, between 4 and 10 percent of the time; the failure rate of diaphragms used without spermicidal substances jumps to as much as 20 percent. The diaphragm fails because it is not used when it should be, because it is inserted incorrectly, because it cannot be perfectly fitted to all changes that occur in the vagina during lovemaking, and because vigorous lovemaking involving multiple insertions of the penis sometimes dislodges it. It is more likely to fail when the woman is on top of the man than when the man is on top of the woman.[13]

The Cervical Cap. Another mechanical device, similar to the diaphragm, is the *cervical cap*. A cervical cap is smaller than a diaphragm, shaped like a large thimble, and made of rubber, plastic, or metal. It is also known as a pessary cap (as is the diaphragm). This device is much more popular in Europe than in America. In contrast to the diaphragm, which covers the cervix and a portion of the end of the vagina, the cervical cap fits only over the end of the uterus, or cervix. Because cervixes differ in size and shape, not all women can use these caps. It takes more skill to insert a cervical cap properly than to insert a diaphragm, but once inserted it can be left in place for days or weeks. As with the diaphragm, it may become dislodged during intercourse, but this is less common. The failure rate for cervical caps is about 8 percent.

The IUD. There are a large number of *intrauterine devices* (IUDs) on the market, and they vary widely in size, shape, effectiveness, and side effects. The use of intrauterine devices goes back to the time of Hippocrates. Following a centures-old practice, Arab camel drivers place a round stone in the uterus of the female camel before a long journey across the desert. During the nineteenth century a variety of intrauterine devices were used for gynecological disorders and for contraception, but in the early twentieth century these devices fell into disrepute. Many early models suffered from high rates of expulsion and often required surgical removal because they damaged the uterine wall, often causing hemorrhaging.

In the 1930s a German physician, E. Geafenberg, developed a coiled silver ring that in his studies produced a failure rate of 1.6 pregnancies per 100 women. Nevertheless, there was strong opposition to his device, and IUDs remained unpopular until 1959. In that year two reports, one by an Israeli who had worked with Geafenberg and one by a Japanese physician, triggered new enthusiasm for the IUD. The failure rates were 2.4 and 2.3 per 100, and no serious complications were reported. These studies involved a total of 21,500 women. In spite of the fact that physicians still do not know why the IUD works, its demonstrated effectiveness and ease of use has made it popular in the United States since 1959.

IUDs are made of various materials and come in many sizes and shapes. The Lippes loop is made of plastic and ranges from 22.5 to 0.30 mm in diameter. A physician inserts this device by stretching the loop into a linear form and pushing it through a plastic tube into the uterus. This procedure is performed through the cervical opening. All IUDs have tiny nylon threads attached to them that hang down through the cervical opening into the vagina. It is possible to determine whether they are properly in place by checking for the presence of these threads. Some of the new models are treated with barium so that they will be readily visible via X rays. The IUD in no way affects the fertility of the woman or the health of the children she might bear when it is removed. If a woman wishes to become pregnant, the IUD must be removed by a physician. After birth it may be repositioned in the uterus until another pregnancy is desired.

	STERILIZATION	PILL	INTRAUTERINE DEVICE (IUD)

How it works	Permanently blocks egg or sperm passages	Prevent ovulation	Uncertain; may stop implantation of egg
Possible side effects	Psychological only	Blood–clotting disorders; dizziness; headaches; bleeding; weight gain; nausea	Initial discomfort and irregular bleeding
Physician assistance required	Operation performed by physician	Must be prescribed by doctor; periodic checkups required	Must be inserted by physician; periodic checkups required
Average pregnancy rate/100 women/year	Hysterectomy: 0.0001 Tubal ligation: 0.04 Vasectomy: 0.15	Combination: 0.1 Sequential: 0.5	1.5–8

	DIAPHRAGM (WITH CHEMICAL)	CONDOM	SPERMICIDAL SUBSTANCES

How it works	Barrier to sperm	Prevents sperm from entering vagina	Barriers to sperm; kill sperm before entering cervix
Possible side effects	Chemical may cause irritation	Loss of sensation	May cause irritation
Physician assistance required	Fitting	None	None
Average pregnancy rate/100 women/year	4–10	10–15	Tablets: 8–27 Suppositories: 5–27 Foam: 3–10

	WITHDRAWAL	RHYTHM	DOUCHE

How it works	Withdrawal of penis from vagina before ejaculation occurs	Abstinence during female's fertile period	Rinses sperm from vagina
Possible side effects	Psychological only	Psychological only	None
Physician assistance required	None	Consultation	None
Average pregnancy rate/100 women/year	20–30	15–31	20–62

FIGURE 8.1 Comparison of various birth control methods.

The current failure rate for the most popular IUD is on the order of 1 to 8 pregnancies per 100 women during the first year of use, with slightly lower rates thereafter. About 10 percent of the women using IUDs expel them during the first year of use, usually during the early months of use and frequently during menstruation. Because the IUD can be expelled without user knowing it, frequent checks to make sure it is in position are important. Only about 75 percent of the women who use the IUD find that they can continue to use it after one year. By the end of 2 or 3 years, only about half of these women continue to use the device.[14]

The Pill. There are two basic types of *oral contraceptives*, or birth control pills: sequential and combination. *Combination pills*, which are the most common type of oral contraceptive, are composed of a mixture of synthetic progesterone and estrogen. *Sequential pills* provide these hormones in sequence rather than in combination. The first 15 pills contain estrogen, while the last 5 contain a mixture of estrogen and progesterone. Enovid, Ortho-Novum, and Norinyl are examples of the progesterone-estrogen combination type of pill. Ortho-Novum SQ and Norquen are examples of the sequential type. Both types prevent ovulation by creating the hormonal balance found in pregnancy. The sequential pills are less effective than the combination pills. While about 0.1 pregnancies per 100 women per year occur when combination oral contraceptives are used, this figure increases to 0.5 pregnancies per 100 women per year with sequential types.

Research has established that high dosages of estrogen are mainly responsible for the pill's side effects. The pills on the market today contain less estrogen than the first birth control pills did. Recently combination pills with still lower doses of estrogen have become available, for example, Demulen, Norestrol, and Lo/Orval. Each of these types—combination, sequential, and low-estrogen combination—has its own effectiveness rate and side effects. The proper matching between a particular woman and a particular pill requires a doctor's evaluation and careful follow-up study. Most commonly, women are advised to change their prescription from time to time in order to reduce the risk of adverse side effects.

Two additional variations have been introduced, primarily to help the woman remember when she is to take her pill. Both techniques are based on a 21:7 sequence. In the first instance, the woman takes 21 pills, stops for 7 days, and then resumes her pills, regardless of when her period began. In the second instance, she takes one pill every day, but 7 of the 28 in the sequence are placebos.

Regardless of its form, the pill is a powerful agent in the human body. It can have both physiological and psychological effects. Therefore, it is difficult to make a definitive statement about which women should use the pill and which should not. A complete medical examination is necessary before a physician can prescribe the proper pill—if one is used. Apparently, women who have very irregular menstrual cycles are likely to experience more complications—particularly with regard to having more children after they have stopped taking the pill—than those with more regular cycles. Also, women who have histories of cardiovascular trouble may experience complications from the use of the pill. Women who have had difficulty with blood clotting, sickle cell anemia, severe heart disease or defect, severe endocrine disorders, or any form of cancer should not take the pill. The adverse psychological effects of the pill are more difficult to detect and predict.

Among the side effects of the pill, the most serious seems to be an increased risk of death from thromboembolic (clotting) disorders. About 3 out of every 100,000 women on the pill can be expected to die as a result of clotting caused by the pill.[15] This is about three times the rate for nonpregnant women who don't take the pill. On the other hand, women using other means of birth control are about 3.5 times more likely than pill users to die from complications caused by pregnancy, childbirth, and postpartum problems, and women who use no contraceptive at all are 7.5 times more likely to die as a result of complications in childbirth than pill users.[16]

Many of the discomforts associated with use of the pill, such as dizziness, headaches, bleeding, weight gain, and the like, have not yet been reliably researched, largely because these symptoms also occur frequently in women not taking the pill. It is difficult to determine what percentages of these cases are caused by the pill. Most of the symptoms pill users experience tend to diminish or disappear after a few months, but many women have become discouraged because of such discomforts.

The advantages of the pill are obvious. It does not interfere with sexual intercourse, does not depend on knowing beforehand that one is going to have intercourse, and when taken properly, has the highest rate of effectiveness of any of the contraceptives currently available. In principle, the pill is 100 percent effective by the second month of use. Missing one pill will not normally have serious consequences if two are taken the next day, but missing two or more pills invites a fair risk of failure. The effectiveness of various contraceptives is compared in Figure 8.2.

In the event that intercourse has occurred without the use of an effective contraceptive, it is still possible to prevent conception by means of three techniques that have been recently introduced. They require the assistance of a physician in most cases. The copper 7 IUD is effective in preventing conception if inserted shortly after intercourse. The "morning-after pill" (DES—Diethylstilbestrol) has been widely publicized. It is a massive dose of synthetic estrogen which some physicians will not use because of the widely noted side effects. Should pregnancy nevertheless occur, an abortion is recommended because of the high risk of fetal abnormality. Finally, menstrual extraction, ordinarily performed in a doctor's office before a pregnancy test has been given, is effective, but some regard it as abortion.

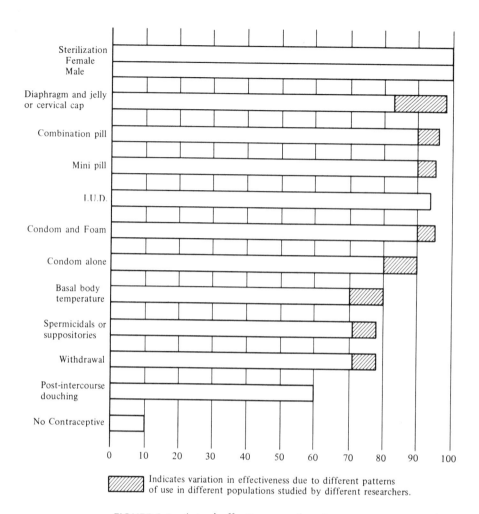

Sterilization
Female
Male

Diaphragm and jelly
or cervical cap

Combination pill

Mini pill

I.U.D.

Condom and Foam

Condom alone

Basal body
temperature

Spermicidals or
suppositories

Withdrawal

Post-intercourse
douching

No Contraceptive

0   10   20   30   40   50   60   70   80   90   100

Indicates variation in effectiveness due to different patterns
of use in different populations studied by different researchers.

FIGURE 8-2 Actual effectiveness of various contraceptives. (Compilation of
data presented in Hatcher et al., *Contraceptive Technology 1980–81*, New
York: Irvington, 1980; *Our Bodies, Ourselves*, Boston: Women's Health Book
Collective.)

STERILIZATION

Sterilization of either the male or the female is a quite different kind of birth
control from those discussed so far because for the most part such operations are irreversible. Nevertheless, voluntary sterilization is becoming increasingly common in the United States: 750,000 vasectomies were performed in 1970 alone. Tubal ligation for the female is a more complex
operation. Nevertheless, sterilization has become the most commonly used
method of birth control for wives between the ages of 30 and 44.[17]

Vasectomy

Vasectomy is a simple procedure that can be done in a doctor's office. It consists of cutting and tying the vas deferens. A local anesthetic is injected into each side of the scrotum and an incision is then made on each side of the scrotum above the testicles. The vas is tied in two places and the segment between them is cut and usually removed.

A vasectomy does not affect a man's sexual response. Some men have difficulty with the idea of voluntary sterilization because they equate masculinity with fertility. Such men may have some emotional problems to overcome should they finally decide on the operation. Occasionally the vasectomy may be reversed. As a surgical procedure it is not 100 percent effective because some men have more than one vas deferens and a second one might be missed. Intercourse should not be resumed until after about the twentieth postoperative ejaculation. If there are no sperm in the last ejaculate, the man can be considered sterile.

Tubal Ligation

Tubal ligation, commonly called "tying the tubes," is the most common method of sterilizing women. This operation is similar in principle to the vasectomy. The cutting of the Fallopian tubes prevents the egg from reaching the uterus. This surgical procedure is far more complicated than a vasectomy, requiring hospitalization for five days followed by three to four weeks of postoperative recovery.

A recent variation for sterilizing women is called *laparoscopic sterilization or laparotomy*. The procedure has been described in the following terms: "The laparoscope is a long instrument that is inserted into the lower abdomen via a small incision below the naval. The tubes are then blocked by cauterization and/or cutting." This operation can be performed on an outpatient basis.

Three other procedures that result in sterility among women are *hysterectomy* (removal of the uterus), *xoophorectomy* (removal of the ovaries), and *salpingectomy* (removal of the Fallopian tubes). They are, however, normally performed to correct various abnormal conditions rather than for birth control purposes.

Sterilization may be either eugenic or therapeutic. A *eugenic sterilization* is undertaken to prevent the inheritance of genetic defects; a *therapeutic sterilization* is undertaken when the person has certain chronic diseases or disabilities. Some couples have themselves sterilized once they have had the number of children they desire. If the male stores some of his sperm in a sperm bank before being sterilized, it becomes possible for the couple to have children after the vasectomy if they change their minds about family size.

ABORTION

In some populations half of all conceptions spontaneously abort before the first period is missed. **Spontaneous abortion** or miscarriage is noticed by the mother in about one out of every ten pregnancies, usually within the first trimester.[18] Strictly speaking, this is not a form of birth control since it is not planned, although it may have the effect of controlling population. **Induced abortion** is a term used to describe intentional termination of a pregnancy.

Historical Overview

Throughout history there have been a variety of attitudes toward abortion. A Chinese manuscript over 4,000 years old is said to record the oldest method of abortion. Within the Judaic tradition there are no laws against abortion in either Talmud or Judaic law, for Judaism, like Japanese Shintoism, believes that the fetus becomes human only when it is born. Aristotle reflected Greek thinking on this matter when he said that abortion was an acceptable means of birth control when other means failed. It is commonly believed that one Greek who dissented from the majority opinion was the physician Hippocrates, for the Hippocratic oath, which was derived from his teachings, includes a clause prohibiting abortion. There is, however, reason to believe that this clause is based on a misunderstanding of Hippocrates, who formulated his oath primarily to prevent physicians from participating in political intrigues by administering potions to members of the ruling classes, and did not intend the oath to bind physicians to defending life under any circumstances. Be that as it may, the idea that abortion is a form of murder seems never to have occurred to the ancient Romans, who, like the ancient Greeks, viewed it as simply the removal of a portion of the body. Even when population control became a problem for the Romans (as a result of the fact that the ruling classes practiced abortion so extensively that the ratio of citizens to slaves declined alarmingly), attempts to outlaw abortion met with only partial success.

Today the strongest and most vocal opponent to abortion is the Roman Catholic Church. It is not widely known that the Church's position on abortion has varied over the centuries. In the twelfth century abortions were allowed if the fetus was not over 40 days old if it was male and 8 days old if it was female. (The Church did not say how in those days it was possible to make a determination of the sex of the fetus.) Four centuries later, in 1588, Pope Sixtus V pronounced all abortions a form of murder. Three years later, Gregory XIV reverted to the earlier law. Gregory's pronouncement remained canon law until 1869, when Pius XI condemned all abortions. The present attitude of the Church thus is only about 100 years old.

Public opinion has gradually come to favor liberalized abortion legislation. By 1972 eighteen states had greatly liberalized their abortion laws, following the American Law Institute's model code, and four (Alaska,

The heated confrontation between those who advocate "choice" and those who are "pro-life" often obscures as much as illuminates the subtle issues involved in abortion. (Charles Gatewood; Catholics for a Free Choice)

Hawaii, New York, and Washington) had made abortion a matter of choice by a woman in consultation with her physician, provided that the abortion was performed early in the pregnancy.[19] A Gallup poll in 1972 showed that 64 percent of the American public, including a majority of Roman Catholics, favored liberalization of abortion laws.[20] In 1973 the United States Supreme Court ruled invalid all existing state laws prohibiting abortion. This ruling permits abortion in the early months of pregnancy at the discretion of the doctor and the patient. It makes abortion a medical matter rather than a legal one. Nevertheless, much opposition to abortion on demand remains, and efforts to reduce its occurrence sometimes take violent form, as in the destruction of clinics and harassment of their personnel. A 1976 Supreme Court decision declared that the states should determine the conditions under which abortion was to be performed.

Hazards of Abortion Without Proper Medical Supervision

In the past, because of legal restrictions, women who wanted abortions had to resort to illegal means. As a result, many abortions were performed under nonsterile conditions by unskilled people. Understandably, the death rate under those conditions was very high. With the legalization of abortions, which permits them to be performed under sterile conditions with proper medical supervision, there is reason to believe that the death rate will be much lower. Indeed, abortion under such conditions is less dangerous than childbirth. For example, in Czechoslovakia, where abortion is legal, there was not a single death in 140,000 abortions during 1963–1964.[21] More recent figures estimate that the death rate from abortion under proper medical supervision is about 1.5 per 100,000 abortions. In contrast, childbirth causes death in about 8.3 out of 100,000 pregnancies.[22]

Four medical abortion procedures are available today: (1) dilation and curettage, (2) vacuum extraction, (3) the saline method, and (4) hysterotomy. The first two methods can be used up to the twelfth or thirteenth week of pregnancy. A fifth method, which makes use of chemicals called prostaglandins, is in the experimental stage.

Abortion is not something that a woman can bring about herself without running serious risks. Many women believe that they can terminate a pregnancy by taking a pill or by some mechanical means such as falling downstairs, pounding the abdomen, or inserting some foreign substance into the uterus. Although amateur attempts at abortion often succeed in terminating the pregnancy, they commonly do so with grisly results for the woman, causing permanent and serious injury in many cases and death in many others. There is no way short of surgery that a pregnancy can be terminated without grave risks to the woman. The folk wisdom that says pregnancy can be terminated by taking a "black pill" (ergot) neglects to mention that the dosage necessary to terminate the pregnancy may also terminate the mother's life.

Of course, the liberalization of abortion laws should not be permitted to lead to a situation in which abortion becomes a major means of contraception. It should be reserved for use when all other contraceptive techniques have failed. The most rational, humane, and healthy social approach is to prevent conception in the first place if children are not desired.

SEXUALLY TRANSMITTED DISEASE (STD)

A number of diseases are commonly transmitted during the intimacies of lovemaking. Until recently, gonorrhea and syphilis were the source of most concern. The incidence of gonorrhea has begun to decline, however, but syphilis is again on the upswing. Both are readily treatable. Two other diseases have recently made the headlines; herpes simplex type II or herpes genitalis is thought to be in epidemic proportions in the United States, and there is great dispute over what to do about it, since there is no known cure at present. It is normally not contagious when there is no visible rash on the skin. The rash is the most common symptom, but there are serious complications, including an increased risk of cancer, and deleterious effects on newborn babies of mothers who have the disease. The second recent newsmaker is apparently not widespread but has created alarm because of its serious consequences—loss of normal immunity—and its association in the minds of the public with homosexuality. AIDS (Acquired Immune Deficiency Syndrome) is now thought to be transmitted by a virus and can apparently infect someone who is the recipient of blood donated by another who has the disease. In destroying the body's immunity, AIDS renders the person vulnerable to infection from many sources.[23]

The risk of catching some form of **sexually transmitted disease** is higher for teenagers than adults (some studies say four times as great a risk is run by teenagers). It therefore behooves one to take precautions to prevent STD. These include care in selecting a sexual partner. The more sexual partners, the greater the risk of STD. Avoid contact with sores, rashes, or discharge around the genitals, anus, or mouth. Some contraceptives—condoms, and vaginal foams and creams—provide some protection for both men and women. Wash sexual organs with soap and water before and after contact and urinate soon after intercourse. If there is any reason to suspect infection, have a checkup. If you are sexually active with more than one partner, have regular checkups and ask the physician to check for STDs. This is not a part of a regular physical. If you should become infected, notify all your sexual partners so that they can be treated immediately.

SUMMARY

Contraception is not synonymous with birth control. This chapter has treated four major techniques to control birth: contraception, sterilization, abstinence, and abortion. Each one has its place as an effective and appropriate technique, given the circumstances under which the decision to use a particular birth control method must be made. Obviously, if one is going to prevent birth it is better to do so before conception. Since the effects of contraceptives are generally reversible, contraceptives are likely to be preferred over sterilization in most cases. Abortion is more risky and raises many more ethical issues, but it too has its place as a means of birth control. For some individuals abstinence may be the preferable form.

The most reliable contraceptives require a doctor's prescription. Both the pill and the IUD are theoretically 100 percent effective and come close to this level in practice in certain populations. However, not everyone can use them, and therefore the diaphragm or cervical cap, both of which are slightly less effective in practice, may be the best option.

Of the contraceptives that are available without a prescription, the condom is the most effective in preventing venereal disease. Spermicidal substances vary greatly in effectiveness and tend to interfere with lovemaking. Douches are virtually ineffective. Since only one-third of all women have menstrual cycles that are regular enough to make use of the rhythm method effective, about all that can be said for this technique as a contraceptive is that it is the only one that is officially endorsed by the Roman Catholic Church.

The rapid increase in STD, particularly among those of high school age, is cause for genuine concern. While almost all cases can be effectively treated if caught soon enough, many people are still reluctant to undergo a physical examination. A more helpful attitude is to view these diseases like any other disease and seek quick and effective care. The symptoms described in this chapter should provide some clues, but among people who are sexually active in nonmonogamous relationships, routine clinical checkups are advisable.

NOTES

1. Paul Blanchard, "Christianity and Sex," *The Humanist*, (March–April 1974): 27–32.
2. James Leslie McCary, *Human Sexuality: A Brief Edition* (New York: Van Nostrand Reinhold, 1973), p. 87.
3. Ibid.
4. The Alan Guttmacher Institute, *11 Million Teenagers: What Can Be Done About the Epidemic of Adolescent Pregnancies in the United States* (New York: The Alan Guttmacher Institute, 1976).
5. The Alan Guttmacher Institute, *Teenage Pregnancy: The Problem That Hasn't Gone Away* (New York: The Alan Guttmacher Institute, 1981).

6. Ibid.

7. Melvin Zelnick and John F. Kanter, "Sexual and Contraceptive Experiences of Young Unmarried Women in the United States," *Family Planning Perspectives*, 3 (1977): 55–71.

8. J. R. Lundy, "Some Personality Correlates of Contraceptive Use Among Unmarried Female College Students," *Journal of Psychology*, 80 (1972): 10–14; A. P. MacDonald, Jr., "Internal–External Locus of Control and the Practice of Birth Control," *Psychological Reports*, 27 (1970): 206; Baroff D. Settlage et al., "Sexual Experience of Younger Teenage Girls Seeking Contraceptive Assistance for the First Time," *Family Planning Perspectives*, 5 (1973): 223–26.

9. Don Byrne, "A Pregnant Pause in the Sexual Revolution," *Psychology Today*, 11 (1977): 67–88; Meg Gerrard, "Sex, Sex Guilt, and Contraceptive Use," *Journal of Personality and Social Psychology*, 42 (January 1982): 153–58.

10. Farida Shah and Melvin Zelnik, "Parent and Peer Influence on Sexual Behavior, Contraceptive Use, and Pregnancy Experience of Young Women," *Journal of Marriage and the Family*, 43 (May 1981): 339–48.

11. J. Forfeit and K. G. Forfeit, "Risk-Taking and Contraceptive Behavior Among Unmarried College Students," *Population and Environment: Behavioral and Social Issues*, 4 (fall 1981): 174–88.

12. David J. Kallen and Judith Stephenson, "Perceived Physician Humaneness, Patient Attitude, and Satisfaction with the Pill as a Contraceptive," *Journal of Health and Social Behavior*, 22 (September 1981): 256–67.

13. Mary S. Calderone (ed.), *Manual of Family Planning and Contraceptive Practice*, 2nd ed. (Baltimore: Williams and Wilkins, 1970), p. 234.

14. Donna Charniak and Allan Feingold, *Birth Control Handbook* (Montreal: Montreal Health Press, 1975), p. 57.

15. Celso-Roman Garcia, "Clinical Aspects of Oral Hormonal Contraceptives," in Mary S. Calderone (ed.), *Manual of Family Planning*.

16. Calderone, p. 318.

17. Charles E. Westcoff and Norman B. Ryder, *The Contraceptive Society* (Princeton, N.J.: Princeton University Press, 1977), pp. 333ff.

18. Much of the material in this section was taken from McCary, *Human Sexuality: A Brief Edition*.

19. Ruth Roemer, "Legalization of Abortion in the United States," in Howard J. Osofsky and Joy. Osofsky (eds.), *The Abortion Experience: Psychological and Medical Impact* (New York: Harper & Row, 1973), pp. 284–86.

20. As quoted in McCary, *Human Sexuality*, p. 82.

21. Lawrence Lader, *Abortion* (Boston: Beacon Press, 1966).

22. Charniak and Feingold, p. 46.

23. Michael Castleman, "The Mystery of 'AIDS,'" *Medical Self Care* (spring 1983): 32–33.

Many years I have wandered through the land of man, and have not yet reached an end of studying the varieties of the "erotic man." . . . There a lover stamps around and is in love only with his passion. There one is wearing his differentiated feelings like medal ribbons. There one is enjoying the adventures of his own fascinating effect. There one is gazing enraptured at the spectacle of his supposed surrender. There one is collecting excitement. There one is displaying his "power." There one is preening himself with borrowed vitality. There one is delighting to exist simultaneously as himself and as an idol very unlike himself. There one is warming himself at the blaze of what has fallen to his lot. There one is experimenting. And so on and on—all the manifold monologists with their mirrors, in the apartment of the most intimate dialogue.

—Martin Buber

9 the *Art* of *Lovemaking*

The main reason for writing a chapter on the art of lovemaking in a text such as this is that in spite of all of our recent concern about sex, in our culture we have devoted less time to the cultivation of the art of lovemaking than we have to the art of cooking. Any art is far more than mere technique. Lovemaking requires dedication and practice and a deep respect for one's partner and oneself. It involves the whole being of both partners and the total setting in which they make love. With humor and playfulness, it can re-create us. While it presents the possibility for heartbreak and tragedy as well, there are few areas of human experience in which so much can be gained with a comparable amount of risk. Learning to make love well can be fun, and is a lifelong adventure that need not be hurried.

We begin with a discussion of fantasy, erotica, and sexual desire. The mind is the most sensitive sexual organ of all, and its ability to play with these images shapes our experience of lovemaking in significant ways. So does the opinion of the experts who contribute to our performance fears that we may not be living up to their standards of good lovemaking. Only the barest outline of the art of lovemaking can be presented in the sections on the setting, stroking, pleasuring, and techniques. Happily there are now many good books on these subjects, and you are encouraged to add some to your library.

CONTEXT

Sexuality means many different things to different people. Human sexuality is not simply natural or instinctive. It is learned. Sexual intercourse is not simply "the union of two souls and the contact of two epidermises." It is "a secret coming together of two human bodies [in which] all society is the third presence." Our cultural heritage is the overarching context within which sexual intercourse occurs.

In the past this heritage has been characterized by woeful ignorance. There are signs, however, that the sexual renaissance may be changing many of our ideas, giving us a much more positive attitude toward sexuality. More and more people are coming to recognize that human sexuality can communicate more than simple erotic attraction. It is becoming increasingly clear that any intimate partnership can be enhanced by an open and genuine sex life.

The warm glow of erotic intimacy need not necessarily be conducive to dialog and open communication, as the remarks of Martin Buber at the beginning of this chapter suggest. But sexual exploration can be a means of communicating as well as pleasuring. We tend to think of communication, openness, and the giving of oneself as occurring primarily through words, but if words are the only way a couple express who they are to each other, they have been cheated. The revelation and self-disclosure of two people in love and in bed together go far beyond what can be put into words. This self-disclosure and joy in finding each other can continue throughout a relationship if a couple do not take their lovemaking for granted. Routine and monotony in lovemaking can easily develop in any long-term partnership, but this need not happen. Viewing lovemaking as an art leads one to anticipate and prepare for the pleasures it brings. Knowing how to make love skillfully enhances these pleasures. But discovering how truly to give each other pleasure in sexual relationships is not simply a matter of technique, however varied and elegant the techniques may be. It is a matter of openness, honesty, and communication as well. The longer and more deeply two partners have known each other and the more vital their love, the more they have to bring to their lovemaking.

Fantasy, Erotica, and Desire

Sexual arousal is the result of a number of factors that are interrelated in complex ways. Cultural conditioning shapes our images of the beautiful or the erotic sexual partner and helps to define the social cues that trigger arousal. Our state of health, and mind, previous erotic experience, the skill of our current partner, and our own knowledge and acceptance of our erotic needs affect how we are turned on. It may not be possible to know all the reasons why a particular person so excites us or a particular situation seems so appropriate for lovemaking, but for most of us, at least some of the time, fantasy and visual imagery play an important role.

Sexual fantasies may occur before, during, or after sexual experiences. They may assist in arousal or inhibit it. They may trigger orgasm or prevent it. They may enrich the afterglow of lovemaking, or chill it. But there is little evidence that these images compel us to sexual behavior as those opposed to pornography are inclined to argue. They have a value all their own in the playing out of the possibilities of sexual adventures in our minds. Thus a woman fantasizes

Two men are undressing me. One slowly unbuttons my blouse, while the other unzips my skirt and lowers it to the ground. They caress my body as they work, one above the waist and one below. The one man removes my brassiere, while the other takes down my waist-slip and pants. Then they join forces to undo my suspenders (garter belt) and, when I am naked, they lift me onto a big bed and lie, one on either side of me. I give myself up completely to them. My pleasure is doubled, for every part of my body gets twice the amount of attention it would normally receive. First one, then the other climbs between my legs and makes love to me.[1]

and a man dreams

I am in a luxurious brothel where the girls are lined up for my inspection. I sit in a big chair before them and beckon them, one by one, to come to me. In turn, each girl stands in front of me and lifts her skirts. Underneath they are naked and I gaze at each one before making a selection. It is a very difficult choice but finally I settle on one girl and we go into a bedroom. I throw up her skirt and take her quickly, then send her off with instructions to send another girl to me. In this way, I manage to work through them all, one by one, until I am finally satisfied.[2]

Fantasies are fantasies because they stand in such a precarious relationship to observable reality. They might depict an insatiable desire, a need to dominate or submit that could not be tolerated in sexual behavior, an ability to satisfy the sexual partner that far exceeds the ability of the fantasizer. Mark Twain in his *Letters From the Earth* is amazed at the extent to which men have been able to impose their fantasies on women in the commonly accepted social customs of his day.

> Now if you or any other really intelligent person were arranging the fairness and justices between men and women, you would give the man a one-fiftieth interest in one woman and the woman a harem. Now wouldn't you? Necessarily. I give you my word, this creature with the decrepit candle has arranged it exactly the other way. Solomon, who was one of the Deity's favorites, had a copulation cabinet composed of seven hundred wives and three hundred concubines. To save his life he could not have kept two of these young creatures satisfactorily refreshed, even if he had fifteen experts to help him. Necessarily almost the entire thousand had to go hungry years and years on a stretch. Conceive of a man hardhearted enough to look daily upon all that suffering and not be moved to mitigate it. He even wantonly added a sharp pang to that pathetic misery; for he kept within those women's sight, always, stalwart watchmen whose splendid masculine forms made the poor lassies mouths water but who hadn't anything to solace a candlestick with, these gentry being eunuchs. A eunuch is a person whose candle has been put out. By art.[3]

Sexual fantasies and social customs intertwine in endless ways, as suggested by the world's mythologies and Twain's critique. But sexual fantasies can be entered into as playful possibilities to be enjoyed for their own sake without feeling the compulsion to act them out or impose them on others. Their power seems to be of short duration as erotic stimuli—two to four hours of exposure in the case of erotica.[4] After this amount of exposure, they seem to lose their arousing capabilities. Internalized imagery may have more long-lasting effect. Alex Comfort offers some guidelines on putting fantasies into practice in loving partnerships:

> There are after all only two "rules" in good sex, apart from the obvious one of not doing things which are silly, antisocial, or dangerous. One is "don't do anything you don't really enjoy," and the other is "find out your partner's needs and don't balk them if you can help it."[5]

Unrealistic Expectations

Although the changes in sexual mores generally described as the sexual revolution have helped many young Americans get over some of their hangups, these changes have produced some new problems. People today are coming to understand their sexuality as a rich and rewarding means of communication and a pleasure in its own right. They also are beginning to understand that women not only can find pleasure in sex, but indeed have much greater physiological potential to enjoy it than men. It is not common any more to think of sex in marriage as the man's pleasure and the woman's obligation, for the contemporary woman enjoys increased freedom to make her own demands. On the negative side, however, these generally beneficial changes have contributed to increased fear of poor performance in many people. In the past thirty years various "experts"—many of whom are no more qualified than the average experienced adult—have offered numerous descriptions of what is expected of both partners in lovemaking. A rather humorous, but basically devastating, description of these changing expectations is found in Gina Allen and Clement Martin's book *Intimacy:*

Once the goal was orgasm for him (essential for health). For her it was "satisfying him" (to keep him at home and preserve the marriage).

Then the goal was "satisfying her" for him (to prove he was a genuine sexual jock, not a run-of-the-mill athlete). Her goal was reaching orgasm (to prove her femininity). To prove she was also mature, it was necessary for her to reach "vaginal orgasm." That was a change in both rules and goals that unfortunately occurred just after the man had learned to find the clitoris. At first, reaching vaginal orgasm was thought to be her problem. But later, it became his problem, too, as he was expected to keep an erection and keep thrusting (and keep his mind off what he was doing) long enough to bring her to a mature, nonclitoral climax. Otherwise, he wouldn't earn his letter.

The stakes were later raised to a mutual climax, which if you were a real jock would shake the world. . . . Quantity rather than quality became the basis for scoring, with each player pitting himself against vague and varying national averages or healthful weekly requirements.

In the meantime, her performance was to be judged in a new way—as if competing for the Academy Award. She wasn't required to have an orgasm. (She got as much pleasure from pleasing her partner, the experts said.) But she was required to simulate an orgasm to make his performance look and feel better. To keep either partner from scoring too high, the experts gave him hints to tell if she was faking. Both lost points if her deception was detected.

And then came multiple orgasm (quantity still counts). Now he was able to give her at least three orgasms in the place of one. The first one of several could be clitoral, a pre-intercourse warmup. Then a mature vaginal climax or two after intromission. And finally—back to the mutual orgasm. A truly super performance by two superjocks!

The name of the game is Sexual Freedom, because it has freed sex from the bonds of reproduction, marriage, and love. The advertised prizes are health, happiness, and an end to anxiety.[6]

The demands made on both partners by such unrealistic criteria for "excellent performance" may well have contributed to the increasing rates of impotence that are now being recorded. Masters and Johnson state that "fear of inadequacy is the greatest known deterrent to effective sexual functioning" simply because it severely reduces an individual's ability to be receptive to the sexual stimuli that occur naturally in lovemaking.[7] No set of criteria can adequately measure the sexual performance of a couple save their own mutual pleasure. In lovemaking, as in all aspects of intimacy, being oneself rather than living up to the expectations of others is more likely to produce such pleasure.

Setting

The immediate setting in which lovemaking takes place affects its quality, tone, and meaning.[8] Making love spontaneously under the pine trees in a secluded woods, on a sailboat in the privacy of a quiet lagoon, or hurriedly in the back seat of a car gives richness and variety to a relationship. Conversely, people who find it necessary—perhaps because both partners live with their parents—to confine their lovemaking to such unappealing places as motel rooms often find that the setting gives their sexual relationship a somewhat degrading quality.

Various physical features can be as important in their own way as the general ambience of the setting. A waterbed, for example, gives quite different rhythms to lovemaking than a feather bed or a standard mattress. Showering or swimming together during or after lovemaking may contribute to the comfort and pleasure to be found in making love. For some lovers the haste of a clandestine affair seems particularly appetizing, whereas others relish the intimate leisure of a long Sunday afternoon with the telephone off the hook and no visitors expected.

The couple who have an enduring partnership and the ability to select a permanent place in which to make love have the opportunity to see to it that certain amenities are present in their setting. A bed that is firm and large enough for adequate movement without undue noise is usually desirable, although lovemaking on the floor of the study or living room after the children have gone to sleep is sometimes a refreshing alternative for married couples. Pillows that are full and able to provide support, should they be called upon, are helpful additions. A chair that is sturdy

Setting often makes a great deal of difference in how we express our feelings for one another. (Ken Karp)

enough to hold two people can add to the variety of positions to be enjoyed in intercourse. A great deal of effort can be put into making the bedroom of an ordinary apartment a much more comfortable and esthetically pleasing setting for lovemaking than it ordinarily is. This list of amenities that can enhance sexual relations could be extended indefinitely. The point is simply that where you make love does matter, so that efforts to improve the quality of the setting in which you make love generally will be amply rewarded.

DISCOVERING EACH OTHER

A great deal of the joy two people experience in coming together in a sexual encounter is the discovery of each other's bodies. In the last analysis we *are* our bodies. As George Downing observes, "Our emotions, our outer perceptions, our spiritual life, and even our conceptual understanding of the world around us all begin and end with this intimate shadowy mass which is our being."[9] The sense of touch is as important as the sense of sight in communicating pleasure. Indeed, our bodies are constantly communicat-

Discovering each other's body is a primary pleasure often much neglected in our more restricted styles of lovemaking. (Arthur Tress, Photo Researchers, Inc.)

ing, whether we are aware of it or not. One of the skills of lovemaking is making use of the sense of touch to create physical pleasure and excitement.

Exploration

Exploring the other's body heightens each person's awareness not only of the other but also of his or her own inner self. Touching can express tenderness, respect, understanding, trust, and of course, the sheer sense of mutual pleasure. When lovers caress, there is a fullness that can never be obtained through words. Touching and exploring each other can be an expression of deep self-giving, not simply a mechanical technique of arousal. But before this can become a reality, one must have developed some awareness of both oneself and one's partner.

Most of the time our bodies are covered and held in reserve. Lovers, though, come to each other without clothing. If they take this condition of nakedness as simply a convenient way of facilitating access to their sexual organs, they will miss out on the opportunity their intimacy provides for exploring each other through exploration of each other's bodies.

One's feelings about one's body are an important part of one's self-image. People who are not comfortable with their own bodies therefore find something threatening in the openness that is required for exploration and discovery. They tend to have a somewhat reserved attitude in their lovemaking, for their low self-estimates lead them to "hold back." Conversely, people who are at ease with their own bodies find it easier to be open and revealing with their partners. Often negative self-images are formed quite early in life, but a loving partner who convincingly conveys the sense of excitement he or she feels at discovering the partner's body can contribute greatly to repairing the damage done by low self-regard. A person who fears that he or she is undesirable often can be convinced otherwise by sincere expressions of desire.

Pleasuring

Sex clinics such as Masters and Johnson's are constantly treating people who are uncomfortable with each other as lovers. They do not know how to give each other pleasure, are fearful of their inadequacies, and come to the clinic to get help. An important part of the therapy Masters and Johnson prescribe for many sexual dysfunctions is called *pleasuring*. Basically, it is a simple means by which couples learn to become open to each other through touching. Initially, the couple is asked to engage in nongenital exploration. Commonly, the man rests against a pillowed headboard and the woman rests against him. If he is to give pleasure to her, she guides his exploring hands over her body and indicates by touch or sound what is pleasureable to her in his touching. Masters and Johnson describe the technique as follows:

> The partner who is pleasuring is committed first to do just that; give pleasure. At a second level in the experience, the giver is to explore his or her own component of personal pleasure in doing the touching—to experience and appreciate the sensuous dimensions of hard and soft, smooth and rough, warm and cool, qualities of texture and, finally the somewhat indescribable aura of physical receptivity expressed by the partner being pleasured. After a reasonable length of time . . . the partners are to exchange roles of pleasuring (giving) and being pleasured (getting), and then repeat the procedure in similar detail. [10]

They thus come to experience the pleasure of giving as well as that of receiving by becoming more attuned to each other. This technique makes sure couples learn to communicate with each other at a very basic level. It assumes something most couples do not—that an individual becomes an expert lover by discovering his or her partner as a unique individual with specific sexual desires and a body that experiences sexual pleasure in a specific way. This process of discovery depends on having a partner who is willing and able to respond to what is felt as pleasurable, who can say in effect, "I like that." This ability to respond openly to sexual stimuli is something many people have never learned because of their cultural conditioning.

The common assumption that men are supposed to know by some infallible instinct what pleases a woman sexually is grossly in error. Nor is it true that sexual expertise ought to be a man's responsibility. Both women and men are quite capable of developing their distinctive sexual tastes and communicating their desires to their partners. But effective communication of sexual desires requires considerable skill of both partners. Our cultural conditioning works against this communication by assuming that sexual expertise is primarily a man's domain and that he can readily discover how to please his partner even if she herself is unaware at one moment of what might please her a moment later. [11]

Pleasuring seems to be a good general technique for a couple who are discovering each other as lovers. It requires openness about oneself and one's body and willingness to provide the much-needed feedback that increases the pleasures of lovemaking. Many couples discover through pleasuring each other that their whole bodies can become "erogenous zones."

MAKING LOVE

Knowledge of one's own erogenous zones is essential if one is to move toward one's full capacity for sexual responsiveness. One learns sexual responsiveness through experimentation and experience in a process that begins with acceptance and knowledge of one's own body. The full flavor of sexual responsiveness is discovered only by a person who has developed "a sensuous enjoyment and appreciation for the sight, smell, taste, feel and use of [his or her] body in all its infinite capacities." [12]

Kissing

The erotic kiss, the most universal form of human lovemaking, has many variations. A kiss enables the lovers to taste as well as touch each other. In the intimacy of their embrace they can smell the fragrance of hair, perfume, and natural body odors. In a deep kiss the experience of penetrating and being penetrated becomes part of their awareness of each other. Light stroking, tentative tongue caressing, gently nibbling, and sucking are all part of their mutual exploration and discovery. With such a varied form of expression, sensitivity and timing become in themselves a show of responsiveness. Kissing can range over the entire body, greatly increasing the discovery and significantly stimulating both partners. The nape of the neck, the ears, the breasts, the palms of the hands, fingertips, thighs, feet, genitals—indeed any part of the body will respond to a lover's kisses. During this exploration lovers come to discover the pleasantness of their own natural body odors.

Some lovers find the genital kiss especially stimulating. Since the genitals are particularly sensitive to erotic stimulation, the genital kiss often proceeds to further exploration of the genital area. For some lovers such activities are psychologically very beneficial, for they encourage them to become intimate with parts of the body that the puritan strain in our tradition teaches us to regard as unclean and unacceptable. On the other hand, some people find oral-genital stimulation repulsive. But if the genitals are clean, there are no hygienic grounds for such repugnance.

Intercourse

Intercourse has many forms. Experimentation and discovery of new and satisfying positions enrich a couple's lovemaking and reveal different aspects of each partner. Taking the initiative, being dominant or submissive, being aggressive or tender, imaginative or creative—all are possible in the various positions of lovemaking. "Marriage must continually vanquish the monster that devours everything, the monster of habit," the French writer Honore de Balzac observed. Creative and imaginative couples who are free with each other can deal rather effectively with the monster of habit. The use of a variety of positions also provides a wide array of different sensations and can enable couples to continue their lovemaking in spite of pregnancy or various mild illnesses that might make intercourse in a particular position uncomfortable for one of the partners.

Although there are many variations in the positions couples can assume while making love, there are four basic positions on which one can improvise by rolling, sitting, or standing. There is no "normal" or "natural" position, although the so-called matrimonial or missionary position enjoys wide acceptance in the United States. The four basic positions in lovemaking can be varied almost indefinitely to suit the couple's tastes. The variations are very subtle and cannot possibly be described adequately in terms of simple mechanics and techniques. They must be arrived at through exploration, discovery, and sensitive communication between loving partners.

Face-to-Face, Man-Above. The face-to-face, man-above position is most commonly employed in the United States, but its use tends to be rare in many non-Western cultures. In this position—also known as the "matrimonial" or "missionary" position—the woman lies on her back with her legs apart, sometimes with her knees bent. The man, lying above her and supporting himself on his elbows and knees, can easily achieve intromission. Once his penis has been inserted, he is basically in control of the couple's body movements because the weight of his body on hers tends to restrict her movement to some extent. It is important for him to keep in contact with the clitoris. This may be accomplished by putting pressure on the pubic bone or by the woman's adjusting her position so that the clitoris is stimulated by the tensions in the clitoral hood. (Indeed, the clitoris is indirectly stimulated by the tensions in the clitoral hood in almost all positions of intercourse, including rear entry.)

Although, as noted earlier, the woman's body movements are somewhat restricted in this position, she is relatively free to vary the position of her legs. During intercourse she may pull her legs up toward her shoulders, lock them around her partner's body, place her heels behind his knees to give her more control over her pelvic thrusting, or place her legs either inside or outside of his. By putting a pillow under her lower back and drawing her knees up toward her shoulders, she can receive the deepest penetration. Thus, by changing the position of her legs she can alter the depth of penetration, relax, change the rhythm of the thrusting, and alter the amount of tension on the clitoral hood.

The advantages of this position are that it is one of the easiest to learn and one of the most adaptable. In addition, because the partners are facing each other they may express their feelings with their eyes and erotic kissing. This is also the position in which couples are most likely to conceive children because of the proper pooling of the ejaculate in the vagina. To increase the possibilities of conception, the woman should remain in this position after intercourse and the man should not withdraw hurriedly.

There are drawbacks to this position, however. The man's weight can be a burden for the woman, who is also hampered in her movements, particularly the movements of her pelvis. What is more, because he must support himself, he is not free to caress, fondle, and stimulate his partner.

Face-to-Face, Woman-Above. The woman-above position provides a great deal more freedom for the woman. In this position she can control and vary the speed of the couple's movement and the depth of penetration. Clitoral contact is frequently more intense in this position, which gives the woman primary control over this important source of stimulation. It is said that this position is less sexually stimulating to men, yet it does allow the man to be more relaxed. He also has easier access to his partner's body and is able to see, touch, caress, and kiss many more areas of her body than in the man-above position. Because she normally can rest her entire weight on him— whereas in the man-above position, his weight may be too much for her to support comfortably—she is equally free. By the same token, the man's body movements are not restricted as much by the woman's weight as the woman's are by the man's weight in the man-above position. Thus, the man frequently is able to delay ejaculation longer in this position.

The woman may, if she wishes, lie full length against the man with her legs inside or outside of his, attaining a fuller sense of body contact. Or she may more or less sit astride him. In this approach the man also may vary his position. By resting on his elbows, he may raise himself closer to her body. By raising his legs, he can provide his partner with a backrest.

An advantage of this position is that many women find it easier to experience orgasm. On the other hand, there are certain disadvantages that appear to be caused by psychological factors. With the woman on top, some men feel threatened by appearing to be placed in a passive or subordinate position. There are certain indications, however, that this attitude is far less common than it used to be.

Face-to-Face, Side Position. The face-to-face, side position offers the opportunity for mutual control of body movements during intercourse. The couple lie on their sides facing each other. Often this position is arrived at by rolling from the man-above position. A thoughtful couple who plan ahead will have the freedom of their arms, legs, and hands after they have rolled over. They then have an infinite variety of opportunities for touching, caressing, and exploring. Because this is the most relaxing position for both partners, it is often possible to engage in intercourse for long periods in this fashion. After intercourse in this position, a couple can lie together in the warmth of each other's bodies for some time and may even fall asleep without separating.

A variation of this position is recommended by Masters and Johnson, who encourage couples to try it because it permits the woman to vary her pelvis thrusting with more ease while at the same time allowing the man great ejaculatory control.[13] Despite the fact that this position may be difficult to get into for inexperienced couples, it has the advantage of neither partner's having to support the weight of the other. This position is especially advantageous if one partner is considerably taller than the other. Although penetration is normally shallower and the movements less active, the leisure and tenderness normally associated with this position make it desirable.

Rear Entry Position. Because animals typically copulate in a rear entry position, many people feel this is an inappropriate position for human beings.[14] Nevertheless, this position can offer a great deal of pleasure to both partners. Many variations are possible: the woman sitting on the man's lap with her back to him; the woman lying on her stomach or kneeling; or both partners lying on their sides. The rear entry position offers the man greater freedom to caress the woman's breasts, clitoris, back, buttocks, legs, and almost all of her upper body. It also offers a wide variety of depths of penetration, depending on the variation employed. As the couple move from a distended position to a more seated position, the depth of penetration increases. Even in variations that offer only slight penetration, some women find great pleasure in the stimulation of the introitus, and either partner is able to compensate manually for any clitoral stimulation that is lacking. The position is restful in most of its variants, and although there is lack of eye contact, many of the other satisfactions of this position can compensate for this lack. In the rear entry position the man can massage and caress his partner's back with much greater ease than in any other position.

Afterglow. Caring partners do not simply end their lovemaking perfunctorily after orgasm. Part of the great joy of lovemaking comes from

Lovemaking is also caring for each other in the little things of life. (Susan Rosenberg, Photo Researchers, Inc.)

bathing in its afterglow. Being together, recognizing what has happened to each other, caressing, lying in the warmth of each other's bodies are all part of the total experience of loving—a feeling that was captured by the poet Dylan Thomas when he wrote, "Let me lie shipwrecked between thy thighs." Less dramatically, the aftermath of orgasm may merge into foreplay and the cycle of lovemaking may be continued after an interlude. Thinking about lovemaking that has ended and anticipating lovemaking that is yet to come is a vital part of a partnership.

Lovemaking Roles

In the past much lovemaking has been tied up with our culture's understanding of masculine and feminine roles. Western culture traditionally has ascribed dominance to males and submissiveness to females, but today there is evidence suggesting that this sort of role stereotyping can be very crippling to the art of lovemaking.[15] A man and a woman in partnership should be free to define their own roles in terms of their own needs and the needs of their partners. Fortunately, there are some indications that this is becoming possible for an increasing number of people—thanks in no small part to the efforts of the women's movement, which has succeeded in making large numbers of men and women sensitive to the problems created by restrictive definitions of sex roles.

NOTES

1. E. Barbara Hariton, "The Sexual Fantasies of Women," *Psychology Today* (October 1977): 43.
2. Ricardo Barros, *Sexual Fantasy* (London: Luxor Press, 1970), p. 47.
3. Mark Twain, *Letters From the Earth* (Greenwich, Conn.: Fawcett, 1963), p. 44.
4. John Money, *Love and Lovesickness: The Science of Sex, Gender Difference, and Pair-Bonding* (Baltimore: The Johns Hopkins University Press, 1980), p. 101.
5. Alex Comfort, *The Joy of Sex* (New York: Crown, 1972), p. 15.
6. Gina Allen and Clement Martin, *Intimacy: Sensitivity, Sex and the Art of Love* (Chicago: Contemporary Books, 1971), pp. 1–2. By permission.
7. William H. Masters and Virginia Johnson, *Human Sexual Inadequacy* (Boston: Little, Brown, 1970), p. 13.
8. Setting has always been an important factor in human lovemaking—in contrast to animal behavior, which is much less affected by this concern. See Bronislaw Malinowski, *The Sexual Life of Savages* (New York: Harcourt, Brace & World, 1929), and Margaret Mead, *Sex and Temperament* (New York: Mentor Books, 1952).
9. George Downing, *The Message Book* (New York: Random House, 1972), p. 134.

10. Masters and Johnson, p. 73.
11. Ibid., p. 87.
12. Ibid., p. 76.
13. Ibid., pp. 310–11.
14. In the Kinsey study, *Sexual Behavior in the Human Male* (Philadelphia: W. B. Saunders, 1953), only about 15 percent of the respondents reported having used this position.
15. Masters and Johnson, pp. 159–60.

Today a female can do almost anything she wants to do without damaging her own sense of femininity. Limits imposed on her are apt to be pragmatic rather than social. . . . The real factor that is being obscured by the clamor of the women's lib movement is that women are far more emancipated than are men. The one bright spot is that men do appear to be shaking off a number of their inhibiting patterns without any sense of loss of masculinity. . . . We are men and women, but first we are human beings and have human roles to play as human beings rather than as males or females. I think society should welcome the achievement of such attitudes, for they would nullify the effects of militancy and hostility between the sexes.

—Mary S. Calderone

10 Gender Roles and Social Interaction

When we consider what it means to be a man or a woman in our society, we confront a host of issues that cluster around what seems at first to be such a simple distinction: Women are different from men. We must consider how they are different and—most important—what we are to make of these differences.

The most pressing social issue is the demand that women and men be treated equally as citizens before the law, on the job, at home, in school, and in all walks of life. The Constitution did not really accomplish this when it declared "All men are created equal . . ." (Note that it did not say all persons are created equal or all men are created identical.) Equality does not imply identity. It calls for a fair and just recognition of the dignity, privilege, and power of women as persons in spite of whatever differences may exist between the genders. And, of course, we have made a great deal out of the differences between women and men in the past. Some would argue that we have cultivated these differences in order to establish women as the subordinate sex.

Freud declared "Anatomy is destiny," and in so doing affirmed more than the obvious fact that male anatomy differs from female. He declared that this anatomical difference affects the person's whole life in profound ways. We must engage the world by means of bodies that have distinctive physical characteristics which undoubtedly affect how we think, feel, intuit, and experience the world with our senses—as well as how we are treated by others. Those who have undergone the psychosocial, physiosurgical transformation of gender tell us what we know from another perspective. Male bodies feel different from female—from the "inside" as well as from the "outside."

The process of normal psychosexual differentiation from conception to adulthood through which we become male or female is not unambiguously determined by genes. Its product is not definable in terms of a simple dichotomy, male or female. There are many mixed cases. Anatomy may seem like destiny because Western societies have, by and large, reinforced the anatomical differences with social expectations about what it means—or should mean—to be masculine or feminine. We have discounted all those whose anatomy is mixed or ambiguous, and discriminated against all those who have failed to live up to our social expectations of behavior appropriate to men and women. These "deviants" now demand justice, and all those who have chafed under the rigid expectations of traditional gender roles seek greater flexibility.

The matter is engaged in yet another dimension when we strive to fulfill our own potential. Whatever the structure of our anatomy, our self-actualization demands the acceptance of both the masculine and the feminine "within" us. Freud thought the phallus was a symbollic expression of the penis and the natural possession of the male, but Jung saw that women must also make use of such an instrument. The world of the soul as expressed in dream, fantasy, and mythology distinguishes between maleness and femaleness, but not on the basis of anatomy. We encounter this symbolic distinction in a somewhat different mode whenever we learn the gender of words in a foreign language.

What we will do in this chapter is provide some insight into these issues without resolving them. We begin with a brief discussion of psychosexual differentiation, move to a consideration of some of the social psychological differences between women and men in the light of the need for equality, and conclude with an account of some recent issues in self-actualization pertaining to the "soft" male.

MASCULINITY AND FEMININITY

Men and women are different, although exactly why they are different remains something of a mystery. The Bible says, "God created them male and female," and for some people this pronouncement has closed the question for good: Men and women are different because they are born that way and that's all there is to it.[1]

Our sense of the nature of these differences includes the classification of the characteristics we identify as masculine and feminine. Every word, every action, every nuance of behavior is affected by this elemental system of classification. When a mother says to her young son, "Little boys don't cry," she is telling him something very important about what it means to be a boy. When she says to him, "Little boys don't hit little girls," she is saying something to him about how men behave toward women. When a mother feels distressed about her daughter's desire to play baseball instead of playing with dolls, she communicates her sense of what constitutes the appropriate development of a woman. When a little girl is interrupted in a brawl with her brother and told, "Little girls shouldn't fight," she gets another clue as to how appropriate feminine behavior differs from appropriate masculine behavior. In all, it seems safe to say that no aspect of our behavior remains unaffected by these expectations of what is properly masculine and what is properly feminine.

As we grow up, these expectations become the "oughts" of our behavior. Generally speaking, we measure ourselves against these social standards, only rarely questioning their validity or appropriateness. Our feelings of self-worth and our comfort in relating to others depend in large part on how we evaluate ourselves by these standards. And yet more and more people are coming to suspect that these standards are neither biologically determined nor socially necessary. In other places and at other times in history, masculinity and femininity have been understood in radically different ways. The discovery that masculinity and femininity are not unalterable characteristics of human nature frees us to enter into the process of changing them to better meet our needs today. It allows us to treat others as human beings first, with human roles to play according to their individual abilities, and then as women or men with certain gender-related differences.

Psychosexual Differentiation

The process by which we become male, female, or mixed is called **psychosexual differentiation**.[2] It begins at conception and continues through to the establishment of an adult gender identity. Although there is a certain powerfully established predisposition for the adult gender identity to be congruent with genetic gender, (that is, that an individual with a 46XY genotype is likely to have a masculine adult gender identity), the genetic inheritance does not determine this. Indeed, the primary role of the gene is to determine the way in which the gonads develop. Under the influence of the H-Y antigen of the XY genotype (male), the gonads develop into testes beginning about the sixth week after conception. Without this antigen (in the normal development of the XX genotype, female), the gonads develop into ovaries after another six weeks.

After the development of the gonads into testes or ovaries, the further differentiation of the embryo is largely under the control of the hormones they excrete. Without any gonadal tissue at all, the embryo will develop into a female. (The Eve principle states that nature's first preference is to develop a female.) The androgens secreted from the testes in the male and the MIS (the Mullerian inhibiting substance) must be added to the embryo's prenatal environment if a male is to develop a penis. (The Adam principle states that if a male is to be developed, something must be added to the prenatal environment at appropriate stages of development.)

The Adam principle applies not only to anatomical development of the genitalia, but also to the development of certain neural pathways in the brain—particularly in the hypothalamus. A genetic female developing in an androgen-rich environment, for example, can become a kind of "tomboy" as a result of the effect of the androgen on her brain structure.

The original gonads are hermaphroditic, and it is possible for nature to produce mixed combinations of traits at each stage of prenatal and postnatal development. We normally apply the term *hermaphrodite* to the 1 to 2 percent of all babies who are born with mixed genitalia. We may not recognize many of the other mixtures until later in puberty or perhaps even adulthood, as in the case of the transsexual. At birth, the normal genitals provide a cue to everyone handling the infant that it should be treated in ways appropriate to its gender. Most of these expectations are informal convention, but they create observable differences in the ways in which adults interact with their babies, sometimes even in the case of parents who are trying hard not to sex-stereotype their baby.

Our Common Understandings

The process of changing our common understandings of appropriate sex role behavior is very complex. In contemporary American society much of the impetus for change comes from the women's movement, which calls for radical changes in how men and women are treated. This call is a plea for redefinition of what it means to be a woman or a man. To better understand why such changes are felt to be necessary, let us look at our common expectations about masculine and feminine behavior. When these expectations are subject to change with changing circumstances and attitudes we will call them *gender roles*; when we want to suggest they are sometimes held rigidly in spite of information or experiences that contradict them, we will call them *stereotypes*.[3]

"It's a Boy!" Both men and women in our society tend to have very strong expectations of what it means to be a man. Masculinity means aggressiveness, self-assertion, roughness of manner, fearlessness, adventurousness, rationality, and the ability to control one's emotions. In multimedia advertisements men are shown in the great outdoors, engaging in dangerous sports, fighting against nature, enduring physically strenuous activities, and winning out. They are interested in tools and have highly developed mechanical skills. They are oriented toward rational pursuits such as the sciences, mathematics, and engineering. They are competitive beings—in sports, in business, and in every endeavor they engage in. Finally, men are task-oriented and see their worth in the world in terms of what they can produce.

Men generally accept these expectations and try to fulfill them. They are encouraged to do so by the people around them, who tend to reward them for becoming more "masculine" and to punish them for failing to develop in this direction. Because men are supposed to be rational, achievement-oriented, and competitive, for example, they are urged to become professionals. As a result men dominate the professions, and their

Within the past decade more women than men are entering college—a fact that will have an effect on our gender-role expectations. (Liamute E. Druskis)

position of dominance gives them the power to encourage other males to follow this path and to discourage females who are foolhardy enough to try.[4] Thus, men are $7\frac{1}{2}$ times more likely than women to hold doctorates and twice as likely to have master's degrees.[5] In 1981, however, women constituted 50.2% of all persons enrolled in college.[6] In this way the common understanding of what masculinity means not only shapes the personal lives of individuals, but also produces the conditions that permit perpetuation of the stereotype.

The extent to which stereotypes permeate our culture is reflected in the responses men and women give on personality tests. Men score higher than women in such traits as dominance, suspiciousness, sophistication, experimentation, and self-sufficiency.[7] The fact that many men develop in conformity with the stereotype—that is what gives the stereotype both its validity and its force—tends to make life difficult for those who do not match the standard picture. Thus, the man who finds pleasure, excitement, and fulfillment in artistic endeavors may find it difficult to gain acceptance among people who assume he is not "masculine" enough. In his formative years he will have to deal with his parents and his peers, who may be confused and troubled by his interest in the arts. He may even begin to wonder whether there is something wrong with him, because all the cues he receives say he is not behaving in the prescribed manner. If he persists in following his own line of development, he is likely to run into problems with women, who also may assume that a man who prefers painting to football is not adequately "manly." Whatever our personal abilities and preferences might be, there is growing evidence that we are evaluated in terms of assumed gender differences.[8] This is stereotyping in its classic expression.

To be sure, the situation is not as simple as this picture may suggest. Numerous exceptions come to mind. The poet Dylan Thomas succeeded in being accepted as "masculine" in spite of his poetry because Irishmen are supposed to be somewhat romantic, and besides, Thomas was notorious as a hard drinker and barroom brawler. Sports such as gymnastics place a high value on both strength and gracefully coordinated body movement. Male gymnasts thus gain recognition by mixing what are commonly thought to be masculine and feminine traits.

These exceptions, though, only reinforce the general principle that for a man success in interpersonal relations—including both sexual relations and business relations—often depends on conformity to the stereotype. What is more, a process of natural selection is at work here: Successful men tend to conform to their society's expectations; because of their success, they serve as role models encouraging the next generation to conform; and so on. In short, stereotypes work as a sort of vicious circle: The more people conform to them, the more power they have to enforce conformity; and the more power they have, the more people conform to the stereotype.

Fortunately, the strength of a vicious circle is also its weakness, for once a stereotype starts to crumble, the process of collapse is self-accelerating. For example, if you are the only boy in your high school who likes reading Shakespeare, you are likely to keep quiet about it. If a few others join you, it becomes less necessary to hide this "unmanly" taste, and each successive defection from the conventional role makes it that much easier for the next boy to break rank. Indeed, precisely this process seems to be in operation in America today, largely under the pressure of the women's movement, which has been insisting on the absurdity of our stereotypes. Whereas twenty years ago most men would have been afraid to be seen doing the family wash at the laundromat, today the number of men who are willing to undertake a fair share of the household chores is increasing, and as it becomes apparent to more and more men that doing a load of wash does not cost them their virility, the stereotypical belief that such tasks are "women's work" will become harder to maintain.

"It's a Girl!" Unfortunately, our stereotypes of women are little more than the opposite of our stereotypes of men. This limitation to some degree reveals our lack of appreciation of maleness and femaleness, for ideally we should be able to describe what the two sexes are like without feeling compelled to compare one with the other.

Our common conception of femininity is that women are compassionate, sympathetic, tender, fastidious, esthetic, emotionally sensitive, passive, and beautiful. They are in touch with their emotions and are permitted, even urged, to express them. (Of course, they are then told that they are too "emotional" to hold most of the important jobs.) Their greatest skills are those of sociability, popularity, and attractiveness; they are most interested in domestic affairs. Paradoxically, unattractive women sometimes find it easier to enter the competitive "man's world" of business and professional life. Men can easily cope with the fact that a "plain" girl might want to enroll at MIT and become an engineer: They assume she is "compensating" for her inability to succeed as a woman. But when a pretty young woman makes this decision men feel threatened by it and are at a loss to explain it: "Why should a lovely young thing like you want to be an engineer? You could have any man you wanted?"

Our common conception of women pictures them as homemakers, helpmates, mothers, and adornments to the household. If a woman does have an interest outside the home, it is assumed she will be engaged in the helping professions—caring for the young, the helpless, the aged, and the infirm. As far as sex is concerned, it is often assumed that women do not know much about it and are not particularly interested in it. They are expected to come to marriage as virgins and to participate in sex at the behest of the male.[9] In sex as in everything else, the woman's role is to be long-suffering, patient, and supportive of the goals established by her husband.

As we have seen in the case of the stereotype of masculinity, there is evidence to suggest that the same kind of self-fulfilling prophecy is at work in the case of femininity. Thus, on personality tests women score higher than men in outgoingness, sensitivity, conscientiousness, eccentricity, and excitability.

Few of the married women who work, do so in such "masculine" ways as this woman. (A.T.&T. Co. Photo Center)

More than half of all married women who are living with their husbands work.[10] On the surface this would seem to indicate that a major portion of women are career-oriented. In fact, however, most of these women work to help their husbands provide for their families. Rather than breaking the stereotype, they are simply extending their maintenance function, normally exercised within the family, to work outside the home. They work in service or clerical jobs rather than in the professions. Those who had appropriate training before marriage are likely to work in teaching, nursing, or social work—occupations that are simply extensions of the commonly prescribed female role.

There is no denying that women are, in effect, forced to spend the majority of their time taking care of their families. A thoughtless response would be to say they are doing this because they are naturally more dependent, compassionate, sensitive, and concerned about people. This simply is not true. Women tend to be weak in "masculine" traits because any sign of competitiveness, rationality, and so forth in a woman is discouraged. A woman who is intelligent, competent, attractive, and achievement-oriented will find these qualities to be liabilities rather than assets. She will have to deal with the misgivings of her friends and acquaintances.

If she chooses to exploit these qualities, she may have to do so with little help from models whom she knows personally. She can emulate famous women, but she is likely to find very few friends who can share her interests and her understanding of what it means to be a woman. Breaking the stereotype and becoming a unique person can be costly when the people around you accept the stereotype without question. A woman who attempts to do so may have a particularly difficult problem finding a man who can accept her as the intelligent, competitive, achievement-oriented person she is.

Our Introduction to Sex Roles

We are introduced to sex roles from the moment we take our first breath. In most instances the primary group in which this learning takes place is the family. The amount of time, energy, and interaction that takes place between a mother and her child or a father and his child constitutes the child's basic learning experience. From a very early age, a young girl has her mother as the model of femininity. Normally, she will spend long periods with her mother in intimate situations. The passive, dependent role she is expected to play as a wife is not too difficult from her early childhood ex-

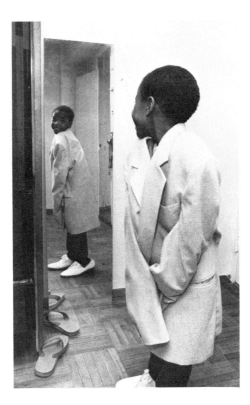

Gender roles are deeply impressed upon us by subtle factors in our development. (Ken Karp)

periences, for it duplicates not only her mother's role as her father's wife, but also her own role as a dependent member of the family.

Men become masculinized in quite a different way. Because fathers tend to be absent from the family for considerable amounts of time, boys are often influenced by images of masculinity presented in the mass media or by their peers.[11] What is more, whereas girls experience "femininity" (passive dependency) as something they have always had, boys have to achieve a masculine identity. A boy has to break away from his dependence on his mother and develop such "masculine" characteristics as aggressiveness, independence, and self-assertiveness. But girls whose mothers are working are likely not only to have less stereotypic views of sex roles, but also to be more aggressive than daughters of nonworking mothers.[12]

By the age of 20 months, girls and boys in our society know the appropriate selection of toys for their sex.[13] They also can classify adult items as appropriate to one sex or the other. By the age of 6 to 8 years, children can tell us about their concepts of what is masculine or feminine. Boys are seen as stronger, larger, darker, dirtier, more angular, and more dangerous than girls. These early images are consistent with our adult images of masculinity and femininity. The fact that these stereotypes appear so early helps convince us that they are natural. In fact, however, there is no biological inevitability that turns an infant with a penis into an aggressive, self-assertive, and independent adult while an infant with a vulva remains permanently in a state of relatively passive dependency. A very important step in achieving equality between the genders will be taken when men assume equal responsibility with women for the care of infants and small children.[14]

THE SOCIAL SHAPING OF SEXUAL BEHAVIOR

The awareness of sexual attraction arises in different contexts for men and women and is expressed in different ways. Among males there is an emphasis on doing things together apart from females, so men tend to learn about sex from their peers to a greater extent than women do. As boys get older, they show increasing interest in the techniques of sexual seduction and sex play.[15] Girls are interested in sex also, but their conversation most frequently centers on the problems raised by the sexual advances of their boyfriends in dating situations, the threat of public exposure, expressed regret for sexual transgressions, or the justification of sexual activities as an expression of love. Conversation among boys tends to consist of boastful accounts of sexual conquests.[16] The conversation of girls therefore tends to reinforce a romantic view of sex, while boys encourage each other to see sex as a competitive game. Sex slang is more common among males than among females, and such slang expressions are frequently derogatory toward women.[17]

These basic differences in our approach to sexuality arise quite "naturally" out of the experiences we have with other people. Men act out their sexuality in terms of personal gratification and conquest. Sex becomes, for them, a further means of proving their masculinity. Women discover their sexual responsiveness in the context of a romantic relationship. Because of the difference between these two approaches to sexual attraction, there is considerable likelihood of conflict and misunderstanding. As Richard Udry observes:

> Sex emerges as something which boys "do to" girls, which girls "let them have" or which boys cheat girls out of. Accounts of boys' early coital experience with girls show the boys have been unconcerned with and largely unaware of the girls' own behavior. . . . It is sexual conquest.[18]

Changing Attitudes

A number of studies have documented changing attitudes toward sex role stereotypes. In general, they support the claim that we are moving toward a more egalitarian view of the relationship between men and women. One study found that there has been a considerable movement toward more egalitarian role definitions between 1964 and 1974, with the changes occurring equally among the various social classes.[19] Most researchers agree there has been considerable redefinition of women's work roles, but there is considerable disagreement about the extent to which changes have occurred in their domestic role.[20] Alan Bayer concludes that a sexist ideology is still supported by a substantial number of young adults. The sexist is likely to be male (although a substantial number of women still endorse traditional roles), black, older in comparison to the rest of the college peer group, from a lower-class rural background, less academically successful, and inclined to study business, health studies, or education.[21] Finally, it should be noted that traditional sex roles have once again been adopted in the *kibbutzim*—at one time the source of Israel's most vocal advocates of equal rights for women.[22] Schlesinger concludes that as the division of labor in the *kibbutz* community becomes more complex, "members . . . must examine its current structure and reevaluate its goals if they want to preserve its unique identity and rekindle its ideal of equality between the sexes."[23] Thus, while there has undoubtedly been a trend toward greater egalitarianism, it is not all-pervasive in scope, nor is it clear, if we take seriously the example of the *kibbutz*, that such a trend will continue.

Research Bias

Some critics have accused researchers who study male and female differences of perpetuating, rather than weakening, social stereotypes. These critics insist that so-called masculine and feminine traits are outgrowths of these stereotypes, not vice versa, and that people should be studied as people rather than as members of one sex or the other.[24] The vocabulary of social science also sometimes encourages stereotypical treatment of male and female differences. For example, the term *mothering* strongly implies that only women can manifest the trait in question and that *fathering* is a different sort of skill, whereas *warmth* can be manifested by either sex. Researchers speak of "father absence" and "mother deprivation," when in fact children need both parents equally. Ordinarily, this bias results from the importance attached to the reproductive role of the female. If the researcher is inclined to think of this role as very important, then social data will tend to be interpreted stereotypically.

Finally, in our society sex stereotypes are linked to our assumptions of what it means to be a good member of a family. This association gives the stereotypes added support because many people still believe that the survival of the nuclear family is of critical importance. The traditional roles are linked to the effort to establish the **nuclear family** as the basic building block of our society. Such an understanding of the family is similar to the nineteenth-century physicist's understanding of the atom as the elemental building block of the universe. With the coming of relativity theory, patterns of interdependence, rather than universal particles or laws, became more appropriate concepts. Such an advance has not yet generally occurred in the social sciences.

TOWARD GREATER FLEXIBILITY

The findings of researchers have clear social implications for developing relationships. Young people learn about their own sexuality in heterosexual relationships before marriage. If the Masters and Johnson findings about women's sexual capacity and its repression under the double standard are correct, and if indeed we value sexuality and what it can bring to our relationships, then the destructive aspects of the double standard must be overcome. This means at the very least that women must have the same freedom to develop their sexuality as men. Indeed, all people should have the freedom to adhere to the sexual code that best fits their developing sexuality as they understand it.[25] Such freedom depends on informed awareness of the costs, the promises, and the risks of any choice that is made.

Gender roles, we know from experience, describe much of what we know about masculinity and femininity. The concept of gender roles, however, is misused when it is taken to mean not merely a reasonable description of what is, but an assertion about what ought to be. In their quest to find general social laws, social scientists are likely to be quite conservative in their attitude toward change and quite insensitive to human needs. Others in the field are genuinely disturbed by the conservative use to which gender role theory is put; they object to the conversion of descriptive material into general laws of social behavior.

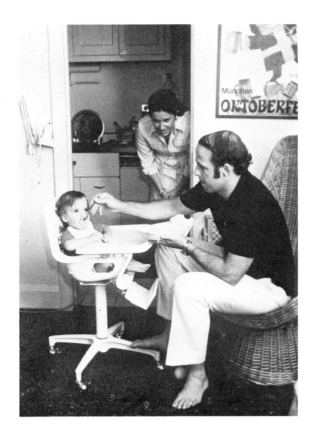

Men are beginning to assume more responsibility in caring for younger children, but they have a long way to go before they assume as much responsibility as do women. (M. Faust, United Nations)

The man who knows there is more to his existence than aggressive competitiveness may very well suffer from the application of stereotypes. The woman who knows there is much to be lost in a state of passive dependency is faced with an uphill struggle against those who would enforce conformity to the stereotypes. Such people know that gender roles need not be the standards by which they measure themselves. Why, for example, should male children be socialized for independence and self-assertion while females are left in a passive, dependent state? Other cultures, such as that of the Tchambuli, reverse this process. Tchambuli men are passive, dependent, sensistive, and artistic; Tchambuli women are aggressive, self-assertive, and independent. Such cross-cultural data indicate that there is no one "natural" way of defining masculinity and femininity.[26]

Some social scientists approach the study of gender roles by looking at their function.[27] They see, for example, that a woman is called upon to keep the family living peacefully together. This means that her major role is to be the "expressive leader" in the household. The man is identified as the provider and the person who is concerned primarily with the economic well-being of the family. He is therefore described as the "instrumental leader" of the family. But the notion of instrumental and expressive leadership comes out of the study of small groups. Researchers have found that small groups that are able to accomplish the tasks for which they are established seem to need these two types of leadership roles. Social scientists assume, therefore, that the family also needs these two types of roles. But the family is anything but a task-oriented small group. Even if these two roles were needed, it is not reasonable to assume that the roles should be assigned on the basis of gender within the family when they are not assigned in this way in small groups. Indeed, in small groups the two roles are not even mutually exclusive; not only can men be the expressive leaders and women the task leaders, but the same individual can serve in both capacities or change roles in the course of the group's life. We need the same kind of flexibility within the family.

Masculine Emancipation

Since the male of the species has generally been the apparent benefactor of a patriarchial tradition that has subordinated women, it may seem strange to talk about the emancipation of men. And yet, as Mary Calderone pointed out in the epigraph to this chapter, "women are far more emancipated than men." The white middle-class male over 30 who has been stereotyped as the aggressor or at least the benefactor of this heritage of male domination has less of a role model today than his female counterpart. The social and economic factors that have supported his role and that he has largely taken for granted are eroding, albeit more slowly than many women would prefer. The Marlboro Man is still around, but he is even more an image of the past. What does it mean to be a man in today's world?

Many middle-class men are discovering their expressive or "soft" side. They can express feelings when appropriate without feeling a sense of shame. The value of cooperation and community over rugged individualism is appreciated. They are becoming ecologically sensitive and socially responsible as well as democratic in their dealings with their families. These are positive accomplishments and a sign of emancipation. But, it appears to some observers, what is lacking is a sense of decisiveness and—more fundamentally—energy. The macho male, for all his shortcomings, seemed in admirable possession of these "masculine" traits, and the "soft" male is struggling to discover how to manifest these traits in new ways.

A story that is a favorite among Zen monks illustrates the predicament. A very famous monk—perhaps it was Basho—came upon a village that was being terrorized by a huge serpent. Whenever any villager set out on the trail to the spring from which the village obtained most of its water, she or he was set upon by the serpent. Many lost their lives. In response to the pleading of the villagers, Basho agreed to go to the serpent and try to pacify it. He approached the lair of the serpent with caution. The great snake came out to meet him, hissing terribly and belching fire from its nostrils, but Basho held his ground and soon converted the serpent, leaving the village in peace.

A few years afterward, Basho returned this way and found the serpent battered and bruised by the wayside. "What ails you, O snake?" asked Basho. "Oh most holy one," said the serpent, "since you left I have lived after your teachings and have been compassionate in all my ways, but the villagers have taken advantage of me. They take great joy in bringing their children out to see the great snake that once terrified their village and the children delight in hitting me with rocks and spitting at me. They have beaten me without mercy and I am about to die of such compassion."

Basho looked at the snake in pity and said: "Poor snake, when I told you that you must live without violence, I did not say that you must give up your terrible hissing." In the imagery of the Grail quest, the myths suggest that we must always be able to "flash our swords," even when sworn not to use them. The energy and decisiveness symbolized by the flashing of a sword, aped by the macho male and corrupted in the foreign policy of "carrying a big stick," is what the "soft" male lacks for a more complete emancipation. Modern women have discovered how to do this better than modern men, and the men are just beginning to recognize their shortcoming and in their consciousness-raising groups set out to do something about it.

SUMMARY

Anatomy has seemed like destiny for the better part of this century because our society has reinforced biological differences between the genders with social expectations that have simply assumed women to be the subordinate sex because of their natural desire to be penetrated. Such social expectations are subtly built into the way in which we raise our children, even when we try consciously not to discriminate between boys and girls.

But as we come to understand the process of psychosexual differentiation—the process by which we become male or female—we discover that from the moment of conception the developing embryo is affected by its environment (prenatal and postnatal) in such a way as to provide many mixed cases. Gender is not simply a dichotomous phenomenon determined by the genes, as was once thought.

Along with our changing expectations of gender roles, we are redefining sexuality as something both men and women can enjoy. The baby boom generation's parents thought of sex as something that a boy did to a girl, appropriately only after marriage, and that good girls and loving wives were inexperienced and generally uninterested in sex. Such attitudes have biased the research of even the most diligent.

In seeking greater flexibility in gender role definition, we can find examples from other societies that can assure us we are not somehow violating human nature. Both men and women can be expressive as well as instrumental. As Mary Calderone observed, "women are more emancipated than men" in their understanding of new possibilities of gender role. The "soft" male must discover how to be decisive and energetic without falling into the macho mode.

NOTES

1. Genesis 1:27.
2. John Money, *Love, and Love Sickness: The Science of Sex, Gender Difference, and Pair Bonding* (Baltimore: The Johns Hopkins University Press, 1980), pp. 15–42.
3. John Money and Patricia Tucker, *Sexual Signatures: On Being a Man and a Woman* (Boston: Little, Brown, 1975), pp. 11–12ff, provide a delightful description of these stereotypes and relate them to a theory of psychosexual differentiation that is very readable and quite informative.
4. U.S. Bureau of the Census, *Statistical Abstract: 1982–83* (Washington, D.C.: U.S. Government Printing Office, 1983). In 1972, women made up 39.3 percent of "professional, technical, and kindred" workers, and in 1977, 42.6 percent. However, most of these women were employed as accountants, computer specialists, librarians, personnel and labor relations workers, nurses, health technologists, and teachers. They were especially poorly represented as engineers, lawyers and judges, life and physical scientists, chemists, physicians, social scientists, and religious workers.
5. Richard J. Udry, *The Social Context of Marriage*, 2nd ed. (New York: Harper & Row, 1971), p. 33.
6. *Statistical Abstract: 1982–83*, p. xx.
7. Udry, p. 34.
8. Eleanor E. Maccoby, *Social Development* (New York: Harcourt Brace Jovanovich, 1980).
9. This component of the stereotype is changing rapidly, especially for college-educated women. Such a stereotype best fits working-class women today.
10. *Statistical Abstract: 1982–83*, p. 34.
11. Udry, p. 67.
12. Shirley M. Miller, "Effects of Maternal Employment on Sex Role Perception, Interests and Self-Esteem in Kindergarten Girls," *Developmental Psychology* (May 1975): 405–6.
13. Greta Fein et al. "Sex Stereotypes and Preference in the Toy Choices of 20-Month Old Boys and Girls," *Developmental Psychology*, (July 1975): 527–28.
14. Dorothy Dinnerstein, *The Mermaid and the Minotaur* (New York: Harper & Row, 1976); Nancy Chodorow, *The Reproduction of Mothering* (Berkeley: University of California Press, 1978).
15. Winston Ehrman, "Premarital Dating Behavior," in Harold Christensen, ed., *The Marriage Handbook* (Chicago: Rand McNally, 1967), p. 339.
16. Ibid., p. 340. See also Donald L. Grummon and Andrew M. Barclay, eds. *Sexuality: A Search for Perspective* (New York: Van Nostrand Reinhold, 1971). p. 76.

17. Nancy G. Kutner and Donna Brogan "An Investigation of Sex Related Slang Vocabulary and Sex-Role Orientation Among Male and Female University Students," *Journal of Marriage and the Family*, (August 1974): 474–83.

18. Udry, p. 78. The account discussed comes from Lester Kirkendall, *Premarital Intercourse in Interpersonal Relationships* (New York: Angora, 1971).

19. Karen Oppenheim Mason et al., "Change in U.S. Women's Sex-Role Attitudes," *American Sociological Review* (August 1976): 573–96.

20. Mason concludes that work roles and demand roles are becoming more closely related. Stan L. Albrocht et al., "Changing Family and Sex Roles: An Assessment of Age Differences," *Journal of Marriage and the Family* (February 1979): 41–49, conclude that the egalitarianism is more common in work situations than in domestic ones. Brent Ropert and Emily Labeff, "Sex Roles and Feminism Revisited: An Interpersonal Attitude Comparison," *Journal of Marriage and the Family* (February 1977): 113–18, conclude that their sample was more favorable toward feminist attitudes concerning economics and political-legal issues than those concerning domestic issues.

21. Alan E. Bayer, "Sexist Students in American Colleges: A Descriptive Note," *Journal of Marriage and the Family* (May 1975): 391–97.

22. Yaffa Schlesinger, "Sex Roles and Social Changes in the Kibbutz," *Journal of Marriage and the Family* (November 1977): 771ff.

23. Ibid.

24. See, e.g., Anne Constantinople, "Masculinity—Femininity," *Psychological Bulletin* (November 1973): 403–4; Arlie Hochschild, "A Review of Sex Role Research," *American Journal of Sociology*, 78, (January 1975): 1015–29; and Stephanie A. Shields, "Functionalism, Darwinism and the Psychology of Women: A Study in Social Myth," *American Psychologist*, 30 (July 1973): 739–54.

25. There are a number of very thorough books about the ethics of sexual behavior. Among the best are Rustum Roy and Della Roy, *Honest Sex* (New York: New American Library, 1968); Frederick C. Wood, *Sex and the New Morality* (New York: Association Press, 1967); John Charles Wynn (ed.), *Sexual Ethics and Christian Responsibility: Some Divergent Views* (New York: Association Press, 1970) See also Money, "Destereotyping Sex Roles," *Society* (July/Aug., 1977).

26. Margaret Mead, *Sex and Temperament* (New York: Mentor Books, 1952); *Male and Female* (New York: Mentor Books, 1955).

27. Talcott Parsons, Robert Bales, and Morris Zeldich, *Family Socialization: An Interaction Process* (New York: Free Press, 1955).

Romantic love as it occurs in our civilization, inextricably bound up with ideas of monogamy, exclusiveness, jealousy, and undeviating fidelity, . . . is a compound, the final result of many converging lines of development in Western civilization, of the institution of monogamy, of the ideas of the age of chivalry, of the ethics of Christianity.

—*Margaret Mead*

11 Marriage in Historical and Cultural Perspective

"Giovanni Arnolfini and His Wife," a painting by Jan van Eyck (see p. 233, depicts an ideal marriage in early fifteenth-century Europe. The young couple are exchanging vows in their bridal chamber surrounded by symbols signifying the sacredness of marriage. The bridegroom has removed his shoes because he stands on holy ground. The little dog is a symbol of faithfulness; the single candle signifies Christ, the all-seeing guest.

What strikes the modern eye first, however, is the bride's protruding abdomen, which suggests pregnancy. The idea that a marriage is not truly consummated until the wife has conceived is more appropriate to the fifteenth century than to the twentieth. Today sterility may be grounds for divorce in some states and married couples are expected to have children, but even so we do not find it appropriate that a bride should come to her wedding "great with child."

This chapter will sketch some of the relevant themes in our understanding of how sex, love, and marriage are related to one another.[1] Our account cannot be exhaustive, only suggestive. It is important to include such an account, however, because how we think about these things today is, in part, fashioned by how our forebears have thought about them in the past. Modern behavior is not completely divorced from ancient belief. We will also briefly contrast our changing beliefs with some of the ideas anthropologists have proposed as a result of their study of other cultures, and we will comment quickly on the factors, other than beliefs, that are shaping marriage today.

LOVE AND SEXUALITY IN WESTERN EXPERIENCE: HISTORICAL PERSPECTIVE

During the third century a lovely and talented lecturer in philosophy at the Alexandrian Museum, a virgin named Hypatia, expressed what was in her day a prevalent attitude toward sexuality. When one of her students professed passionate love for her, she hoisted her dress above her waist and exclaimed contemptuously, "This, young man, is what you are in love with, and not anything beautiful!"[2]

Her words and actions give evidence of the influence of Christian thinking, for by the third century the Christian conception of love had developed strong overtones of asceticism and antifeminism. Celibacy was being widely proclaimed as superior to marriage. Thus, Ammon, a young man of Alexandria, was so strongly influenced by the teachings of St. Paul that he decided to remain chaste in order to lead a more perfect life. When he was forced into marriage by his father, he promptly persuaded his bride that they should purify their marriage by jointly taking a vow of celibacy. They lived a life of rigorous sexual denial without ever consummating their marriage. The fame of Ammon and his wife spread throughout the land, and monks came to live near their separate huts in the desert to bask in the radiance of their purity.

During the same period many clergy chose to demonstrate their devotion to chastity and spiritual love by sleeping with naked virgins who, according to the record, in most cases remained virgins. It is difficult today to understand what these priests were trying to demonstrate. In blatant contrast to the practice of earlier societies, where temple prostitutes provided a means of worship through sexual intercourse, the Agapetae—spiritual sisters or spiritual wives—provided a means of worship through sexual denial. They dramatically portrayed the tearing apart of sexuality from spirituality.

Of course, this antisexual bias is just one of the many images of love that have guided attitudes toward loving and lovemaking in Western civilization. For contrast, consider the following quite different picture, which appeared seventeen centuries later in a work of fiction by an American novelist:

> And as they remembered, Angela and Adam, lost in each other's flesh, acted out the unceasing cosmic life drama. Slowly awakening to each other's touch, and responding to the amazing, panting wonder of being each other, they made love with a joyous laughing surrender that would dance in their heads for hours. And then lying in his arms, because their love had no before or afterwards but was continuous, Angela was partially aware that her charm for Adam was her own subconscious necessity to sway on the windseeds of his ideas, not losing her own roots as a person, but coming alive and blossoming for him and herself because neither of them alone could provide the cross-fertilization.[3]

Between these two extremes—on the one hand Ammon's view of sexual love as an evil from which one must purge oneself in order to enjoy spiritual love, and on the other hand the contemporary novelist's view of the intimate link between spiritual and sexual expressions of love—lie all the various conceptions of love that have dominated the thinking of Western men and women.

The New Testament Tradition

We need not be surprised that Ammon and Hypatia regarded sexuality in the negative way described earlier. The Christian conception of love has been inordinately influenced by unmarried men. Jesus and Paul are prime examples. Although scholars have been able to uncover interesting information about the sexual adventures and misadventures of the church fathers and the celibate clergy and theologians who followed them, the historical record concerning the sexual behavior of Jesus and Paul is completely blank. What is more, we know very little about their attitudes toward sexuality. To be sure, they did speak about love, but the love they proclaimed as an ideal was the love generally described by the Greek term *agape*, meaning "God's love for man, or spontaneous altruistic love."[4] Christianity took this term from Greek society, in which it meant the kind of love directed toward members of the same household who were not related by blood or marriage, and centered it in the person of Jesus, the Christ. The life of the community that arose in response was built on this notion of love. Agapetic love is expressed as a kind of openness to all people, as a kind of joy or warmth. Some contemporary theologians speak of it as a love arising out of our perception of being. But it is decidedly not sexual. As experienced between men and men—or between women and women—it is the sort of love we associate with the concept of brotherhood or sisterhood. As experienced between men and women, it corresponds to what we commonly call

Platonic love. While we can differentiate love into many forms, *agape* is thought of as sustaining all forms.

There has been a tendency in the West to look at the New Testament as a book about ethical teachings.[5] To a considerable extent this view does not correspond to the intention of its authors. They were more interested in proclaiming the "Good News" of Christ's coming, and inviting their hearers and readers to a new fullness of life, than they were in offering ethical instruction. Of course, the New Testament does contain numerous prescriptions or ethical teachings, particularly in the epistles of St. Paul. These teachings, however, were colored by Paul's belief that the world was going to come to an end very soon—probably before he died. His basic advice, therefore, was to prepare for the end. This is the context of such Pauline statements as "To the unmarried and the widows I say that it is well for them to remain single as I do. But if they cannot exercise self-control, they should marry. For it is better to marry than to be aflame with passion."[6] The negative attitude toward heterosexual partnerships implicit in this statement may be traceable to the fact that Paul did not think there was time to work things out. The statement does not indicate that Paul would have looked with favor on Ammon and his wife, who married but chose to remain chaste. Their approach placed excessive and unnatural demands on even the devout. Indeed, a view like Ammon's could seem credible as a response to Paul's teachings only because Ammon lived three centuries after Paul and thus did not consider his teachings about chastity in the context of his view of the imminent end of the world.[7] Thus, a teaching that was intended to reflect priorities that were relevant to a time when the end of the world was at hand was distorted into an absolute proclamation of the desirability of chastity for all people at all times.

If the New Testament is read as a proclamation of the "Good News" that Jesus is indeed the Christ and his presence in this world manifests the love of God for His creatures, its statements about spiritual love (*agape*) take on a completely different meaning. Christianity in its essence is an incarnational religion, for its central doctrine is that God chose to become incarnate in the world: God so loved the world that he took on our flesh and dwelt among us. Paradoxically, this religion based on a doctrine of incarnation produced a group of followers who saw it as their duty to struggle to escape from bondage to the flesh. Indeed, this struggle to escape from the flesh has characterized Christianity throughout most of its history.

The theologians who have left their mark on Western thinking about love have been intellectuals and scholars. On the whole, they were heavily influenced by Aristotle and Plato, so that the Platonic sense of love (*Eros*) as a love of ideas has never left our tradition. Thus, the Greek conception of *agape* fused with the Christian understanding of the agapetic and asexual love of God and one's fellow human beings to produce the dominant elements in Western thinking about love. To the extent that Christians have thought of themselves as a special people who are saved because they have done the right things—rather than because all people are saved because they are loved by God—the ethical teachings have been seen as more important than the "Good News." These ethics are strongly influenced by a fundamentalist asceticism.

Augustine

St. Augustine, a fifth-century Catholic bishop, had an enormous influence on Christian thinking about marriage, sex, and the sins of the flesh. After a lusty youth in which he apparently caroused extensively and with abandon, he converted to Christianity at the age of 27. He was ordained as a priest four years later and was consecrated as a bishop four years after that. In *The City of God*, his major work, he made a distinction that has had immense consequences for fifteen centuries. The sinfulness in human sexual intercourse, Augustine argued, was not to be found in the act of procreating offspring. It was, rather, in the passion that had to accompany the act. In it, a man and a woman lost control of themselves for the moment and thus were fair game for the constantly vigilant Satan. This passion Augustine labeled "concupiscence." By confining concupiscence within the context of the sacrament of marriage, however, this danger could be overcome because it was now divinely directed toward a good end—procreation. To Augustine, marriage is far more than a social contract between two parties; rather, it is a divine sacrament necessary for transforming the sinful passion of concupiscence into a divinely sanctioned procreative act.

For Augustine, then, it was not so much sex itself as erotic passion that stood condemned. This becomes clear in the following passage, in which he fantasizes about the passionless nature of intercourse in Eden before the Fall:

> Those members [*genitals*], like the rest, would be moved by the command of his will, and the husband would be mingled with the loins of his wife without the seductive stimulus of passion, with calmness of mind and with no corruption of the innocence of the body because the wild head of passion would not activate those parts of the body but, as would be proper, a voluntary control would employ them. Thus it would then have been possible to inject the semen into the womb through the female genitalia as innocently as the menstrual flow is now ejected.[8]

In this fantasy Augustine made clear a distinction that has had profound consequences for Western sexual thought: Procreation is exalted as a necessary and divinely ordained duty, but sexual passion is a "corruption of the innocence of the body." The major thrust of Augustine's thought has been largely ignored, however. His primary argument against sexual passion was that it was such a near-at-hand pleasure—as near as the enjoyment of one's own body—that it could become a goal in itself. The problem was not having a body or enjoying the pleasures of that body, but placing more importance on that bodily pleasure than it deserves. If one loved God first, one could do as one pleased—whatever one pleased. The point was to love God first.

Aquinas

By the Middle Ages the Church had pushed Augustine's notion of marriage as a divine sacrament even further. St. Thomas Aquinas (1225–1274) asserted that the sacramental nature of the marriage bond meant that a couple, once joined, could never be separated except by death. Thus, the sacrament of "holy matrimony" indelibly establishes a relationship between those who enter into it. According to Aquinas, the Christian should engage in sexual activity of any sort only with the right person (his or her spouse), for the right reason (procreation), in the right way (heterosexual intercourse with the man on top). The purpose of sex was procreation. Any sexual activity that did not have a chance of producing offspring was a perversion—a crime against nature. He gave the opinion that this perversion occurred, in ascending order of gravity, in masturbation, coitus in an unnatural manner (oral or anal intercourse), bestiality (intercourse with animals), and homosexuality. Much of our condemnation of homosexuality today derives from this kind of ranking. There were less serious sexual crimes, in Aquinas's opinion. Seduction or rape occurred when a woman was violated while under the authority of her father. Adultery occurred when a woman experienced intercourse with someone other than her husband—and thus violated his authority over her. The fact that a man's property rights in a woman were violated was a very important element in these definitions of seduction and adultery. "Kisses, touches, caresses are only sinful if inspired by a wrong motive such as enjoyment of forbidden pleasure."[9]

Much of our understanding of traditional marriage comes directly from Aquinas. For example, the widely held sentiment that sex is a legitimate activity as long as it occurs for the right purpose, with the right person, in the right way is a direct reflection of his teachings; similarly, the belief that marriage is the proper context for sexual intercourse for the purpose of procreation derives from the teachings of both Augustine and Aquinas. But in the Roman Catholic tradition, chastity was still much preferred to marriage for the devout.

The Reformation

When Martin Luther broke from the Roman Catholic Church, he enthusiastically embraced the idea of the "married state." Marriage is "God's gift to man, a heavenly and spiritual state, a school of faith in love in which every menial task, every trouble and hardship, is a means of religious education."[10] Although he still saw sexual intercourse as a troubling and vexing problem, a source of temptation that could lead people to forget the spiritual side of their nature, his thinking on marriage represents an advance over the Church's traditional position in that he emphasizes the companionship between the partners as an important element in marriage.

John Calvin was more original in his view of marriage. For Calvin, sexual intercourse was holy, not unclean. Marriage was a high calling whose primary purpose was to fulfill needs for belonging and acceptance. It was important that each adult person belong to a family, for families were the elemental building blocks from which the religious community was built. In this system woman was ordained to be man's companion throughout the gamut of his experience, and her specific calling was motherhood.

The preceding discussion obviously cannot do justice to the richness of the New Testament tradition. We have only touched on some of the central elements of the teachings of only a few of the prominent thinkers who have contributed to this tradition. Nevertheless, we can make the following broad generalizations about the impact of this tradition on our understanding of love, sex, and marriage:

1. "Being" or altruistic love (*agape*) is held up as the highest form of love. It is divinely given and is held to be superior to the love men and women experience when they "make love" (erotic love).
2. Erotic love (*Eros*) is rooted in our humanness. It arises out of our capacity to feel, to sense, to be filled with passion. Whereas spiritual love can and should be extended to all humanity, erotic love should be confined to marriage. In spite of its usefulness in the act of procreation, erotic love is often portrayed as self-seeking, for in it each person is seen as expressing merely his or her own passion. Erotic love is based on the perceived lovable or attractive characteristics of the beloved.
3. The only acceptable context for erotic love is one's relationship with one's spouse. Implicit in this view is the belief that the erotic satisfactions that derive from erotic love should always be subordinate to procreation—the natural function of sex. Thus, all forms of sexual behavior that do not offer the possibility of procreation are condemned.

No one who has been brought up in the Western tradition can escape being influenced by these ideas. Whether we can identify their source or not, whether we agree with them or not, they are part of our heritage. They affect how we feel, behave, and think in partnerships, even if only to the extent that we find ourselves in conscious rebellion against them.

Amour

Mainstream Christianity tended to oppose spiritual love (*agape*) and carnal passion (*eros*), but during the late Middle Ages another distinctive kind of love emerged in the West. Joseph Campbell describes the situation thus:

Marriage in the Middle Ages was almost exclusively a social, family concern—as it has been forever, of course, in Asia, and is to this day for many in the West. One was married according to family arrangements. Particularly in aristocratic circles, young women hardly out of girlhood were married off as political pawns. And the Church, meanwhile, was sacramentalizing such unions with its inappropriately mystical language about the two that were now to be of one flesh, united through love and by God: and let no man put asunder that God hath joined. Any actual experience of love could enter into such a system only as a harbinger of disaster. For not only could one be burned at the stake in punishment for adultery, but, according to current belief, one would also burn forever in Hell. And yet love came, even so, to such noble hearts . . . and it was the work of the troubadours to celebrate this passion, which in their view was of a divine grace altogether higher in dignity than the sacraments of the Church, higher than the sacrament of marriage, and, if excluded from Heaven, then sanctified in Hell.[11]

This love celebrated the *experience* of love in the context of human existence. It was a celebration of life in its wholeness, in defiance of a convention that devoutly sought to compartmentalize it. Those who could not stand the pain and suffering required of a gentle heart (in order to rise above the urgings of mere lust) could not enter onto this love's thrashing floor.

Unlike *agape, amour* was discriminating. It was not a love for humankind, it was a love for a particular person in all that person's perfection—and imperfection. Indeed, it came to be appreciated that it was the beloved's imperfections that made the beloved distinctive—more so at least than the much-admired perfections. In contrast to simple sexual desire, such love was not mere impulse or instinct. The whole point of the trials and tribulations of the lovers yearning mightily after each other over long periods of time was to prove that their love was not simple sexual passion. It was *amour*. The fact that the word was the reverse of *Roma*, source of the Christian sacrament of Holy Matrimony, was thought to be particularly appropriate. No priest was required to sanctify the union of Parsifal and Condwiramurs. The noble *amour* alone sanctifies their marriage, and loyalty to the beloved confirms it. Under these conditions, it was most appropriate to consummate *amour*.

Such a celebration of the experience of love demanded a great deal of the lovers. Their sorrow and suffering were overcome by their love, but not eliminated by it. Given the break with tradition, the lovers abandoned all hope of heaven, and some anticipated an eternity in hell. Indeed, Dante saw all the famous lovers of history (Helen, Paris, Cleopatra, Tristan) whirling around in a burning wind in what he took to be endless pain. But Campbell notes:

His point of view was that of an outsider; one, furthermore, whose own love was bearing him onward and upward to the summit of the highest heaven. . . . the point about Hell—as well as of Heaven is this: when there, you are in your proper place which, finally, is exactly where you want to be.[12]

Had not Tristan exclaimed, when his servant warned him that the love potion from which he and his beloved drank would be the death of them both, "So then God's will be done, whether death it be or life. For that drink has poisoned me sweetly. I do not know what the death of which you tell is to be, but this death suits me well. And if delightful Isolt is to continue to be my death this way, I shall gladly court an eternal death."[13] Love is not confined to heaven—it extends to hell as well. A Persian tradition even has it that Satan is the most noble lover of all. He was cast out of heaven by God because he would not bow down to humanity and is sustained in hell by the last words he heard from his beloved: "Be Gone!"

Clearly this kind of love is not for everyone. Indeed, the love that the troubadours sang of was mimicked in the royal courts of Europe in a form of courtly love that broke with tradition on some counts, but preserved it in the most important. The beloved may have been someone else's wife in many cases, but the love—if it were true love—could not be consummated in sexual union. Much of our understanding of romance comes from this tradition.

The essence of romanticism is the distinction between "true love" and "false love." In a curious echo of the Christian distinction between agapetic love, which is nonsexual, and erotic love, which is confined to

Our tradition has put love, sex, and marriage together in very different ways as this fifteenth century picture of a pregnant bride clearly shows. (Art Resource)

marriage, romantic theory held that true love is experienced with a lover and not with one's spouse. True lovers could kiss, touch, fondle, even lie naked together, but they could not consummate their love. Should a lady give herself in sexual intercourse to her lover, she was no longer an appropriate object of his adoration. Thus, although the object of true romantic love was a member of the opposite sex, their love was supposed to be as asexual as agapetic love in the Christian tradition. What is more, sexual love was confined to marriage, as it was in Christian thinking, and was held to be inferior to nonsexual love.

This strange ethic may have arisen, in part, in response to the fact that in the Middle Ages marriage had come to be more or less a business proposition. It involved land, loyalties, and the production of heirs and future defenders.[14] As Morton Hunt has written, "The average Renaissance husband looked upon his wife with eyes which appraised rather than adored."[15] Romantic love thus offered an alternative to the mundane relationship of marriage. Lovers fought with their rivals, performed many acts of bravery and self-sacrifice, and yearned mightily and publicly for their beloved, and the fact that the union could never be consummated only added to its appeal. Thus, the rewards of courtly love were basically to be found in the suffering, striving, and yearning of unrequited love.

Although the courtly love convention may seem somewhat bizarre to us, it introduced into emotional relationships between men and women in the West many elements that are familiar today. As Hunt observes:

> It brought into them tenderness and gentleness, exaggerated and sometimes absurd in form, but important nevertheless. It opened within a framework of adultery, yet it stressed as never before the importance of the fidelity of one man and one woman each to each.[16]

The Nineteenth Century

The nineteenth-century husband enjoyed a status in society rarely surpassed in other eras.[17] He was a master of the ship of state and the king of the domestic castle. His wife was cultivated for her economic uselessness. To the extent that he could afford it, she did nothing to support the household—she did not even cook the meals. She acquired social graces for entertaining and skills such as embroidery and needlepoint to help her pass the time and to contribute to the culture of the home, but he was responsible for the income of the household and its major expenditures as well. Middle-class wives were symbols of their husband's skill at conspicuous consumption.

The family world was a world of respectability and religious piety sharply separated from the outside world. Although there is some evidence that some Victorian women experienced and regularly enjoyed sexual intercourse, it was the exception rather than the rule.[18] Whereas in previous centuries sexual indiscretions were confessed to the priest, in the nineteenth

In the nineteenth century the family was a world of respectability and religious piety sharply separated from the outside world. (The Metropolitan Museum of Art, Gift of Frederick H. Hatch, 1926)

century they were told to the psychiatrist, who studied them intensely. Sexual science was born in this century, and in the streets pornography flourished. It promised excessive gratification of every sexual desire prudery prohibited.

Before the law, women were largely nonentities. They legally became "one flesh" with their husbands and could not own property, sue for divorce, vote, or establish precedent for their grievances before the courts in most cases. They could not legally deny their husbands access to their bodies, as this would be a violation of the male's conjugal rights. It is no wonder that women began to organize.

LOVE AND SEXUALITY: THE CROSS-CULTURAL PERSPECTIVE

When we compare the traditional Western understanding of love, sex, and marriage to the beliefs and practices found in other parts of the world, it becomes clear how truly unique our views are.[19] The word *love* is rarely found in the indexes of anthropological studies of primitive peoples. It plays a far less significant role in the affairs of other men and women than it is proclaimed to play in our own tradition. In many cultures personal attraction or individual preferences are not taken into consideration in the selection of a mate. Anthropologists have a difficult time identifying anything similar to what we call love.

Sexual relationships are evident everywhere, and marriage—even monogamous marriage—is a widespread phenomenon common to many cultures, but analogs to the Western understanding of love are quite rare. Indeed, in many primitive socieities love relationships between husband and wife are suppressed on the ground that they tend to estrange the couple from their kin. Because kinship relationships are often the basis of the social order in primitive societies, any exclusive tie of the married couple to each other would have serious disruptive consequences for the entire society.

Perhaps the most important difference between our view of marriage and the more common pattern found in other cultures is that marriage is not seen as the primary regulator of sexual behavior. Thus, for example, in most societies premarital intercourse is an acceptable part of growing up. It does not follow, however, that it is "OK" to conceive a child outside marriage, for most societies prohibit this. Since sexual passion is not bad, as we have traditionally thought, it does not need a sacrament of matrimony to bless it. But since children are heirs to property and privileges that are handed down from generation to generation, it will not do to bring an "illegitimate" child into the world.

Furthermore, since it is biologically evident that women give birth to children, some anthropologists see marriage as the primary means of licensing fatherhood. Every child should have one father and one father only. Now since some societies, such as the Trobrianders in the early part of this century, do not know that sperm from a man play an important role in the conception of a child, the father of a child need not be the man who sired it. Thus, anthropologists distinguish between the social father, or **pater**, and the biological father, or **genitor**. So delicate is the father's role, some will argue, that the primitive custom of the **couvade** (common among African and South American tribes) was invented to secure this role. In the couvade the father is thought of as having given birth to the child, not the mother. He lies in and gives evidence of experiencing birth pains, while she gives birth in the fields. In a half-hour or so she returns and puts the child in his arms. Old men with wrinkled faces are often spoken of by women as follows: "You should have seen him before he gave birth to so many children."

Other anthropologists contend that marriage is the essential social institution because it is the primary means of bonding kinship groups in reciprocal exchanges of rights and privileges. Thus, Lévi-Strauss argues that marriage is the only universal social institution but that the family founded on this bond may take many forms. The **conjugal family** or small family similar to ours is in his view only a transitory stage between the mother-child dyad and the large extended family containing hundreds of people. Marriage in such societies is primarily an economic institution and is commonly arranged by the elders.

Finally, although monogamy is the most common form of marriage in the world today, it is not the most preferred. Muslims are entitled by Islamic law to have four wives. Mormons still practice polygyny in Utah today, although this practice is illegal and was once severely suppressed. **Polygyny** (plural wives) is the form of marriage that most societies prefer when economic conditions permit it. In contrast, **polyandry** (plural husbands) is associated with economic hardship. Societies in which it is necessary for many men to work hard in order to establish a family and raise children are likely to endorse polyandry. A fourth form of marriage—**group marriage**, in which several men and several women are married to one another—is extremely rare. What is most important is that most societies permit more than one form of marriage, although in their norms they prefer a single form. In regard to marriage and family forms (as opposed to norms), all societies are pluralistic and always have been.

The sociologist William F. Goode suggests that love is not such a desirable state in other societies as we consider it in our tradition. He points out that many societies have evolved elaborate institutional patterns to control the potentially disruptive consequences of love.[20] He identifies five such patterns in common use:

1. *Child marriage.* Among the Tiwi of Australia a man may promise his firstborn daughter in marriage even before she is born.[21]
2. *Mate selection predetermined by the kinship structure.* In societies that use this system people in a given kin relationship automatically marry each other and the only decision the elders must make is to determine when the marriage is to occur. For example, a preferred choice of mate in many societies is a cross cousin—a mother's brother's child or father's sister's child. In societies like the Murngin (an Australian aborigine people), cross cousins automatically marry each other simply because their position in the kinship structure decrees that they should.[22]
3. *Institutional isolation of young women who are possible mate choices until the time of their marriage*, as among the Manus (a tribe on the Admiralty Islands of the Pacific).
4. *Close supervision by duennas or close relatives*, as among some Spanish-speaking peoples. Where such a tradition is in effect, young couples are constantly chaperoned because it is assumed that if they were not there would be a natural tendency for them to engage in sexual intercourse.
5. *A system in which love relationships are encouraged and in which the choice of mates is formally free, but in which there are informal constraints.* Our own society is an example of this system insofar as economic, ethnic, religious, and regional factors limit the choice of mate to a socially approved field of eligibles. For example, although we insist that love is the decisive criterion in selecting a mate, very few marriages are contracted between blacks and whites. The fact that we do not have formal rules determining who should marry whom does not diminish the effect of social expectations on our choice of mate.

MARRIAGE IN AMERICA TODAY

Marriage, as social scientists look at it today, is primarily a social institution. It can be defined as follows:

> Marriage is the established institution for starting a family. . . . There is often an exchange of economic goods in a marriage, and involved is a legal, physical and moral union between a man and a woman, continued through the raising of children. Marriage regulates relations between the sexes and helps establish the child's relation to the community. It is usually associated with a ceremony . . . which formalizes the group's approval. In marriage, the children produced by the woman are usually accepted as the legitimate offspring of the married couple.[23]

This definition, taken from a dictionary of anthropology, is intended to cover all known cases—including group marriage, polygamous marriage, and monogamous marriage. It does not define *how* the institution regulates relationships between the sexes; it does not specify the nature of the legal, physical, and moral union. Nor does it describe the characteristics of the ceremony that formalizes the group's approval. It merely describes the basic function of marriage, whatever its form: a formally sanctioned economic institution that regulates procreation.

Modern Beliefs

The preceding general definition can be compared with what most contemporary Americans would consider a minimal definition of marriage as it is found in our society. The majority of Americans probably think marriage is a lifelong, monogamous union between a man and a woman involving exclusive sexual rights in the spouse, minimal acceptance of patriarchy, and the expectation of children. This conception fits the general definition well: It sees marriage as a union for the purpose of procreation; it establishes patriarchy as the primary form of descent; and it establishes monogamy as the form that regulates relations between the partners.

Let us examine this definition of the contemporary American understanding of marriage in greater detail. In the first place, we note that marriage is expected to be a lifelong union. Of course, we all know perfectly well that, factually speaking, this is not the case. One hundred years ago or less, when divorce involved extremely expensive legal procedures and was granted only on a limited number of grounds, and when any divorced person—male as well as female—was an object of social scorn, it would have been reasonable to speak of marriage as a lifelong partnership in fact as well as principle. Today, however, divorce is common enough to make it no longer accurate to speak of marriage as a lifelong relationship.

Nevertheless, the idea that marriage represents a permanent commitment to a partnership persists as an ideal that exerts considerable influence on people's attitudes. Although many young people today are realistic enough to recognize that they will be able to terminate their marriage if it doesn't "work out," they still regard permanence as the ideal toward which they are striving. Anything short of permanence is regarded as a failure.

The next stipulation—that marriage must be monogamous—is relatively straightforward. Monogamy is the only form of marriage that is legally valid in the United States. Occasionally one hears of various forms of group marriage involving three or more partners, but such relationships have no legal standing at all. This sort of pseudopolygamy is interesting from a sociological standpoint, but experiments in this direction have so far had little influence on our attitudes and ideals. They have had no influence whatsoever on the legal requirement that marriage can exist only between two people of opposite sexes. (In this connection it is interesting to note that various groups of homosexual activists have been fighting in courts and legislatures for legal recognition of their partnerships—so far without success.)

Next we turn to the common belief that marriage is a union "involving exclusive sexual rights in the spouse." Generally speaking, these rights exist both positively and negatively. On the negative side, our conventional understanding of marriage holds that both partners are prohibited from giving themselves sexually to anyone but their spouse; on the positive side, it means that each party enjoys the right to receive satisfaction from his or her partner. Although in most states both the positive and negative sides of these rights are legally enforceable—that is, both adultery and nonconsummation may be grounds for divorce or annulment—conventional understandings of what these rights imply vary considerably. For example, in some social circles these rights exist primarily for the benefit of the male. Thus, many people maintain that when a woman marries she incurs an obligation to satisfy the sexual demands of her husband, but the people who hold this belief rarely feel it important to add that the husband is obliged to satisfy his wife. This difference results from the myth that women are sexually passive whereas men are sexually active. On the negative side, too, conventional understanding in some social circles favors the husband, whose infidelity is often tolerated as one of the facts of life a wife must learn to live with, whereas infidelity on her part would be regarded as a serious breach of the marriage contract.

What does it mean to say that marriage in the United States is minimally patriarchal? **Patriarchy** is a social arrangement in which the father serves as supreme authority in the family and in which heredity is reckoned in the male line. In our society this is reflected in the widespread practice of having the woman adopt her husband's surname upon marriage; children, too, tend automatically to be given the husband's surname, so that the family as a whole is identified in terms of the male. It should be noted, however, that this naming convention is not legally obligatory in 49 of the 50 states (Hawaii is the exception). In California, for example, the state's attorney general recently found it necessary to answer a complaint by women who objected to the practice by pointing out that they were under no legal obligation to adopt their husbands' names. A married woman is perfectly free to keep her "maiden name"—that is, her father's surname—if she desires to do so. What is more, just as our patriarchal naming conventions are not legally binding, so in many states the laws governing the holding and transmission of property in a marriage partnership are not notably patriarchal. In this regard we have come a long way from the nineteenth-century British system—common also in many parts of the United States—in which all of a married woman's property belonged to the husband, including property she held in her own name prior to marriage and income she earned in any way while married. Today such blatantly patriarchal laws are practically nonexistent, and a number of states have community property statutes that make any property held by either member of a marriage partnership the joint property of both partners.

Nevertheless, American marriage can still be described as a patriarchal system in terms of the general social and psychological expectations we bring to it. **Egalitarian** marriage is, of course, quite possible, but it is still the exception rather than the rule, a trend rather than a reality. Unless a couple explicitly agrees, either before marriage or in the course of their partnership, that they are to relate to each other as equals, male dominance tends to "go without saying." A situation commonly used to illustrate this point concerns decisions as to where the family is to live. Generally speaking, if both partners have careers, the practice is for the family to live where the husband can pursue his career to best advantage. If a husband gets an attractive job offer that requires the family to relocate, we consider it perfectly normal for the wife to give up her job, but only in abnormal situations do we consider it appropriate for the husband to give up his job if the shoe is on the other foot. This is a clear reflection of our patriarchal bias, which assumes, even when both partners are employed and earning equal salaries, that financial support of the family is the male's obligation and that the female's contributions in this area are optional and voluntary.

Finally, our definition stipulates that marriage is a partnership involving an expectation of children. Here, of course, the norm is not legally binding at all, but this is nevertheless one of the most important of the conventional attitudes and ideals that we bring to marriage. Advances in contraceptive technology have brought us a long way from the day when the birth of children was regarded as inevitable if a couple continued to make love. Except among the poor (especially the rural poor) and those whose religious beliefs preclude contraception, modern American society can be described as sophisticated in its understanding of the techniques for controlling birth. For most people, however, the ability to practice birth control means they can determine when they will have children and how many they will have. Most people do not see it as a choice of whether to have children or not.

Family and peer pressures in this area can be immense. The couple who postpone the birth of their first child for a considerable time are often told in no uncertain terms what is expected of them. Many married partners who are quite comfortable in their two-person partnership succumb to these pressures and decide to have a child without ever being able to articulate their doubts about whether raising a family is right for them. Thus, although couples are frequently free to remain childless if they decide to do so, it is safe to say that when two people get married they generally expect to have children as a matter of course, without giving the question any conscious thought. What is more, even if they give it some thought, their decision is likely to be heavily influenced by the expectations of interested onlookers—especially the couple's parents.

These, then, are some of the major beliefs that color and shape the expectations people bring to marriage in our society. Of course, no institution actually functions precisely the way a generalized and abstract picture of it would lead us to expect. Our attitudes and ideals tell us only what we expect the institution of marriage to be like, just as an organizational flow chart tells us only how a business institution is supposed to operate. The institution of marriage must cope with a changing world, changing attitudes, and individual differences. In the remainder of this chapter, therefore, we will examine the reality of marriage as it is evolving in America today. In some ways, this reality will conform to common expectations; in many ways, it will not.

The Evolving Reality

A 14-year-old acquaintance of the authors was able to identify at least five different life styles simply on the basis of her babysitting contacts. These were as follows:

1. A traditional monogamous marriage, with its characteristic balance of authority and permissiveness in childrearing and a traditional involvement by the married couple in the "straight" social sense.
2. A divorced woman with children whom our informant described as a "swinging single." She takes a traditional approach to childbearing but makes no attempt to keep from anyone the fact that she spends weekends away from her children with various boyfriends.
3. A divorced woman who is living with a man "without benefit of clergy." In all outward aspects this partnership seems no different from any successful marriage in which the partners are bound to each other by the usual religious and/or legal forms.
4. A young upper-middle-class couple whose apartment consists mostly of makeshift furniture and has few of the mechanical comforts associated with modern living. These individuals are deeply involved in mystical religious experiences; they seem to entertain a wide array of friends under a wide variety of circumstances, but our informant was not able to provide details.

240

The character of marriage in America is suggested by the diversity of our marriage ceremonies. (Bruce Roberts, Photo Reserachers, Inc.; Alice Kandell, Photo Researchers, Inc.; Ken Karp; Eugene Gordon; Bill Bachman, Photo Researchers, Inc.)

5. A couple in which both partners have children by previous marriages in addition to offspring from their own union. This family is structured along traditional lines, with a normal middle-class social life, but there are occasions in which the tattered remnants of the previous marriages intrude on the current relationship. All the members of the family seem to be aware that the children can be divided into "his," "hers," and "theirs."

There is nothing representative about these styles and structures, but clearly they are all around us. The fact that they are not often differentiated in studies of marriage does not mean that they do not represent significant departures from our common ideals or that they do not demand different responses from the pariticpants. They are a part of the rich variety of styles and structures that testify to the fact that the institution of marriage is changing and evolving.

In the nineteenth century people were often amazed and appalled at the variations in marriage and family styles discovered by anthropologists. Now it is becoming increasingly clear that the greatest variation is to be found not in primitive cultures, but in modern industrialized societies where affluence, leisure, and a critical stance toward one's culture both foster change and give increasing numbers of people the capacity and the motivation to try out new alternatives.

Some of the changes that are altering the structure of marriage in our culture result from conscious attempts to try out new styles of living together, new forms of marriage and family life. The number of people involved in intentional alterations of the traditional marital life style is probably quite small, however, although the public that sympathizes with such deliberate experimentation is undoubtedly considerably larger. Much of what is changing marriage today is not intended.

Why Is Marriage Changing?

The shortest answer to this question is "Because our society is changing." To see how social change affects marriage, let us briefly examine some important dimensions of such change as they affect the character of the marriage partnership in America today. These are (1) the declining influence of religion; (2) the widespread use of products such as the birth control pill and the automobile; (3) the increasing antipersonalization of our society; (4) the creation of an enormous job market for women;[24] (5) the increasing demand for advanced training, which tends to increase the period of premarriage and encourages a critical stance toward our culture; (6) demographic changes; and (7) a changing ethic.

The Declining Influence of Christianity. When social scientists talk about the declining influence of religion, they are not so much concerned with church attendance as they are with the decline in importance of the sacred or holy in people's lives. Primitive people saw the entire world as essentially sacred, but with the advance of science and technology the sphere of the sacred has diminished drastically. Today many people do not have a sense of the sacred or holy.

In addition to a decline in the sense of the sacred, there has been a decline in the influence of the Christian tradition. At least since the time of Augustine, marriage has been regarded as a sacred contract, as indicated in the traditional wedding formula, "What God hath joined together let no man put asunder." By the Renaissance marriage had come to be less a sacred contract and more a social contract with important implications as a business transaction.[25] In the former view, one was obliged to fulfill one's marriage contract much as one was obliged to obey any of the other precepts of one's faith; in the latter view, breaking the marriage bond was as unthinkable as any violation of the norms of ethical business conduct. In the one case divorce was a sin against God; in the other it was violation of the social order. Today, however, most people regard marriage as primarily a personal contract between two individuals. Thus, neither the religious nor the secular community can have much influence on a couple who decide to terminate their marriage. The recent expansion of Evangelical Christianity may soon change all this.

Some Pertinent Products. Modern technology has given us many products that affect both the style of courtship and the character of partnership. Perhaps none have had more significant repercussions on the institution of marriage than the automobile and the birth control pill.

The automobile has affected courtship and partnership patterns by increasing the autonomy of the young couple. Prior to the advent of the automobile, couples courted in the parlor; after it, they courted in the back seat. Greater freedom from parental supervision enabled couples to develop their own style of courtship, which generally included a much greater degree of sexual intimacy than was possible in the parlor. The automobile also increased the likelihood that a partner would be selected who lived at some distance—perhaps even across town or in the next town. This change created problems that did not exist when mate selection was limited, for all practical purposes, to the boy or girl "next door," for couples are not as likely to share a similar background. Finally, the automobile has made it relatively easy for couples to establish their residence at some distance from both job and kin. The implications of this separation will be discussed later.

The birth control pill, along with other efficient contraceptives, has made it possible effectively to separate sexual pleasure from conception. The increased incidence of premarital sexual intercourse is directly related to the development of better contraceptives. Moreover, the ability to separate sexual pleasure from conception has shaken our assumptions regarding the naturalness of the love–marriage–sex–reproduction sequence, which is the basis of our traditional understanding of marriage.

An Antipersonal Society. To a considerable extent, the professional person's view of life militates against intimacy. This view is detached and impersonal, and is intended to be. Although young professionals are supposed to be able to adjust, to move from the world of their work to the world of their families with ease, most people do not do this well. The two worlds overlap in their concerns, and when this happens the world in which one earns one's living tends to dominate. This is particularly true in the middle class, where a large portion of the population is employed in a professional capacity, but it is also true, although to a lesser extent, in working-class families.

On the job people are rewarded for aggressive competition, in which they must manipulate people in order to further their personal objectives. The job places a high value on things and rewards behavior that is effective in producing those things.[26] At present males generally receive greater rewards for productivity than females.

The personal world of most American men has two centers: the home and the work place. Normally, these are located in different places and generate quite distinct settings within which the man acts out his daily routine. The lives of women, on the other hand, typically have but one focus: the home. They may leave it for a number of reasons, but they do not ordinarily establish a separate setting within which they may try on new roles and fulfill different expectations. Thus, in spite of the successes of the women's movement, it remains true that in the typical case masculinity in America is defined primarily in terms of the expectations governing the job or career, while femininity is defined primarily in terms of the expectations associated with childrearing and domesticity.

The net result is that men, because of the "cool" stance they are encouraged to adopt in their work and because of their preoccupation with their careers and with the necessity of providing for their families, are less able to enter into intimate relationships than women. Equally important is the related fact that marriage has a different valence for men than it does for women. For middle-class men, marriage is important for full social acceptability; it also provides the middle-class man with a means of demonstrating his professional competence through the standard of living he provides for his wife and children. For most women, on the other hand, marriage is a necessary step on the way to personal fulfillment. Because many women still see motherhood as essential for their fulfillment, they also see marriage as a necessity because in our society it provides the only legitimate context in which a woman can become a mother.

Working Women. About 51 percent of all married women who live with their husbands are employed outside the home.[27] This figure has tripled since World War II. To the extent that women work outside the home and to the extent that such employment provides them with some degree of economic independence, marriage has less utilitarian value for them. A woman who is able to support herself does not have to remain in an unhappy marriage for economic reasons; her financial independence gives her an alternative.

It should be recognized, however, that the statistics on the number of employed women do not give an accurate picture of the extent to which women have achieved economic independence from their husbands. The average working woman's income is considerably below that of the average man, so that in most cases if a working couple were to separate, each to live on his or her own income, she would be much less well off than he. Nevertheless, the fact remains that the more income a woman is able to command, the more she is free of the necessity to remain married for financial reasons. What is more, as more and more women are realizing the importance of pursuing careers rather than merely holding jobs, and as more and more worthwhile jobs are becoming available to women, the force of the financial compulsion to marry will disintegrate. Sheer economic necessity was never a very good reason to remain in a partnership, but it was a real one. The progress of women toward economic equality with men makes it less so.

The Need To Be Trained. The amount of training required for many jobs and careers has been increasing steadily for decades, and this has had a considerable effect on the institution of marriage. This factor is particularly pertinent to the success-oriented upper middle class, but it applies also to the working class, although to a lesser degree. The decade of post-high school professional training involved in graduate education is an extreme case, but college education or technical training is becoming an accepted part of life for a huge portion of the population. In 1979, 12 million Americans over the age of 25 had at least one college degree—well over twice the number that had obtained a college degree in 1961.[28]

Undoubtedly, the most important reason why advanced education affects marriage has to do with the fact that it postpones the time when young people are economically independent. Because many men are reluctant to marry unless they can support a wife and a family, increases in the number of years of schooling have the effect of postponing the age at which people marry. In turn, this leads to more premarital sex and an increasing number of nonmarital partnerships. What is more, a college education often provides students with the intellectual equipment that makes possible a critical stance toward their culture and a greater degree of openness to alternate ways of doing things. This is reflected in the fact that college-educated people are considerably more likely than their non-college-educated peers to look favorably on freedom and experimentation in marital life styles.

A Nation Growing Older. The so-called population explosion, particularly the postwar "baby boom," has added an enormous number of people to our society. Although the *rate* of growth for the nation as a whole is approaching zero, the *size* of its population will continue to increase as a result of the larger base of females of childbearing age. The median age of the U.S. population is 30 years, and the over-65 age group is one of the fastest-growing segments, accounting for 11 percent of the population in 1980.[29]

Experimentation, innovation, and new departures always have been prerogatives of the young, but in the past young people could not help but feel that their ideas were more or less transitory. Young men and women were well aware of their minority status in a world populated mostly by older folk. Thus, although they might feel free to depart from the norms by "sowing their wild oats," they tended at the same time to be aware that this was simply a phase they were passing through on their way to taking their place in the adult world. Today, however, young people constitute a significant minority of the population. Of great importance here is the fact that they are probably the largest and most influential group of consumers of cultural products such as music, literature, motion pictures, and television, so that to a considerable extent they are the trend setters in matters of taste. We still idolize the young even as the nation ages.

Thus, instead of having a situation in which young people learn how to behave in the adult world, we have a situation in which the junior members of society establish the fashions and their elders struggle to keep up. This was clear as long ago as the early 1960s, when middle-aged people tried to master the Twist. Half a century ago, a typical 20-year-old man probably would have been working somewhere where he was surrounded by workers twice his age or older. Today, a typical 20-year-old male is likely to be in college, surrounded by hundreds of students his own age and taught by instructors half of whom may not be 30 years old themselves. In a nation of younger people, in short, the unconventional behavior that characterizes the young in their approach to social institutions such as marriage can itself become a norm. As we continue through the 1980s, however, the sentiments of older segments of the population are beginning to be heard. We will soon learn what happens to the "now" generation when—for whatever reasons—it becomes established.

A Changing Ethic. In 1973 the world's economy was hit by rapidly rising oil prices, and some analysts believe this event marked the end not only of cheap oil, but also of the long-term expectations held by American parents that their children would naturally do better than they did. For many, it now appears that they will be lucky to do as well as their parents did economically. And there are ecological as well as economic reasons why a return to a society based less on material consumption and more on interpersonal growth and development is desirable. Daniel Yankelovich notes in his *New Rules* that 47 percent of his sample were deeply involved in a search for community in 1980—an increase from 32 percent in 1973. Two out of five of his respondents said they had fewer friends now than they did in the recent past. There are social as well as ecological reasons for such a trend.[30]

During the recent past America has been split, in Yankelovich's opinion, between a small minority still adhering to the work ethic and the ethic of self-denial, and another small minority exploring the new ethic of self-gratification, with the majority of us in the middle picking and choosing between the extremes. Yankelovich believes that the self-gratification ethic was personally disappointing and socially unacceptable. True self-fulfillment, he rightly perceives, demands commitment to others. Given the need to develop personal relationships and the social incentives to validate ourselves in nonmaterial ways, Yankelovich believes we can learn from the misguided efforts at need gratification and find greater satisfaction and personal fulfillment in a new ethic of commitment. This ethic has two components: the high value placed on deep personal relationships and the cultivation of reverential thinking—a return to the sacred sense of life. Both are important if we are to find personal fulfillment, and there is evidence that we are turning toward this ethic. To the extent that we do, we will be very much in tune with the approach taken in this text toward the cultivation of partnerships.

SUMMARY

Many Americans still think about sex, love, and marriage essentially the same way St. Thomas Aquinas did 700 years ago: Sex is to be experienced only with one's spouse and primarily for the purpose of procreation. Although most of us are persuaded that sex in marriage ought also to be enjoyable, we still tend to feel that any sexual behavior that cannot at least potentially lead to reproduction is perverted. The idea that virtuous women should enjoy sex, even in marriage, is very recent.

To a large extent we have defined *agape*—"being" love—as "good" and erotic love as "bad" because rationality is lost in the process of lovemaking. The idea of concupiscence is traceable to St. Augustine, who felt that the dire consequences of concupiscence (damnation) could be averted if passion were redirected through the sacrament of marriage toward the goal of procreation.

From a cross-cultural perspective we have seen that many peoples feel that erotic love threatens to disrupt the social structure by isolating the lovers from their kin. Goode was able to describe five ways in which societies attempt to control the potentially disruptive aspects of love: child marriage, arranged marriages under rules of endogamy, institutional isolation of young people until the time of marriage, close supervision of young couples (especially young women), and informal norms that define a field of eligible mates, as in our own society.

In most societies it is "OK" to have sex before marriage, and many people accept extramarital sex. However, few accept the notion that it is "OK" to conceive a child outside marriage. Most societies see marriage as an economic and social bond between kin groups. In such societies marriages are arranged by elders, who know which mates are appropriate for their children. Monogamy is the most common form of marriage around the world, but polygyny is the most preferred.

Today marriage is changing because our society is changing. The declining influence of conventional religion, the increasingly antipersonal nature of our society, the use of products such as the birth control pill and the automobile, the creation of an enormous job market, the increasing demand for advanced training, and an aging population have all contributed to changes in norms and behaviors. Consequently, even a 14-year-old can identify differing life styles. The number of people who are intentionally experimenting with alternatives to traditional marriage probably is quite small, but one thing seems certain: The basically antisexual outlook of Aquinas no longer dominates our morality or our behavior the way it did not too long ago.

NOTES

1. A more detailed discussion of the sexual aspects of this period is found in David A. Schulz, *Human Sexuality* (Englewood Cliffs, N.J.: Prentice-Hall, 1984), chap. 3.
2. Hunt, *The Natural History of Love* (New York: Knopf, 1959), p. 102.
3. Robert H. Rimmer, *Thursday My Love* (New York: Signet, 1972), p. 257.
4. *Webster's New World Dictionary of the American Language, 2nd College Edition* (New York: World, 1970). The Greeks had another word for love in addition to *agape: Eros*. We retain something like the Greek concept of *Eros*, of course, in our notion of erotic love, except that for many intellectual Greek men the most desirable object of erotic love was a young man. Plato's *Symposium* thus is a hymn to homosexual love.
5. There are, of course, many understandings about what the Bible really is. As the authors see it, the Bible is a book written by many people over almost fourteen centuries of human history. It is a changing account of their encounter with their God and reflects numerous understandings about what that encounter meant. The New Testament, written over a period of about 200 years, tells how this understanding was dramatically changed by the man Jesus of Nazareth, whom the Apostles called the Christ. The Apostles and those who followed them saw that Jesus proclaimed the good news, "I have come that ye shall have life and have it more abundantly." Exciting interpretations of what this good news can mean are found in such books as Paul Tillich, *The Shaking of the Foundation* (New York: Scribner's, 1948), and *The Courage to Be* (New Haven, Conn.: Yale University Press, 1952); Joseph Fletcher, *Situation Ethics: The New Morality* (Philadelphia: Westminster, 1963); John Robinson, *Honest to God* (Philadelphia: Westminster 1963); and John S. Dunne, *A Search for God in Time and Memory* (New York: Macmillan, 1969).
6. Corinthians 7:8–9.
7. The notion that Paul was writing an "interim ethic" did not emerge until the nineteenth century. It arose out of the scholarly practice of seeing the Bible as a product of its own time—a stance fostered by a school of critics who developed methods for interpreting the Bible in historical terms.
8. St. Augustine, *The City of God*, bk. 16, chap. 26.
9. Derrick Sherwin Bailey, "Sexual Ethics in Christian Tradition," in John Charles Wynn, ed., *Sexual Ethics and Christian Responsibility* (New York: Association Press, 1970), p. 148.
10. Ibid., pp. 150–51.
11. Joseph Campbell, *Myths to Live By* (New York: Bantam Books, 1982), p. 162.
12. Campbell, p. 165.
13. Quoted in Campbell, p. 164.
14. Hunt, p. 137.
15. Ibid., p. 190.
16. Ibid., p. 192.
17. Interesting accounts of the nineteenth century can be found in Steven Marcus, *The Other Victorians* (New York: Basic Books, 1966); Michal Foucault, *The History of Sexuality*, Vol. 1 (New York: Vintage Books, 1980); and
18. Carl N. Degler, *At Odds* (New York: Oxford University Press, 1980).
19. More detailed comparisons are made in David A. Schulz, *The Changing Family*, 3rd ed. (Englewood Cliffs, N.J.: Prentice Hall, 1982).

20. William F. Goode, "The Theoretical Importance of Love," *American Sociological Review*, 1959, p. 40.

21. C. W. M. Hart and Arnold R. Pilling, *The Tiwi of North Australia* (New York: Holt, Rinehart & Winston, 1960).

22. Lloyd Warner, *A Black Civilization* (New York: Harper & Row, 1937).

23. Charles Winick, *A Dictionary of Anthropology* (New York: New World Library, 1964).

24. U.S. Bureau of the Census, *Statistical Abstract of the United States, 1982–83* (Washington, D.C.: U.S. Government Printing Office, 1983), pp.

25. Hunt, p. 190.

26. See especially Jules Henry, *Culture Against Man* (New York: Random House, 1963), pp. 11–12; and Erich Fromm, *The Art of Loving* (New York: Bantam Books, 1970).

27. *Statistical Abstract*, p. xx.

28. Ibid., p. 133.

29. Ibid., p. xviii.

30. Daniel Yankelovich, *New Rules: Searching for Self Fulfillment in a World Turned Upside Down* (New York: Bantam Books, 1982), p. 284.

In the view of the wise, Heaven is man and Earth
    woman: Earth fosters what Heaven lets fall.
When Earth lacks heat, Heaven sends it; when she
    has lost her freshness and moisture, Heaven restores it.
Heaven goes on his rounds, like a husband foraging
    for his wife's sake;
And Earth is busy with housewiferies: she attends to
    birth and suckling that which she bears.
Regard Earth and Heaven as endowed with
    intelligence, since they do the work of intelligent beings.
Unless these twain taste pleasure from one another,
    why are they creeping together like sweethearts?

—Rumi

12 Husbands and Wives

The poet Rumi beautifully describes how, in his view, the ancient roles of husband and wife are related to one another. The verses introducing this chapter were written over seven centuries ago, yet their understanding of this relationship still speaks directly to many couples today. This chapter will examine the implicit expectations of the marriage contract and how these are changing. Today as always, the institution of marriage accommodates a wide range of interpretations of what it ought to be. Perhaps the most unusual aspect of our discussion of marriage is the extent to which these are openly discussed and widely accepted.

All styles of partnerships, marital and nonmarital, have their benefits and their costs. This is no less true of traditional styles than of innovative ones. People entering any kind of partnership must decide what they are willing to give, what risks they are willing to take, and for what benefits. The ideals and norms of traditional marriage are no more unrealistic or unrewarding than any other style. This is why large numbers of people find them satisfactory.

This chapter will explore some of the creative aspects of marriage as it is conventionally defined. A successful traditional marriage, like any viable partnership, must be a dynamic process rather than a static condition. A man and a woman who are committed to one another will constantly be aware of the opportunities to confirm each other's self-actualization. The social conditions supporting the conventional marriage norms change, and these changes will affect the norms. Thus, the expectations that a couple share after fifteen years of marriage will most likely be different from those they had when they began. Much of the joy—as well as the sorrow—of marriage derives from coping with these changes and renegotiating what marriage means to a couple.

We will look first at some of the more lasting expectations about marriage and then examine some of the changes that have taken place. Increasing numbers of married women work outside the home. Renegotiating the marriage contract to encourage wives to have careers, and managing the new state of affairs that results when a couple take this step, is not easy. But many couples feel that the benefits are worth the effort. Changing norms governing sexual behavior have encouraged some couples to open their marriage to intimate friendships that may or may not involve sexual relationships. The range of acceptable behaviors available to marriage partners in many areas seems to be increasing.

As a durable—yet flexible—contract, marriage continues to offer the possibility for nondependent living, personal growth, and individual freedom to those who are willing to stick to their commitment to each other and work together to realize those benefits.

THE IMPLICIT MARRIAGE CONTRACT

While most couples talk about what they expect of each other before they get married, they rarely take the time to write these expectations down in a formal contract. Because the conventional norms governing what marriage is supposed to be are still fairly widespread, many people feel comfortable with the intention to be "a good husband" or "a good wife" without going into what this means in any detail. Behind the wedding vows is a more or less implicit contract or understanding about what marriage should be like. The basic elements of this implicit contract are lifelong **monogamy**, exclusive sexual rights in the spouse, common residence and economic independence from parents and relatives, a distinctive—if no longer very convincing—understanding of what is man's work and what is woman's work, the expectation of children, and the need for togetherness.

Lifelong Monogamous Union

The central expectation of traditional marriage is that it is an indissoluble monogamous union. This understanding of marriage derives from the Judeo-Christian tradition of marriage as a sacrament in which the ceremony makes the union indissoluble before God and humanity: "What God hath joined together, let no man put asunder." Even though marriage has been transformed, to a large extent, from a religious sacrament to a civil contract and then to a personal affirmation, it remains a symbol of the deep commitment of a man and a woman to each other. For many people this symbol still has validity.

For example, we know a couple who lived together for years without being married. After they got married, they reported that the marriage

Even with the increasing rate of divorce, most Americans still expect that their marriage will be for life. (Ray Ellis, Photo Researchers, Inc.)

produced beneficial results for their partnership. "Sometimes we'd go through difficult periods," the husband explained,

> and when we'd have a fight maybe it would end with one of us moving out for a few days. We always got back together again but it could get kind of scary. Whenever this happened there was a sense that maybe this time would be it. It tended to make both of us a little reluctant to bring up things that were bothering us; we were afraid to start a fight because of what it might lead to. But when we got married we more or less said to each other that we wanted to stay together for good. Instead of someone walking out when things get tough, we have to stay there and work the thing out. So it seems like we can be more open with each other now because by getting married we sort of said to each other, "Look, if there are any problems, they're *our* problems. We've got a good—a beautiful—relationship and we're not going to let any temporary problems break us up."

Indissoluble monogamous marriage points toward a growing relationship in which two people look forward to time together in various stages of their lives. It offers them the exciting possibility of continued discovery and interchange as they mature together. It sees the human personality as a rich and ever-changing resource. It assumes that there will always be mystery in the other partner that can constantly be discovered and can give new joy to the partnership. Part of the commitment to such a contract is the expectation that the partners will change and that they will share their changing selves with each other. The public affirmation of this commitment "before God" or "before family and friends" is not only a statement of intention, but also a source of support. When others who love you know of your intentions to live together "forever," they can often help without being asked. Your knowing that others know about your relationship can make you less willing to dissolve it in the face of adversity. These supports should not replace the basic commitment of the couple, but they can reinforce that commitment.

Exclusive Sexual Rights in the Spouse

Traditional marriage involves an expectation of exclusive sexual rights in the spouse. This expectation reinforces the notion of monogamy as a lifelong commitment and emphasizes the uniqueness of the relationship. At one time, not so long ago, it was popularly believed that there was only one person in the world who was meant to be one's spouse. Whether it derived from the religious or the romantic tradition, such a notion helped support the exclusiveness of the relationship.

As with lifelong monogamy, there is considerable variation in people's understanding of this expectation. In working-class families today, for example, the understanding is often that the husband has such rights over his wife, but that she does not necessarily have them over him.[1] Sometimes a distinction is made in which casual sexual encounters, such as with a prostitute, are permissible but long-term affairs are not. In some upper-class social circles, extramarital sexual affairs are permitted for both husband and wife, with the couple understanding this clause in the implicit marriage contract as requiring only that they conduct themselves with propriety and not in a blatant manner. In many modern middle-class marriages, the understanding is often that the wife's rights in this matter are the same as the husband's; that is, either both are free to engage in extramarital sexual activity or neither is.

Although it is often charged that the idea of exclusive sexual rights in the spouse necessarily implies a possessive relationship, this need not be so. On the contrary, it can simply be an indication of the dedication of the partners to each other. Traditionally, exclusive means exclusive. Any sexual relationship outside the marriage is a violation of the marriage contract—though such indiscretions may occur. If they occur, there is a "guilty party."

Common Residence and Economic Independence

The assumption that the marital partnership will be economically independent from any outside support, together with the assumption of common residence, gives a distinctive economic identity to the married couple in modern American society. These assumptions, which probably derive from the characteristic American emphasis on "rugged individualism," place an enormous responsibility on the husband—and now increasingly on the wife. Although many studies have shown that few American marriages are completely cut off from kin support, the extent to which we take it for granted that couples must "go it alone" is probably greater than the extent to which most other societies hold this view.[2] Although it is not uncommon for young people to marry while they are still in school and to depend on parental support in the early years of their marriage, the general acceptance of the idea that marriage entails economic independence often leads such couples to feel that their marriage is not really complete—that they are merely "playing house" together—until they are on their own.

Division of Labor

Many changes are taking place in the traditional **division of labor** within marriage. It is possible to describe at least five patterns that women commonly follow in the assumption of their role obligations; at present men have fewer alternatives. Although each pattern is a variation on how the work is to be divided up, all the patterns mentioned here tend to assume the other expectations of traditional marriage described earlier.[3]

The Maternity–Homemaking Pattern. In this pattern the husband accepts the entire responsibility for providing for the family, while the wife assumes all the responsibility for housekeeping and childcare. Under this arrangement it is not possible for the wife to work outside the home, but she makes a major economic contribution by processing food for the home and doing all the cleaning and domestic chores—with the help of her children when they are old enough. For this reason, large families can be an advantage when this pattern is in effect. The pattern is still widely followed in rural America, but in urban and suburban settings it is less common and is less likely to be successful.

The Companionship Pattern. In this pattern the maternal and economic roles of the wife are less important than they are in the maternity-homemaking pattern. Instead, the wife's attention and time are focused on her husband's interests and activities. In this pattern a wife might be expected to spend a great deal of time making herself attractive in order that she may respond in a sexual, recreational, and therapeutic manner to her husband, in whom she finds her fulfillment. Her social role as hostess to her husband's friends and business associates is also emphasized. This pattern, which is common in the upper middle class, has been a target of the women's movement because it seems to center on the male. This criticism is undeniably valid, but there is no denying that in such relationships women tend to have a great deal of power. Some men and women find intrinsic value in such a division of labor and do not feel that it makes the wife's role inferior in any way.[4]

A recent study of the social standing of "housewife" as an occupation found that the status of this occupation was strongly dependent on its context. Overall, "housewife" ranked in the middle of the NORC prestige scale—only the professions and semiprofessions, the arts, and managerial and official positions (all of which require training or experience) scored higher. Housewives and people over 35 years old tended to rank it higher than working women and people under 35. The author concluded that the role may be retaining its status because it is becoming a luxury item. This is especially true in the working class, in which the husband's income alone is rarely adequate to support the family.[5]

The Career Pattern. The career pattern is the other side of the coin from the maternity-homemaking pattern. Small families are favored, and the birth of children probably will be planned so as not to interfere with careers. Outside help is employed for child care and domestic chores. The wife assumes considerable responsibility for the support of the family and seeks part of her fulfillment in her career. In this pattern, as compared to any of the others, the husband is more likely to be assigned a share of the household tasks. This style of partnership within traditional marriage is emerging as a dominant middle-class pattern. It is not to be confused with the working-class situation, in which a wife works because she has to in order to maintain the family's standard of living or simply to pay the bills, for a job is not the same thing as a career. People take jobs for money and other fringe benefits, whereas in a career they are likely to be looking primarily for personal fulfillment. One way to distinguish between these roughly similar situations is by asking whether the wife would continue working if the husband's income were sufficient to satisfy the family's financial needs.

Although it is sometimes tempting to conclude that finding a job outside the home will in itself help women to find personal satisfaction and fulfillment, the evidence supporting this notion is mixed. Several recent studies find that working women are indeed more satisfied with their lives than housewives.[6] However, six large national surveys conducted by the National Opinion Research Center over the years 1971 to 1976 fail to support such a hypothesis. Wright finds no significant differences.[7] There are costs and benefits to both roles. Working women enjoy additional outside income and some increases in independence. If they are working in careers that are intrinsically rewarding, they undoubtedly have this source of satisfaction. But they pay for these benefits in reduced leisure—particularly when their husbands do not pick up many of the domestic chores. Working women are likely to lead much more complicated lives and experience a more hectic pace than nonworking women.

Relatively little attention has been paid to the effect of a wife's working on her husband. One study suggests that husbands of working wives were less satisfied with their marriages than husbands of nonworking wives.[8] It was suggested that while the wives enjoyed an increase in status because of their working, their husbands experienced a reduction in status insofar as they did more work around the house. Whatever the status of a housewife may be, there is little evidence that men generally perceive domestic chores as a source of personal fulfillment. A man may enjoy an improved relationship with his children, derive some satisfaction from seeing his wife develop, and feel more competent as a family member. However, in a society in which a man's status is still generally based on his ability to function in the intellectual, business, or industrial world, domestic work has generally lower status.

Thus, both husbands and wives receive benefits as well as costs from living in a dual-career family. Even in the best situation from the point of view of the couple, in which the wife works because she finds satisfaction in her work and the couple earn enough so that someone else can be hired to do the domestic work, there are problems in adjusting to a more complicated life style that must be taken into consideration. Dual-career marriages offer exciting possibilities for both partners, but they should not be considered an automatic route to personal satisfaction in marriage for either partner.

The Family-Plus-Partial-Career Pattern. In this pattern childcare, child-bearing, and household responsibilities are high priorities. Some or all of these tasks may be delegated to outside employees or agencies, but if these become unavailable or inadequate the wife is expected to relinquish her career. This simply means that the wife considers, or is expected to consider, her family interests first and her career second. A common variant of this pattern is for the wife to have a career until the birth of the first child, suspend that career until the last child reaches a certain age, and then resume her career as best she can. Naturally, this variant is easiest to follow if the wife's career is one in which continuity of employment is not essential. In general, the family-plus-partial-career pattern, like the full-career pattern, is primarily a middle-class life style.

The Role Segregation Pattern. None of the patterns enumerated so far seems accurately to describe what Elizabeth Bott has called the "role segregation pattern" typical of the working class, although the closest approximation is the maternity-homemaking pattern.[9] The distinctive feature of the role segregation pattern is that husband and wife really do not seem to see themselves as complementing each other's activities. Men typically engage in recreation with other men and women with other women. The sharp distinction between the "man's world" and the "woman's world" separates not only their major occupations—his job, her homemaking—but also their outside interests, hobbies, and social habits.

Women are achieving increasing equality with men. They outnumbered men in college enrollment for the first time in U.S. history in the late 1970s.[10] Over half of all married women work. However much they are discriminated against in wages at present, women are developing an independent economic base outside the family, and this must affect how power is distributed within the family. One study has found that a large majority (72 percent) of all Americans prefer a marriage of shared responsibility in which husband and wife share work, childrearing, and homemaking responsibility. The traditional marriage in which he is the breadwinner and she is the homemaker is preferred by only 27 percent.[11]

The "Two Worlds" of Work and Family. The patterns of role relationships just described indicate that the worlds of work and family cannot be separated. Yet both in theory and in practice there is a strong tendency to pretend that they can and should be. Thus, family sociologists rarely look at the work situations of family members, and social scientists who study work rarely look at family life patterns. Similarly, corporations have assumed that what happens in the family is largely none of their concern because whatever occurs there should not affect performance on the job. It is common to assume that the priorities of the work world should take precedence over the priorities of the family, and family members are expected to adjust to any change in job requirements the company imposes on its employees. Increasingly, however, we are coming to see that these distinctions are arbitrary and that they mask very basic issues that should be of concern to us.[12]

One interesting study of the interface between the worlds of family and work suggests that there are personality differences between husbands and wives in one-career and two-career families.[13] Working wives have significantly lower scores than nonworking wives on scales measuring needs for inclusion, control, and affection. Husbands of working wives also score lower on these scales. A measure of the couple's preference for taking an active or passive role in relating to others indicates that housewives are more passive than working women and husbands of housewives more active than husbands of working women. This latter finding supports the notion that the stereotypic roles are more commonly found in the single-career family. Burke and Weir were not able to determine the cause of these personality differences. It is not clear, for example, whether people with such personality traits would prefer such family styles or whether the wife's experience at work changed the personality traits of both partners by changing their role expectations.

Another study suggests that managers discriminate against working women in that they do not expect them to be as able as their husbands to balance home and career responsibilities and do not expect the husband of a working woman to sacrifice his career opportunities for hers.[14] Thus, working women are perceived of as offering a greater risk to the employer and are not as likely to be considered for jobs involving travel. These managerial attitudes are likely to generate conflict between the marital partners. The wife is placed in a second-class role on the job, and her career expectations are more likely to be frustrated. Her husband also must suffer the effects of discrimination if he attempts to cooperate and adjust his career expectations to accommodate his wife's. His manager will find him less competitive than men who do not hold such egalitarian attitudes toward working women.

The Balance of Power

Much has been written about the balance of power within the traditional household.[15] This, too, is changing. Thus, although patriarchy was an almost universally accepted norm a few decades ago, its acceptance has declined markedly since World War II. To be sure, most middle-class husbands still make the major decisions about moving, buying a house or a car, deciding when to take a vacation, and so forth, but today it is considered far more acceptable for the wife to have an input in such decisions. Although the husband may still have the last word in many families, he generally can expect less support for an unpopular decision than, say, his father or grandfather would have expected in the same situation. The movement toward a companionship type of family has opened many of these decisions to debate within the family, even though in the last analysis it is still common for the father to make the final decision.

The Blessing of Children

The expectation of children is an important ingredient in the traditional understanding of marriage. Without children, it is often said, a marriage is not a family, and although a family has its good points and its bad points, it cannot be replaced with any other kind of relationship. Traditionally, large families of five or more children were thought of as highly desirable. Today, even though smaller families have become more popular, it is still widely felt that a marriage without at least one or two children is incomplete.

Togetherness

One of the more exciting experiences we can have as individuals is the sharing of events, interests, and ideas with others. To laugh with someone who has come to know you intimately because she or he has shared so much of your life is to understand the private humor of personal involvement. Engaging in a common task, whether it be fixing up the house or going on a picnic, is not only rewarding but also just plain fun. To have a spouse to whom you can turn in the midst of disappointment, frustration, and agony is one of the deepest and most significant rewards of intimate partnership. Cuber and Harroff capture a great deal of the positive value of the norm of togetherness in their example of a "total" relationship. In the following passage a consulting engineer describes his pleasure in being able to share part of his job with his wife:

> I invariably take her with me to conferences around the world. Her femininity, easy charm and wit are invaluable assets to me. I know it's conventional to say that a man's wife is responsible for his success, and I also know that it's often not true. But in my case I gladly acknowledge that it's

Doing things together has long been a part of what we consider to be a good marriage. (Ken Karp)

not only true, but she's indispensable to me. But she'd go along with me even if there was nothing for her to do because we just enjoy each other's company—deeply. You know, the best part of a vacation is not what we do but that we do it together. We plan it and reminisce about it and weave it into our work and our play all the time.

His wife comments:

It seems to me that Bert exaggerates my help. It's not so much that I only want to help him: it's more that I want to do these things anyway. We do them together even though we may not be in each other's presence at the time. I don't really know what I do for him and what I do for me.[16]

In these statements the husband and wife have captured an aspect of togetherness that is often overlooked in superficial descriptions of doing things together. For Bert and his wife, however, their togetherness represents the fact that they enjoy a relationship in which communication takes place at a deep level.

When we speak of togetherness, therefore, as one of the expectations implied in what we have been calling the implicit marriage contract, we should distinguish between togetherness as a norm for conduct and togetherness as a product of a relationship. When people get married they often regard togetherness as a norm; that is, they consider the kind of interested sharing described here as something they are entitled to from their mates and something they are obliged to give in return. They feel that this is a part of the contract. Such expectations can be damaging insofar as they deny the partners their unique, autonomous individuality. But this does not mean togetherness is undesirable. On the contrary, when two people come to have genuinely mutual interests arising out of a pattern of intimate sharing, the result can be a deepening of their experiences compared to what they would have encountered if each had followed only his or her own interests.

BECOMING MORE FLEXIBLE

We have repeatedly noted that traditional marriage is undergoing some dramatic changes. The divorce rate is increasing, but until recently the remarriage rate was increasing even faster. Counselors tell us that about half of the marriages in America are failures as measured by the partners' own assessment of their relationship. It is safe to say that a large number of marriages could not be considered vital, growing partnerships and are not considered such by the people involved.

At the very time when an impersonal society is making increased demands on marriage to fulfill the needs of its members for intimacy and a sense of belongingness, many people find the traditional institution incapable of satisfying their needs. Although this situation has led to some gloomy predictions about the future of marriage, many observers feel that

Couples can learn greater role flexibility by sharing and exchanging chores. (Mimi Forsyth, Monkmeyer Press Photo Service)

the problem is not some weakness in the institution itself, but rather the fact that people often bring to marriage unrealistic and outdated expectations that are no longer relevant to the task of living together in today's world. There seems to be a need to make our expectations about marriage—and our marriages themselves—more flexible, more in tune with our own unique needs and desires.

People who take this approach generally see their efforts as an affirmation of monogamous marriage, not a repudiation of it. They are operating on the assumption that the institution of marriage is worth saving. This affirmation comes at a time when others are contending that marriage has outlived its usefulness. What is more, it comes from people who are in touch with one another and care about each other rather than from partners who find themselves in a deteriorating relationship in which they have lost touch with one another. That to say, the various attempts we see all around us to make marriage more flexible are not necessarily the desperate effects of couples on the verge of divorce or of unhappy people looking for some alternative to their situation. On the contrary, those who want to improve marriage, to make it more responsive to their own needs and desires, tend to be couples who already have a reasonably good partnership and want to make it better.

Such people are attempting to build a vital relationship in which the growth of the partners is an important consideration. Good communication between the partners is essential if this end is to be achieved. So is a creative effort to transcend the conventional roles of married life when these roles are felt to inhibit personal growth and the growth of the partnership. Role transcendence is aimed toward the ideal of nondependent living—that is, a way of living together in which the relationship between the two individuals does not force either one to give up so much that she or he becomes dependent on the other. People striving for more flexible marriages also place a high priority on the personal growth of each partner and recognize that individual freedom is a necessary ingredient of such growth. Each individual, they feel, must have the freedom to decide for himself or herself what the most creative use of his or her time might be. And finally, most immediately related to role transcendence is the ability to be flexible in the definition of the roles of husband and wife.

Nondependent Living

According to popular lore and popular songs, the aim of marriage is for two people to live together "as one." But according to the ideal of nondependent living, each partner in a marriage should strive to become more of a person in his or her own right and avoid surrendering his or her own personhood to the partner. As each partner becomes more of a person by developing his or her own talents and interests, the two of them avoid becoming dependent on one another. Each one brings to the relationship a growing, many-faceted personality that could, if the occasion called for it, stand alone and manage the problems of everyday life.

Loss of self in a relationship follows naturally from efforts to live up to the ideal of two people "becoming one." In order to succeed in this aim, either both partners must surrender a part of themselves, or one of them (in our society this is generally the woman) must surrender entirely. Because such relationships generally meet with social approval, especially when it is the woman who is called upon to renounce her personal development, the loss of autonomy frequently goes unnoticed.

It is very important that partners be alert to the importance of retaining their distinctiveness and personhood. They should look for such signs as habitually deferring to the other person's wishes or trying to assess what the partner thinks about something before venturing to express their own views. As the poet Kahlil Gibran wrote in *The Prophet*, "Let there be spaces in your togetherness!"[17] Without a significant degree of personal autonomy, it makes no sense to talk about freedom or personal growth. In order for two people to "come together," there first must be *two people*.

Personal Growth

Personal growth is the movement away from simple conformity with social expectations toward the discovery that each of us has an internal center of evaluation that can provide us with adequate guidance. Personal growth involves coming into contact with the vast array of feelings, emotions, ideas, and attitudes that are within us, and responding to the world in terms of this complexity. It is discovering how we feel personally about the world and cultivating the courage to act on these feelings. It means that as we grow we have available to us a rich variety of possible responses to any situation.

To illustrate what we mean by personal growth, consider the fact that most people have the capacity to engage in simple athletic skills such as swimming, baseball, tennis, and skating. Although a lot of instruction has been lavished on young children who are trying to master these skills, no child is ever going to learn an athletic skill until he or she tries it. Then the child's own sensations and perceptions will enable him or her to perform successfully. Indeed, a few afternoons at a baseball park will convincingly demonstrate that few of the really good hitters have batting stances that look like the stances illustrated in the "how-to" books. Over time they have developed styles of their own that suit their own specific talents best.

In much the same way, personal growth in partnerships requires reliance on how one feels in the partnership rather than concern about how one "ought" to feel. In one of Carl Roger's case studies, Roy and Sylvia convey how they feel about their growing partnership:

> We want our relationship to be such that each is given the freedom and encouragement to develop his (her) full potential. We want our marriage to be an exciting exploration of new avenues. We want to share so deeply that even the forbidden, the shameful, the jealous, the angry feelings that we have are as fully expressed and as much accepted as the tender and loving feelings. . . . We want to be the complexity of our feelings, which are by no means always simple and clear.[18]

It is important to note at this point that although personal growth often entails willingness to disregard or defy convention, it is not a matter of simple rebellion. Personal growth is the process of becoming one's real self, and this means following conventions where one is comfortable with them as well as rejecting them where one is not. Rebellion for the sake of rebellion is not personal growth. Personal growth involves awareness and affirmation of the meaning of one's behavior. In partnerships in which personal growth is taking place, Rogers observes, "a worthy partner [is] not a slave or a slaveowner, not a shadow or an echo, not always a leader nor always a follower, not a person to be taken for granted, and certainly not a boring person."[19]

Individual Freedom

The ideals of nondependent living and personal growth imply that the partners in a marriage have a considerable degree of individual freedom. At the simplest level this freedom means willingness to dissolve what Nena and George O'Neill call the *couple-front*—a term they coined to describe acceptance of the norm that married partners should always manifest solidarity, at least outwardly.[20] Acceptance of the couple-front as a norm means that the couple should always go places together, do the same things, and not allow any other person to have intimate access to either partner. Inevitably, this demand legislates against individual freedom.

To counter the notion of the couple-front the O'Neills coined the term **open marriage** to suggest it was possible to be much freer in a marriage. True individual freedom does not mean merely the time and resources to do things separately. Equally important is an awareness that the partners are free to make contacts, cultivate friendships, and develop separate interests and activities. As one of the O'Neills' respondents remarks:

> Both of us have shared interests along with different individual interests. So how can we live our whole lives attached to one another? Her to me, me to her? Is she going to get all her humor from me, all her sympathy, all her intellectual interests from me? Christ, I can't fill that role. I'm smart, but let's face it, I'm not God. So when you get down to it, what does it mean, that I can't be everything to her? It means she has to live with other people too. So if she meets another person, another man, say, who is a musician, it's all right for her to go to dinner with him. Is it all right for her to go to a ballet or a concert with him? Sure. Sometimes we go to the ballet together, too. But I can't possibly supply the same type of stimulus and companionship at a ballet or concert that she can get with a musician.[21]

We are well aware that for many readers this husband's statement conjures up the specter of sexual infidelity. Indeed, the O'Neills' book *Open Marriage*, from which this statement is taken, is widely assumed—by people who have not read it—to be a defense of a new style of marriage in which the partners are free to engage in sexual activities with people other than their mates. To a large extent this mistaken interpretation of the O'Neills' views about individual freedom in the context of marriage is a result of sensationalist journalism, which has singled out the most lurid implications of their argument.[22] But to an equally large extent this misinterpretation of the idea of freedom in marriage derives from the suspicion, widely held in our society, that close personal friendships of a nonsexual nature are not possible between men and women. Americans in general tend to be quite cynical on this issue, imagining that the husband just quoted is being hopelessly naive: If he thinks his wife can go to concerts, ballets, and dinners with another man, he is, such people would say, asking for trouble.

In a sense these skeptics are not completely wrong, for their dire predictions can tend to be a self-fulfilling prophecy. That is, in a society in which married men and women are not trusted to socialize freely with members of the opposite sex, even totally "innocent" contacts are likely to be looked at suspiciously, and as a result the individuals involved may feel it necessary to be somewhat furtive about their relationship. What is more, this sort of furtive secrecy, which is natural in illicit sexual relationships, makes it easier for the relationship to turn into a sexual one—even though that was contrary to the original intentions of the man and the woman.

Consider, for example, the case of a male college teacher who finds he can enjoy the stimulating conversations about his academic specialty with a certain female colleague. They find themselves spending five or six hours a week together after classes "talking shop." If his conversational companion were another male he probably wouldn't give this a moment's thought, and neither would his wife. But socializing with a woman is another matter. Perhaps his wife shows signs of jealousy, or perhaps he imagines them; in either case he reasons—quite rightly—that he has done nothing wrong and that there is no reason to terminate his friendship. But he doesn't want to upset his wife, and he especially doesn't want people to "start talking," so he and his female colleague stop meeting in public places and he begins to lie to his wife about where he spends his afternoons. He justifies the lying by telling himself that the truth in this case would only upset his wife needlessly. But the point is that he is no longer honest in his relationship with his wife and has transformed a perfectly innocent friendship into something he feels guilty about. Psychologists tell us that people frequently engage in behavior they know is wrong in order to "justify" feelings of guilt; children who misbehave because they feel they deserve punishment are an example of this phenomenon. In the situation just described, this mechanism may well work to drive the teacher and his colleague into an affair neither of them really wants.

On the other hand, if the man in this case had felt perfectly free to form whatever close friendships he felt were required for his development as a person and as a professional, his association with his female colleague would not have been surrounded with an aura of guilt, and insofar as it was guilt that led him to escalate a friendship into an affair, this outcome would have been much less likely. This is not to say that sexual infidelity will not occur in a marriage governed by the principle of individual freedom. But when we recognize that in American society today the norms are generally against the freedom of a married person to form friendships with members of the opposite sex, and that nevertheless about 50 percent of married people report they have engaged in extramarital sexual activities at one time or another, the conclusion that limiting freedom is not an effective way to secure marital fidelity is inescapable.

In general, if individuals have experienced sexual intercourse before marriage they are more likely to approve of sexual intercourse outside marriage as well.[23] Religious individuals are likely to disapprove of extramarital sexual intercourse in most cases. Only those who are most liberal or radical in their beliefs are likely to condone such behavior.[24] In restrictive cultures, one study suggests, women tend to feel confined to the formal family, from which they nevertheless feel psychologically alienated.[25] They disapprove of extramarital sex, but once they have experienced such behavior they tend to become emotionally involved. Hence the many beautiful Chinese love poems to someone else's spouse.[26]

From an ethical point of view, it seems clear that sexual exclusiveness practiced in a context of freedom is far more valuable and meaningful to the couple than the same exclusivity when it is a result of enforced seclusion from members of the opposite sex. The man or woman who secures his or her partner's sexual fidelity by making sure the partner is never alone with a member of the opposite sex may get the desired result, but such fidelity does not express the value the partner places on the relationship. Indeed, in an intimate partnership any act that is not a result of free choice is meaningless as a communication of how the partners feel about each other.

Role Flexibility

It is impossible for any individual to be completely free from the influence of social expectations about appropriate behaviors or roles. Roles provide the framework within which social interaction can take place, even among strangers in the same culture. They are accretions of past experiences that lend stability and order to social living. Despite their obvious value, however, simple acceptance of established social roles leads to domination by those roles. On the other hand, awareness of the roles one is called upon to fulfill and reflection on them in terms of one's own unique situation enable people to make their roles more flexible and better suited to their own individual needs.

At the simplest level, that of daily living, role flexibility means willingness to share and exchange chores. Role flexibility in an intimate partnership means the man becomes more involved in childrearing, cooking, and other domestic tasks while the woman takes on decision-making responsibilities that have traditionally been reserved for the male. Some couples are deliberately experimenting with role reversal over extended periods. One such couple devoted an entire year to reversal: The wife went to work and paid the bills while the husband stayed home and took care of their two children. They reported that the process resulted in increased understanding of each other, and they believed it had made a creative contribution to their marriage. The O'Neills observe that "any task normally undertaken by one mate can be exchanged with the other. None is likely to be glamorous, but all are necessary, and by shifting these chores back and forth, marital partners can relieve boredom, learn something new, become more versatile, and gain additional respect for the other's efforts." Scandinavian countries such as Sweden have given experiments in role reversal extensive testing.[27] Predictably, both partners usually take several weeks or months to become adjusted to the new routine, but the results are generally gratifying. The wife seems to be better able to adjust to the job than the husband to the home and domesticity.

Openness. Couples striving for greater flexibility generally replace the norm of togetherness with an emphasis on mutual trust and expansion through openness. One of the couples in the O'Neills' study defines trust as follows:

Glenda: Trust is a confidence you have in the other person, a belief in him. I believe in Robert, he believes in me. Sure, it takes time, but we love each other enough to be honest with one another. If we weren't honest with each other, it wouldn't be possible.

Robert: You know, trust is freedom—a lack of fear. When you get down to it, trust is really faith. We have a faith in the fact that what we have together is much more than any temporary relationship could ever be. So we aren't afraid of one another's relationships with other people.[28]

The fact that Glenda's and Robert's relationship is open and honest and based on mutual trust gives it a kind of vitality rarely possible in partnerships limited by conventional role assignments. They share an exciting experience of the sort that builds confidence in one's partner and in oneself. In such a partnership, the partners know that the relationship has durability, and the inner security they derive from this knowledge gives them the freedom to expand and grow in an open and trusting way. That is to say, in an intimate partnership trust has a spiraling effect: The more it is given and reciprocated, the more secure the partners become in the essential soundness of their relationship, and hence the more trusting they can be.

Openness involves the capacity to hear, understand, and realize who another person is. It means assuming responsibility for yourself first and then sharing that self to whatever degree seems appropriate. Every couple must define these limits for themselves, for openness means not only communicating freely with one's partner, but also respecting the partner's need for privacy and his or her need to have an independent, autonomous life, parts of which he or she may not wish to share. The couple who pride themselves on the fact that they "have no secrets from each other" may not have as open a partnership as they imagine they do. What is missing in this case is the freedom to have a private life.

We can realize how important this is by considering the case of a wife who has a friend who would like to confide some personal secret to her but does not want the husband to know. If the friend is aware that the husband and wife "have no secrets," she will be reluctant to talk confidentially, knowing that anything she tells her friend will pass directly to her friend's husband. She finds it impossible, therefore, to treat her friend as an autonomous individual; instead, she has to regard her as merely half of a husband-wife duo and can share with her only thoughts that she would be willing to share with him. This simple but rather common case involving an outsider indicates how easily the ideal of openness and sharing can be misunderstood and pushed too far. Openness should never become a pretext for invading the individual privacy of the partner. Properly understood, the ideal of openness means not only the freedom to communicate fully with one's partner, but also the freedom not to communicate when one does not want to.

Another important ramification of the concept of openness involves the controversial subject of whether or not opening up marriage to outside sexual contacts is beneficial. We will return to this subject in our discussion of the role of jealousy in intimate partnerships, but for the time being we should like to observe that there is some evidence to suggest that in some cases expanded sexual relations can indeed bring new life to individuals and to their partnership. Raymond Lawrence, a therapist, provides an example in his case study of Susan, a patient in her mid-20s who had been married for over six years when she came to him for therapy.[29] "She was thinking of having an affair with a young pediatrician and she felt she needed to talk to someone about it," Lawrence explains.

Over a series of sessions, various areas of Susan's marriage were explored. It was revealed that Susan's husband was deeply immersed in his work and was able to spend little time with her. Throughout this time in her marriage, Susan felt herself deteriorating and her feelings about herself becoming less and less positive. Although her meetings with the pediatrician were accidental at first, she found that they had the effect of making her feel more and more stimulated and excited about life.

During the sessions with Susan the therapist sought to examine whether she was acting out a desire to communicate something to her husband, to even the score with him for her sense of dullness, to be revenged on him for something that he might have done, or simply to get his attention. None of these typical motivations seemed to be present behind Susan's desire to have an affair with the pediatrician. Susan revealed a commitment to her marriage, even with its limitations. "Susan is like innumerable married persons who have come to me for counseling," Lawrence observes. "They are . . . stifled and burdened by the total and exclusive dimension of the marriage contract."[30]

After having secured reasonable assurance that there were no ulterior motives and that the projected affair was not an assault on her husband, the therapist explored the whole area of guilt with Susan. He tried to help her understand the serious moral questions involved in her interest. He asked Susan to consider whether she was capable of bearing the guilt feelings such an affair was likely to entail. At the end of this careful process of guided self-examination, Susan decided to have the affair. It lasted six months. During that time marked changes in her appearance, manner, and functioning within her family became apparent. These changes evoked increasing interest and response from her husband. He exhibited some anxiety and at the same time began to focus more attention on her and on their marriage. Both Susan and her husband were pleased with the new vitality in their marriage.

From this case history we can understand something of the contribution outside relationships may bring to a partnership under certain conditions. It must be noted, however, that in this case the therapist explored many possible ulterior motives, unconscious drives, and other psychological mechanisms that could have been used to turn this affair into a very destructive liaison for all involved. The same sort of caution should always be employed whenever the question of engaging in sexual intercourse outside marriage is approached, because this is an area in which hidden psychological motivations are likely to be at work. It may not always be necessary to seek professional guidance, but a careful examination of one's own feelings is advisable if one is to feel confident that the end result will be an opening up of the relationship to greater freedom rather than a plunge into a tangled situation involving self-deception and feelings of guilt.

Coping with Jealousy

Jealousy is an integral component of our understanding of love. The extent to which we feel jealous is often taken as a measure of our love. If the husband or lover does not experience jealousy when the beloved bestows her time and attention on another, then he must not love his partner very much. What is more, anthropologists tell us that jealousy seems to be a fairly widespread phenomenon in human experience; it occurs even among co-wives in polygamous households.[31] Nevertheless, there is little evidence to support the assumption that jealousy is a learned response. Far from being a natural way of indicating the depth of one's love, it is a learned technique for expressing the insecurities that arise in possessive relationships. As the O'Neills observe,

> The idea of sexually exclusive monogamy and possession of another breeds deep-rooted dependencies, infantile and childish emotions and insecurities. The more insecure you are, the more you will be jealous. Jealousy, says Abraham Maslow, "practically always breeds further rejection and deeper insecurity." And jealousy, like a destructive cancer, breeds more jealousy. It is never, then, a function of love, but of our insecurities and dependencies. It is the fear of a loss of love and it destroys that very love. It is detrimental to and a denial of a loved one's personal identity.[32]

The fact that jealousy is a deep-rooted tradition in our culture and that, in personal terms, it may express unconscious feelings, does not mean that it is natural, inevitable, or something to be encouraged. Many people have been able to overcome it in their efforts to achieve trusting and open partnerships. Such people often report that their struggle with jealousy has been successful to the extent that it does not prevent them from developing meaningful and loving relationships outside the primary partnership of their marriage. They have come to view outside relationships as a natural right to be enjoyed by themselves and their spouses.

When two partners in an intimate relationship are secure in their own self-identity and are capable of trusting each other, each is free to know, enjoy, and share relationships outside the marriage that can actually serve to augment the primary partnership and make it more creative. Occasionally, the partners may even agree that their outside relationships may include sexual intercourse. At present this extreme form of openness is relatively rare, and the situation is difficult to discuss objectively because of the deep feelings many people have on the subject.

The most important point to be borne in mind is that openness means a relationship based on mutual trust and equality; in an open relationship there is no room for jealousy as a measure of love because the feelings of insecurity and possessiveness out of which jealousy grows are reduced. Thus, it may well be that some couples with an open partnership can enjoy outside sexual contacts the enable them to bring back to their marriage the love and pleasure experienced in those contacts without their partnership's being disrupted by jealousy.

On the other hand, recognizing that openness can be of immense value in creating a dynamic and growing partnership should not blind us to the fact that there are many good reasons why a couple may choose to limit their sexual activities to each other. Many people find that their sexual pleasure and their ability to communicate through sex are heightened by the fact that it is a private communication between just the two of them. For such people, sexual exclusivity would not be inconsistent with an open relationship. But when exclusivity is based on proprietary feelings about one's partner, openness is impossible. In short, the couple who want an open and trusting relationship should strive to eliminate feelings of possessiveness and jealousy from their interactions. But this does not mean they have to or even should open up their sexual relationship to outside contacts. On the contrary, sexual exclusivity can be an important and meaningful part of an open and creative partnership as long as it is not based on jealousy and possessiveness.

Flexibility as a Social Issue

It is not easy to become more flexible in a partnership. All of us want to feel good about ourselves, and one important way we do this is to live up to the expectations of others. When these expectations are role expectations about what it means to be a good husband or a good wife, not following them means we must be able to find a sense of self-worth elsewhere or suffer the sense of worthlessness. Loving partners can help us change in spite of social expectations by confirming what is valuable in our experimenting with new ways of living. A wife who can confirm her husband's emerging capacity to feel emotions and acknowledge his vulnerability and a husband who can encourage his wife to assert herself and establish her independence are not merely dealing with each other, however. They are taking on the entire society.

In order for him to express his feelings openly and acknowledge his vulnerability, he must normally either compartmentalize his life so that he does this only at home or pay the price for appearing less competent or competitive on the job. Emotions run counter to the professional image of objectivity and the working man's ideal of manliness. Few of us can find jobs that allow us to be the same person at home and at work. We must live with the tensions that result, and when we are trying to do something different, tensions increase.

The wife's independence and assertiveness are not simply her personality traits, they are reinforced by the social opportunities available to her. It makes much less sense to talk about autonomy when you have no adequate source of income—and an adequate source of income is normally contingent on jobs being available. Sometimes we become aware of these structural inequalities in unexpected ways. One man in his forties told Nena O'Neill:

> I've been through it all—my former marriage was built on all the old expectations, and when my wife wanted to be liberated, it didn't work. So then I divorced and I was free, but there was the bitter pill—I still had to support the kids. OK fine, I love them and want to support them and I have to, but there is always argument over the fairness of it. Now I've remarried and it's entirely different. We both have jobs, and I think our marriage is fairly liberated. But I still have to support my kids. My point is that for all the liberation women are supposed to have, the economic pressure still remains on the man.[33]

The economic pressure remains on the man to the extent to which women cannot or do not find jobs that can adequately support them. Such jobs are often unavailable not only because many men do not believe women should have equal job opportunities, but also because current economic growth makes the generation of new jobs difficult or impossible. One of the little-publicized aspects of the current employment situation is that, although the unemployment rate has risen to a postwar high, the total number of persons employed has also steadily increased.

Realizing social equality for women means generating millions of new jobs and/or changing our cultural expectations about work so that job sharing and part-time work are more rewarded. But work is not merely a means of earning a living, it is also intimately tied to our sense of self-worth. It may be that we cannot solve our employment problem until we have revalued leisure and can find ways for more and more people to make creative use of it. Our current understanding of leisure time depends on notions about conspicuous consumption, having fun, and engaging in activities that cost a great deal and help make use of the enormous amount of commodities we produce as well as providing jobs for others in the service sector of the economy. Contemplative activity does not consume much and therefore is not valued highly. A veritable cultural revolution is required to change these valuations. Such change is not impossible—indeed there is evidence that it is already underway—but it will not come about easily. A great deal of personal courage, compassion, and commitment are required of all of us if we are to become flexible in our partnerships.

SUMMARY

This chapter began with an examination of the implicit marriage contract, which is the set of expectations that determine the roles, rights, and obligations that married partners generally expect to see fulfilled in their relationship. A partnership that follows the norms described in the implicit contract will be characterized by (1) lifelong monogamy, (2) sexual exclusivity, (3) economic independence of the partners from outside support, (4) a division of labor that will vary from case to case but generally will follow one of several broad patterns, (5) a pattern of dominance in which the husband generally holds the balance of power, (6) the expectation of children, and (7) acceptance of the ideal of togetherness.

Although there is nothing wrong with any of these conventional expectations, it seems to be generally true that a couple can increase the chances of building a dynamic and growing relationship by adapting the conventional expectations to their own situation. By becoming more flexible, a couple can achieve a relationship characterized by nondependent living, personal growth, individual freedom, role flexibility, mutual trust and expansion through openness, and freedom from jealousy.

NOTES

1. Ivan Nye and Felix Berardo, *The Family: Its Structure and Interaction* (New York: Macmillan, 1973), argue that the sexual revolution has created a new obligation for the husband—to satisfy his wife sexually.

2. See William N. Stephens, *The Family in Cross-Cultural Perspective* (New York: Holt, Rinehart and Winston, 1963), pp. 197ff.

3. A fuller discussion of this role expectation can be found in Nye and Berardo.

4. See the response of 120,000 female readers of *Redbook* on this point. A significant *minority* favored the traditional roles. "How Do You Feel About Being a Woman?" *Redbook* (January 1973): p. 1.

5. Linda Burzott Nilson, "The Social Standing of a Housewife," *Journal of Marriage and the Family* (August 1978): 541–47.

6. M. Ferrea, "The Confused American Housewife," *Psychology Today*, 10 (1976): 76–80, and "Working Class Jobs: Housework and Paid Work as Sources of Satisfaction," *Social Problems*, 23 (April): 431–41. Ronald J. Burke and Tamara Weir, "Relationship of Wife's Employment Status to Husband, Wife and Pair Satisfaction and Performance," *Journal of Marriage and the Family* (May 1976): 279–86.

7. James D. Wright, "Are Working Women *Really* More Satisfied? Evidence from Several National Surveys," *Journal of Marriage and the Family* (May 1978): 301–13.

8. Burke and Weir, pp. 285ff.

9. Elizabeth Bott, *Family and Social Networks: Roles, Norms, and Extended Relationships in Working Class Families* (London: Tavistock Publications, 1957).

10. U.S. Bureau of the Census, *Statistical Abstract of the United States: 1982–83.* (Washington, D.C.: U.S. Government Printing Office, 1983), p. xx.

11. M. W. Osmond and P. Y. Martin, "A Contingency Model of Marital Organization in Low Income Families," *Journal of Marriage and the Family,* 40 (May 1978): 315–29.

12. Jean R. Renshaw, "An Exploration of the Dynamics of the Overlapping Worlds of Work and Family," *Family Process,* pp. 143–64.

13. Ronald J. Burke and Tamara Weir, "Some Personality Differences Between Members of One-Career and Two-Career Families," *Journal of Marriage and the Family* (August 1976): 453–58.

14. Benson Rosen, Thomas H. Jerdee, and Thomas L. Prestwich, "Dual-Career Marital Adjustment: Potential Effects of Discriminatory Managerial Attitudes," *Journal of Marriage and the Family* (August 1975): 565–72.

15. See William Goode, Elizabeth Hopkins, and Helen M. McClure, *Social System and Family Patterns: A Propositional Inventory* (Indianapolis: Bobbs-Merrill, 1971), pp. 558–61, for a list of references. See also S. P. Douglas and Y. Wind, "Examining Family Role and Authority Patterns: Two Methodological Issues," *Journal of Marriage and the Family,* 40 (February 1978): 35–47; and J. Scanzoni, "Contemporary Marriage Types," *Journal of Family Issues,* 1 (March 1980): 125–40.

16. John F. Cuber and Peggy H. Harroff, *Sex and the Significant Americans* (Englewood Cliffs, N.J.: Prentice-Hall, 1965), p. 59.

17. Kahlil Gibran, *The Prophet* (New York: Knopf, 1952), p. 16.

18. Carl Rogers, *Becoming Partners* (New York: Delacorte Press, 1972), p. 69.

19. Ibid, p. 208.

20. George O'Neill and Nena O'Neill, *Open Marriage: A New Life Style for Couples* (New York: Evans, 1972), p. 166.

21. Ibid., p. 167, Copyright 1972 by Nena O'Neill and George O'Neill. Reprinted by permission of the publisher, M. Evans and Company, Inc.

22. Nena O'Neill helps set the record straight in her book, *The Marriage Premise* (New York: Evans, 1977).

23. Lee H. Bukstel et al., "Projected Extramarital Sexual Involvement in Unmarried College Students," *Journal of Marriage and the Family* (May 1978): 337–40.

24. Singh et al., "Extramarital Sexual Permissiveness," *Journal of Marriage and the Family* (November 1976): 711.

25. Minako K. Maykovich, "Attitudes Versus Behavior in Extramarital Sexual Relations," *Journal of Marriage and the Family* (November 1976): 693–98.

26. O'Neill and O'Neill, p. 158.

27. Olaf Palme, "The Lesson from Sweden: The Emancipation of Man," in Louise Kapp Howe (ed.), *The Future of the Family* (New York: Simon & Schuster, 1972), pp. 247–58.

28. O'Neill and O'Neill, p. 226.

29. Raymond Lawrence, "The Affair as a Redemptive Experience," in Robert Rimmer (ed.), *Adventure in Loving* (New York: Signet Books, 1973), p. 65.

30. Ibid., p. 66.

31. George Peter Murdock, *Social Structure* (New York: Free Press, 1965), p. 294; William N. Stephens, *Comparative Perspectives on Marriage and the Family* (New York: Holt, Rinehart and Winston, 1963), p. 59.
32. O'Neill and O'Neill, p. 240.
33. O'Neill p. 144.

I now start . . . with the needs of infants and young children for a sensitive, enthusiastic kind of care if they are to develop into warmhearted, creative people. They can receive this from loving fathers, mothers, grandparents. But each year it is harder to hire a full-time substitute caretaker whose personality and attitude approach those of good parents. . . . If neither parent is willing to take part time off from a job for a few years, they might do better without children.

—*Benjamin M. Spock*

13 Parents and Children

By common understanding children make a family. In some areas of the world, such as rural Sweden and among the Swazi of Africa, a marriage is not considered consummated until the wife has borne a child. This idea has been very common in our own past. Even today a young couple very often do not really feel married until they have children. Thus, many young people look forward to growing up, getting married, and having children as the normal and natural sequence of events in their lives. The idea of not wanting to have children seems unnatural and even perverse. Some misguided marriage counselors have even advised people who were having trouble in their marriage to have a child, apparently on the assumption that this would "bring them back to normal." This is common folk advice. But parenthood has been even more romanticized than love in American society. Whether or not the addition of a child to a couple's marriage is best described as a transition or as a crisis, it is clear that children are an additional responsibility and burden that bring with them trials, tribulations, and sorrow as well as happiness and joy.

In this chapter we begin with some arguments for and against having children. We assume that, in our time especially, this should be a conscious choice, not an automatic next step. Some consideration is given to preparing for parenthood once the decision to have children has been made, and a bit of the joy and sorrow of family life is suggested. Even after they have weighed all the evidence, it is likely that most readers will decide to have children, for the decision not to have them is a very difficult one to make in a society convinced that every couple should have children. For most couples it is likely that the real question will be whether to have two or three children rather than none at all. Whatever decision a couple might make, the social and psychological factors discussed here will undoubtedly influence that decision.

DO WE REALLY WANT CHILDREN?

Most couples can have children. The question is, Do they really want them? To raise the question in this way may be misleading, for it implies that a couple can somehow know enough to answer it rationally. In fact, however, the consequences of whatever decision is made are hard to know beforehand. Couples in the second year of their marriage have different resources and liabilities than couples in their fifth or fifteenth year of marriage. Their personalities change; their life chances and life styles change; and the world in which they live changes. Then how is it possible to answer such a question with any assurance that the answer will still seem right a number of years in the future?

Although it is difficult to reach any answer with certainty, an important step is taken as soon as the question is raised. In the past the factors that seemed to have had the most influence on whether or not couples had babies were economic. During the Depression, for example, the birthrate fell drastically, presumably because people were fully aware of the economic hardships of raising children in such hard times. It rose again after World War II, when prosperity produced a "baby boom."

After declining throughout the 1970s, the birthrate has begun to increase slightly in the 1980s.[1] This apparently short-term "mini" baby boom reflects a number of factors, among them the change of heart of women in their thirties who decide to have children "before it is too late" when previously they thought they did not want them. Certain religious groups such as the Seventh-Day Adventists value large families and are growing rapidly. The much-touted economic recovery may contribute to

Having children should be a matter of careful consideration rather than a thoughtless acceptance of convention. (Ed Lettau, Photo Reserachers, Inc.)

this trend, but it must first put people back to work in significant numbers. The perception of parents that jobs are relatively easy to find seems to influence their decision to have children. But what specific factors actually influence these decisions in particular cases? And on what basis can a couple have reasonable assurance that they have made the right decision?

One of the interesting things about asking the question "Do we really want children?" is that very few people have bothered to offer arguments in favor of having children. It is simply assumed that nine out of ten couples will want children, and that is that. As a result, there is little research on this question, for until quite recently neither researchers nor the general public saw the issue as critical. As the arguments against having children have become more and more pronounced, however, the counterarguments in favor of children have had to be developed consciously.

Thus, we have a paradoxical situation in which having children is still assumed to be the natural choice for married couples, but the arguments in favor of this decision may tend to seem idealistic and a bit unconvincing. Conversely, it is easy to argue convincingly that the public interest is best served by controlling the number of children, but the decision not to have children is a difficult one to make. The question of whether or not to have children is complicated by the fact that a great number of factors must be considered in arriving at an answer. The first of these concerns the health and biological capacities of the partners and their prospects for a normal birth. Second, in light of the increasing concern for population control, the choice to have or not have children cannot be made responsibly without some awareness of the issues involved in controlling the world's population. Third, the changing life style of women, particularly those who want to pursue careers, adds new dimensions to the choice, inasmuch as having children usually places some constraints on the mother's career development. Fourth, the teachings of various religious denominations may come into play if one belongs to a faith that limits one's options as far as birth control and abortion are concerned.

It is important that the decision to have children or not be a mutual one. Recent court cases between divorced persons raise the issue of paternity in cases where the husband claims his wife deceived him by not using contraceptives when they had agreed not to have children, but the courts have not yet determined that this is sufficient ground to contest paternity.[2] More important, the decision to have children or not should not be part of a power struggle between spouses or involve deception in any way. It must be based on mutual consent if it is to contribute to the growth of the partnership.

Finally, the decision to have children involves a long-term commitment of resources. It is difficult to specify how the conditions of life will change during the period of the child's growing up, but once a child is born the decision is irrevocable. On the other hand, under most circumstances the decision not to have children can be reevaluated at any time, although of course increasing age diminishes the effectiveness of such a reevaluation. Most couples would probably find it very difficult to decide to have children after 40.

Most people who decide to have children today do not really sit down and weigh the alternatives before reaching a decision. The costs of having children, or more children than one can afford, may lead to a conscious and rational decision *not to have* children, but in most cases the decision to *have* children is not made on the basis of such explicitly developed reasons. This is why we think it important that the arguments both for and against children be sketched out, so that either decision can be reached on a rational basis that will satisfy any particular couple's needs, values, and desires.

In Favor of Children

Among the factors that affect the decision to have children, probably the most significant is the fact that society normally expects two people who get married to have children. Childless marriages are commonly subject to criticism, and there tends to be a general suspicion that there must be something wrong, either physically or psychologically, with a married couple who do not have children after a reasonable length of time. Because of these expectations, many women feel that fulfillment as a woman depends on giving birth to a child and experiencing motherhood. Thus, women frequently decide to have children because they believe it is necessary for them to do so in order to fully realize their own identity. What is more, for both men and women, accepting the responsibility of parenthood is ordinarily regarded as clear evidence that one has reached maturity.

In addition to these social factors, there are many personal rewards that derive from the roles and expectations of parenthood. In a very real sense, the decision to have a child is really a decision to begin developing a new and different kind of an environment in which to grow. Being one member of a couple certainly can provide a feeling of group identity and belongingness, but being a member of a "family," even a small one, multiplies the possibilities for intimate interaction. **Self-actualization, self-respect**, and **self-esteem** can develop within families to a richer and fuller extent than in dyadic (two-party) relationships simply because the web of intimate connections is fuller and more complex. For this to happen, however, the children must be regarded as participants in the companionship system of the family, not simply as dependents. When children enjoy participant status, their contribution to the growth and development of their parents can take place at several levels. Simply by interacting with their parents they may bring about a deeper understanding of what it means to be a person. Children often feel freer than their parents to express such basic human emotions as affection, love, and respect. Contact with them thus often serves to help adults get back in touch with their feelings. What is more, children's awe and wonder at the commonplace, and their curiosity about all things, often provide their parents with refreshing opportunities to see the mundane world in a different and more exciting way. In this sense children can create a richer environment within which growth can take place, so that it seems fair to conclude that the family is a socializing agency for the parents as well as for the children.

A final reason for having children is the elementary fact that the propagation of the human species appears to be an intrinsically worthwhile goal. Implicit in the commandment to "be fruitful and multiply" is the assumption that procreation is beneficial both for the species and for the couple. Indeed, some people see this as the overarching reason for having children. In this context even the contemporary recognition of the need to control the size of our population is not an injunction against having any children at all. On the contrary, it is a recognition of the fact that it is necessary for some people to limit the size of their families or to have no children at all if we are to provide the best possible environment for the species as a whole. But of course this does not mean that *no one* should choose to become a parent. The fact that many people are making the choice to have few or no children means those who want children are freer to have them without feeling that their decision is socially irresponsible.

In a recent article J. E. Veevers documents six meanings of parenthood that she contends are widespread in our culture. They are (1) the moral meaning, in which parenthood is a religious obligation and being a parent is being moral; (2) civic responsibility, in which parenthood is a civic obligation; (3) parenthood is a natural, instinctive phenomenon; (4) sexual identity and sexual competence are demonstrated through parenthood; (5) parenthood is the meaning of marriage—it improves marital adjustment and prevents divorce; (6) being a parent contributes to maturity and personality stability—it is an indication of normality and mental health. Now, these social meanings support the arguments we have given for having children. It is easy to see, however, that if they are held onto as the only reasonable choice that couples can make, they make it very difficult for any couple to choose not to have children. To not desire to become parents then becomes (1) a flouting of religious authority, a sign of immorality; (2) an avoidance of civic responsibility; (3) an unnatural state; (4) a rejection of gender role and a sign of sexual incompetence; (5) a stand in the way of marital adjustment, an invitation to divorce; and (6) a sign of immaturity and emotional maladjustment.[3] These latter points are often made by those who claim to be "pro life" under the implicit assumption that life under virtually any circumstance is to be sustained. It fails to consider the possibility that one can honor life by caring well for the living and by restricting their number so that this is more likely to occur.

Against Children

The arguments against having children seem to be gathering some strength today because of concern about the population explosion. People who are worried about the population problem generally argue that young couples should learn to *want* fewer children, not that they should have fewer than they want. Insofar as this general argument serves to reduce the pressure on couples who are really hesitant about having children for a variety of reasons, it tends to increase the number of couples who do not in fact have children. But it is not an argument against having children per se.

By far the most powerful arguments against having children are linked to attempts to overthrow the myth that motherhood is instinctive and that women cannot fulfill themselves unless they have children. The simple truth of the matter is that some people, perhaps a large number of them, should not have children because they are not suited, either socially, psychologically, or biologically, to the role of parent or because having children and raising them can effectively destroy or at least hamper careers they value more than they value parenthood. At present, day care facilities are not adequate to permit many parents to find suitable substitutes for parental care at a price they can afford.[4] Given this state of affairs, the choice to pursue a career may reasonably exclude the choice to have children.

Because of the belief that the maternal role is in some sense natural or instinctive, the decision to say no to motherhood is regarded as a nonconforming choice and earns the woman who chooses this option little social support and few rewards. Although this situation is slowly changing, making it easier for some middle-class women to opt against motherhood, this is still by no means an easy choice for a couple to make. The choice not to have children places both the man and the woman in relatively unexplored territory as they experiment with the rather new style of voluntary childlessness. The guidelines are not as clear; the expectations are not as precise; and the social benefits—ranging from tax advantages to social approval—are not as great as the benefits deriving from parenthood.

Children place numerous constraints on their parents. Parents are not as free as nonparents to move, change jobs, travel, change life styles, or engage in various recreational activities. Children demand time and resources, and any significant change in the family's living conditions must be considered in terms of how it is likely to affect the children. Thus, people who do not want to accept these constraints are provided with a powerful argument against having children. Unfortunately, couples who decide to remain childless for this reason are often denounced as selfish and self-indulgent. They should recognize that this criticism—which can be quite disturbing, especially when it comes from the couple's parents—has absolutely no validity. Seeking to find personal satisfaction through a childless life style is not necessarily more self-indulgent than seeking personal fulfillment through parenthood.

In light of our society's interest in training and education, it is surprising that Americans spend so little time and effort training people to be parents. At a time when more is expected of parents than at any other time in our history, parents have few resources to fall back on and often find themselves feeling inadequate in the role. In the past, when extended families were common and young couples tended to live with or near their own parents, new parents could count on readily available guidance. Today this is less likely to be the case, and the trend for young couples to establish residence in suburban communities consisting largely of their peers means that in all likelihood inexperienced parents will be surrounded by friends who are no more experienced than they are.

It is easy enough to tell the young couple who doubt their competence in this role that "everybody feels this way" and "you'll get over it," but it is not necessarily clear that it is wise to do so. Obviously, anyone beginning a new experience is likely to feel somewhat apprehensive about it. In some cases these apprehensions may be no more than natural nervousness about a new role, but in other cases feelings of inadequacy may be quite justifiable. When one considers how many disturbed and unhappy children there are in our country, one cannot help wishing people had not always been so eager to convince couples who doubted their ability to be good parents that their doubts were unfounded. Parenthood is undeniably a

Parenthood is undeniably a difficult and demanding task that has been unduly romanticized in our society. (Ed Lettau, Photo Researchers, Inc.)

more difficult and demanding role in our fluid and changing society than it was in the relatively more stable social situation of a few generations back, yet the psychological rewards it offers have remained unchanged. The fact that there has been an increase in the costs and no compensatory increase in the rewards tends to make it less attractive than it used to be. There is no reason why couples who do not find parenthood appealing should be encouraged to become parents.

Economic considerations often provide an important reason not to have children. As a rough guide to cost, we can estimate that it takes three times the annual family income to raise each child to the age at which he or she achieves economic independence. Thus, a family earning the medium income of $23,000 will spend about $69,000 on each child, including education.[5] This is a heavy expenditure that will increase as inflation, expectations for an even more comfortable style of life, average years of schooling, and the cost of education rise. What is more, the money lost from the wife's income if she stops working or reduces her work schedule to care for the baby must be taken into account. Campbell estimates that for families living at poverty levels this cost is about $2,000 annually; for middle-income people it would, of course, be much higher.

Many contraceptive techniques are available to couples who choose not to have children. Some of these means (such as sterilization) make the choice essentially nonreversible, but with most techniques a couple can change their minds later in the marriage. Now as never before, intentionally childless marriage has become an available and viable life style option for increasing numbers of people, either for part of their marriage or as a lifelong arrangement. The choice to remain childless should not be seen in negative terms. The decision not to have children requires thinking and examination of alternatives, but giving this matter thoughtful consideration also means that the decision to have children—if and when it is made—becomes a more conscious choice.

PREPARING FOR PARENTHOOD

We have just examined some of the arguments for and against having children. As time passes, young couples in our society are more and more likely to make the matter of having or not having children a conscious decision rather than simply assuming that it is natural to have children. As matters stand at present, however, about nine out of every ten married couples will have one or more children. And in most cases in which couples do not have children it will be because they cannot have them.

In practice, the decision whether or not to become a parent seems to be based on a number of considerations. Given the strong norms in favor of having children, those who decide not to have them must redefine the meaning of sex, marriage, and family life. They may do this by minimizing social contacts with parents and friends and seeking new friends in organizations such as the National Organization for Nonparents (NON) that support their decision not to have children.[6] Women generally are more inclined to want children than men. One study found that contentment was much more strongly associated with motherhood among women than with fatherhood among men.[7] One study suggests that a husband's family size preference depends in part on the amount of income his wife commands and on the extent to which her feelings about the number of children to have are shared by the husband.[8]

Two to three children are widely considered ideal; larger or smaller families are difficult to defend. The decision to have a third child seems especially to be influenced by beliefs and by the perceived consequences of having that child. In this sense it appears to be a more rational choice than the decision to conceive a child in the first place.[9] Thus, at present the *rate* of growth in the U.S. population is near zero, or replacement, but because it is felt that the job market will improve in the near future, some analysts are predicting that another baby boom is on the way.[10] In the past there has been some correlation between the ability of young people to get jobs and the size of the family they produce. Whether this will hold in the future is uncertain.

There is very little preparation for parenting in our society, though there is increasing interest in preparing for childbirth. Some researchers conclude that the birth of the first child can appropriately be described as a crisis for the typical young couple.[11] Others consider it to be a problem, but one that is best described as a transition.[12] Black families seem to have more difficulty making this transition than white families, according to one study.[13]

Despite common assumptions to the contrary, learning how to be a parent does not come naturally. Bringing children into the world and raising them can be exciting and interesting, but it can also be a very difficult and arduous task. In our society these difficulties are often glossed over, for parenthood is romanticized even more than marriage. This romanticism can intensify the problems that new parents face, inasmuch as it leads them to approach parenthood with a great many naive and misguided notions. Thus, many young parents are terrified and frightened when they first experience intense negative or even hostile feelings toward their screaming infants. They have been taught that good parents always love their babies, and they are not prepared for temporary lapses from this norm. Young mothers and fathers often find it difficult to cope with the complex feelings that arise in response to the new person who is making demands on their lives.

In one sense there is not much a young couple can do to prepare themselves psychologically for the arrival of their first child. Caring for an infant of one's own is so unlike any other experience that in most important respects it will be something entirely new for the couple. Even people who grew up with younger brothers and sisters and may have assumed a fairly heavy share of responsibility in caring for them do not have an experience that is really analogous to having one's own child. For example, we have already mentioned the fact that new parents often go through periods during which they resent intensely the demands placed on them by the infant. But the fact that they may have had similar feelings toward a younger brother or sister does not really provide them with guidelines for responding to their own baby, for our social values tell us that it is quite acceptable to resent a demanding younger sibling but quite unacceptable to resent the demands of one's own child. Thus, familiarity with the feelings does little or nothing to assuage the sense of guilt that they are likely to generate.

In this regard perhaps the most important thing young couples can do to help themselves prepare for or adjust to parenthood is to get as unromantic and realistic a picture as possible of what is involved. Something like consciousness-raising sessions for new parents can be quite helpful, as can serious conversations with candid and honest people who have experience with children. The candidness is the key ingredient here, for many people are reluctant to admit the existence of certain problems. Such people, far from providing helpful information, can deepen the new parents' sense of confusion, disorientation, and guilt by reinforcing unrealistically rosy and romantic expectations about what parenthood is like.

Another appealing idea, which seems far less radical today than it did a mere decade ago, concerns something called **trial marriage** or "marriage in two stages."[14] The idea of trial marriage is to break the link that connects childbearing and marriage as though one were the inevitable consequence of the other. In trial marriages couples agree to marry simply for the sake of becoming partners and discovering each other. Children are specifically *not* part of the contractual expectations at this stage. (Divorce from such a marriage should be relatively easy to obtain because no children are involved.)

Only after satisfying themselves that the "trial" was successful would a couple approach the decision as to whether or not parenthood is a desirable step for them. If it is, then the couple would remarry, this time on the basis of a marriage contract that included an expectation of children. Divorce from the second stage of this marriage should be more difficult to obtain, but because of the great amount of thought that went into making a specific contract for parenthood it is reasonable to assume that divorce would be less likely to occur than in conventional one-stage marriage. Of course, if the couple should decide to remain childless after living in such a trial marriage for a number of years, then there is no reason why they should not be free to perpetuate the partnership on its original basis.

It is not unlikely that something like trial marriage will become a legal reality in the not-too-distant future. It makes good sense from a number of points of view. Some published marriage contracts attempt in effect to establish a trial marriage by stating that the couple do not at this time wish to have children and that they believe that any children they might have in the future should be by choice rather than chance.[15] Such private marriage contracts do not yet have legal status, but they are useful in making explicit the intentions of the parties involved.

LIVING WITH CHILDREN

With the advent of their first child, a young couple face a totally new situation. Many adjustments will be necessary. Simply because there are now three people instead of two, there is a more complicated interaction pattern in the family and a more complex network of relationships. What is more, a growing child needs to be treated differently at different stages in her or his development. Thus, the parents must continually learn new response patterns. And as the child's world expands through school, friends, and other outside contacts, the parents will be drawn into more active participation in the society outside their family.

One of the most demanding aspects of parenthood is the exercise of parental authority. Growing children continually test their parents'

One of the most demanding aspects of parenthood is the exercise of parental authority. (Richard Hutchings, Photo Researchers, Inc.)

authority to make and enforce rules to guide the common life. In patriarchial societies, including some in our own past, the authority of the father over the household was supported by religion and custom. The _pater familias_, the status of the father in the ancient Roman family, was set by his role as trustee for the lineage; he could legally kill his wife or children for disobedience. The modern father has a much different status—fortunately. He ideally shares authority equally with his wife. They seek to increase their children's responsibilities and privileges in the family as the children become able to do more and more things. The establishment of rules and their enforcement and modification under such shared responsibility is a much more difficult undertaking requiring a great deal of insight, forbearance, and compassion. It is very easy to characterize a macho male who takes an authoritarian stance in his family, or a milk-toast male who lacks all authority, but mutually responsible parenting offers fewer opportunities for stating general principles. It is acquired through experience more than precept.

When a family contains three people instead of two, it becomes possible for **coalitions** to be formed, and this possibility by itself is enough to bring about changes in the family power structure. A mother and her child can easily drift into an alliance that effectively excludes the father; a father and his child may form a coalition that leaves the mother out of the action; or a husband and wife can join forces against their child, producing what may well become a psychopathological condition called **scapegoating**.[16] If another child is added to the family, the potential for two-party relationships increases from three to six and it becomes possible for three-party coalitions to emerge. The larger the family, the greater the increase in the complexity of this family interaction network. Coalitions can emerge simply as a function of the increasing size of the family and may have little or nothing to do with the particular characteristics of their members. They can come about simply because it is now possible for them to occur.

Lest the reader become alarmed about what sounds like a frighteningly tangled situation, we should point out that in most cases coalitions between family members are not stable, long-term alliances. Most coalitions arise on a issue-by-issue basis. There is nothing wrong with coalitions of this sort; in fact, they are unavoidable. If a family is undecided about even such an elementary matter as whether to eat at home or go out for a pizza, the simple mathematics of the situation tell us that two members will favor one option and one will favor the other; after all, if all three agreed there would be no decisions to make. This means that a coalition forms between the two who are in agreement. Such a coalition, however, probably will not last beyond dinnertime; by then a different coalition may have been formed about some other matter such as what television show to watch.

Coalitions become a problem only when consistent patterns begin to emerge. For example, imagine a marriage in which one of the partners generally prefers an active social life while the other favors spending most evenings at home. When such a couple have no children, they probably will work out some compromise in which sometimes the more active partner goes out alone and at other times they take turns going along with each other's desires. With the arrival of a child, however, the situation changes. Many small children do not like their parents to go out and leave them with babysitters. Thus, it becomes very easy for the more socially passive partner to form an alliance with the child, who quickly learns that it is possible to keep Mommy and Daddy home through strategic intervention in discussions about whether to go out or not.

Such a situation is dangerous because it can easily escalate into a permanent arrangement. At first it may be limited to one recurring issue, such as going out or staying home, but as one parent—say, the mother— grows to resent the persistence with which her child and her husband "gang up" against her, she may deepen the alienation, thereby generating further coalitions. When children get a sense that one parent is more sympathetic to their desires than the other, it is easy for them to form a coalition with the parent they see as the "good guy" against the one they see as the villain. This situation commonly arises over the issue of discipline, when husbands who are away from the children all day are reluctant to play a role in disciplining them when they get home. The father then becomes the child's natural ally while the mother is cast in the role of enemy. The situation worsens when the father, unconsciously recognizing what is going on, becomes even more reluctant to discipline the child because he does not want to jeopardize his favorable position in the child's eye. Even small children can be remarkably adept at exploiting such situations for their benefit, thus intensifying the alliances and deepening the divisions they cause in the family structure. For this reason, couples are well advised to watch for the emergence of any such patterns. Husbands and wives should listen attentively whenever their partners complain they are being victimized by this sort of "ganging up." Coalition patterns arise so naturally and easily, often without any conscious intent, that the aggrieved party is very likely to be right on this score. Fortunately, most coalition patterns can easily be broken if they are caught before they harden into destructive antagonisms.

The birth of a child not only changes power relationships within a family, but also necessitates the reorganization of many other aspects of the family's life style. Some studies indicate that the birth of the first child is a crisis for a couple regardless of whether the child was planned or not.[17] This crisis involves reorganizing the spending and often the earning of the family income. It involves new demands for space, time, and attention. What is more, the partners must renew the intimacy and renegotiate the patterns of responsibility and privilege, power and authority that may have been disrupted by the period of pregnancy and postpartum abstinence from intercourse. The young husband may become increasingly aware that the demand that he earn a living may be in conflict with the demand that he be present as a family member as much as possible. The young wife becomes increasingly aware that child care can become a full-time occupation and may resent the unexpected extent to which her other interests have to be pushed into the background.[18]

The birth of a child makes it necessary for the couple to reestablish a satisfactory sexual relationship under different circumstances. Because of increased demands on their time and energy, both partners are more likely to be tired when they come to their lovemaking. The infant's cries and the toddler's demands may interrupt sexual activity. The preservation of intimacy thus becomes more difficult. Conversation between partners tends to get more disciplined; some research has indicated that young parents talk to each other only half as much as newly married couples do and that when they do talk they tend to talk about the children rather than about themselves or their relationship.[19] In sum, the frequency of intercourse declines, as does the amount of shared leisure. Under these circumstances any difficulties the couple may already have in their sexual relationship may become magnified. If they are handled properly, however, none of these problems need result in family crisis or marital dissatisfaction. In this regard perhaps the best defense is knowing what to expect. The couple who imagine that having a baby will mean turning the study into a nursery but will not otherwise affect their life style are in for some shocking surprises that they may not be prepared to deal with creatively.

There has been much discussion regarding the extent to which parents are able to socialize their children adequately—that is, raise them to be useful members of society. Studies that document intergenerational differences in attitudes and opinions frequently talk of a **generation gap**. The younger generation does seem to have different attitudes and beliefs when compared to the older generations.[20] But when parent-child comparisons are made, the differences diminish. A general consensus characterizes much parent-child belief systems. Specific areas of disagreement relate to the sex of the offspring, his or her college class level, and the social background of the father.[21] Another study found that the extent to which students held conventional views about life was strongly related to the extent of their identification with their parents, their political conservatism, and church attendance.[22] Similarly, another study found that runaways differed from nonrunaways in the extent to which they held values different from those of their parents and in the extent to which they perceived their parents as unwilling to listen.[23] Parents who listen continue to have a strong influence on their children, even though their children may not agree with them on all counts. But listening to children is a skill that is not easily acquired.

SUMMARY

Most Americans are less prepared for parenthood than they are for marriage. Our folklore has done us a great disservice in romanticizing parenthood as an unqualifiedly happy experience and as capable of bringing a couple together if their marriage is in difficulty. Like marriage, parenthood is commonly taken for granted as natural. As a result, most couples tend to have children as a matter of course whether they are qualified for parenthood or not. The proposal that marriage be made a two-stage contract is one way of dealing with this situation. In the first stage the partners marry each other, but children are definitely not part of the contract. After they have experienced marriage, the couple may make a second contract to become parents if they so desire. Because no children are involved in the first stage, it should be possible to obtain a divorce without much trouble, whereas obtaining a divorce in the second stage would be much more difficult.

Coping with the problems of children is a difficult task. Studies demonstrate that the first child presents many problems of adjustment for the young parents, whether the child is planned for or not. The possibility of forming two-party coalitions against the third member of the household becomes a reality. What is more, time and resources must be rearranged to meet the demands of the new member of the household. The intimacy that may have been developing between the parents must be developed further under trying circumstances such as reduced emotional capacity to cope with frustration as well as interruptions in the couple's private time.

Because we tend to take it for granted that couples should have children, the arguments that might be advanced in favor of them seem trite or unpersuasive to increasing numbers of people, who view the population explosion and the pressure on resources as cogent social reasons for not having children. The decision to not have children is becoming a more personal one because the social expectation that married people should have children is losing some of its force.

NOTES

1. U. S. Bureau of the Census, *Statistical Abstract of the United States: 1982–83* (Washington, D.C.: U.S. Government Printing Office, 1983), p. xix.
2. "Casenotes: Hughes vs. Hutt, Supreme Court of Pennsylvania, Decided January 28, 1983," *Delaware Law Forum*, 10 (May 1983): 10.
3. J. E. Veevers, "The Social Meanings of Parenthood," *Psychiatry*, 36 (August 1978): 291–310.
4. Urie Bronfenbrenner, *The Ecology of Human Development* (Cambridge, Mass.: Harvard University Press, 1980).
5. *Statistical Abstract: 1982–83*, p. xxi.
6. Marcia G. Ory, "The Decision to Parent or Not: Narrative and Structural Components," *Journal of Marriage and the Family* (August 1978): 531–32.
7. Michael Humphrey, "Sex Differences in Attitude to Parenthood," *Human Relations*, 30 (December 8, 1977): 737–49.
8. Susan H. Cochrane and Frank D. Bean, "Husband—Wife Differences in the Demand for Children," *Journal of Marriage and the Family* (May 1976): 297–306.

9.   Paul D. Werner et al., "Having a Third Child: Predicting Behavioral Intentions," *Journal of Marriage and the Family* (May 1975): 348–57.

10. Paul Glick, "Demographic Changes and the Family," paper presented to the Groves Conference on the Family, Washington, D.C., April 1978, pp. 1–3.

11. E. E. LeMasters, *Parenthood in America*, 2nd ed. (Homewood, Ill.: Dorsey Press, 1974), pp. 8–32; David Beauchamp, "Parenthood or Crisis: An Additional Study," Masters Thesis, North Dakota, 1968; E. D. Dyer, "Parenthood as Crisis: A Restudy," *Marriage and Family Living* (May 1963): 196–201.

12. Daniel E. Hobbs, Jr., and Sue Pack Cole, "Transition to Parenthood: A Decade Replication," *Journal of Marriage and the Family* (November 1976): 723–30.

13. Daniel F. Hobbs and Jane Maynard Wimbish, "Transition to Parenthood by Black Couples," *Journal of Marriage and the Family* (November 1977): 677–88.

14. The notion of a trial marriage has a number of well-known advocates. See esp. Judge Ben V. Lindsey, *Companionate Marriage* (New York: Boni & Liveright, 1927); and Lord Bertrand Russell, *Marriage and Morals* (New York: Bantam Books, 1968).

15. "Marriage Contract of Harriet Mary Cody and Harvey Joseph Sadis," *MS*, June 1975, pp. 65ff.

16. Ezra Vogel and Norman W. Bell, "The Emotionally Disturbed Child as the Family Scapegoat," in Bell and Vogel (eds.), *A Modern Introduction to the Family* (New York: Free Press, 1960).

17. E. E. LeMasters, "Parenthood as Crisis," *Marriage and Family Living*, 19 (1957): 325–55.

18. Helen Z. Lopata, *Occupation Housewife* (New York: Oxford University Press, 1971). See also the response to *Redbook's* questionnaire, "How Do You Feel About Being a Woman?" *Redbook* (January 1973): 1.

19. William F. Kenkel, *The Family in Perspective* (Englewood Cliffs, N.J.: Prentice-Hall, 1966), p. 455.

20. Kingsley Davis, "The Sociology of Parent-Youth Conflict," *American Sociological Review* (1940): 523–35.

21. R. Brook Jacobsen et al., "An Empirical Test of the Generation Gap: A Comparative Interfamily Study," *Journal of Marriage and the Family* (November 1975): 841–50.

22. Edwin Yost and Raymond J. Adamek, "Parent-Child Interaction and Changing Family Values: A Multivariate Analysis," *Journal of Marriage and the Family* (February 1979): 115–21.

23. Linda Blood and Rocco D'Angelo, "A Progress Research Report on Value Issues in Conflict Between Runaways and Their Parents," *Journal of Marriage and the Family* (August 1974): 486–90.

Developing Families

Every society consists of [people] in the process of developing from children into parents. To assure continuity of tradition, society must early prepare for parenthood in its children; and it must take care of the unavoidable remnants of infantility in its adults.

—Erik Erikson

Old age is not a disease—it is strength and survivorship.

—Maggie Kuhn

14 *Developing Families*

When a meaningful partnership such as marriage is established, the lives of many people are changed. Parents become in-laws, and some old friends either lose their position of importance in the life of one of the partners or take on new importance to both partners. Relatives approach the couple in a new way. All these changes are bound to affect the way the partners relate to one another.

Because marriage is a socially approved partnership with a long tradition behind it, it gives both the young couple and those who come into contact with them a set of guidelines that help shape their behavior, thus easing the couple's transition into a new set of relationships. Couples without such guidelines must improvise with care if they are going to retain valued external relationships and still develop their partnership. For example, when a daughter invites her parents to meet the young man with whom she has been living for a number of months, how should the parents behave? How should the young man respond? What can the daughter reasonably expect of any of them in this situation? As yet, there are no clearly defined norms governing such situations, which as a result tend to be fraught with anxiety and confusion.

Like any enduring partnership, marriage changes over time. Some of these changes result from the ongoing process of mutual discovery as the partners get to know each other more intimately and the relationship grows in maturity and depth. The birth of a child, or the addition of another member to the partnership, also sets up a whole new set of demands and interactions that change the nature of the relationship; as the child grows and develops, the parents must change the way they relate to the child and to each other. An expanding family with several children of different ages is quite a different kind of environment than a family with only one child or no children. What is more, as the partners themselves grow older, their needs and expectations with regard to one another and their partnership change.

Finally, when the children have all left home, their parents enter what is commonly called the "empty nest" period. In this period both partners, but particularly the mother, must make some dramatic readjustments in their life style. Just as the transition to the empty nest phase is often particularly difficult for the American woman, so preretirement and retirement generally tend to be difficult times for the American man. In most cases his job or career has been the center of his life—just as in most cases the children have been the center of his wife's—for such a long time that it is difficult for him to adjust to not being needed on the job. A great deal of patience and understanding is demanded of both partners at this stage of their relationship.

In this chapter we will examine some of the tasks that are common to families in the beginning years, the middle years, and the post-childrearing years. More attention will be given to the problems of the beginning years, on the assumption that these are of most immediate interest.

BEGINNING FAMILIES

There is a wide variety of schemes for describing the family life cycle. The number of stages in models of development may vary from as many as ten to as few as four.[1] Recent research suggests that the most important considerations covered in this approach are the presence or absence of children and the length of marriage, suggesting the possibility of a two- or three-stage model.[2]

Beginning families are commonly thought of as newlyweds before they have to tackle the problem of childrearing. Most couples spend about 1.5 years in this stage.[3] During this time they can focus on the problems of beginning a lifelong partnership. Among the **developmental tasks** that are common to beginning families, the following six seem especially important and will be considered in some detail: (1) developing competence in decision making; (2) working out realistic, mutually satisfying ways of getting and spending the family income; (3) adjusting to the status of being "married"; (4) developing appropriate ways of expressing and accommodating differences; (5) developing satisfactory relationships with relatives, particularly both partners' parents; and (6) working out satisfactory household routines and schedules that facilitate smooth functioning in the worlds of work and pleasure.[4]

These are common tasks all couples must face in one way or another. How they deal with them depends on their personalities, the constraints placed on them by their social situation, their self-understanding, and the kind of life style they wish to develop.

Decision Making and Planning

All couples must work out some satisfactory way of making the decisions they must make together. Decision making is not simply a matter of getting the job done or the problem solved, for the whole style of a couple's life together is affected by the way they make their decisions. This style of the decision-making process and the style of the partnership are closely related. Couples must decide what areas they want to be subject to collective decision making. Will they each have areas of interest or activity in which only their own decisions will count? For example, will he have anything to say about how the household budget is spent, or will she have anything to say about the kind of car they will own? Will they have joint or separate bank accounts? These considerations involve more than just a discussion of skills or areas of privacy. They are tied closely to the couple's notion of an appropriate division of labor in the home.[5] In recent tradition the husband has enjoyed greater power in the decision-making dimension of marriage, but the trend is toward more egalitarian patterns.[6]

Using decision making as a planning process is important to some couples and not to others. Some people are quite organized about the way they handle their lives; others favor a more spontaneous approach. If two partners are at opposite ends of this spectrum, they will have to come to grips with the difference between their decision-making styles. The young man who calls his wife from the office on Friday afternoon and says, "Honey, let's see if we can get someone to take care of the kids and we'll go away somewhere for the weekend" may not meet with an enthusiastic response if his partner feels that a weekend trip should be a carefully planned event.

Shared Decision Making. In the early years of a marriage, shared decision making very often comes quite naturally. This initial period is often characterized by a sense of excitement and mutuality. Yet the use of shared decision making at this stage does not always foretell the couple's future decision-making pattern. Shared decision making requires time, energy, and a spirit of accommodation. All things considered, it is a "costly" way of reaching decisions. In the early years of a marriage, a couple might derive a great deal of pleasure and excitement from deciding on a piece of furniture for their living room, but after a number of years this approach may come to seem too time-consuming and inefficient. If shared decision making is not a conscious mode of behavior to which the couple is committed, it tends to slip into a pattern of unilateral decision making as the partnership matures.

The fact that equality between the members of an intimate partnership is an important value often leads people to assume that shared decision making is always to be preferred over unilateral decision making. This is not necessarily the case. In general, shared decision making seems to be preferable under two conditions: (1) when both partners want to have a say in the decision and (2) when both partners have an equal or nearly equal interest in the outcome of the decision. The first condition is simply another way of saying that it is not necessary for partners to feel obligated to take part in all decisions simply for the sake of keeping the decision making on a shared basis. In our furniture-buying case, for example, the husband may have learned from experience that he tends to favor furniture that looks good in the showroom but doesn't wear well at home. He has learned to trust his wife's judgment in this area and to be suspicious of his own. In such a situation his choice to refrain from participating in the decision-making process certainly seems reasonable.

The second condition concerns the question of what "right" each partner has to involve himself or herself in a particular decision. The simplest case occurs when one partner is not in the least concerned with the outcome; here, obviously, the partner who is concerned should be free to decide unilaterally. But most situations are not that simple. What if a wife wants to enroll in a late-afternoon class at the local university? In itself, the decision as to whether or not to take a course involves her alone, but if she decides to take it she will be unable to prepare dinner on the three days a week when the class meets. This means that the husband too is concerned. But is his interest in the outcome of the decision the same as hers? It doesn't seem, on the face of it, that the inconvenience entailed in eating frozen dinners a few nights a week is as important as the opportunity to engage in a fulfilling educational experience; he therefore has less right to shape the final decision than she does. This is not to say that the couple should not discuss the situation, but it is to say that in many situations it is more appropriate for one party to have the "last word" than for the decision to be mutual.

Decision Making as a Process. There are different styles of decision making appropriate to different types of decisions within the family. Here we are concerned with decisions both partners deem important and in which both perceive themselves to have a roughly equal investment (such as moving, changing jobs, having children, buying a home). We also assume that both are interested in making use of the decision-making process as a means of growth for the partnership, and not simply as an efficient way to resolve a problem. Decision making is a process, not simply a choice at a particular point in time. Every decision involves the past history of the person or couple, their wishes at the moment, their perceptions, and their feelings. Hence, in most families decision making is not the cool, rational process it is often thought to be. It involves feelings about ourselves and who we are, feelings about our partner and who he or she is, and feelings, either distorted or realistic, about the limits placed upon us in the particular situation, including an assessment of the costs and benefits of each of the available alternatives.[7] An adequate decision must take all these dimensions into consideration.[8] The following account of a young couple in a small Midwestern town faced with a decision about moving and changing jobs illustrates the complexity of the decision-making process:

> The new job is a junior executive position with an advertising company in a large West Coast city. Jim and Shirley have lived in their hometown all their lives, except for a period away from home attending the state university. Their four parents and numerous other relatives are an important part of their lives. They are prominent people in their hometown. Their social circle tends to be closed and comfortable.
>
> Jim and Shirley have to explore numerous areas, including some self-examination, if they are to make an adequate decision. An adequate decision in this case would be reflected in their ability to move to the large West Coast city, knowing that they personally could survive, that their relationship could stand it, and that their work would contribute to their growth. Or it could be a decision to stay and achieve some of the same goals in their hometown; this decision would be based on a recognition that they value the life style they have achieved more highly than they value the sort of career advancement that is at stake.
>
> In the process of reaching a decision, Jim will have to come to some understanding of himself, some perception as to whether he is the kind of person who could make a contribution in the demanding field of advertising in this much larger cosmopolitan community. Does he have the stamina, drive, and creativity required? Does he see himself in this role, or does he find the small-scale, low-pressure life that he lives more in keeping with who he is? Shirley, too, has many questions to answer. Does she have the strength to leave the comfortable social circle she already knows? Is she the kind of person who is comfortable developing new friendships and discovering new modes of entering into relationships? How will she take the new experience? Is the source of her strength her close friendships and relations with her relatives? How will she fare without this support?
>
> Moving to a new community will require them to sell their modest home

and live in an urban apartment. The new job will require them to live in the city, which means that the pleasure they enjoy in small-town life will be taken away from them. In making a decision, therefore, they must assess the constraints and limits that the new job will place upon them.

In their new home Jim and Shirley will have to cope with the fact that at first they will not know many people and will not have a familiar social scene in which to move. They will have to learn how to live in an urban situation, which demands a different style of life from what they are used to in a small town where they knew everybody and had a clear sense of their status. The promise is, however, that this may be a starting point from which Jim can develop many of his potentials, which he felt were not being adequately used in his hometown. The job holds the possibility of advancement and greater economic rewards.

As Jim and Shirley face this decision, they will have to weigh the costs on the one hand against the promises on the other. Does Jim's career have higher priority than the life style they had established in their hometown? Can they make an adequate adjustment to the new life style? Will he really develop his potential?

Because this is a decision that deeply affects both partners, it seems appropriate that it be made jointly rather than unilaterally. In making the decision, therefore, each should contribute not only his or her knowledge and feelings about the objective situation, but also his or her feelings about both of them. Jim must have some sense of how Shirley will react to the new situation, just as Shirley probably has some assessment of how well Jim will adjust to the new job. They both face many unknowns, but each can help the other understand the situation as fully as possible.

It is impossible to know everything about a given situation, so there is always an element of risk in any decision. But if a couple have developed a method of decision making that is a creative process for both of them, they stand a good chance of making adequate decisions and are in a good position to cope with the situation in case their decision turns out to have been an inappropriate one. It is simply easier to live with a troublesome situation if one can feel confident that the decision that brought it about was the best that could have been made under the circumstances. For this reason, building a decision-making process in which one can have confidence is an important task for all couples, regardless of the particular decisions they will have to face.

Some Common Patterns. Although it is important for a young couple to develop a style of decision making that suits their own unique partnership, a great many studies on decision making in marriage have uncovered the following patterns and trends:

1. Personality characteristics have some influence on family decision making, especially the peculiar combination of both partners' traits.[9]
2. For the vast majority of couples, age has little or no influence on decision-making power, but in those cases where there is considerable difference in age (say ten years or so), the older spouse has the greater power.[10]

3. Ordinarily, the mate with more education is more influential in the decision-making process. In the working class, however, wives, with more education, generally do not have more power.[11]
4. A wife who is employed outside the home normally has more influence in family decision making than a wife who does not have outside employment.[12]
5. The husband dominates the decision-making process more in high-status families than in low-status families.[13]
6. Several studies have shown that marriages in which all decision making is left in the hands of the wife tend to be unhappy. Researchers interpreting this finding generally assume that the wife's dominance is a result of the unhappiness and not its cause.[14]
7. There is a discernible trend among young couples toward the development of separate fields of authority. The more competent tend to make the decisions in the area of assumed competence.[15]
8. Very little is known about the influence of children on the family decision-making process, but clearly they have a considerable impact. Presumably, the older the child, the greater the influence.[16]
9. Finally, couples in the early stage of their marriage tend to be "syncratic" in their decision making; that is, they decide by means of discussion and resolution. As the family expands, however, the wife's influence declines, although it is partially restored as the children leave and the parents approach middle age. Middle-aged married life is almost as egalitarian as the preparental stage.[17]
10. The spouse who is most in love and most in need of love has less power.[18]

These patterns are closely related to the traditional understanding of sex roles and the traditional nuclear family structure. In partnerships that differ significantly from these norms, the patterns just described may not be in evidence.

Income Management

One of the most important tasks facing the beginning partnership concerns income management. Mutual decisions must be made about ways of acquiring income and spending it. These decisions must be sufficiently in tune with reality to allow the couple to survive financially. Except for this constraint, the partners are free to decide who should earn the money and how it should be spent. What is important, however, is that they both freely consent to whatever division of labor they decide on.

Getting the Income. At the beginning of a marriage in which the husband is the sole producer of the income, it is very often the case that the wife must accept a lower standard of living than she is used to. If both partners are working, however, this is not likely to be the case; indeed, young couples starting out with both partners working often enjoy more disposable income than at any other time in their relationship. The arrival of children, often accompanied by home mortgage costs and other indebtednesses along

An important task of beginning families is deciding how the family income will be earned. (Erika Stone, Photo Researchers, Inc.)

with loss of the wife's income, often puts a severe strain on family resources. At the other end of the development spectrum, although disposable income may be higher than ever after the children have left the family, the need to plan for retirement and to provide for the uncertainties of old age often leaves older couples without much financial flexibility. Thus, ironically, young couples often find themselves in one of the most favorable economic positions of married life, although frequently they fail to appreciate this fact and do not adequately plan ahead for future demands on their income.

Women are increasingly contributing to family income. In 1900, about 5.6 percent of married women worked outside the home; by 1981, about 51 percent did so.[19] For the first time, in 1979 more women than men entered college.[20] Clearly, these changes have important implications for role assignments with regard to housework and child care. Indeed, many factors may enter into the decision as to who will engage in income-producing work, and often income itself is not the most important of them. In cases in which financial necessity dictates that the wife must work, the only decisions to be made will concern compensatory arrangements so that she is not saddled with the double workload of housekeeping and employment while her husband is responsible only for his job. But in cases in which financial needs do not make it necessary for both partners to work, factors such as the personal satisfaction that may derive from a career, a suitable distribution of the domestic workload, and the benefits of added income must all be weighed.

In a truly egalitarian partnership it may be felt that the decision as to whether the wife works should be made primarily by her. After all, there is no inherent reason why the husband should be given first crack at the choice between making an income and doing housework. Yet this is, in effect, what most commonly happens. That is, the partners recognize that they are faced with the twofold task of supporting and running a household; the husband automatically undertakes the support function; the wife is then free to work only if the couple can reach a mutually satisfactory agreement about how the household is to be run. Most of us would consider it almost unthinkable, when two gainfully employed people marry, for the wife to tell the husband, "I'm keeping my job; let's figure out whether we can afford a housekeeper so that you can keep yours too." The fact that this statement sounds unfair should be an indication that it is just as unfair when it is said by the husband to the wife.

Once we look at the issue in this light, we can see that the solution is for each partner to decide, on the basis of his or her preferences, whether or not to work. If one decides to work and the other chooses not to work, the division of labor between running the household and supporting it is automatically settled. (Under these conditions the wife might decide to work and the husband to stay home. Why not?) If both decide to work, they must divide the housekeeping responsibility. This should not be regarded as a matter of his choosing what areas of housework he will undertake to "help her out"; if both partners are working, the housekeeping responsibility belongs to both of them and he is no more "helping her out" when he does the dishes than she is "helping him out" when she does the laundry. Whichever partner works, it is probable that the more rigid requirements of the job will affect his or her life satisfaction in basic ways. One study concludes that men typically redefine their notion of happiness to be consistent with their position on the job.[21] Women are less likely to redefine happiness.

The issue of earning money and spending it—a subject to which we turn in a moment—is often the question around which the autonomy of the partners comes into focus. Many cultural factors shape the expectations that help or hinder a young couple in deciding on a division of labor that is appropriate for them. Parents, friends, and professionals are all too ready to give advice, whether they are asked for it or not. In this context a creative step for the young couple is to establish their own priorities and follow them.

Spending the Income. In the beginning of a partnership one of the things each partner learns quickly is the spending habits of his or her mate. Spending habits vary not only by personality but also by class, region, and ethnicity. Despite the facts that money problems are almost inevitable and that money may well be the most common source of conflict within marriage, a recent study on engaged couples indicates that they were "almost completely unaware of potential differences over the use of money."[22]

In our society the problems faced by young couples as they learn to manage their money are exacerbated by the cultural emphasis on spending. Even economic experts have been known to advise young couples to overcome their prejudice against going into debt. Banks and credit card companies advertise services that make it no longer necessary for people who want an expensive product to take into consideration whether they can afford it or not. Very often one partner will be caught up in this consumption orientation and the other will not. Such differences can lead to heated showdowns unless the partners take the trouble to work out mutually satisfactory ground rules for spending the family income.

There are many ways in which couples can divide up the task of spending their income. Duvall and Hill have described five common types of spending patterns:

1. *The Dole System.* In this system, one of the partners hands out small amounts of money at a time to the other partner and to other family members.
2. *The Family Treasurer System.* In this system, each member is allowed a certain amount of money to spend as he or she sees fit; one member dispenses these allowances and keeps the rest of the family's income for paying bills and for making the majority of the family's purchases.
3. *The Division of Expenses System.* In this system, the various spending tasks are assigned to either one partner or the other, with an appropriate amount of money allotted to each. For example, the husband may be responsible for the mortgage, the insurance, and the automobile while the wife is responsible for the food, clothing, and recreation. Any other spending is undertaken after a joint decision.
4. *The Budget System.* The couple plan together in advance what their expenses will be and establish this as the basis of their spending.[23]

Each of these systems has certain advantages and disadvantages. For example, both the dole system and the family treasurer system have the advantage of simplicity and clear accountability in that there can be no doubt about who is responsible for keeping the family on a stable economic basis. They have the disadvantage of giving one partner more power than the other over disposing of the income. If the wife is the treasurer, for example, and her husband wants to buy a new suit, he must ask for the money, whereas she does not have to ask anyone's permission to buy a new dress. The joint-account system has the advantage of providing greater equality in the power to spend along with the disadvantage of unclear lines of responsibility.

Each couple should weigh the various advantages and disadvantages of these systems and develop the system that best preserves their individual needs for autonomy and best meets their day-to-day need for control over their spending habits. Because the two partners may come from homes in which different systems were employed, deciding on an appropriate system may be difficult. Nevertheless, it is important that this difficulty be faced. With patience, a great deal of inexperience in managing money can be overcome, and the partners can learn a great deal about each other in the process.

Being Married Is Different

Marriage is a social as well as a personal event. For couples who go through the normal stages from courtship through engagement to marriage, a good part of the engagement period ordinarily is devoted to working out the wedding arrangements and making plans for a new home. A certain amount of mutual exploration and adjustment is possible during this period, but being engaged is not the same as being married. Unmarried cohabitation is probably the closest approximation to marriage, but even here there are some subtle but nonetheless real differences. The fact that many unmarried couples who are living together decide to get married is clear proof that, at least in their eyes, marriage is different.

From one perspective the marriage ceremony itself is a superb labeling process. It impresses on the "just married" and their friends, neighbors, and relatives that a contract has been negotiated that involves public as well as personal expectations. Even though Americans do not generally put much emphasis on ritual, a wedding makes a definite impression on most of the people who attend it. What is more, even though we are not a particularly religious nation, three-fourths of the couples who marry prefer a church wedding.[24] Curiously, there is a weak but significant correlation between "success" in marriage and having been married in a religious ceremony, although it is not clear why this is so.[25] It is probable that this correlation reflects the conforming or conservative character of those who prefer church weddings more than it reflects any sort of independent commitment to marriage.

Weddings dramatize the commitment of the couple to each other and to their social and familial responsibilities. One theory holds that the heavier the responsibilities the couple is expected to assume, the more elaborate the ritual of the wedding and its associated events. It is clear, of course, that weddings also provide an occasion to display publicly the wealth of the families that are being related by this event—particularly the status of the bride's family, which is expected to pay for most of the wedding.[26]

To a young woman, the label "Mrs." and the adoption of her husband's surname provide a shorthand way of referring to a whole set of expectations regarding the role behavior that is now demanded of her. The man, of course, does not undergo such a dramatic transformation of identity—a fact that has caused feminists to denounce our society's naming customs as symbols of the possessive nature of the marriage relationship. The woman, these critics point out, becomes immediately identifiable as the man's wife upon marriage, but nothing in the way the man identifies himself indicates that he is her husband. For this reason it is becoming increasingly common for young women to retain their "maiden" names after marriage and to use the label "Ms.," which avoids identification in terms of marital status.

Even without the name change, however, marriage often entails a more dramatic change for the wife than for the husband. This change is especially marked when a woman retires from her career or job upon marriage and becomes a full-time housewife. The couple therefore should not be surprised if the wife experiences somewhat greater difficulty than the husband in adjusting to the new situation.

The tradition of a honeymoon trip was probably designed primarily for the purpose of easing the transition into the new roles that both partners are expected to assume when they marry. During the honeymoon the couple can begin to adjust to each other as husband and wife in a setting where they will not be bothered by the more pressing problems of everyday life. The honeymoon is one of the few socially sanctioned occasions for "dyadic withdrawal." Philip Slater interprets the pranks that are often attached to this event as signs of society's anxiety that the couple will "drop out" more permanently and forget their social obligations.[27]

Dealing with Differences

Although the mate selection process tends to favor couples who are similar in such areas as religion, socioeconomic class, ethnicity, age, and community background, thus producing a situation in which the partners who come to a marriage tend to be alike in a great many ways, nevertheless the personalities of the two partners inevitably will differ in significant and critical ways. The problem of learning to cope with differences in spending patterns has already been suggested.

Even though few households are three generational, kinship ties remain very important to us. (John Isaac, United Nations)

Relating to Relatives

Beginning a marriage means establishing some kind of relationship with in-laws and redefining relationships with other relatives. Kinship ties normally are maintained most closely through the mother-daughter relationship, a fact that is reflected in the folk saying, "A son's a son till he takes a wife, a daughter's a daughter for all of her life."[28] Probably as a result of this situation, the wife is more likely than the husband to feel that in-laws are a problem.[29] Indeed, the classic situation of conflict in the American kinship system is the relationship between mother-in-law and daughter-in-law.[30]

The importance of kinship ties varies with socioeconomic class in a curvilinear fashion.[31] Kin are most important in the lower and upper classes and less important in the middle class, where friendships often play a role in the couple's life analogous to the role played by kin in other socioeconomic classes.[32] Several studies suggest there is a positive relationship between marital happiness and establishing good relationship with in-laws.[33] Thus, couples who make a reasonably good adjustment in other areas of their partnership and develop a sense of working together as partners tend to have fewer problems with their in-laws than couples who are less well adjusted to each other. On the other hand, disagreements over how to relate to in-laws are frequently cited as a source of marital unhappiness.

Kin are the people to whom marital partners are most likely to turn when they need help or support that they cannot get from their mates. This is true even in middle-class marriages, in which kinship may otherwise be relatively unimportant. Bott's classic study of working-class England showed that couples who did not share very much with each other commonly shared a great deal with their kin.[34] This seems also to be the case with lower- and working-class Americans, although to a lesser degree than Bott found in her English population. Thus, the kinship network is related to the nuclear family unit in a complex way and has subtle effects on the patterns of marital interaction.

When couples are asked to identify the source of in-law problems, both partners tend to name the mother-in-law most often. The reason for this is quite obvious. In our society the mother is the parent who is specifically oriented to caring for the children, and it is not easy for her to relinquish this role when they marry. Very often this tendency is exacerbated when one of the partners has not fully separated himself or herself from the mother-son or mother-daughter role. The husband who wants his wife to cook the way his mother did is inviting his mother to interfere in her daughter-in-law's kitchen; the wife who turns to her mother rather than to her husband for advice in establishing her new home is likely to make her husband resent his mother-in-law, whose presence, he may be justified in feeling, is an intrusion in the couple's privacy that is all the more irksome because his wife actually seems to welcome it.

For these reasons and many others, three-generational households are very difficult to maintain satisfactorily in our society. They are typically resorted to when there is no other economic alternative to having the parents move in with their children; less frequently, the children "come home" to live with the parents. Part of the problem comes from the fact that our society has no specified way of dealing with the allocation of authority in such a household. Is the daughter to have authority over the household and its chores, or does she relinquish these responsibilities to her mother when she moves in? And what if it is her husband's mother rather than her own mother with whom she must live? Each couple must work out their own arrangements for coping with such situations, and we must frankly confess that none of those arrangements seem to work very well in our society.[35]

Working Out the Routine

In the early years of their partnership, young couples are seldom aware of how many hours of just plain routine will go into their relationship. Caring for bodily needs, cleaning the house, buying the food and preparing it, picking up after each other—these and many other mundane matters consume a great deal of time. Because these aspects of living involve deeply ingrained habits that are often taken for granted, partners can find themselves struggling through a great deal of conflict without really knowing why they are getting angry at one another. Yet a great deal of marital conflict arises out of things that may seem too unimportant to matter.[36]

The problem of dealing with these questions of detail and routine is half solved as soon as it is realized that they are not unimportant. If persistent feelings continue to point up a disturbing pattern, this should be brought out into the open and discussed in such a way as not to offend the other person. Often these "little things" (such as leaving underwear hanging in the bathroom to dry or never filling up the car until the tank is practically empty) are laughed at before marriage; thus, the offending partner may feel that the other has understood his or her idiosyncracy and can live with it. But after marriage the humor fades rapidly and the matter becomes a source of constant irritation.

The development tasks described in the preceding sections may or may not be adequately met in the beginning stage of a partnership. If they are adequately met, the assumption is that the partnership will develop smoothly and the partners will be relatively free to deal with new tasks that confront them as their relationship matures. If they are not adequately met, however, the partners are likely to experience increasing tensions that may disrupt their partnership or slow its development. In either case, however, if the partnership endures, it is quite likely that the issues discussed in the first stage will fade from prominence as new ones arise and require the couple's attention. The later stages in the developmental sequence will be discussed briefly in the remainder of this chapter.

FAMILIES IN THEIR MIDDLE YEARS

The time after the children have left their parent's home and become independent has been called the **empty nest** stage in the developmental sequence through which the parents are passing. This stage covers the period from the departure of the last child to the beginning of retirement—an average of about fifteen years. If the trend toward earlier retirement continues—as seems likely—then this stage will become shorter.

The use of the phrase "empty nest" to describe this stage in the family's life cycle suggests that it is a bleak and lonely period, especially for women. Evidence is beginning to accumulate that this is not necessarily so.[37] There is a period of adjustment, yes, but most of the effects of the last child's departure have dissipated after two years.[38] A middle-aged woman with a small child still in the home is generally likely to be less satisfied with her marriage than a woman whose children have left home.[39] While there is a continuing debate over the importance of the findings, a number of studies support the view that a couple's satisfaction with their marriage begins high, slumps slightly during the childrearing years, and rises again after the children have left home.[40] These years are clearly a time for renegotiation of the marital contract and an opportunity to reestablish the importance of the marriage in the couple's lives.

Couples in these middle years have an opportunity to experience a new sense of independence, to rediscover each other, and to achieve greater intimacy. Middle-aged people today are generally healthier and more vigorous than people in this age group were at the turn of the century. What is more, their income is apt to be near its maximum. On the other hand, the

When couples reach the end of childrearing, there is the opportunity to begin a new partnership with each other. (Hella Hammid, Photo Researchers, Inc.)

couple may find that their relationship has changed during the period of childrearing and that they have grown apart. When she tries to return to her career, the wife may find it is impossible for her to compete with younger people and with people her own age who did not drop out to raise children. What is more, the couple may discover that they have lost the ability to spend leisure time creatively. Thus, time may weigh heavily on couples in their middle years. This problem is likely to affect women more than men. The wife who can no longer find her fulfillment in bringing up children, finds no particular pleasure in housework, and cannot return to a job or career is faced with a major problem of adjustment.

Most couples enter the middle stage of their marriage around the age of 45 or 50. Before the turn of the century it was not common for couples to have many years together after the children had left home, for the average life expectancy simply was too short. As a result, we do not have well-defined, traditional expectations about what such couples should do. They must face the fact that children can no longer be the center of their lives and that they have reached the stage in their lives when their economic status is pretty well established. Either they have "made it" or they have not. A man must accept the fact that he is no longer a promising young executive on the way up; at 45 he has either "peaked out" or (in most professions) should be able to make a reasonably good estimate of how much farther up the ladder of success he is likely to climb. If he has realized his personal objectives, he can take satisfaction in his accomplishments; if not, then he should adjust himself to the fact that he is not likely to have another chance. The self-awareness required for each adjustment often comes as quite a jolt to working-class men, who at 45 may find themselves earning less than their sons who went on to college—in fact, less than their sons who went to work right after high school but are more valuable to employers than the "old man" because of their youth, greater agility, and greater strength. In the lower levels of the working class, men are often laid off or "retired" early so that companies can avoid paying maximum pensions—if there is a pension program—and can keep the payroll down by minimizing the number of higher-salaried, more experienced workers.

For women, menopause marks the transition to later life as dramatically as retirement does for men—perhaps more so. With menopause, women end their childbearing period and must cope with the effects of aging that become apparent as a result of changes in hormone balance. For many women, the end of their menses symbolizes the end of their youth. Often this is a traumatic time in which the woman may come to doubt her own womanliness. These doubts may be aggravated by suspicions that her husband is losing interest in her. Most women adjust to this new stage in their lives, but this does not mean that the psychological pain often associated with menopause should be taken lightly. A husband is no more entitled to assume that "it's just something she'll get over" than a wife is entitled to disregard the husband's gloomy feelings of uselessness and obsolescence as he faces retirement. In both cases, an understanding partner is an invaluable aid in getting through what sometimes tends to be a rather tough transition.

The physical process of aging, of course, changes the character of both men and women. Bodies lose their tone, their shape, and begin to wrinkle. Physical stamina declines. Men and women may accept these changes as inevitable and take reasonable steps to minimize the rate of aging by such means as exercise, diets, cosmetics, and a change in the types of clothing worn. Or they can strive to "maintain their youth" by not admitting what is happening to them. In either case the physical process of aging will continue, so the former strategy is clearly preferable in that it enables the person to cope with an inevitable situation.

During the middle years the need to plan for retirement becomes evident. Awareness of this need is often quite limited in earlier years, as is evidenced by the fact that the majority of American couples do not prepare adequately for retirement.[41] Couples with limited resources often find it simply impossible to prepare for this stage of life. Thus, a large majority of couples have made no provision for retirement income. Social security is a very inadequate source of retirement income, yet it remains the source on which most retired couples depend.

Providing for an adequate income is only one aspect of the problem of planning for retirement. For most men, retirement means coming to grips with the fact that they are no longer useful to society. To avoid this feeling of uselessness, it is better to retire *to* something than to retire *from* something; if possible, therefore, hobbies, community activities, and avocations should be cultivated during the middle years. Unfortunately, even in our "affluent society" many American families can afford neither the outside activities that can lend a sense of purpose to the retirement years nor the luxury of being able to put aside savings for the time when employment income disappears. For countless families retirement means poverty, and that in itself is a lonely and frightening prospect.

AGING FAMILIES

A couple fortunate enough to have adequate income in their retirement years generally can look forward to good health and several more years of life together. The average life expectancy at birth for males born in 1980 was 69.8 years and for females 77.5.[42] Because of the longer life expectancy of women, the wife can expect to be the survivor and can anticipate a widowhood of eleven years (on the average). The problems of aging families are closely tied to the problems of our economy, which tends to produce workers who accumulate like the waste products of industry, to be disposed of or discarded when the industrial system is through with them. Severe economic constraints are placed upon the elderly, either as a result of their own lack of planning or as a result of society's inability to provide adequate income through earnings, social insurance, or outright grants.[43] Descriptions of this phase in a couple's life often seem to gloss over the hardships and emphasize the autonomy of the aging couple.

With all this information, it is not difficult to see that one of the primary tasks facing an aging couple is to recognize that they can be useful people and to find a way to express this fact. Often, however, the husband simply retires into the home when he loses the one thing that gave his life meaning—his job. Having no other outlets through which to express himself, he may slouch around the house and meddle in his wife's established routine, which has not undergone such radical changes. Very often he loses his sense of purpose and meaning in life.

Because a husband and wife usually spend more time together after his retirement, many conflicts that used to be suppressed or ignored now become very important. What is more, the formerly independent breadwinner loses status and the formerly dependent wife gains in status and power, producing role changes to which the elderly couple may have difficulty adjusting. Another common pattern is for the aging couple to become increasingly dependent on their children. All these hazards must be dealt with if the couple is to stand any chance of enjoying the retirement period.

A happier scenario is recorded in the case of husbands who are able to find a sense of usefulness and purposefulness in their retirement years by participating more actively in the household chores and being loving, affectionate companions to their wives and children. Middle-class men generally are able to make this role change more readily and more effectively than lower-class men. Because the upper-middle-class man is likely to have experienced some degree of role flexibility prior to retirement, he is often able to change roles with a fair degree of self-confidence while basking in the afterglow of his successful career. If his success and self-esteem are secured, he can look forward to this kind of role change as an opportunity to participate in an expressive life style and to explore feelings he may have overlooked during his climb to success. If the relationship is one of caring and understanding, both husband and wife can evoke from each other a new sense of purposefulness during this stage of their marriage.

A big part of the problem faced by aging citizens is overcoming the stereotypes of aging.[44] Not very long ago the generally accepted model of normal aging declared that old people disengaged gradually from the things of this world as they prepared for death, the inevitable departure. Now this disengagement is seen as an illness, not a normal part of aging. Similarly, it was once thought that intellect and sexual desire were greatly diminished in old age. Now it is recognized that older citizens can remain sexually and intellectually active. The discovery that a great deal of vigor and vitality can sustain healthy aging people living independent lives is a great emancipation for many. When the majority of people in our society come to recognize the resources the elderly can provide and stop thinking of them as "wrinkled babies," a very great change will have occurred in our way of life.

SUMMARY

From the developmental point of view, partnerships such as marriage face certain critical tasks at various stages. Beginning families must develop decision-making patterns and adjust in other ways to the uniqueness of the married state. Families with children face the task of incorporating new members and dealing responsibly with these individuals. During the "empty nest" period the partners need to rediscover each other and prepare for the retirement period.

In this chapter we touched briefly on all these stages but devoted most of our attention to the first stage. In particular, we explored six tasks that are of major importance at this stage: (1) developing competence in decision making; (2) working out realistic, mutually satisfying ways of getting and spending the family income; (3) adjusting to the status of being "married"; (4) developing appropriate ways of expressing and accommodating differences; (5) developing satisfactory relationships with relatives, particularly both partners' parents; and (6) working out satisfactory household routines and schedules.

NOTES

1. The approach to marriage taken in this chapter is called the developmental approach. This way of looking at partnerships such as marriage sees them as passing through several stages of development. There can be as many as ten or as few as four stages, depending on who is doing the research. At each stage there are certain tasks that must be accomplished in order for the relationship to develop smoothly. The three-stage model used here is a condensation of the eight stages proposed by Evelyn Duvall, *Family Development*, 4th ed. (New York: Harper & Row, 1972), p. 151. A much more sophisticated treatment of this approach is found in Roy Rogers, *Family Interaction and Transaction: The Development Approach* (Englewood Cliffs, N.J.: Prentice-Hall, 1973).

2. Steven L. Nack, "The Family Life Cycle: Empirical or Conceptual Tool," *Journal of Marriage and the Family* (February 1979): 15–25.

3. Paul C. Glick, "Updating the Life Cycle of the Family," *Journal of Marriage and the Family* (February 1977): 5–13.

4. William F. Kenkel, *The Family in Perspective* (Englewood Cliffs, N.J.: Prentice-Hall, 1966), p. 409.

5. James L. Hawkins et al. "Marital Communication Style and Social Class," *Journal of Marriage and the Family* (August 1977): 479–89 suggest that the communication style of a partnership is more likely to involve open self-disclosure if the partners are better educated, but all classes seemed to prefer these styles.

6. S. P. Douglas and Y. Wind, "Examining Family Role and Authority Patterns," *Journal of Marriage and the Family*, 40 (February 1978): 35–47.

7. Boyd Rollins and Stephen J. Bahr, "A Theory of Power Relationships in Marriages," *Journal of Marriage and the Family* (November 1976): 619–26 suggest that power in the family is a function of social interaction rather than

attributes of individual personality. Power and control exist when there is a conflict between the goals of the married partners, and does not exist independently of perception. It does not suffice, therefore, to simply discover who makes the decisions. It is very important to determine how each partner feels about the decision as well.

8. Again, this process is concerned with adequacy more than with efficiency or verification of data. Most decisions of consequence, it would seem, are made with inadequate information. We must nevertheless invest a great deal of ourselves in the decision and assume responsibility for the consequences. This is risky. Emphasis on the adequacy of the decision-making process helps us cope with the risks. The kind of decision making described here is more appropriate for "commitment-type" choices involving long-term consequences than it would be for simple choice situations such as what cereal to buy.

9. W. J. Doherty and R. G. Ryder, "Locus of Control, Interpersonal Trust, and Assertive Behavior Among Newlyweds," *Journal of Personality and Social Psychology*, 37 (December 1979): 2212–20.

10. J. Scanzoni and K. Polonko, "A Conceptual Approach to Explicit Marital Negotiation," *Journal of Marriage and the Family*, 42 (February 1980): 31–44.

11. D. L. Gillespie, "Who Has the Power? The Marital Struggle," *Journal of Marriage and the Family*, 33 (August 1971): 445–58.

12. J. Scanzoni, "Contemporary Marriage Types," *Journal of Family Issues*, 1 (March 1980): 125–40.

13. F. Philip Rice, *Contemporary Marriage* (Newton, Mass.: Allyn and Bacon, 1983), p. 197.

14. Richard Udry, *The Social Context of Marriage*, 2nd ed. (New York: Harper & Row, 1973), pp. 315–18.

15. G. H. Conklin, "Cultural Determinants of Power for Women with the Family: A Neglected Aspect of the Family Research," *Journal of Comparative Family Studies*, 10 (spring 1979): 35–54.

16. M. W. Weil, *Marriage, The Family and Society* (Danville, Ill.: Interstate, 1971).

17. R. A. Lewis, "Satisfaction with Conjugal Power over the Family Life Cycle," Paper presented to the National Council of Family Relations, 1973.

18. G. W. McDonald, "Family Power: The Assessment of a Decade of Theory and Research, 1970–1979," *Journal of Marriage and the Family*, 42 (November 1980): 841–54.

19. U.S. Bureau of the Census, *Statistical Abstract of the United States: 1982–83* (Washington, D.C.: U.S. Government Printing Office, 1983), p. xxi.

20. Ibid., p. xx.

21. Joseph Harry, "Evolving Sources of Happiness for Men Over the Life Cycle: A Structural Analysis," *Journal of Marriage and the Family* (May 1976): 289–96.

22. Judson T. Landis and Mary G. Landis, *Building a Successful Marriage*, 6th ed. (Englewood Cliffs, N.J.: Prentice-Hall, 1973), p. 358.

23. As described in Richard H. Klemer, *Marriage and Family Relationships* (New York: Harper & Row, 1970), p. 271.

24. Leonard Benson, *The Family Bond: Marriage, Love and Sex in America* (New York: Random House, 1971), p. 173.

25. For an excellent survey of the factors social scientists consider important predictors of marital success, see William F. Stephens (ed.), *Reflections on Marriage* (New York: Harper & Row, 1968).

26. Benson, p. 174.

27. Philip Slater, "Social Limitations on Libidinal Withdrawal," *American Psychological Review*, 25 (June 1963): 339–64.

28. Udry, p. 337.

29. Ibid.

30. Ibid.

31. See the discussion of the American kinship system in relation to the conjugal family in David A. Schulz, *The Changing Family: Its Function and Future*, 3rd ed. (Englewood Cliffs, N.J.: Prentice-Hall, 1982), pp. 117–21.

32. Udry, p. 337.

33. Landis and Landis, p. 296.

34. Elizabeth Bott, *Family and Social Networks: Roles, Norms and Extended Relations in Orderly Families* (London: Tavistock Publications, 1957).

35. Klemer, pp. 277ff.

36. Peggy Marcus, "In-Law Relationships in Couples Married Two or Eleven Years," *Journal of Home Economics* (January 1951): 35–37.

37. Norval Glenn, "Psychological Well-Being in the Post Parental Stage: Some Evidence from National Surveys," *Journal of Marriage and the Family* (February 1975): 105–9.

38. Elizabeth Bates Harkins, "Effects of Empty Nest Transition on Self-Report of Psychological and Physical Well-Being," *Journal of Marriage and the Family* (August 1978): 549–55.

39. Glenn, "Psychological Well-Being."

40. Boyd C. Rollins and Harold Feldman, "Marital Satisfaction over the Family Life Cycle," *Journal of Marriage and the Family* (February 1970): 20–28; Boyd C. Rollins and Kenneth L. Cannon, "Marital Satisfaction over the Life Cycle: A Reevaluation," *Journal of Marriage and the Family* (May 1974): 271–83; Graham Spanier et al., "Marital Adjustment over the Life Cycle: The Issue of Curvilinearity," *Journal of Marriage and the Family* (May 1975): 263–75; Rosalyn Weiman Schram, "Marital Satisfaction over the Family Life Cycle: A Critique and Proposal," *Journal of Marriage and the Family* (February 1979): 7–12.

41. Harold Shepard, "The Poverty of Aging," in Ben B. Seligman (ed.), *Poverty as a Public Issue* (New York: Free Press, 1967), pp. 86–87.

42. *Statistical Abstract: 1982–83*, p. xix.

43. F. Ivan Nye and Felix Berardo, *The Family: Its Structure and Interaction* (New York: Macmillan, 1973) p. 578.

44. Alex Comfort, *A Good Age* (New York: Simon & Schuster, 1976), and Maggie Kuhn, "Liberating Aging," *New Age* (February 1979): 34–39.

Money is very much a state of mind like the states of consciousness that you see on an acid trip. . . . To really understand the extent to which money is a dream listen to the economists's definition of money, it is: part of a system of relative pricing and an accounting store of value. . . . It is a record of previous transactions like your savings account, your checking account, credits of energy or inheritance that you have built up. It is a store of imaginary value.

—Michael Phillips

15 Family Money Management

Managing money is perhaps more difficult than earning it. In any case, a great deal of the strife and conflict in partnerships such as marriage results from inability to agree on how this should be done. This inability derives not only from lack of knowledge about how to manage money, which seems to be endemic in our society, but also from disagreement or confusion over whether it should be managed at all. The fact that most couples do not manage their money at all is most curious in a supposedly materialistic society like ours.

This chapter will approach the issues raised by money management from two perspectives. First, we will raise some questions about what is valuable and why, and attempt to distinguish economic choice from other kinds of choice. Economics is a "dismal science" only when it contends that its image of a human being as a threatened small businessperson is adequate to describe the human condition in general. Its notion that everything has a price and that all valuable things can be reduced to a cash value is likewise limiting. In this framework nothing can have intrinsic value, and the tools of money management, the concern of the second part of this chapter, cease to be tools in the hands of a creative person. They become rules to live by.

Developing a budget, making good use of credit, planning a savings and investment program, handling income tax matters, and other practical considerations of good money management presuppose a stable economy and tend to foster a commitment to an economic way of life that many people are challenging today. In this chapter we cannot resolve these issues, but we will consider them. It is simply not true that money management is merely a business matter unrelated to other issues of life style. Indeed, we will argue, the fact that the management of money raises fundamental issues of life style, personal responsibility, and moral choice is one reason why some people have difficulty discussing money management in the first place.

We will begin, then, with a discussion of the broader concept of valuation within which the issues of money management can be considered. Few people would argue that the ability to spend money for what is truly needed is not a desirable skill. The problem is, What do we want and why? And how is this management of personal finance likely—or unlikely—to accomplish our broader objectives?

THE PROBLEM OF VALUE

Classic economic theory assumes that the "invisible hand" of the free market will establish the value of goods and services and the value of the labor necessary to provide them. A person's labor or a dozen eggs are worth what the market will pay, and no more. Such is the conviction expressed in the so-called law of supply and demand. The value of everything is determined relative to the value of everything else through the medium of the market. Everything has its price.

Economic theory has some utility as an explanation of how things are given a price, but when it becomes expanded into a world view or a philosophy of life, it is grossly inadequate. From the point of view of an individual trying to make sense out of life and wanting to give everything its proper value, market valuations will not do. We know intuitively that some things cannot be given a price. The most baffling item on this list of things is self. "How important am I, anyway?" It doesn't help to ask the flip question "Relative to what?" The question of how valuable I am is another form of the question "Who am I?" When I ask this question, I am not interested in what I can earn. I am not really interested in how important others may think I am. I am interested in how important I really am in the scheme of things. I raise the question as to whether I have *self-worth*—intrinsic value—or not.

Those who have explored issues of self-knowledge over the centuries have not generally assumed that the question of "Who am I?" or "What am I worth?" can be answered once and for all. The affirmation that I am intrinsically valuable will not solve all the problems of life. The best that can be said is that how a person stands on this matter will determine a basic perspective within which these other problems can be solved. Many people assume that the self is infinite and that, therefore, the quest for self-understanding is endless. And yet there is a sense in which the value of self is determined before the journey has begun. Each new insight adds another dimension to an already experienced reality. Existentialist philosophers like Søren Kierkegaard thought that the most important choice we make in life is to affirm or reject it. He added to the Delphic Oracle's "Know thyself" the critically important "Choose thyself!" I can choose to accept or reject myself and my life, or I can choose to remain ambiguous, afraid to affirm or deny. Whichever fundamental choice I make, my life style is deeply affected.

It is possible to take the question "Who am I?" or "What am I worth?" out of the marketplace. The major religions of the world have done just this by grounding the sense of self-worth in a continuing encounter with an ultimate reality or ultimate value, commonly called God. A common thread running through the major religions of the world is the affirmation that through meditation and prayer it is possible to experience one's place in the scheme of things and to know the answers to the questions of self-knowledge and self-worth. To the extent that a person is able to accept his or her intrinsic worth through a direct encounter with that which is ultimately valuable, to this extent it is unnecessary to try to establish the sense of one's importance through socioeconomic evaluation. Paradoxically, the world's religions seems to answer the question of the intrinsic worth of the individual in diametrically opposite ways. Buddhism stresses the unity of all things and the comparative insignificance of the individual as such. On the other hand, it asserts, "Thou art that," meaning "Thou art God," or thou art an expression of the divine in the world. Christianity proclaims the infinite value of the individual soul through its doctrine of the resurrection of the body. You will remain recognizably and essentially you throughout all eternity. You are not God, but God has made you infinitely valuable.

When the matter of self-worth becomes simply a matter of negotiation (as the expanded model of the market suggests), an individual is cast adrift on a sea of relativity. In such a situation it is tempting to find some security by placing one's confidence in things that others find valuable—gold, stocks, expensive homes, and so forth. In society, a person's worth is frequently judged from the size of his or her estate. A lot of the pretense about how much is saved and how much spent on the car and how much on the house is an effort to inflate one's social importance. Social status is one measure of how important a person is in our society. But however tempting the retreat to social prestige might be, it quickly becomes unsatisfying. We know there is no necessary relationship between how we feel about ourselves, our importance in the scheme of things, and what others say about us. We establish whatever relationship might exist through our affirmation of ourselves. The social and economic evaluations are ultimately hollow, but they immediately attract us. It is also tempting to resolve the question of self-worth by joining a group of people who seem to be pretty sure about their answers to this question. Cults like the People's Temple and the Church of Hakeem are made up of people who listen as true believers to leaders who tell them who they are and what they are worth.

We must now turn to a discussion of the situation that seems to be more common in our time. Most of us find that our management of money is intimately tied up with our efforts to establish a sense of self-importance. Madison Avenue has striven mightily to encourage us to believe that we are important and valuable because of what we own or what others say about us.

Money Management and the Question of Self-Worth

It is difficult to manage money when what we want or think we need in life continues to increase. In most industrial societies, most people earn more than enough to ensure their survival, and a great many earn enough to provide themselves and their families with an ever-expanding array of luxuries. In the preceding section we argued that it is not simply an insatiable longing for creature comforts that drives us to spend. More fundamentally, we spend because in spending we seek to resolve what for most of us is an unresolvable question, that of how valuable and important we are. Social standing in an urban society does not depend as much on personal knowledge of another's ability as it does on the cues the other person gives off about how wealthy or powerful he or she is. Since most of us are not well known by the majority of the people with whom we come into contact each day, our social presentation of self revolves largely around impression management—the cues we give off in our behavior, dress, and possessions that associate us with a particular class of people. Although most people will state that they are members of the middle class, most also aspire to be as high on the status ladder as possible.

The successful advertisement campaign aims at providing readily recognizable status symbols in the company's products, or cues suggesting that the owner of their product is competent, self-assured, or tasteful—in short, that the buyer of the product stands to gain a great deal more from purchase of the product than its functional utility. This is known as "selling the sizzle rather than the steak." These campaigns do not necessarily create the conditions that are favorable to such sales pitches; they may simply take advantage of the fact that most of us do not seem to have adequately resolved the issue of self-worth. Uncertainty about our own worth is not the only noneconomic factor that influences our money management. We may spend or manage money as a form of entertainment. We may use money to put others down or to relieve a sense of guilt. When the issue of self-worth is faced directly, however, these other issues are more likely to come into perspective.

An Alternative to Conspicuous Consumption

Social scientists at Stanford University Research Institute have created considerable concern in the business community with their publication of a report entitled "Voluntary Simplicity."[1] **Voluntary Simplicity (VS)** is not, in their view, the latest social fad. It is a growing social movement that has attracted the interest of at least half the adult population of the United States and by the year 2000 will be practiced by about 120 million Americans as a way of life. They see VS as a major transformation of American cultural values.

The values of VS are contrasted with the dominant world view in a number of ways. Whereas contemporary values stress material growth, VS strives for material sufficiency and personal growth. Human beings can be thought of as inhibiting two worlds: the outward world, where worth is a matter of social prestige and productivity, and the inward world, where worth is established through direct experience. VS turns inward, believing that personal growth is more important for a satisfying life than building an estate. Although these two activities need not be mutually exclusive, they frequently are. This emphasis on personal growth has led VS advocates to turn to religion and the humanities, especially Eastern thought, with its emphasis on direct experience of reality through meditation. Human beings are not thought of as pitted against nature in a struggle for the survival of the fittest; rather, they are viewed as living harmoniously and cooperatively with the natural environment. Therefore, ecology and conservation are prime concerns. Cooperation and enlightened self-interest is opposed to rugged individualism and narrow economic self-interest. Finally, an intuitive mode of knowing is added to the rational mode that is considered sufficient by most people in the West.

These values are reflected in a number of social characteristics. VS is against conspicuous consumption. It favors reducing the gadget load rather than increasing it. VS favors smaller, less complex, energy-conserving housing, an environmentally appropriate (less polluting) technology, greater role flexibility both on the job and off, much greater acceptance of cultural and interpersonal diversity, and a more relaxed stance toward life. In short, VS favors creating an abundant life by being satisfied with less.

VS must not be confused with poverty. It is advocated by those who have made it or who live comfortably because their parents have made it. The people who make the headlines are those who "drop out" of a very successful career to live the simple life. "The motivation of such people tends to be highly private and specific—desire to escape the rat race, personal disillusionment with success, boredom with the job, the desire to live a less plastic life." The largest group of VS advocates, however, are predominantly young (20s–30s) and single, almost exclusively white, from a middle–upper-middle-class background, politically independent, and urban. These young people are motivated toward VS largely because of the social problems mentioned earlier. They are drawn by the promise of personal fulfillment. Although VS can be traced to the counterculture of the 1960s, it is by no means limited to this group. It includes a broad spectrum of middle-class Americans. Poor people and minorities who have not yet entered the mainstream of American life do not commonly advocate or practice VS.

We have sustained our way of life in the West not only through the incentives of material reward and the bogus promise of self-fulfillment they offer, but also by accepting the notion that only in modern industrial societies is the good life possible. People in primitive societies, it is commonly thought, must spend most of their time struggling to survive. The fantasy of the South Sea Island where you don't have to work very hard to stay alive and can lie around on the beach making love all day is believed to be just that, a fantasy. Yet anthropologists are beginning to understand that the contrast between the life of luxury offered by industrial societies and the struggle for existence demanded by primitive ones is much too simple.

Primitive Affluence. Indeed, the Machiguengans of the Amazon rain forests live more leisurely and less stressful lives than middle-class people in France. "One of the paradoxes of modern life is the persistence of suffering and deep dissatisfaction among people who enjoy an unparalleled abundance of material goods."[2] Along with the Buddhists, anthropologists are coming to see that there are two paths to affluence: to produce more or be satisfied with less. Being satisfied with less is not as punitive as we are inclined to think, judging from what we can learn from the Machiguengans. French men and women spend more time working outside the home than the Machiguengans. French women spend less time working outside the home than Machiguengan women, but much more time working inside the home. Most significant, Machiguengan men spend more than 14 hours a day engaged in free time, compared to 10 hours for French men. Free time in both cases includes 8.2 hours of sleep.

Life Styles and Socioeconomic Constraints

As conventionally used in sociology, **life style** refers to a standard of living achieved because of a particular command over resources given to an individual as a member of a particular socioeconomic class. It is often assumed that life style is determined by socioeconomic class standing. The truth in such a way of thinking about life style is the commonsense understanding that economic resources significantly shape the opportunities available to us in fashioning the life we desire. Beyond this commonsense observation is a frequently overlooked significant insight: One's socioeconomic status is very often not a simple matter of one's ability. Indeed, for the world's impoverished, personal achievement and native talent have very little to do with their impoverishment. Children born to impoverished parents sometimes do move up the socioeconomic ladder, but most do not—at least not very far up—and certainly not in the situation we now face, in which millions of persons are unemployed because there are not enough jobs for them, regardless of their training. Poverty and unemployment today in the developed countries are more the result of socioeconomic factors beyond the control of the unemployed than any personal failing. It behooves us to examine some of these factors briefly because they affect all of us, even if we feel confident of employment or are already well employed.

After World War II, with relatively minor perturbations called recessions, the economy of the developed nations grew stronger each year until 1973, the year of the Arab oil embargo. The curtailment of oil to the developed countries and the enormous increase in price demanded by the OPEC countries put an end to the era of cheap oil—and perhaps cheap energy as well. The recent announcement of an oil glut notwithstanding, the earth's reserves of fossil fuel are severely limited, and the Arabs have only speeded up the time when we must pay careful attention to this fact. We are now spending over ten times the amount we paid per British Thermal Unit for fossil fuel in 1960, and—in spite of our efforts to cut back our dependence on oil-exporting countries—we are importing over three times as much oil as we did in 1970, before the embargo.[3]

The tremendous increase in the cost of energy, the increasing indebtedness of the federal government due to defense and social welfare expenditures, and the general decline in productivity of the American industrial machine have imposed an enormous burden on the American economy—enough to wipe out half of the income gains of the average American family over the past quarter of a century.[4] In addition, while the current dollar income of the median family continues to rise, the constant

dollar income (a way of accounting for the effects of inflation) has remained relatively steady—and since 1979 has begun to decline slightly. In
effect, while people may think they are earning more than they ever have in
their lives, their real income has not changed much. Indeed, although most
Americans took it for granted that their children would do better than they
economically, after 1973 many have begun to wonder if their children
would do as well. As of June 1983, the economy—by some indicators—
seems to be making a recovery. But the 11.5 million unemployed, the $13
trillion federal debt, and the threat of rising interest rates creates at best a
mood of cautious optimism. It does not seem likely that most Americans
will continue to enjoy the ever-rising level of material well-being often re-
ferred to as standard of living.

There are other factors that may well restrain future economic
growth and a consequent rise in standard of living. These pertain to the
poorly understood but potentially devastating effects of environmental pollution—water, air, and heat pollution being most seriously considered at
present. America's bid to nuclear supremacy in the production of energy
has been severely set back by our failure to find safe ways of disposing of
the deadly radioactive wastes. At present there is no safe way of disposing
of these nuclear wastes, some of which last over a quarter of a million years
and have commulative effects on living tissue. The chemical industry is just
beginning to assume public responsibility for the disposal of its toxic
wastes, and the Reagan administration has just announced its belief that
acid rain is a serious environmental threat that must be controlled. The
most subtle form of pollution of all, perhaps, is heat pollution. The heat
generated by our industrial processes, the generation of energy, and the
operation of our automobiles and homes is slowly increasing the temperature of the earth's waters and atmosphere. An increase in a few degrees
could melt the solar ice caps and inundate the great coastal cities.

Although the industrially developed countries contribute most
heavily to environmental pollutants, the developing countries contribute
most heavily to the rapid increase in the earth's human population. Places
like Mexico City are doubling every 14 years, and although developing
countries such as India and China have birth control programs, their
populations continue to increase rapidly.[5] Needless to say, all the earth's
problems are magnified by increased population growth, and those who
have the least resources with which to control that population are being
called upon to be the most energetic.

Finally, those who are practicing voluntary simplicity are coming
to understand that the good life—however defined—is not necessarily a
function of economic affluence. The rat race required to produce that affluence, which is now demanded of both husband and wife, is not worth it,
nor does the achievement of a high standard of living secure a fulfilled life.
The number of people who are beginning to perceive the poverty of
material abundance and are seeking a more simplified life style in response
may offer one reasonable alternative for the future.

Spending Patterns

Although each household has its own peculiar habits, there are some broad patterns worth looking at briefly. The median family income in 1981 was $22,238—a decline in real income from 1970 of $723.[6] Table 15.1 indicates what it cost a family of four to live in three settings (urban, metropolitan, and nonmetropolitan) under three budget assumptions. Although these figures vary from place to place in the United States (generally being somewhat lower in the South and Midwest), certain figures are helpful. For example, families in the middle income range spend about 13 percent of their income on food, 19 percent on housing, 14 percent on transportation, 5 percent on clothing, 4 percent on health, and 6 percent on gifts and contributions. In general, families in lower income brackets spend a greater percentage of their income on housing, food, and transportation than those in upper income levels. The necessities must be covered before other items can be purchased. However, the amount spent on such nonessentials as alcohol and tobacco remains remarkably constant over this income range. The poorer families spent a much greater percentage of their income on these items than the better-off families. The percentage of income allocated to gifts and contributions amounts to about 6 percent in all cases.

There is no reason why you should endeavor to plan your spending so that it conforms to these average patterns. Your spending should reflect your priorities, not national averages. Nevertheless, it might be interesting to see the extent to which your priorities produce a distinctive spending pattern. Such tabulations can suggest, in rough terms, the extent to which you lead a life distinctively different from that of most people.

The Impact of Inflation

In general, during inflationary times people buy now in the expectation that prices will be even higher in the future, thus increasing the likelihood that they will be. The self-perpetuating nature of such a cycle affects everyone, but some are more hurt by it than others.

Wage Earners. Up until 1973, you were not too disadvantaged by inflation if you were on a wage or salary. These did not fall behind increasing prices because many contracts had cost of living clauses built in to protect the worker from inflation. Thus between 1950 and 1972, for example, production workers' average hourly wage increased by 176 percent while the consumer price index—a general measure of the cost of living—increased by only 74 percent. This would suggest that these workers experienced a real increase in wages of about 102 percent over this period. In more recent years (1965–1972), wages have also kept up. During this period the consumer price index increased by 33 percent, while wages increased for various kinds of workers as follows:[7]

TABLE 15.1 **Budget Costs: Urban Family of Four, 1981**[a]

	Lower Budget[b]			Intermediate			Higher Budget		
	URBAN	METRO	NON METRO[c]	URBAN	METRO	NON METRO[c]	URBAN	METRO	NON METRO[c]
Cost of Consumption, total	**$12,069** / 1,006	**$12,179** / 1,014	**$11,579** / 965	**$18,240** / 1,520	**$18,523** / 1,544	**$16,978** / 1,415	**$25,008** / 2,084	**$25,560** / 2,130	**$22,545** / 1,879
Food	**4,545** / 379	**4,599** / 383	**4,313** / 359	**5,843** / 486	**5,915** / 493	**5,521** / 460	**7,366** / 614	**7,512** / 626	**6,713** / 559
Housing[d]	**2,817** / 235	**2,863** / 239	**2,612** / 218	**5,546** / 462	**5,659** / 472	**5,045** / 420	**8,423** / 702	**8,652** / 721	**7,403** / 617
Transportation	**1,311** / 109	**1,248** / 104	**1,591** / 132	**2,372** / 198	**2,380** / 198	**2,333** / 194	**3,075** / 256	**3,126** / 261	**2,847** / 237
Clothing and personal care	**1,316** / 110	**1,327** / 111	**1,265** / 105	**1,841** / 153	**1,853** / 154	**1,785** / 149	**2,666** / 222	**2,683** / 224	**2,595** / 216
Medical care	**1,436** / 120	**1,475** / 123	**1,266** / 106	**1,443** / 120	**1,481** / 123	**1,274** / 106	**1,505** / 125	**1,544** / 129	**1,331** / 111
Other family consumption	**644** / 54	**670** / 56	**532** / 44	**1,196** / 100	**1,233** / 103	**1,020** / 85	**1,972** / 164	**2,043** / 170	**1,657** / 138
Other costs[e]	**621** / 52	**624** / 52	**606** / 51	**1,021** / 86	**1,031** / 86	**978** / 82	**1,718** / 143	**1,746** / 146	**1,595** / 116
Social security and disability	**1,596** / 133	**1,629** / 136	**1,453** / 121	**4,443** / 370	**4,602** / 384	**3,730** / 311	**9,340** / 778	**9,817** / 818	**7,215** / 601
Personal income tax	1,596	1,629	1,453	4,443	4,602	3,730	9,340	9,817	7,215
Total costs	**$15,323** / 1,277	**$15,481** / 1,290	**$14,619** / 1,218	**$25,407** / 2,117	**$25,893** / 2,158	**$23,238** / 1,937	**$38,060** / 3,172	**$37,117** / 3,260	**$33,338** / 2,778

Source: Adapted from U.S. Bureau of the Census, *Statistical Abstract of the United States: 1982–83* (Washington, D.C.: U.S. Government Printing Office, 1983), p. 465.

[a]A four-person family here assumes a 38-year-old employed husband, a wife not employed outside the home, an 8-year-old girl and a 14-year-old boy.
[b]Not intended to represent a minimum or subsistence level.
[c]Places with 2,500 to 50,000 population in 1960.
[d]Includes the average cost of renter and home owner shelter, house furnishings, and household operations. Lower budgeters are assumed to rent. Small allowance for lodging away from home in higher budget.
[e]Includes gifts, contributions, life insurance, and occupational expenses.

Production workers in private industry	50 percent
Nonproduction workers	42 percent
Service workers	55 percent
Government employees	2 percent

As Figure 15.1 suggests, however, after 1973 things became much more uncertain. The high cost of energy was the most dominant factor affecting both the producer price index (PPI) and the consumer price index

FIGURE 15.1 Family income and price indexes. (Statistical Abstract of the United States: 1982-83.)

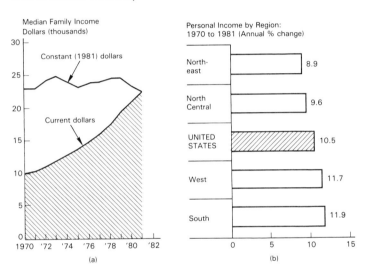

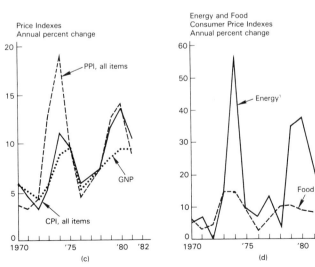

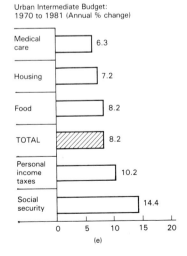

(CPI). Although personal income rose in current dollars over the period 1970 to 1981, in constant dollars it fluctuated and since 1979 has begun to decline. In the 1980s workers have had to forfeit some of their fringe benefits, take reductions in wages, and experience long periods of unemployment. Managing the family income has become much harder for all but the very rich.

The Poor. There are, however, about 32 million poor people in the United States today—about 11 percent of all families. In 1981 a family was poor if it was a nonfarm family of four and earned less than $9,287 a year.[8] These families are extremely vulnerable to inflation. Although two-thirds of such families are headed by workers, their income is rarely in the form of inflation-proof earnings. Cyclical employment, nonunion status, and a low skill level make such workers' jobs very unreliable hedges against inflation. Because such families are also unable to borrow money at reasonable rates, have little money saved, and must devote a high portion of their income to necessities such as food and housing, they have little flexibility in managing their resources. When the value of the dollar depreciates, the amount of loss may be small because their income is low, but it has painful consequences.

The poor receive 45 percent of their income from the government in the form of unemployment pay, workmen's compensation, veterans' payments, and social security. Over the long run these payments have kept pace with inflation, but between increases in congressional appropriations for such payments there are periods of painful erosion of buying power. In

There are about 32 million poor people in the United States today—about 11 percent of all families. (Harry Schlack, Monkmeyer Press.)

the past, inflationary times were usually times of high employment. However, more recently the unexpected phenomenon of "stagflation" has produced a situation in which inflation coexists with high rates of unemployment. A large number of working class and marginally poor families are thus having a doubly difficult time.

The Wealthy. At the other end of the socioeconomic-status ladder, the wealthy are also hit by inflation, but in a somewhat different way. Basically, their problems stem from the fact that they typically hold large amounts of money in the form of bank deposits, notes, mortgages, and insurance bonds. These assets are most susceptible to inflationary erosion because of their fixed rates of return. However, many wealthy lenders can protect themselves somewhat by increasing interest rates. Similarly, some leases include a cost of living provision that automatically insures the lessor against inflation. Thus, while the wealthy encounter some problems during inflationary times, they generally have the resources to cope with them. One crude measure of their ability to cope is the fact that the percentage of the national income accumulated by the top 5 percent of the families has changed very little since the Depression, remaining at about 15 to 16 percent each year.

However, since much of their income is from assets other than salaries, their total wealth is not accurately reflected in these figures. The top 5 percent of all families actually control a much higher percentage of the total national wealth—perhaps as much as 53 percent. (This figure is a rough estimate because it is difficult to assess assets and compare wealth that is both carefully protected and constantly changing.)

The Elderly. Over 26 million people in the United States are over 65. Indeed, the median age of our population is now 30.3 years.[9] This group is more vulnerable to inflation than any other group. Few people over 65 work. They hold a higher portion (23 percent) of their total assets in a fixed form such as private pension plan payments. While social security payments have generally increased twice as rapidly as the inflation rate, in themselves they are not enough to keep people above the poverty level and are not intended to do so. Government pension plans also have built-in inflation allowances. Private plans typically do not, however. If these pensions are not supplemented by income from other sources, one is likely to be in real financial difficulty upon retirement. Some older citizens find that they cannot keep their houses because of increasing costs of living and higher taxes.

The Young. In this category we will include families with heads under 44. Almost all the income in these families comes from salaries and wages. These families are not as likely to possess the material assets of some elderly people, or to retain their assets in a monetary form that is readily eroded by inflation. Their relatively high level of indebtedness is to their advantage, because the payments they make diminish in value while they enjoy the products they have purchased.

Why, then, are the young grumbling about inflation? For the most part, the problem is psychological. Prices should not always be rising. It ought to be possible to do better than simply keep pace with inflation. Seeing each increase in pay eroded by decreased buying power is a psychologically damaging experience even if there is a net increase in buying power. The losses are remembered more than the gains. And, since 1979, real income has declined.

Consumer Attitudes

According to a 1975 survey by General Mills, the typical American family is deeply troubled by economic uncertainty, unemployment, and inflation.[10] Families that have become accustomed to good times have trouble understanding our present predicament. Although most are managing to cope with their financial problems, there is widespread feeling that we are headed for a depression. Over 50 percent feel the government owes them a good standard of living, but also feel victimized by both government and business.

Most families report major cutbacks in utility use, magazine subscriptions, liquor, barbershop visits, and the like. They report that they are economizing by staying home more, repairing things they used to throw away, and postponing medical and dental appointments. There is a large-scale increase in bankruptcy and loans to cover outstanding bills. Almost half the families surveyed report that credit cards make it easy for them to overbuy. Twenty-five percent report they save on a regular basis, but another 25 percent say they have used all their savings to meet current expenses.

The General Mills study found that 54 percent of the couples surveyed argued about money matters. Current arguments seem to focus on the need to economize, the need to stop wasting money, and failure to keep track of where the money goes. The families most likely to argue about money are low-income families, families with children, households with working wives (particularly those who work just for the money), families that rent rather than own their homes, and families in which the head is less than 35 years old. Money fights are most likely to occur when there is uncertainty about the family's financial future. Difficulty in coping with inflation and a sense of failure are also part of the money argument.

In about half of the families interviewed, the adults reported they were unable to communicate frankly and freely with other members of the family about money matters. While most parents (73 percent) reject the notion that children should be spared money worries, there is considerable disagreement over how much they should be told. About one-third of the adults studied felt there was too much talk about money in their families.

Only a minority of the couples interviewed (41 percent) shared equally in making decisions about money. Overall, about 39 percent believe it is up to the man to be the main provider and decision maker, but in financially pressed families support for this view increases to about 46 percent.

Looking ahead, the families studied felt that economic hardship might make them less wasteful (59 percent), encourage them to be better shoppers and money managers (70 percent), and bring them back to basic values (33 percent). The large majority (82 percent) had not given up on their hopes and dreams, but 18 percent had.

COPING WITH FINANCIAL PROBLEMS

Financial problems can be related to the broader considerations of stage in the family life cycle and inflation. These will be considered in the following pages.

Financial Problems and the Family Life Cycle

Table 15.2 defines the family life cycle in two ways.[11] On the left is a commonly used sociological model of the life cycle. It is related to a widely used economic model, shown on the right. Because economic considerations are paramount in this chapter, we will refer to the righthand column in our discussion. Figure 15.2 provides a way of measuring resources available to

Table 15.2 Relationship Between Family Life Cycle and Family Economic Span

FAMILY LIFE CYCLE	FAMILY ECONOMIC SPAN	
1. Married couples without children 2. Childbearing families, oldest child 30 months	1. Foundation years	0–4 years of marriage
3. Preschool children—oldest child 2 1/2 to 6 yrs. 4. With school-age children—oldest child 6 to 13 years 5. With teenagers—oldest child 13 to 20 years	2. Developmental years	5–19 years of marriage
6. Families as launching centers—first child gone—last leaving home 7. Middle-aged parents—empty nest to retirement	3. Assessment, achievement, and readjustment years	20–39 years of marriage
8. Aging families—retirement to death of spouses	4. Retirement years	40 + years of marriage

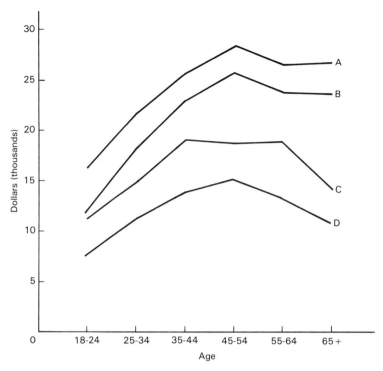

Key: A = Husband employed full time, wife employed.
B = Husband employed full time, wife not employed.
C = Husband not employed full time, wife employed.
D = Husband not employed full time, wife not employed.

FIGURE 15.2 Mean income in several types of husband-wife families by age of head. (Adapted from *Current Population Reports,* "Consumer Income," Series P-60, No. 118, March 1979, Table 21.)

four types of families over the life cycle by looking at median incomes for particular age cohorts.

The Foundation Years: The First 4 Years of Marriage. This is a period in which major goals are formed, decisions on the desirable level of living made, and occupation(s) established. It may be that these first decisions are changed later in the marriage, but during the first years they seem clear and achievable. There is relatively high satisfaction with the financial situation because incomes are reasonably good, there are no dependents, and parents can often be counted upon to help out. The family typically has to make a small outlay for housing—normally an apartment. Expenditures on food, entertainment, and household durables are high, especially if both partners work. The highest fixed expenditures are likely to be for rent, taxes, mortgage, life insurance, and pension plans. Ordinarily, a fairly high percentage of income is available for flexible expenditures. Indeed, the couple may have more discretionary income at this time than at any other time in their lives, although few may appreciate this fact.

Problems associated with the foundation years pertain to the management of these flexible expenditures. In middle-income families the high debt-to-income ratio at this stage in the life cycle points to the problem of managing indebtedness. Couples in this stage are more likely to use credit to meet current expenses and gratify immediate desires, than to save for the future or spend on planned necessities. There is generally an unsophisticated handling of money, in line with lack of previous experience. Twenty percent of families in the first years of marriage have at least $2,000 of installment indebtedness.

The Developmental Years: 5–19 Years of Marriage. Characteristically, few major decisions are made that are peculiar to these years. Rather, decisions made during this stage are built on earlier ones, and effort is directed toward fulfilling goals set during the foundation years. During these years health, housing, furnishing, food, and insurance costs typically rise. The financial problems of these years derive from the fact that most income is absorbed by fixed expenditures. It becomes necessary to reduce savings to meet expenditures. Many families, however, have few cash assets (40 percent have none) to draw upon. About 38 percent of the families in this category have installment indebtedness of $2,000 or more.

However, couples have gained experience in money management by this stage in their marriage and, while their satisfaction with the way their finances are managed may decrease during the early years of this stage, it typically increases during the later years.

The Assessment, Achievement, and Readjustment Years: 20–39 Years of Marriage. For most families the level of living, kind of housing, and degree of financial security or insecurity has been established by this stage. Employment and retirement decisions become crucial, especially when income is low. The use of credit cards is greatest during these years, but the level of installment indebtedness is low. Four percent of families in this stage have at least $2,000 of such indebtedness. This is also likely to be the time during which quarrels erupt over money management. If both partners have pretty much realized their life goals, things might well look rosy. However, if achievement has fallen far short of expectations, it is necessary to cope with a growing sense of failure. The sense of failure is more difficult to deal with at this time than it might have been earlier in life because of the recognition that there is comparatively little time in which to improve. When this is accompanied with growing doubts about one's capacity to learn new tricks or adjust to a different style of life, problems are compounded. Major expenses during this period are likely to be for creature comforts, college education, and weddings.

Family incomes peak during this period of marriage. Over half of all married women are working, and childcare responsibilities have been greatly reduced or eliminated. Housing costs decline and assets rise.

The Retirement Years: 40 Years or More of Marriage. It now becomes necessary for most families to once again make some major decisions regarding their style of life, particularly with regard to housing, level of living, health, and the management of time. Needs for personal services and medical care increase during this period.

For most families, income drops off dramatically. Few people find postretirement jobs. Not many have saved enough to permit them to continue to live in the style to which they have become accustomed. Income now is largely fixed and is subject to radical erosion by inflation. It often becomes necessary to live off assets. There is a tendency to hoard funds rather than spending to meet needs. Most older citizens value their independence and are reluctant to seek help. They are susceptible to fraud and are more readily victimized than at most other times in their lives. On the other hand, only 3 percent have at least $2,000 in installment indebtedness. In most instances, however, this reflects a dramatic curtailment of expenditures rather than adequate earning power.

Many older people own their own homes, and if taxes and the increasing cost of living can be accommodated, they may have a degree of financial security that approximates their expectations of comfortable living. The accumulations of a lifetime are reflected in generally high assets and few debts. Upper-middle-income families may, indeed, enjoy greater freedom to do the things they have always wanted to do. But many older

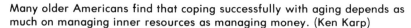
Many older Americans find that coping successfully with aging depends as much on managing inner resources as managing money. (Ken Karp)

Americans find that coping successfully with aging depends much more on managing inner resources than on managing money. The extent to which self-worth has been established independently of what a person is capable of producing or consuming seems to be a critical factor in determining the extent to which the world can be enjoyed and creative contributions made in the later years of life. The debilitating stereotype of old age as a time of disengagement, diminishing vitality, and decreasing usefulness is frequently a self-fulfilling prophecy. Old age is not yet a badge of honor nor necessarily a time of fulfillment, but many people are working to see that it increasingly becomes both.

FINANCIAL MANAGEMENT

Not many people in the United States plan for their future economic needs.[12] Most of us simply assume that our income will increase enough to allow us to live the way we would like to—or we will have to make do with something less. When times are good, as they generally have been, this strategy may work well enough. It fits in with an intuitive method of budgeting on a day-to-day basis. However, when raging inflation cuts away at the dollar's buying power while encouraging people to buy now rather than later, forethought is necessary to avoid financial disaster.

Setting Financial Goals

Financial goals are commonly thought of as either long-run goals or short-run goals. The most common kind of long-run financial goal is the desire to be worth a certain amount of money upon retirement so that the retirement years will be relatively free of economic worries. Thus, if a couple decide that at age 65 they will need $225,000 to live reasonably comfortably, they had better begin setting some money aside now if they are to realize this goal. Most people do not even make such a simple calculation of their needs. Indeed, even people who are responsible for the financial management of large corporations often leave such considerations to the company's retirement plan, trusting that it will provide them with adequate resources upon retirement. Often they are wrong. A wise decision about retirement needs should include the projected benefits that are likely to accrue in whatever retirement plans (including social security) one is covered by, together with a determination of what additional monies are necessary to meet these retirement needs. These funds will have to be provided through savings and investment programs.

In making these estimates of retirement needs, the rate of inflation should be taken into account. One assessment of the effect of inflation declares that a 1976 dollar will be worth 30 cents in the year 2000. It is also predicted that the minimum wage will be at least $19,800 and that a job that pays $25,000 salary in 1976 will pay $112,500 in 2000.[13] Fantastic? Such projections are not certain but they are the best available. It is difficult to determine long-range goals when the whole economic future is likely to be quite different from the present and we cannot even be certain about the *rate* of change. Therefore, long-range goals will most likely have to be reevaluated from time to time. If you are not aware of the need to make such reassessments, it is unlikely that you will arrive at retirement with adequate funds. Notice also that it is conceivable that with age, a person may discover less is best. The amount you plan for, therefore, may not be enough by common economic standards but may nevertheless be quite adequate. In any case, it's nice to be able to choose to live simply rather than having simplicity forced upon you because you did not plan ahead.

Other long-range goals may also need to be taken into consideration. A couple just starting out may be depending on two incomes. Will it be necessary for one or both partners to have more education? When might this be necessary? How much might it cost? What about starting a family? How long will it be necessary to do without at least one salary if the wife cannot have maternity leave with pay? When do you plan on buying a home or condominium? What about the children's schooling? These items can be anticipated and money set aside for them, or they can be negotiated as circumstances permit when the decisions must be made. Some forethought is bound to pay off.

Short-range goals are normally confined to consideration of needs for the year ahead. Expensive items such as tires or large appliances can be planned for, vacations anticipated, and the amount of savings necessary to achieve the long-term goal set aside. If the year's budget cannot be balanced, it may be necessary to change some of these short-term goals or even drop them entirely. One outcome of a well-managed income could be more time to do what you want to do. None of this planning need be considered absolutely binding in its specific details, but given the relatively limited income most couples receive, the overall budget must balance or you will go into debt.

Actually, a certain amount of indebtedness is considered to be a good thing. Wise use of credit cards, for example, to purchase things that are needed now and are on sale at bargain prices makes sense. It makes sense to borrow money for a house or a car in many instances. It is not a matter of not being in debt at all but rather, a question of the nature of one's indebtedness. A person who is in debt because of compulsive buying habits is in a double bind. Not only will that person have to make up the indebtedness; he or she will also suffer as a result of not having thought much about what is really needed. Having a second car when what you really need is a good vacation (and you can't have both) is an unfortunate situation.

Making a Budget

Planning a budget can begin with a determination of anticipated **disposable income** for a given year. This is the money that will be available to pay the bills after taxes, pension plans, and other deductions. Although most of us know pretty much what our gross income will be for a given year, the determination of disposable income is another matter.

If the only source of income is wages or salaries, the problem is relatively simple. Most payroll offices will provide you with a list of your deductions and determine your disposable income for you in advance. Should you receive a raise or be laid off during the course of the year, the resulting changes in anticipated income can be made at the time and your planned expenses altered accordingly. If a considerable portion of your income comes from bonuses, honoraria, royalties, interest on investments, and the like, it is necessary to make a reasonable estimate. It is much better to be conservative and underestimate these figures than to make too high an estimate and find it necessary to cut back. Given the continued struggle with inflation, it may also be helpful to keep a chart of your annual income adjusted to account for the rate of inflation. This will help you understand the extent to which your real buying power has changed.[14]

Keeping a record of what you spend is more difficult, but this should be done for a period of a few months in order to see how well any budget you may decide upon is working. The most important distinction in the early budgets you may make is deciding what expenses you have some degree of control over and what **expenses are fixed.** Rent, mortgage payments, school tuition, and car payments come readily to mind as fixed expenses during any given year. Unless you renegotiate your loans, move, or drop out of school, you are not going to be able to alter these expenses very much. On the other hand, medical expenses, utilities, taxes such as real estate and estimated income tax, and membership dues can be reasonably estimated and are commonly included in the "fixed" expenditures category. It is more likely that you could change the amount of these bills somewhat through your own efforts, but presumably you would not want to cut back on these expenditures unless you absolutely had to because they reflect a way of life that is satisfying to you. Less obvious fixed expenses are allowances, insurance premiums, and interest on loans and savings. Savings should be included as a fixed expense. You should pay yourself first, right off the top.

Now, clearly, the category of fixed expenses reflects a set of priorities about what is important in your life that you feel is still worth affirming. If, upon further examination, you find you can simplify things a great deal by cutting back or getting rid of some of these expenses, by all means do so. But for the moment we are going to assume they are not items you can change easily, nor are they ones you want to change. Each of these fixed expenses should be calculated for the year, then divided by 12 and in-

A typical middle income family spends about 13 percent of its income on food.
(Laimute E. Druskis)

cluded as a monthly budget item. Thus, even though school tuition payments come only twice a year, they should be saved for by setting aside one-twelfth of the total amount each month.[15]

When all your estimated fixed expenses are added up and subtracted from your estimated annual income (we trust that the latter will be larger), what you have left over is money for your **flexible expenses.** If your estimated fixed expenses exceed your estimated annual income, you obviously have a problem. Something must be cut back in an area where it is not easy to do so. If your remaining income is very small in comparison to your wants/needs, you may have a very difficult time making adjustments. If you are very poor, it is possible to budget what you have so you can use it for more important expenses, but the distinction between fixed and flexible expenses will become less and less useful. In the middle income range, there should be some income left over that will stand in a reasonable relationship to your perceived wants/needs or can be made to do so with careful consideration.

Although the process of making a budget may be offensive to some people, it is one method by which people can improve the way they spend their money so that they will be more likely to spend it for what they really want. A budget will not in itself increase one's income or guarantee that all one's wants are satisfied. It is merely a tool that can be used to improve one's spending habits.

Commonly included in the category of flexible expenses are: (1) food, both regular grocery bills and that which is eaten at restuarants; (2) household services and expenses such as repairs and cleaning supplies; (3) clothes, including repair costs; (4) furnishings and equipment; (5) transportation, car payments, maintenance, operating costs, parking fees; (6) medical care that is not listed as fixed expenses because it is not covered by insurance or purchased on installment; (7) personal care, barber, hairdresser, toilet articles; (8) education and recreation, including books, newspapers, magazines, music lessons; (9) gifts and contributions not paid for out of personal allowances; and (10) miscellaneous items that only you can fill in. There may be a certain degree of arbitrariness in assigning expenses to particular categories, but any given item should consistently be assigned to the same category.

These items are listed as flexible expenses because, presumably, they are the ones over which you have the most control. In estimating what you will spend for each of these items over the next year, you may be guided by records of past expenses or simply by your intuitive judgment about what seems reasonable. It is best to be as realistic as possible about what you will spend so that you do not have to expand many items later on, thus ruining your efforts at budgeting at an early stage. If you've been doing reasonably well in managing your money intuitively, a budget may seem a needless bother. Most people seem to turn to budgeting when their intuitive approach fails.

In any case, a budget is not intended to be a straitjacket to keep you from having a good time. Rather, it is intended to be an instrument that, properly applied, can increase the likelihood that you will have a good time because you will be spending for what you want to spend within your ability to spend. It is possible to make use of a budget in such a way only if your wants are under some degree of control before you begin and your income is not greatly out of line with what you want.

Help in Managing Money

There is a growing industry devoted to helping families manage their money. Its practitioners are called financial planning consultants. Even very large companies like Merrill Lynch are getting into the business. They have found that the ten most common mistakes in family finance are the following:[16]

1. Failure to set long-range objectives.
2. Lack of an up-to-date will.
3. "Falling in love" with one's investments so that deadwood is not regularly weeded out.
4. Being too greedy and refusing to sell when a stock has experienced a sharp run-up in price in the hope that it will go even higher.
5. Neglecting insurance protection (both life and homeowner's).

6. Failure to recognize that tax shelters have drawbacks as well as advantages, with the result that risky investments often lose more money than could be saved from the tax collector.
7. Lack of adequate financial records.
8. Shying away from paying for financial advice.
9. Trading or speculating on the market rather than investing.
10. Failure to follow a balanced investment program.

Young couples rarely establish good money management habits until they run into problems that force them to do so. Although most of the companies in the financial-planning business are geared to incomes over $50,000, some are moving into the lower income brackets. There are several companies that can help you with your financial problems. They are listed in the Yellow Pages under "Financial-Planning Consultants" and "Tax Consultants." These sources, however, cannot help you decide what you want out of life. But once you decide on your life style, they can help you realize it.

SUMMARY

Economic decisions should be related to a set of prior decisions about what is really important in life for a particular partnership or individual. The decision to seek an abundant life through increased income and conspicuous consumption is contrasted with a style called "voluntary simplicity," or learning to live with less. Both ways can provide a life of abundance. These basic orientations toward life will affect how one establishes one's financial goals and how one uses a budget.

Financial goals are normally thought of in terms of long-range and short-range objectives. The long-range ones, including retirement income, education funds, a new home, and the like, must be woven into the short-range goals of any given year so that money can be set aside for them. If the determination of fixed expenditures, including savings, is large relative to the income anticipated in a given year, budgeting will be difficult but necessary. A budget ought to provide a partnership with greater freedom in financial matters by ensuring that spending is realistic in light of income and appropriate in terms of needs and wants.

Money management problems vary with the stage in the family life cycle and the rate of inflation. Families in the foundation stage rarely have the expertise and experience in managing money that they will acquire in the later stages. At the same time, they have more discretionary income that could be managed wisely. Families in the retirement stage are likely to be faced with an inadequate income from retirement plans and social security benefits. They will quite often have to cut back at the very time when they have a chance to expand their horizons.

Inflation encourages people to spend now for what they fear will cost much more tomorrow. While a certain amount of indebtedness is a good thing in inflationary times, the tendency to overspend is widespread. Inflation also cuts into the funds available to fixed-income groups such as the elderly and the poor, making it much more difficult for them to survive than for families whose incomes come from inflation-adjusted wages or salaries.

Wise money management will not get rid of all the problems of family finance. It may simply bring some of those problems into clearer focus. Above all, a budget and the planning of financial goals should reflect a continuing consideration of what is important in life and what is the best way to achieve that which is really valuable.

NOTES

1. Duane Elgin and Arnold Mitchell, "Voluntary Simplicity (3)," *Co-Evolution Quarterly*, Summer 1977, pp. 4–18; "Voluntary Simplicity: Follow Up & Commentary," *Co-Evolution Quarterly*, Fall 1977, pp. 52–59. Duane Elgin, *Voluntary Simplicity: Toward a Way of Life That Is Outwardly Simple, Inwardly Rich* (West Caldwell, N.J.: William Morrow, 1981).

2. Allen Johnson, "Search of the Affluent Society," *Human Nature*, September 1978, p. 51.

3. U.S. Bureau of the Census, *Statistical Abstract of the United States: 1982–83* (Washington, D.C.: U.S. Government Printing Office, 1983), p. xxviii.

4. Danial Yankelovich, *New Rules: Searching for Self Fulfillment in a World Turned Upside Down* (New York: Bantam Books, 1982), p. 203.

5. In a commentary called "Earthwatch" in *New Age Magazine* it is noted that 157 countries now have population programs. China has strict enforcement of a one-child policy, which has produced a great deal of problems for female babies, who are aborted or killed in order for the family to have a son. "In an increasingly crowded world, however, responsibility is taking on new meanings." *New Age* (June 1983), p. 12.

6. *Statistical Abstract 1982–83*, p. xx.

7. *The New York Times*, August 5, 1973, pp. 14 ff.

8. *Statistical Abstract, 1982–83*, p. xxi.

9. Ibid., p. xviii.

10. General Mills, *Report on the American Family and Money*, 1976, pp. 23–26.

11. This comparison was developed by my colleague Ms. Karen Stein.

12. "If You Need Help in Planning Your Finance," *U.S. News & World Report*, April 17, 1978, p. 91. I am indebted to Ms. Karen Stein of the College of Human Development, University of Delaware, for her assistance in the development of the material in this section.

13. "What You'll Earn and Pay in 2,000 A.D.," *Nation's Business*, November 1978, pp. 6–8. See also Lawrence J. Gitman, *Personal Finance* (Hinsdale, Ill.: Dyden Press, 1978), p. 62.

14. Sylvia Porter, *Sylvia Porter's Money Book* (New York: Avon Books, 1975), pp. 76–139.

15. Sylvia Porter is followed here, but Gitman, *Personal Finance*, recommends a more elaborate double-entry bookkeeping system in which each expenditure is recorded twice.

16. General Mills, p. 25.

For an unknown, but indubitable large number of people, marriage isn't a comfort, a source of companionship or a means of sexual satisfaction. . . . Making divorce more obtainable is a relief for some people caught in the agony of a hateful marriage, but legal farewells are difficult, unpleasant and sometimes traumatic. A better solution would be to change the institution of marriage to fit the needs and desires of husbands and wives.

—Nicholas von Hoffman

16 Disorganization and Divorce

Although all partnerships must come to an end, in the past in the United States marriages have usually been terminated by death, desertion, or psychological withdrawal. What is new is the increasing prominence of divorce. More marriages end in divorce than through the death of the partners. Since World War II, divorce rates in this country have generally increased to the point where we now have the highest divorce rate in the world: There is now one divorce for every two marriages that take place in the United States. In the past, this rising divorce rate has been partially offset by a rising remarriage rate, but recently this rate has begun to drop.

Some analysts are very concerned about these trends. They most certainly do have personal and social costs. However, there are also some benefits to consider. Marriage has become a very personal contract that must be personally satisfying if it is to be maintained. We expect more of marriage than any other people on earth in this sense. Rather than endure a partnership that has psychologically ended, most couples are now able to legally end their marriage and start a new way of life—often involving another try at marriage.

This chapter will examine the costs and benefits of these trends in divorce and remarriage and will consider their impact on the children who are increasingly involved in divorce.

FAMILY DISORGANIZATION

Sociologist William Goode helps us understand divorce by placing it in the larger context of family disorganization. As Goode sees it, there are at least five major types of disorganized families: the uncompleted family; the empty shell family; the family disorganized by an external catastrophe such as bankruptcy, scandal, or imprisonment; the family disorganized by an internal castastrophe such as illness or death; and the family disorganized by willed departures such as divorce.[1]

The Uncompleted Family

Families that have never been formed in the first place are a part of Goode's classification. These result when a child is born outside of wedlock and the couple fail to assume the socially expected role obligations of parenthood. The child born of such a union creates a fundamental problem for society as it is now structured because he or she has no acknowledged place in that society. This is symbolized by the fact that it cannot reasonably take the name of its biological father. Very often, such a child takes the name of the mother unless he or she is adopted. In this case, the adoptive parents bestow their name upon the child, thereby establishing his or her place in the social structure. This has the practical consequence of permitting the child to inherit from its adoptive parents and legally to expect the support we assume a nonadopted child to have.

Although it is true that a few women openly prefer to be mothers without getting married, most of those who do so with some degree of success are members of the upper class and have sufficient economic power and resources to overcome many of the social handicaps of not having a socially recognized husband and father for the child. A child born outside marriage in the lower class does not ordinarily suffer as much from the stigma of illegitimacy as he or she would in the working or upper classes, but economic hardships are to be expected.

Sociologist Kingsley Davis points out that it is possible to eliminate illegitimacy in one of two ways: Either a society can institutionalize marriage to such an extent that no one can conceive outside it, or it can establish marriage so weakly that few, if any, people marry.[2] In either case, illegitimacy would be no problem. One society, the Tiwi of Australia, has made it impossible for a woman to be unmarried. A female is often bestowed in marriage before she is born (and certainly before she reaches puberty), and if her husband dies before she does, she is remarried at the graveside of her deceased husband. At no time in her reproductive life is she unmarried. Any child born to her is considered to be her husband's, regardless of its biological origins. Thus there can be no such thing as an illegitimate child among the Tiwi.[3]

We do not know of any society that has taken the other option, that of disestablishing marriage to the same extent that the Tiwi have established it. In some Caribbean islands, illegitimacy rates of around 70 percent of live births are not uncommon. These rates are so high because, in addition to the normal number of unwanted or accidental pregnancies that eventuate in live births, the islanders have accepted a visiting relationship in which a man and a woman live together for extended periods and care for each other without getting married.[4] To some extent, these illegitimacy rates are artifically high because of the fact that the government considers only Roman Catholic marriages valid, so that children born to other marriages are considered illegitimate. Nevertheless, the islanders clearly seem to prefer marriage, despite the fact that they are quite willing to accept a nonmarital alternative.

The Empty Shell

By calling attention to the **empty-shell** type of disorganization, Goode recognizes that partnerships may be terminated for all intents and purposes even though the partners continue to live together. Many of the couples described by Cuber and Harroff in *The Significant Americans* as having a "utilitarian" kind of partnership may fit into this category.[5] The utilitarian reasons for staying together—because the pattern of everyday life is reasonably comfortable, the expenses of living together are less than if the partners lived apart, and so forth—may not really compensate the couple who live in an empty shell partnership. They may remain together because they can perceive no other alternative. A heavy sense of dispair may hang over their hopeless situation, or they may simply not have much vitality in their partnership. In either case, the partnership is meaningless.

External Catastrophes

Wars, depressions, floods, imprisonment, bankruptcy, or scandal may cause the termination of a partnership. The stress these events generate may simply be too much for the partners to cope with. Sociologist Reuben Hill

Family disorganization can result from such external catastrophies as floods which severely reduce the family's resources. (Nancy J. Pierce, Photo Researchers, Inc.)

has pointed out that different partnerships handle the same event in quite different ways. After all, the Depression of the 1930s did not cause all marriages to break up, but it disrupted quite a few. On the other hand, it seems to have strengthened some couples as they rose to the occasion and saw it through. In Hill's view, a family's inability to handle a stress-inducing event is a function of six interrelated variables: (1) degree of role conflict, (2) adequacy of interpersonal relationships, (3) extent of cultural diversity, (4) extent of unrealized aspirations, (5) class memberships, and (6) economic resources. Partnerships that have reasonably compatible role patterns, adequate communication channels, similar frames of reference, an adequate history of realized aspirations, and adequate economic and sociopolitical resources are much less likely to become disorganized by stress-inducing events.

Internal Castrophes

Events that occur within the family—such as the illness, disability, or death of one of its members—can also cause family disorganization. The family's capacity to cope with these events follows much the same pattern as its ability to cope with external catastrophes. In the case of a partnership in which there are no children, however, the disabled partner may not be able to participate in the definition or resolution of the crisis, so the dynamics of coping with these types of crises are probably much different in such cases.

Willed Departures

Finally, partnerships such as marriage may be disorganized by the willed departure of one of the partners, as in desertion, separation, annulment, or divorce. At the outset it must be pointed out that the extent to which any given separation or divorce can be said to be willed or intentional varies. This point will be developed in the remainder of this chapter. Here, it is sufficient to note that lower-class partnerships are more prone to such "willed departures" than upper-class partnerships. Taking divorce statistics alone, however, the upper classes rank higher. This is largely a matter of their being able to afford the amenities of a divorce—in other words, desertion is the poor man's divorce. Thus, it seems reasonable to argue that lack of income is as likely to account for the "instability" of low-income marriages as lack of commitment.

A further advantage of viewing partnerships in terms of disorganizing factors is that it becomes apparent that society has more of an interest in one kind of disorganization than in another. We are rightly concerned about rising divorce rates and approve of increased resources to cope with them through family enrichment programs, such as marriage encounters and family therapy, and marital counseling. We have even begun to expect corporations to become conscious of the effects of their demands on their employees. As a result, partners can receive a considerable amount of help in coping with problems that are likely to lead to divorce. At the same time, the rising divorce rate means that more and more divorced people find themselves with others who are in a similar state and can feel freer to talk about their problems. On the other hand, very little is being done about the empty shell type of family. In part, this is because those involved in such relationships are able to conceal this fact from others by withdrawing somewhat from normal social activities. In part, too, it derives from our general unwillingness to probe the private lives of others. This means that people in empty shell partnerships must cope with their problems largely on their own.

DIVORCE

Divorce Rates

At present there is one divorce or annulment for every two marriages that take place each year. In 1981, for example, 2,400,000 couples got married and about 1,300,000 terminated their marriages.[6] Figure 16.1 shows that since 1961 the divorce rate has been increasing more rapidly than the marriage rate. The rate at which couples remarry, however, is rising even more

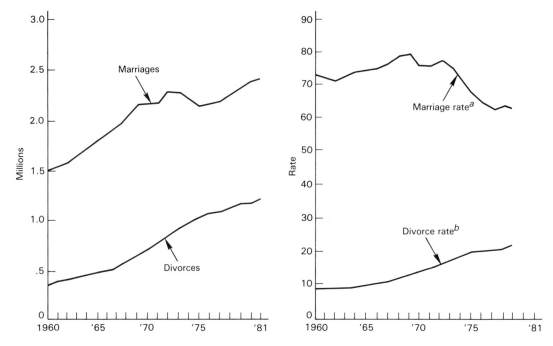

aRate per 1,000 unmarried women, 15 years old and over.

bRate per 1,000 married women, 15 years old and over.

FIGURE 16.1 Marriages and divorces, 1960 to 1981. (Statistical Abstract of the United States: 1982-83.)

rapidly. About 20 percent of all remarriages end in divorce. Alvin Toffler observes that "as conventional marriage proves itself less and less capable of delivering on its promise of lifelong love . . . we can anticipate public acceptance of temporary marriages."[7]

In general, marriages last longer and the rate of remarriage is lower as the income and education of the partners increases. For example, in marriages in which both husband and wife are college graduates, 90 percent of the partners have been married only once. Eighty-three percent have been married only once in marriages in which both partners are high school graduates, and 75 percent of the partners have been married only once in marriages in which neither the husband nor the wife has graduated from high school.[8] If the percentage of marriages in which the partners have been married only once is used as an index of marital stability, the majority of marriages are stable; on the whole, in 1971 about 33 million— or 81 percent of all married people—had been married only once. On the other hand, there is a small but increasing number of couples in which each partner has been married three or more times. In 1971, there were about 200,000 such instances.[9]

A Closer Look

Divorce is becoming part of the experience of more and more people. Thus, while only 2.8 percent of the men and 4.3 percent of the women were counted as divorced in 1973, a recent study by census experts Paul Glick and Arthur Norton indicates that about 15 percent of all men and 17 percent of all women who were 70 years old or older and had ever been married had experienced divorce.[10] People who marry at a younger-than-normal age are more likely to become divorced. For example, white men who married between the ages of 14 and 21 and white women who married between the ages of 14 and 19 are more prone to divorce than those who married at later ages. When these people were studied twenty years after their first marriage, 24.4 percent of the men and 24.8 percent of the women had obtained at least one divorce. One study estimates that 48 percent of those persons who married in 1970 will eventually divorce.[11] The ratio of divorced to married persons has increased at every age level, but it has increased most dramatically in the age group 30 to 44 (Figure 16.1).

The figures for black men and women are notably higher across the board. Forty-six percent of all black men who first married between the ages of 14 and 21 had obtained at least one divorce twenty years later, as had 47 percent of all black women who had married between the ages of 14 and 19. Glick and Norton conclude that "barring marked change in current trends, it seems plausible to expect that during the lifetime of those who are entering marriage at correspondingly young ages, close to one third of the whites and one half of the Negroes will eventually end their marriage in divorce."[12]

When looking at divorce statistics, it is important to realize that marriage is still a durable partnership for most Americans. For example, sociologist P. Krishnan calculates that a married female aged 20 has a chance of 29 in 100 of becoming divorced during her lifetime. She can expect divorce during childrearing at a lower probability of 25 in 100, and thereafter can look forward with confidence to twenty-five years of uninterrupted married life during her nonreproductive years.[13] For those who do divorce, however, the typical first marriage is much shorter.[14] On the average, about 1.2 children are involved in the divorces that take place in the 1980s. This means that about 1.5 million children are involved in a divorce each year. One study estimates that more than 30 percent of all children of school age are not living with parents who are living in a continuous first marriage.[15]

Divorce Laws

The cause of divorce is normally quite different from the legal grounds for divorce. Unfortunately, the law plays only a limited role in controlling divorce. Sociologist Eugene Litwak argues that this is so because marital breakup is such a complex matter that a more adequate matching of a particular type of law with a particular type of breakup is required. The law, for example, can be primarily punitive, as in cases in which the costs of divorce are high and grounds are few; it can be therapeutic, as in cases in which it requires counseling; or it can be primarily educative, as when it requires certain tests before marriage. It is least effective when it is purely punitive.[16] Thus, at least one study concludes that no-fault divorce—divorce proceedings in which there is no need to prove that someone is at fault or to establish legal grounds for divorce—has had little effect on the divorce rate in most states in which it is operative.[17]

One consequence of the predominantly punitive orientation of traditional divorce laws is that the legal grounds for divorce are often faked or trumped up. For example, before New York passed its no-fault divorce law, the only ground for divorce was adultery. The standard procedure in such a case was to obtain a divorce in Nevada or to provide evidence—often deliberately staged—of adultery in New York.

The Uniform Marriage and Divorce Act is not a law at present, but it is intended as a model to guide state legislation. It does not require a couple to produce grounds for a divorce. Rather, it permits them to seek legal redress of grievances when they perceive that their relationship has reached an "irretrievable breakdown." It recognizes that it is more than likely that the couple, not one particular partner, are "at fault." Marriage counselor Marie Kargman comments,

> If unhappily married people could have access to the courts for the dissolution of their marriage before marital infidelity seems the only way out, before desertion seems the only way out, before the hostilities have seriously wounded either one or both partners, before either one or both parties are driven in desperation to dope, to drink, or to mental illness; then the parties could be encouraged to make responsible agreements for their marital obligations, especially when there are children, and the family could be "recycled" with diminished damage to all concerned.[18]

Divorce Counseling

Today marriage counselors are taking a new look at their role in regard to divorce. At least one counselor contends that in reality the term *marriage counselor* is misleading. A better way of labeling the profession would be "marriage and divorce counselor."[19] Adding the word *divorce* suggests the new stance of many counselors. Esther Fisher contends that the role of the counselor is not limited to improving the character and quality of the partnership's dissolution, for the counselor's role must shift as the stages in the process change. Before a divorce has been decided upon, the issue is whether or not a divorce should be sought. During the divorce process itself, support must be provided to one or both partners so they will not take advantage of each other or make hostages of their children. After a legal divorce

Marriage counseling has become more widely identified as marriage and divorce counseling. (Ken Karp)

has been granted, the role of the counselor is to help the client achieve the transition from ex-spouse to single person. Fisher points out that divorce itself can be seen as a three-stage process. Emotional divorce occurs when the couple realizes their relationship has ended. Physical divorce follows upon separation from bed and board. Legal divorce is really an anticlimax; it simply records for posterity what has already been accomplished and permits the divorced person to remarry legally.

Divorce as a Process

Paul Bohannan describes divorce as a process involving at least six stages.[20] It is a complex social phenomenon and can be a traumatic personal experience. Because people often mistrust the emotions associated with the dissolution of a partnership, they tend to withdraw from the situation and allow the crisis to develop slowly so they can more readily manage the unpleasant experience. Socially, this tendency to hide from the situation is reflected in inadequate legislation, support, and role guidelines for people who are in the process of getting a divorce. Bohannan's six stages are the following:

> (1) The emotional divorce which centers around the problem of the deteriorating marriage; (2) the legal divorce based on grounds; (3) the economic divorce which deals with money and property; (4) the co-parental divorce which deals with custody, single parent homes, and visitations; (5) the community divorce surrounding the changes of friends

and community that every divorce experiences; and (6) the psychic divorce, with the problem of regaining individual autonomy.[21]

These six stages are not related sequentially to one another, since some may occur simultaneously. But each stage involves distinctively different tasks.

Emotional Divorce. The first stage is obviously the most significant one in that marital breakdown is taking place. This is what provides the initial impetus for considering the possibility of divorce. Conflict has already taken its destructive toll, and in one way or another the partners have stopped giving themselves to each other. Although they may appear to function adequately in the social sphere, they have ceased to aid each other's growth and are giving each other increasing amounts of divergent feedback. In a healthy, growing partnership two people naturally grow apart to some extent as they mature, but they also continue to build up their interdependence. In emotional divorce, however, two people grate on each other simply because they interpret whatever interdependence remains as hated evidence of dependency.[22] Sadly, two people can remain emotionally divorced from each other for a lifetime without ever obtaining a legal divorce.

Legal Divorce. An emotionally divorced couple may seek a legal divorce. The courts in each state specify the "grounds" for divorce; that is to say, they have determined what will be acceptable reasons *before the law* for obtaining a divorce. The legal grounds for obtaining a divorce, of course, may be different from the "real" reasons for wanting a divorce. This is why divorce proceedings are often a travesty of justice and an additional pain to the couple seeking a divorce. They often have to lie or trump up charges against each other to obtain a legal divorce.

The major problem with having to prove fault in seeking a divorce is that the law makes it very difficult for the couple to part amicably. It is emotionally difficult to "forgive and forget" misdeeds of a partner in marriage and legally imprudent to do so. Although the law warns against chicanery (collusion and connivance), having to prove fault increases the likelihood of their occurrence. A state that will grant divorce only on the grounds of adultery increases the chance that such grounds will be faked, or—worse still—that the partner seeking a divorce will entrap the other partner and provide evidence through photographs.

Several states are modifying their divorce laws and providing for "dissolution of marriage" in a proceeding that essentially asks the court to determine whether there is, in fact, evidence that the marriage cannot be continued; however, forty states have not changed their divorce laws in decades. They still operate on the old "adversary" notion: that one partner must be found "at fault" in order for the divorce to be obtained. New York, California, Florida, and eight other states have adopted no-fault divorce laws in which a couple can obtain a divorce for a nominal fee without a lawyer. In California the present rate is one divorce for every two marriages.

The actual divorce proceedings take but a few minutes; few take more than fifteen. Many divorcees are disappointed, having expected that their grievances would be heard when they had their "day in court":[23]

> I thought there would be more to it than that. My attorney just asked a few questions and the judge asked something without even looking up from the papers in front of him, and my attorney indicated that I should step down. It couldn't have taken five minutes and my marriage has lasted five years. I still feel married.[24]

Nevertheless, despite the problems and hypocrisy involved in divorce proceedings as they are commonly conducted at present, legal divorce does accomplish one thing that cannot be accomplished in any other way:

> Divorce can be varyingly defined as the pronouncement of a court, the paper on which this pronouncement is recorded, or the legal situation which arises from this pronouncement. In this situation the parties, or occasionally only one of them, are free to do something which they could not do before; they are now free to enter upon new relationships capable of being recognized as legally valid marriages.[25]

Economic Divorce. Because couples in the United States are recognized as an economic unit not unlike a corporation, divorce must involve a property settlement. The assets of the couple must be divided in half. This division is complicated by tax laws, so the divorce lawyer must know the details of those laws or make use of an assistant who has this specialized knowledge. Varying kinds of emotional and sometimes irrational decisions are made at the time of the property settlement. Anger and frustration often impede a just settlement. Although most things are clear in terms of separating the household goods, various items of value to which one or the other partner may have an emotional attachment can become critical, conflict-provoking issues.

Involved in the economic settlement is, of course, the matter of alimony. In most cases the husband is required to pay alimony in an amount established by the court. Some recent decisions, however, maintain that in some situations the wife is quite capable of maintaining herself. Alimony is usually based on the wife's needs and the husband's ability to pay. Other factors that are often considered are the wife's educational background and ability to be a breadwinner, her state of health, his state of health, the income tax question, children, and the general life styles of both partners. Very few courts award alimony for the lifetime of the wife.

Child support is figured separately from alimony but on a similar basis. Because both alimony and child support are established by the court, failure to pay represents contempt of court. This is the only legal sanction that can be invoked to ensure that these payments are made, but it is not really adequate in dealing with husbands who refuse to pay. Many postdivorce conflicts arise out of failure to deal adequately with the economic aspects of divorce.

Co-Parental Divorce. Co-parental divorce is necessary if there are children. In 1977, 7.2 percent of all children under the age of 18 in the United States lived with a divorced parent.[26] Perhaps one of the most painful and agonizing aspects of divorce is determining who will live with whom after the household breaks up. Custody of the children is decided by the court on the basis of the child's well-being. The custodian may be either of the parents, or a third party if the court feels such an arrangement is necessary. Traditionally, under English common law the father had absolute property rights in the children, but today it is more common to give the mother custody. The number of children involved in divorces is increasing, as is the number who are living with their fathers. Some women refuse child support on the mistaken assumption that by so doing they can deny the father the right to see his children. In fact, however, his visiting rights are not contingent on child support, but derive from his parental role. Nevertheless, some fathers accept this tradeoff, although it is not likely that it would stand up in court.

Community Divorce. The change in status of the divorced person sometimes means isolation from the community of friends and neighbors, a situation that is difficult to cope with or overcome. Personal inadequacies are now seen in a different context, and loneliness can become all-pervasive. However, the number of options available to single people in our society is increasing, and as a result the surface of this loneliness can be broken much more easily today than in the past.

Psychic Divorce. The most difficult stage in the recovery from divorce, yet probably the area in which one is most free to be creative, is regaining individual autonomy. In one sense a partnership like marriage never ends, particularly if there are children. It may be legally broken, but the ties inevitably go on for a while, sometimes for a lifetime.

The problem of regaining autonomy is related to the extent to which autonomy was given up in the partnership. Men and women who retained a great deal of individual autonomy in their partnership will have less difficulty after divorce. (It is also less likely that they will divorce in the first place, however.) Regaining autonomy means

> learning to live without somebody to lean on—but also without someone to support. There is nobody on whom to blame one's difficulties (except oneself), nobody to short-stop one's growth and nobody to grow with.
>
> Each must regain—if he (or she) ever had it—the dependence on self and faith in one's own capacity to cope with the environment, with people, with thoughts and emotions.[27]

Psychic divorce is in many ways the most difficult because it involves the regaining of individual autonomy which may have been submerged in the marriage. (Timothy Eagan, 1978, Woodfin Camp & Associates)

There is evidence that "divorce breeds divorce" in the sense that restrictions on obtaining divorce influence the rate of divorce, although the data on this issue are far from clear. Nevertheless, the trend toward higher divorce rates need not be cause for alarm. Qualitatively, there is reason to believe that divorce, whatever its frequency, is preferable to conflicted, destructive partnerships. As Max Reinstein observes:

> If we regard family stability as a social good, a situation of high incidence of marriage breakdown constitutes a social evil. Its reduction deserves to be an aim of social policy. But what about divorce? It does not occur by itself but only as a sequel to marriage breakdown. Insofar as divorce opens the door to legitimate remarriage and thus to the creation of new homes

free of any taint of illegitimacy, it is a social good rather than an evil. But if the easy availability of divorce is conducive toward a high incidence of marriage breakdown, good social policy requires that the incidence of divorce ought also to be reduced.[28]

SUMMARY

Because we know so little about how nonmarital partnerships terminate, in this chapter we have chosen to focus exclusively on how marriages end. Following Goode, we can describe five types of family disorganization: the uncompleted family, the empty shell, the family disorganized by external catastrophe, the family disorganized by internal catastrophe, and the marriage terminated by willed departures such as divorce.

Although death terminates more marriages than any other cause, divorce receives the most publicity. Currently, one divorce takes place each year for every two marriages contracted in that year. While 81 percent of all married people have been married only once, about 15 percent of all men and 17 percent of all women who are 70 or over have been divorced at least once. Our study concludes that 48 percent of those marriages made in the 1970s will eventually end in divorce.

Divorce laws are rapidly being modified to better fit the realities of modern marriage and give couples access to legal redress of grievances without having to prove "fault." This change amounts to another factor that is making marriage more voluntary and thus contributes to the increase in the divorce rate. Divorce counselors are beginning to take a more active role in reducing the damage that can be inflicted by divorce.

Paul Bohannan describes divorce as a six-stage process. Each of these stages—emotional divorce, legal divorce, economic divorce, coparental divorce, community divorce, and psychic divorce—involves certain problems that must be faced by divorcing couples.

NOTES

1. William J. Goode, "Family Disorganization," in Robert K. Merton and Robert A. Nisbet, (eds.), *Contemporary Social Problems*, 2nd ed. (New York: Harcourt Brace Jovanovich, 1966), pp. 479–552.
2. Kingsley Davis, "Illegitimacy and the Social Structure," *American Journal of Sociology* (1939): 215–33.
3. C. W. Hart and Arnold R. Pilling, *The Tiwi of North Australia* (New York: Holt, Rinehart and Winston, 1962).
4. Hyman Rodman, *Lower-Class Families: The Culture of Poverty in Negro Trinidad* (New York: Oxford University Press, 1971), pp. 46ff.
5. John F. Cuber and Peggy B. Harroff, *Sex and the Significant Americans* (Baltimore: Penguin Books, 1968).

6. U.S. Bureau of the Census, *Statistical Abstract of the United States: 1982–1983* (Washington, D.C.: U.S. Government Printing Office, 1983), p. 59.

7. Alvin Toffler, *Future Shock* (New York: Bantam Books, 1972), p. 251.

8. *U.S. News & World Report*, October 30, 1972, p. 39.

9. Ibid.

10. Paul Glick and Arthur Norton, Frequency, Duration and Probability of Marriage and Divorce," *Journal of Marriage and the Family* (May 1971): 310.

11. Arlene Skolnick, *The Intimate Environment: Exploring Marriage and the Family*, 3rd ed. (Boston: Little, Brown, 1983), p. 247.

12. Ibid.

13. P. Krishnan, "Divorce Table for Females in the United States," *Journal of Marriage and the Family* (May 1971): 318.

14. Glick and Norton, "Frequency, Duration and Probability of Marriage and Divorce," p. 316.

15. P. C. Glick, "A Demographer Looks at American Families," *Journal of Marriage and the Family*, 37 (February 1975): 15–26.

16. Eugene Litwak, "Divorce Law as Social Control," *Social Forces*, 24 (March 1956): 217–23.

17. Gerald C. Wright, Jr., and Dorothy M. Stetson, "The Impact of No-Fault Divorce Law Reform on Divorce in American States," *Journal of Marriage and the Family* (August 1978): 575–80. California and Florida are exceptions to the general findings. These states have significantly higher divorce rates than the national average. G. G. Gunter, "Notes on Divorce Filing as Role Behavior," *Journal of Marriage and the Family* (February 1977): 95–97, suggests that the increase in the divorce rate after Florida passed its no-fault law was in part a result of major changes in male-female role behaviors.

18. Marie Kargman, "The Revolution in Divorce Law," *The Family Coordinator*, 22 (April 1973): 245.

19. Esther Fisher, "A Guide to Divorce and Counselling," *The Family Coordinator*, 22 (January 1973): 55. Dorothy Fahs Beck, "Research Findings on the Outcomes of Marital Counseling," *Social Casework* (March 1975): 153–81 provides evidence of the generally positive outcome of marital counseling.

20. Paul Bohannan, *Divorce and After* (Garden City, N.Y.: Doubleday, 1970).

21. As quoted in Marcie E. Lasswell and Thomas E. Lasswell, *Love, Marriage, Family: A Developmental Approach* (Glenview, Ill.: Scott, Foresman, 1973), p. 475.

22. Ibid., p. 476.

23. Lasswell and Lasswell, p. 482.

24. Fullerton, *Survival in Marriage* (New York: Holt, Rinehart and Winston, 1977), p. 406.

25. Max Reinstein, *Marriage, Stability, Divorce and the Law* (Chicago: University of Chicago Press, 1972), p. 266.

26. Paul Glick, "Demographic Changes and the Family," paper presented at the National Conference on Work and Family, Hauppauge, N.Y., 1978, p. 11.

27. Lasswell and Lasswell, p. 488.

28. Reinstein, p. 267.

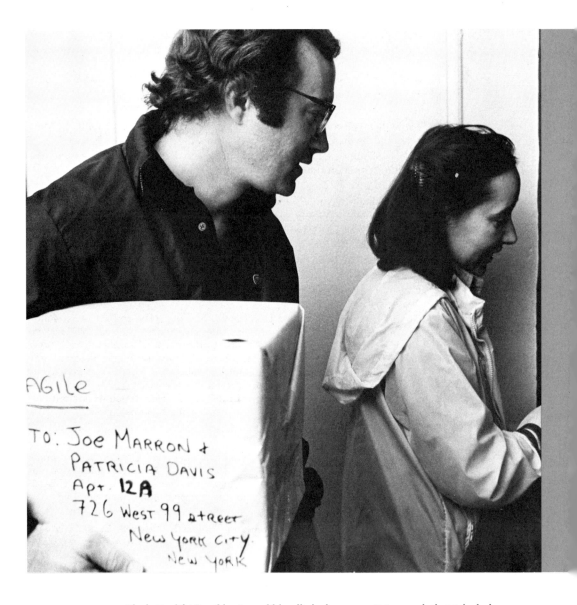

On the box: FRAGILE

TO: Joe Marron + Patricia Davis
Apt. 12A
726 West 99 Street
New York City.
New York

The better life! Possibly, it would hardly look so, now; it is enough that it looked so then. The greatest obstacle to being heroic is the doubt whether one may not be going to prove one's self a fool; the truest heroism is, to resist the doubt; the profoundest wisdom, to know when it ought to be resisted, and when to be obeyed.

—Nathaniel Hawthorne, Blithedale Romance

17 Alternative Life Styles

As we have seen, marriage is the most durable partnership in the United States, even though there is increasing acceptance of different marital styles such as the two wage-earner or dual-career family, the voluntarily child-less, and an overall trend toward greater equality between husbands and wives. In this chapter we will consider several other alternatives: remaining single for life, living communally or in multilateral marriages. Less attention will be paid to communes and multilateral marriages, because they remain an option for a relatively few people in practice. Most attention will be given to the singles, because the number of unattached individuals is a significant minority of the present adult population and one of the most rapidly growing life styles.

Under the category "single" we will consider the never married, the divorced, and the widowed with and without children not because these are in any sense absolute categories, but because they present distinctive problems to those who would fashion a life style after having experienced them. In a strict sense, of course, it is not possible to study the never married until after they are dead. They are better called, perhaps, the not yet married, since many of these persons will eventually marry. A small but growing minority, however, do find the prospects of being single a lifetime life style, especially if this means merely "not legally married."

WHO ARE THEY?

We do not know much statistically about how the average American goes about establishing partnerships other than marriage. Therefore, it is not possible to provide an estimate of the amount of time people spend without entering any kind of partnership at all. The average length of marriage for those who do divorce, however, is about 6.8 years.[1] It has been estimated that divorced people who remarry live in partial families—that is, families consisting of one parent plus dependent children—for an average of 5.9 years. Three of these years are spent in a state of either legal or de facto separation prior to divorce; the other 2.9 years follow the legal divorce. Widowed people live in partial families for an average of 3.5 years.[2] Some people in each category, of course, never remarry.

The overall figure of about 56.8 million people over the age of 18 who were not married in 1981 includes a sizable number who are going to get married as soon as they can.[3] Between 1965 and 1981, the percentage of men and women under the age of 35 who remained single generally increased. The percentage of people age 35 and older who remained single, on the other hand, decreased during those years. Many of them already had their marriage partners picked out, and some undoubtedly were engaged. Within five-year age cohorts from 15 to 34, however, the percentage in each age cohort who have never married is increasing and is projected to continue to do so through 1990 by the Joint Center for Urban Studies.[4]

The figure of 56.8 million also includes all divorced and widowed people without children and a number of individuals who will never marry, either because of circumstances beyond their control or because they really never intended to marry. One study estimates that there are at least 8 million females over 18 in our society who are *involuntarily* single. There were about 23.8 million widowed and divorced people in 1981.

Thus, although in any given year the fraction of the population who are without marital partners is about 35 percent of the total number of people over 18, the total number of individuals who have lived for a significant part of their adult life without a marital partner is much larger.[5] As the pressure to marry diminishes with society's increasing recognition of the value of nonmarital partnerships, the number of people who choose not to marry—or not to marry again—will continue to increase.

The Divorced

The single person who has been married one or more times brings to the single life style a distinctive heritage, for good or ill, arising out of the fact of having been married. Determining the marital status of one's partner is one of the first pieces of information one collects in a developing relationship, and "divorced" has certain implications in this context. "Whenever a guy hears that I am a divorcee, he thinks that I am ready to go to bed with him at the drop of a hat," a divorced woman reports. "When I go out with a woman and tell her I am divorced," a man testifies, "I can see the wheels start turning immediately. Before she's willing to let herself get interested in me she wants to find out what my problem is. She's afraid maybe I'm impotent or have a violent temper or something like that."

Divorce frequently carries with it an aura of failure that affects both divorced people themselves and those around them. Thus, a certain insecurity is frequently part of the heritage of divorce. "After being married to George for thirty years, I really don't know how to respond fully to other men," one woman laments. "God, I don't even know how much soap to put into the washing machine," a divorced man says, expressing what he obviously sees as a symbol of his general incompetence. On the other hand, divorce offers some people a new lease on life: "I never really knew I was such a sexual person until I started dating other men"; "I didn't realize how much I lost track of the meaning of relationships during those twelve years." Divorce has a different significance for different people, depending on whether it occurs when they are relatively young or when they are in middle or old age, on whether they were married for many years or only a few months. It makes a difference if children are involved, particularly if the family is poor. In the 1960s well over three-fifths of all divorcing couples had minor children.[6] Only divorced people without children will be considered in this section.

How Do We Live? Because of the strong expectations that adults be independent from their parents, divorced people who do not have children rarely return to live in the parental home. "I couldn't possibly go back and live with my parents," a divorced woman explained. "Of course I was very lonely but it was better to be lonely than to burden my parents with my sadness. After all, it wasn't their fault that John and I couldn't get along. I simply would have made them hate John, and that's not fair." If a woman returns home after divorcing or becoming a widow and care is not taken to clearly specify the lines of authority, a dysfunctional family form can result in which the generations become enmeshed in continuous conflict.[7]

If the couple followed a traditional division of labor during their married years, the requirement that they now live on their own will mean that each has to develop the skills formerly contributed by the spouse or pay for such services. A man who moves into an apartment usually buys as many domestic services as he can afford. He eats out, sends his clothes to the laundry, and hires a housekeeper. If he is paying alimony, this means, in effect, that he is paying for the running of two households. The woman's predicament in this regard is usually more serious than the man's if during the marriage she limited her work to performing housekeeping duties. While it is possible for him to continue in his specialty—earning the income—and hire someone to provide the services that she used to provide, it is not possible for her to hire someone to support her while she remains a homemaker. If there is no alimony or if the amount is inadequate for her needs—or as often happens, it is not paid regularly—she must seek employment, even though her inexperience as a worker puts her at a disadvantage in the job market. The woman who worked during marriage, on the other hand, is in a position not unlike that of the divorced husband.

What Do We Do about Friends? Divorce means not only the loss of a partner; over time it usually means the loss of some of the friends the partners knew as a couple. Divorce can create an awkward situation for the friends of a formerly married couple. The problem from the friends' point of view is, "Which one do we invite?" Often friendships between couples are really two friendships—one between the wives and another between the husbands. When one of the couples get divorced, therefore, it is likely that the husband in the still-married couple will favor maintaining relations with the ex-husband while the wife wants to keep the friendship of the ex-wife. Settling this difference may produce a strain that is most easily resolved by cutting off relations with both divorced partners. "I'd like to have you to dinner more often, Helen," the friend of a divorced woman might explain, "but my husband thinks it wouldn't be fair to Bob."

To a large extent, divorced people are unable to control such developments. Over the course of about a year, they will find that their friendship patterns have changed radically. "After eight months I began to realize that I was getting fewer and fewer invitations to go out. I still had occasions for luncheon with my old girlfriends, but I was spending more and more time alone at night," a divorced woman explained. At this point the divorced person usually recognizes the need to discover new friends. Although this is no easy task even today, it is getting easier all the time. Compared to single women aged 25, divorced women are more likely to marry.

What is more, divorced women with children are more likely to remarry than those without children, and statistics show that they are able to do so in about the same amount of time. In fact, children seem to be an incentive to marry. The problems they create for divorced people—especially divorced women—will be discussed in a later section.

But what if the divorced person really doesn't want to remarry? Two-fifths of them do not remarry. What kind of a life can they expect to realize as single people? Again, times are changing. Any one of a number of organizations can provide social and recreational opportunities that formerly were not available to single people in our society. This is truer, perhaps, for divorced people under 35 than for older people. It is also truer for people who are more gregarious. The life style of the young unmarried single, to which the young divorced person could return, is discussed later.

A less frantic sort of life style can be substained by making use of activities provided by churches such as the First Singles Church and various civic organiations.[8] Many places of entertainment are now open to single men and women, whereas in the past they catered largely or even exclusively to couples. The problem of getting to know people is not so much a matter of where to go as one of money and incentive. If the divorced person is young and has at least a middle-class income, there are numerous opportunities for social contacts of many sorts. Without money, the problems are quite different. Because most low-income individuals who become divorced have children, their style of adjustment will be discussed in the section dealing with single-parent families.

What about Sex? Although at one time it was popular to expect divorced people to abstain from sexual intercourse just as they were supposed to have done before marriage, it is now becoming widely recognized that this is nonsense. As attitudes toward sex are changing, it is becoming increasingly easy for divorced people openly to acknowledge their sexuality. The fact that divorced men and women are not expected to be sexually "innocent," the way never-married single people are, may be one of the real advantages they enjoy over the never married as they attempt to adjust to a single life style.

Living with a Label. In spite of the opportunities for divorced people to make a better reentry into single life (and to achieve a better remarriage, if they want one), there are still many problems associated with the role of divorced person. The label "divorced" still means failure both to society at large and to the divorced person. Although this can be beneficial, in the sense that one's expectations of partnerships like marriage may be more realistic "the next time around," it can also mean that the divorced person feels less sure of himself or herself in social and intimate interactions.

It is unfortunately true that not many divorced people are permitted to emerge from the experience with their sense of themselves as solidly intact as the woman who gave us the following testimony:

> Look, getting divorced is a lot like getting married in some ways: both are voluntary decisions to change your living arrangements. Sure, in a lot of cases people get divorced unwillingly—I mean, their husbands or wives divorce them against their will or their marriage is so bad they feel they have no choice. In those cases, I suppose, people should sympathize with them. But my husband and I both decided to get divorced. It wasn't anything that happened to us, it was something we decided. I don't want people's

sympathy and I don't think Andy does either. When we got married people had the courtesy to assume we knew what we were doing. They didn't say, "Oh I'm sorry things didn't work out for you when you were single"; they said, "Congratulations." Well, this is a decision to change the way we're living, too, and I wish people would take it that way. When someone I haven't talked to in a while calls and I tell them I'm divorced, they always say, "I'm sorry to hear that," or "Oh, that's too bad." Well, it's not too bad; I think it's the best thing for both of us.

In the same vein, many divorced people do not feel they should be stigmatized as having failed in marriage, which is how they are most commonly regarded and the way they are encouraged to regard themselves. "I don't think my marriage with Diane was a failure just because it didn't last forever," one man reported.

We had a lot of good years together; we helped each other a lot and we grew a lot with each other. That's not what I call failure. We just reached a point when we stopped growing and we both felt we could do more with ourselves if we each went our own way. I look at it this way: a person learns a lot in college, but it reaches a point when college doesn't have all that much more to offer him. He graduates. Does that mean that he was a failure at college because he couldn't go on learning there forever? I know the analogy doesn't really fit, because when you enroll in college you only intend to go four years but when you get married it's supposed to be for the rest of your life. But that only means we were wrong about that part. It doesn't mean our relationship was a failure.

Both statements indicate that the stereotype which labels divorced people as individuals who "couldn't make a go of it" in marriage is, like all stereotypes, often inaccurate and contributes to the problems divorced people face in our culture by encouraging them to see themselves as misfits. This is not to deny that in a great many cases divorce does represent a traumatic failure of one sort or another; for example, divorced people have higher death rates and suicide rates than married people.[9] One study found that death rates were higher for single people than for married people. In this study, mortality rates were highest for nonmarried individuals who were not living in households and lowest for married people with children.[10]

Clearly, divorce can have a significant negative impact on an individual's performance and health. On the other hand, for many people divorce is a positive step toward reestablishing themselves as autonomous, growing individuals. The decision to get divorced, because it is viewed so critically by many people, sometimes requires great courage and may be more difficult than the decision to remain in an unsatisfactory or unfulfilling relationship. Summoning up the courage to make this decision, therefore, may be a significant triumph in an individual's development. In this sense we do divorced people an injustice when we think of them as failures.

The divorced person without children can cope with the stress and disorientation often involved in divorce by traveling, "losing" herself or himself in a job, moving to a new location, dating new people, or becoming a hermit and simply suffering for a time. The divorced person with children obviously does not have as many options, for he or she must consider the impact of all these decisions on the children. Because the children most often live with their mother, it is usually the divorced women who must cope with this problem.

The Widowed

Although death can come at any age, the widowed population is, as one might expect, on the average considerably older than the divorced population. For every five divorces that occur among people in their late twenties, for example, there is one widow. Because of the different life expectancies of men and women, bereavement is more commonly experienced by women than by men. Forty percent of all women between the ages of 65 and 74 are widowed.[11] In 1977 there were 12.8 million widowed people over the age of 18 in the United States, of whom 10.8 million were women.[12] In the past men survived their wives with greater regularity than they do now. The tombstones of New England bear witness to the death of many women in childbirth and note with awe the man who survived several wives. Today, a man's life expectancy is about seven years less than his wife's, and the average widow outlives her husband by eleven years. But the fact that women

Widows and widowers must cope with myriad experiences for which they may not be prepared. (Richard Frieman, Photo Researchers, Inc.)

are widowed more often than men is really beside the point. The point is that, except in the relatively rare and generally accidental cases in which two partners die simultaneously, all couples can expect that one partner or the other will have to go through a period of bereavement.

Grief Work. When a spouse dies, the widow or widower must cope with myriad experiences for which she or he is not prepared. Our society tends to deal with the question of death in a most inadequate way, for unlike other cultures we do not have the heritage of a rich and complex ritual response to death. Not only do widows and widowers not know what their role in mourning should be, but on top of this, they must handle this lack of knowledge on the part of the majority of people who have known the deceased partner. Because of the lack of guidelines and the anxieties provoked by the crisis of death, most people want to do something, but the fact of the matter is that there isn't that much to do. Thus, the widowed person is forced to become in some respects a "project director" for consoling friends and relatives.

In "grief work" there is an initial period of unreality when the bereaved is not quite sure what has happened. A kind of automatic response to the situation helps the bereaved person make the decisions that need to be made, but she or he may not remember having made them. A decided memory lapse is not uncommon among the newly widowed, who also often feel a need to place blame for the partner's death somewhere; as a result, they fluctuate between guiltily blaming themselves and lashing out at others. Much has been written about grief work, and in general psychologists agree it is important for the psychic health of the bereaved that grief be expressed; if it is not, it will frequently result in neurosis.[13] Bereavement itself, rather than the simple fact of living alone, has been shown to be the major cause of depression in widows.[14]

Once the widowed person has performed the appropriate grief work, she or he in some sense joins the ranks of the singles. Although widowed people are generally older than the average divorced person (over 88 percent of the widows in 1981 were over 55; more than 69 percent were over 65), the widowed and the divorced face many of the same problems of reentry into the single life style.[15] Both widows and widowers have a lower probability of remarriage than divorced persons at all age levels.[16] Those who do remarry, however, do so within a shorter time than the typical divorced person (if the period of separation from the spouse is included in the computation of remarriage time for divorced people).

What About Friends? Old friendships tend to dwindle for the widowed person, partly owing to the death of friends and partly as a result of a pattern similar to that experienced by divorced people. The upper-class woman who has been involved in a great many activities outside her marriage will have a less difficult time maintaining friendships than the lower-class woman or the woman for whom marriage has been the center of her being. The widowed form a large portion of the impoverished population of our society, and thus the widowed person with inadequate income often faces old age and death in a terrifyingly lonely environment.

Coping with Inadequate Income. The problems of most widowed people are compounded by inadequate income—a result of the fact that most couples in America are financially ill prepared for old age. They come to retirement with little more than social security as a dependable source of income, and this is rarely sufficient for their needs. For some time it was widely believed that older people really need less than younger people (because they have already bought most of the things they need in life; besides, they are less active than younger people and therefore their expenses are necessarily lower). Yet it is clear that, given adequate income, older people can put it to good use. They can travel, buy condominium apartments, move to warmer climates, and generally maintain a level of social interaction not too different from that which they experienced in middle age. This is especially important for widowed older people, for whom the resources that make an active social life possible provide an opportunity to rebuild a life that was probably seriously disrupted by the death of the spouse. Indeed, the needs of the widowed elderly may well be greater than those of the elderly in general, if for no other reason than the fact that the pleasures of companionship, which cost nothing, may be missing from their lives. It therefore is often necessary for them to get out of the house if they do not want to be alone, and most outside activities cost money. Several studies suggest that poverty is the cause of a number of psychological and social disorders attributed to bereavement. These include less social participation, greater loneliness, and anxiety and lower morale.[17]

Single-Parent Families

The problems of all solo parents seem similar, even though some of them may be single because they have never married, some because they have been divorced, and some because they are widowed. Whatever the cause, the solo parent must cope with the task of trying to raise one or more children without the help of a spouse. This requires a considerable commitment of the parent's time while she or he is also striving to provide an adequate income. (Divorced women may have it a bit easier on this score because child support is commonly available to them, whereas, obviously, it is not available to the never married and the widowed.) Single people with children are not nearly as free to make choices about partners, residence, and how they will spend their own time as single people without children.

About 11 million families are headed by a single parent. By far the larger number of single-parent families are headed by women.[18] Ways of coping with solo parenthood vary by class. Lower-class men rarely assume responsibility for heading a family without a spouse because they have very

Single-parent families are increasingly common in the United States and an increasing percentage of them are headed by males. (Ken Karp)

few resources for housekeeping or for earning a living; besides, most of our welfare legislation favors families headed by women. Upper-class professional men may head a partial family, in which case they usually compensate for their spouse's absence by buying the services of a maid, housekeeper, or "nanny."

Broken Families. Single-parent families are often thought of as "broken," "partial," or "disorganized" nuclear families. It is commonly argued that both parents are necessary to socialize the child properly. In particular, "fatherless families" have been correlated with increased rates of schizophrenia in children, juvenile delinquency, inability to delay gratification, and a host of other disorders.[19] In recent years, however, it has become increasingly clear that many of these studies are based on faulty and inappropriate comparisons. As Nye points out, the assumption that "any father is better than no father at all" is commonly held by psychologists but often denied by sociologists.[20] The family in which there is conflict and continuing tension between the spouses is clearly not to be preferred to a single-parent family in which there is warmth and acceptance. Frequently, studies of fatherless families overlook the extent to which there is, in fact, a viable male role model in the house. This is prticularly true of lower-class black families in which a boyfriend assumes the role of a quasi-father.[21]

In sum, a good case can be made for abandoning pejorative labels such as "broken" when describing single-parent families. Many single-parent families provide their members with as complete and unbroken a family environment as many two-parent families. The term *broken* simply does not do justice to the successful efforts of numerous single parents who are performing the demanding task of raising their children in a society in which two-parent families are decidedly the norm.

Boyfriends. Recent sociological studies of lower-class black families reveal that boyfriends are frequently much more supportive of a woman and her children than had previously been imagined. The boyfriend may not "live in" with the family, but in his care and concern for all the members of the family he clearly demonstrates that his relationship to the family is not simply limited to his tie to the mother as a sexual partner. "He believes in survival for me and my children," one mother said in describing the concern of her boyfriend. This care may take the form of purchasing a significant part of the week's groceries, buying furniture, taking the family to the movies or the park, and helping the mother with her young children when she is sick. Boyfriends often discipline the younger children and are generally respected in the household. Given their concern, it seems reasonable to assume that more such couples would marry if they had an adequate and dependable source of income and the welfare laws in various localities did not make it disadvantageous for them to do so.

Having a boyfriend allows the low-income woman to make a better assessment of the man's ability to care for her and her family in a context in which this is not easily determined in any other way. Women who have been disappointed in one marriage do not find it easy to commit themselves to another when there are fewer social constraints to keep the marriage together and many factors that tend to pull it apart. Therefore, they frequently say, "If he wants to love me he has to love my kids first."

Aid to Families with Dependent Children. The problems of providing aid to families with dependent children have been with us since the 1930s. Today, 10.5 million households receive this assistance at a cost of over $12 billion.[22] It seems clear that many of the greatest difficulties of single-parent families are directly related to the fact that they often lack an adequate income. Nye observes:

> Our society seems to be saying: "We will support life in these families and nothing more."
> Sociologically, the question may be stated: Do the roles of child care, socialization and housekeeping constitute an adequate occupation for a woman who has no husband for whom she may render these and other services?
> Currently, it seems American society has not accepted the maternal role as a sufficient contribution to society and, in effect, by providing a submarginal level of subsistence for partial families, it tries to motivate them to become self-supporting. However, it has not yet provided the institutions that are necessary for the solo parent to function sufficiently and to share in the rewards of the society.[23]

Undoubtedly, the most significant of the institutions society could provide to benefit solo parents at all income levels is an adequate day care program. Without some such program, solo parents with dependent children are placed under severe stress, both economic and psychological. Working would be almost counterproductive for a single parent who could expect only a low-income job and would have to pay a large portion of that income for child care. What is more, time away from the children is important to all parents, but particularly to solo parents who, in the absense of a spouse, cannot find companionship with other adults in the family setting. Lack of adequate day care facilities ties the single parent to his or her children, making both work and a healthy social life nearly impossible.

The Influence of the Absent Spouse. The question of how to handle the absent spouse can be a vexing problem for divorced parents. If the children are young—say, under the age of 6—when the divorce occurs, and if the parents have been relatively open about their conflicts and disagreements, they may not be very close to their biological father or mother and can therefore accept a stepparent more readily. Presumably, they also might not have a great deal of difficulty accepting any other kind of partnership the mother or father might wish to establish. Older children are more likely to find it difficult to accept another intimate partner for their solo parent.

It has been argued that divorce laws should be modified in such a way as to minimize damage to the children's relationship to their parents. When the conjugal bond is broken in divorce, it is not in fact necessary to sever the parental bond. Indeed, in most instances it seems highly desirable for all concerned to cultivate these parental relationships even after divorce. If a divorce is to be minimally harmful to the children involved, the following guidelines should be observed:

1. The responsibility for the decision to divorce must belong to the adults and not the children. Some couples on the verge of divorce consult the children in order to solicit their feelings on the subject. Unless this is done very carefully, it can have the effect of making them feel responsible for the decision when it is made—a tactic which is hardlly fair to a child.
2. The divorcing couple should agree on realistic reasons for the divorce.
3. They should share this information with their children in an understandable fashion.
4. The divorcing couple should work out their settlement with as wide an understanding of their personal needs as possible; flexibility and responsiveness to the children's needs should be the primary consideration in establishing visiting patterns.
5. The departing parent will help his or her child if he or she continues to show interest in the child; some visible symbol of their continuing relationship is often helpful in this regard.
6. The separated couple should continue to plan together for the children's future. Important decisions about the children—such as decisions about schooling—should not be left exclusively to the parent with whom the child is living.

7. The parents should be willing to discuss the divorce with the children even after the divorce; both of the former partners should be honest about the facts of the divorce at all times. In this regard, honesty about human frailties can help the children cope with the fact of divorce without blaming either one parent or the other.[24]

The Never Married

In our society about 8 to 10 percent of the adult population chooses never to marry. Since the 1960s the needs, wants, and tastes of single people have been given increasing attention. Singles housing, bars, clubs, and dating systems, along with a deemphasis of "couples only" requirement in restaurants, excursion cruises, and other public recreational facilities, have brought about many new opportunities for singles to get together in groups or as individuals.[25] This public recognition that there is an alternative single style of life has also encouraged a kind of "singles" consciousness that enables single people to think positively about their choice rather than to view it as a liability. The greatest amount of singles activity is concentrated in New York and California, the two states with the largest number of adult single people. Many of these individuals are immigrants from small towns or rural areas; a large percentage of them are office workers and professional people.[26]

Housing for Singles. The 1960s and 1970s have seen a rapid increase in the availability of housing for singles only. Closed communities of singles in rather posh settings cater to the housing and recreational needs of upper-middle-class singles. These housing units, often located in suburban communities, offer "a millionaire-like atmosphere with pool, saunas, jacuzzis, air conditioning, outdoor barbecues, recreation rooms and billiards, plus a wild and exciting decor![27] Many of these places also provide a hostess or program director who organizes and manages dances and group games and generally oversees the social life. It should be noted that many young people tend to criticize this particular kind of single life style as little more than an extension of the college dormitory, sorority, or fraternity. Nevertheless, the fact that large sums of money have been invested to develop these complexes indicates that there is a considerable market for them.

In large urban areas, bar hopping has provided a more or less traditional way for single people to meet members of the opposite sex. Many urban areas have "body shops," bars that are well known as places where it is possible to find a sexual partner. Criticism of this side of our emerging new singles society has been widespread. It is often charged that, in effect, such establishments cater to men and degrade women. Rosalyn Moran points out that men in the various bars, complexes, clubs, and other social settings for singles often behave like "buyers at a slave market."[28] Indeed, there is no denying that men in these settings typically do not stop long

Singles bars are popular meeting places. (Jill Hartley, Photo Researchers, Inc.)

enough to develop a conversation, much less a relationship, in their quest for "progress" among the prospective females available.

A Quieter Style. Fortunately, the evolution of the singles life style has reduced the necessity for single people to meet under these circumstances. Many single women and men are pleased with the emergence of a new style of singles club where they can engage in social encounters in a context that is not specifically sexual. What is more, many large cities offer a fairly wide variety of apartments of all sizes and prices, making it increasingly easy for single people to find suitable living accommodations. Thus, it is possible for some single people to work out a rich and varied life style that has little in common with the "swinging" singles scene so widely publicized in magazines and films.

Ann is one such person. Forty-two years old and a graduate of a university not far from her current residence, she has never been married. She has a wide circle of friends of both sexes. Some of her friendships with men date back to her days in the university, some were formed at work, and others resulted from her membership in numerous organizations. Ann dates often and establishes varying degrees of intimacy in her relationships with the men she dates. She travels a lot, particularly for skiing in Europe, which she is able to afford on the salary she earns as a professional. She manages her money well, feels excited about what she is doing, seems to enjoy a considerable amount of freedom in her relationships, and in general seems happy and adjusted in her single life style.

Ann has developed a life style she finds rewarding, despite the fact that her experience runs counter to the prevailing myth that true fulfillment—especially for women—is not to be found outside marriage. There are various factors, of course, that have made it relatively easy for her to do this. Living in a community where the university from which she graduated provides a network of social interactions is important. She is fortunate, too, in that she benefits from a financial position that gives her much flexibility. And finally, the fact that she is apparently at ease with her own sexuality has enabled her to be much freer in her relationships with others than is commonly the case. Her general approach to life enables her to expend her energy on things that help her grow as a person.

Many people like Ann have developed very adequate life styles as single individuals, but even today many of them are unnecessarily burdened by the fact that their society tends to see them as in some sense inadequate because they are single—that is, because they have "failed" to marry.

Changes in sexual mores over the past decade or so may be decreasing the burden placed on single people, but there is no denying that they still face some serious problems. As Rustum and Della Roy point out,

> Traditional monogamy does not deal humanly with its have nots—the adult singles and the widowed and divorced. Statistically, we in America have more involuntarily single persons above the age of 25 or 30 than those who have had no choice about a socially and economically disadvantageous color for their skin. The latter have had to bear enormous legal and social affronts and suffered the subtler and possibly more debilitating psychological climate of being unacceptable in much of their natural surroundings. But this disability they share with voiceless single persons in a marriage-oriented society. Our society proclaims monogamy's virtue at every point of law and custom and practice, as much as it says white is right. Biases, from income tax to adoption requirements and Emily Post etiquette, all point to the traditional monogamists as the acceptable form of society.[29]

COMMUNES AND MULTIPLE MARRIAGES

Throughout history, **communes** have at various times and places offered an appealing alternative to the more common ways of living in families. In our own history, the nineteenth century was a time in which communes flourished. Most of them were religious or ideological communities organized around a passionately held vision of a better life. The Shakers, for example, sought the simple life expressed in their craft, trade, and buildings; denounced sexual intercourse as the cardinal sin of humanity; strictly segregated the sisters from the brothers; and worshiped Ann Lee as an incarnation of God in a religion that has survived in ever-diminishing numbers to the present day. In an age in which divorce was not easy to obtain, and welfare was virtually nonexistent, the Shakers offered many a viable alternative.[30] The Oneida Community of midstate New York practiced a form of Christian perfectionism for thirty years, advocated group marriage, self-criticism, greater equality between the genders, and developed the first eugenics program based on male countenance.[31] In all, about 150 settlements with names like New Harmony, Brook Farm, and the Icarians distinguished themselves by practicing ways of living that as often earned them the scorn of their neighbors as their admiration.[32]

During the past three decades we have seen a resurgence of interest in communes. Hippie communes in the Haight-Ashbury district of San Francisco were among the first to capture nationwide attention as young people disenchanted with middle-class life in an affluent America sought to experience life more freely and authentically. Anarchist and free land communes such as the Morning Star Ranch near San Francisco practiced a radical form of socialism.[33] Although some dropped out of established society, others became more involved in social action. The Farm in Tennessee grew out of a caravan of people who left the Haight. It now has about 1,200 acres of land, 1,500 members, and $1.5 million in assets and sends its members around the world in humanitarian service to developing countries.[34] Twin Oaks in Virginia is one of the best-known communities. It is modeled after a vision of the good life put forth by B. F. Skinner in his *Walden Two*.[35] For over forty years, Koinonia, a Christian fellowship retaining the centrality of the nuclear family, has striven to realize racial equality in the rural South. Young communes around colleges and universities continue to provide economical room and board and to tinker with alternative life styles in the process. Like the anarchist groups, the youth communes are generally of short duration.

Estimates of the number of people involved in communes (which can roughly be distinguished by the common residence and intent to change a whole way of living) vary from about a quarter of a million to a million and a half persons living in some 3,000 to 5,000 settlements.[36] At best this is less than 1 percent of the U.S. population, and the enthusiasm for such life styles seems to be waning. Nevertheless, communes are extremely valuable to a rapidly changing society such as ours because they continually test alternatives that may be critical to our survival in the future and allow some individuals to find greater personal fulfillment today.

To distinguish **multiple marriage** from a commune, it can be said that the former is primarily—if not exclusively—interested in changing the marriage contract rather than a total way of life. The people who lived at Harrad West—a group marriage arrangement inspired by the works of Robert Rimmer—lived otherwise very conventional lives in a California suburb.[37] They simply tried to put into practice the belief that all adults were married to each other and the children were the responsibility of all the members. At work, they behaved like everyone else. Larry and Joan Constantine have conducted the most extensive study of these kinds of living arrangements.[38] They have discovered that, while the triad is common and more durable than most such groups, very few **multilateral marriages** lasted more than five years, and the majority less than two.

SUMMARY

If for no other reason than the simple fact that the number of males is not equal to the number of females in our society, monogamous marriage cannot be a reality for all people. Nor should it be. Yet we live in a society that either covertly or overtly measures people by whether or not they are married—despite the fact that a large portion of our population is unmarried by choice, by accident, or by fate.

In this chapter we have tried first to describe people who are unmarried for a variety of reasons. We have attempted to sketch some of the ways in which single people form partnerships distinct from marriage. In analyzing the various life styles of the different categories of single people, we have used the labels "divorced," "widowed," "single parent," and "never married" to define some of the unique problems single people face as well as some of the opportunities open to them.

A divorced person may bring to new relationships deeper insight into who he or she is along with a deeper longing for a partnership. This wisdom and knowledge may not always be pleasant, but the experience of marriage and divorce certainly offers an opportunity for reflection and growth. The widow or widower, if she or he successfully completes the period of grief work, has a tougher time than the divorced person in adjusting to a single life style because she or he generally becomes single at a later age. On the other hand, the widowed person often brings to the single life style memories of a meaningful partnership. Solo parents have some very practical limitations placed upon them regardless of their economic background, but obviously the difficulties are greater for low-income people than for the more well-to-do. Children are both a hindrance and an aid in forming new partnerships, depending on many factors in the parent-child relationship.

Today never-married individuals are living their single life style at a time when it is becoming possible to think positively about that style of life for the first time in our history. Although the seemingly hectic life style of the singles complex may not appeal to all single people, modern urban settings offer the single person a rich variety of resources to help him or her establish almost any kind of life style.

It is important that our society develop more adequate ways of responding to all types of "singles" life styles. Being single can no longer be taken to mean being a second-class citizen in a society that prides itself on recognizing individual differences and affirms the right of all men and women to develop freely in a style of life best suited to their own unique personhood.

For most Americans, communes and multiple marriage are radical alternatives to conventional life styles. Indeed, many aspects of these alternatives—particularly their styles of marriage—are illegal in most American states. Nevertheless, communes have existed in Western experience since at least the second century B.C. One of the most famous experiments in

America history, the nineteenth-century Oneida community, introduced the notions of complex marriage and mutual criticism to many individuals in the modern commune movement through the numerous books that have been published about this perfectionist community.

Multiple marriages differ from communes in that people who live in group or multilateral marriages are interested primarily in redefining marriage, but not necessarily in establishing a whole new style of life. Practitioners of multilateral marriage characteristically live in suburbia, retain professional jobs, and remain in close contact with the society surrounding them.

NOTES

1. U.S. Bureau of the Census, *Statistical Abstract of the United States: 1982–83* (Washington, D.C.: U.S. Government Printing Office, 1983).

2. Ivan F. Nye and Felix Berardo, *The Family: Its Structure and Interaction* (New York: Macmillan, 1973), p. 529.

3. Ibid., pp. 1,3,5,36

4. George Masnick and Mary Jo Bane, *The Nation's Families: 1960–1990* (Cambridge, Mass.: The Joint Center for Urban Studies of MIT and Harvard University, 1980).

5. *Statistical Abstract: 1982–83.*

6. Nye and Berardo, p. 475.

7. Paul F. Dell and Alan S. Applebaum, "Trigenerational Enmeshment: Unsolved Ties of Singles Parents to Family of Origin," *American Journal of Orthopsychiatry* (January 1977): 52–59.

8. "First Singles Church, U.S.A.," *Newsweek*, June 12, 1972.

9. Nye and Berardo, p. 520.

10. Francis E. Kubrin and Gerry E. Hendershot, "Do Family Ties Reduce Mortality? Evidence from the United States 1966–1968," *Journal of Marriage and the Family*, (November 1977): 737–44.

11. *Statistical Abstract: 1982–83*: p. 39.

12. *Statistical Abstract: 1982–83*: p. 38.

13. Stanley G. Stergis, "Understanding Grief," *Menninger Perspective*, April–May 1970.

14. Paula T. Clayton, "The Effect of Living Alone on Bereavement Symptoms," *American Journal of Psychiatry* (February 1975): 133–37.

15. Derived from *Statistical Abstracts, 1982–83*, Table 49. The comparable figures for divorced women are 28 percent and 8 percent.

16. Nye and Berardo, p. 606.

17. Robert Atchley, "Dimensions of Widowhood in Later Life," *The Gerontologist* (April 1975): 176–78, and Carol Harvey and Harold M. Bahr, "Widowhood, Morale and Affiliation," *Journal of Marriage and the Family* (February 1974): 97–106.

18. *Statistical Abstract: 1982–83*, p. 43.

19. Thomas F. Pettigrew, *Profile of the Negro American* (Princeton, N.J.: D. Van Nostrand, 1964), p. 1.

20. Nye and Berardo, *The Family.*
21. For a more detailed discussion of the role of the boyfriend, see David A. Schultz, *Coming Up Black: Patterns of Ghetto Socialization* (Englewood Cliffs, N.J.: Prentice-Hall, 1968).
22. *Statistical Abstract: 1982–83*, p. xxii.
23. Nye and Berardo, p. 5.
24. Jack Westman and David W. Koine, "Divorce Is a Family Affair," *Family Law Quarterly*, no. 5 (March 1971).
25. Computer dating, a popular fad in the 1960s, has declined in popularity, largely as a result of the many abuses associated with it. See Rosalyn Moran, "The Singles in the Seventies," in Joann Delora and Jack Delora, (eds.) *Intimate Life Styles* (Pacific Palisades, Calif.: Goodyear, 1973), p. 338.
26. Moran, p. 338.
27. Ibid., p. 341.
28. Ibid., p. 339.
29. Rustum Roy and Della Roy, "Is Monogamy Outdated?" *The Humanist*, March–April 1970. By permission.
30. William Kephart, *Extraordinary Groups* (New York: St. Martin's Press, 1980).
31. Maren Carden Lockwood, *Oneida: From Community to Corporation* (Baltimore: The Johns Hopkins University Press, 1971).
32. Raymond L. Muncey, *Sex and Marriage in Utopian Communities* (Baltimore: Pelican, 1974).
33. Richard Fairfield, *Communes U.S.A.: A Personal Tour* (Baltimore: Penguin Books, 1971).
34. Judson Jerome, *Families of Eden* (New York: Seabury Press, 1974).
35. Kathleen Kinkade, *A Walden Two Experiment: The First Five Years of Twin Oaks Community* (New York: William Morrow, 1972).
36. Jerome.
37. Fairfield, pp. 297ff.
38. Larry and Joan Constantine, "Where Is Marriage Going?" *The Futurist*, April 1970, pp. 40ff. See also Robert Rimmer, *Adventures in Loving* (New York: New American Library, 1973).

Ultimately all social change involves moral doubt and moral reassessment. If we refuse to consider change while there is still time, time will pass us by. Only by examining and taking stock of what is can we hope to affect what will be. This is our chance to invent and thus to humanize the future.

—Suzanne Keller

18 *Fantasies, Forecasts, and Trends*

Looking into the future is not something social scientists do with any degree of accuracy. Unlike astronomers who study the movement of the heavenly bodies and can reasonably expect to be able to predict their precise positions as far into the future as we might desire, or experimental scientists in laboratories who can predict in large measure because they can control the environment that influences their experimental subjects, social scientists have enjoyed little success in predicting.

Human beings have been writing about their partnerships with one another since history began, and there is an accumulated wisdom regarding the joys and hazards of human loving in the works of many writers. But there is nothing comparable to the cumulative body of observations available to astronomers or natural scientists. Our observations on human loving to date are more like anecdotes and aphorisms whose context must be sketched out fully before their truth can be appreciated, than universal laws governing human behavior. Social scientists not only have little control over the object of their investigation, they are intimately involved in the human enterprise in such a way that their own dreams and desires influence their vision of the future—even when they claim they are merely stating the facts.

Nor will the past admit to better treatment. Understanding what has been characteristic of partnerships in the past has some advantage over predicting what they may be in the future in that some evidence of these past partnerships remains for our examination. And yet history is not dead. It changes with the new insights, information, and techniques available in the ever-changing present. It is never simply the accumulated facts that concern us, but their meaning and value as well. And these things change as our attitudes change, what was once considered virtue is now considered vice.

What it means to love one another and enter into enduring and ever-changing partnerships to better express that love is not merely a reflection of historical and socioeconomic trends that place great constraints on our choice of life style, it is simultaneously an affirmation of the human spirit in freedom. Our families and partnerships are at one and the same time responses heavily contingent on the resources at hand—our money, self-esteem, friends—and an effort to realize a personal or shared vision of a better life. Where there is no vision, the people perish just as surely as where there is no bread—though it may take a bit longer for them to do so.

In this chapter we will consider the continuing controversy over the future of the family and the rights of women in the light of some new information on the past and with an eye to what the future might bring. We will look at the prospects for the more radical alternative life styles as well as suggest the changes that now seem most likely to occur. Such an approach is undertaken not because of any particular confidence in our better capacity to predict, but because of a deep need to assess where we are and where we might like to go in our partnerships. Given the information we have provided about styles of our loving in this book, we need to affirm what seems to be their benefits and acknowledge their costs. Whatever the pressures of the moment might be, we should not be, we believe, mere pawns in a predetermined process, but active agents committed to discovering what it means to love one another in an ever-changing context.

LOOKING BACKWARD

When the world is as uncertain as it is today and the guidelines for engaging in loving partnerships are often contradictory or nonexistent, it is tempting to try to reduce the uncertainty by restoring a way of life that is remembered as being better. Much of our concern about the crises of the conjugal family today is based on a "family of American nostalgia" which is assumed to have flourished not so long ago when the world was much better off that it is today. The family in which "father knew best," children were obedient and respectful of their parents, and mothers were good cooks, homemakers, and raisers of children—the family that went regularly to grandmother's house for Thanksgiving and Christmas—is an image in our collective consciousness that symbolizes domestic tranquility and the happiness of the hearth.[1]

Our need for such an image is the same need that encourages all of us to say that we have had happy childhoods while forgetting the problems and frustrations we also faced while growing up. But having an image of the ideal partnership in our minds also increases our worries about what is happening when most partnerships—particularly our own—do not seem to be that way. There have been few—if any—times in history in which people have not worried about what is happening to "the family."[2] This concern existed alongside the recognition that, in fact, there are many kinds of acceptable—if not always preferable—alternatives available in everyday life that sometimes differ dramatically from the ideal image in our minds.

From the founding of our country throughout most of the Nineteenth century, the authority of parents over their children was never

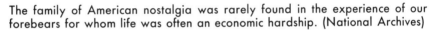

The family of American nostalgia was rarely found in the experience of our forebears for whom life was often an economic hardship. (National Archives)

absolute and was always subject to factors beyond the parent's control. The most prominent of these was the opportunity offered to the young by the American frontier.[3] Unlike their European contemporaries, they did not have to wait upon inheritance; they could (and did) leave home at an early age and homestead their own property. The American experience was liberating to the young of immigrant families in yet another way. More often than not, these children were better able to adapt to the new country than their parents. Although the frontier closed around 1895, immigrants continued to pour into the country well into the twentieth century. The Industrial Revolution also contributed to the undermining of parental—particular paternal—authority in that sons could often find work quicker and earn more than their fathers because they had more strength and energy and because the new machines did not put as much premium on skill as the old crafts and professions had. The establishment of labor unions and seniority rules reduced this trend somewhat during the middle of the twentieth century.

Women on the frontier had greater equality than women in the Eastern cities through the eighteenth and early nineteenth centuries. Their labor was as necessary to the frontier homestead and as irreplaceable as that of their husbands. It is no accident of history that they received the right to vote in Western states before the Nineteenth Amendment of 1920 granted it to all women of voting age.[4]

The 1920s was a notable period of crises for the image of what a family should be as the women who won the right to vote exercised their equal citizenship by seeking divorce more often than their spouses and by establishing their right to sexual expression.[5] The increasing divorce rate and the decreasing birthrate were often interpreted as alarm signals that something was wrong with "the family"—whereas, in fact, it could equally be said that something very right was occurring in the increased equality being granted to women and their ability to exercise greater freedom of choice in their lives. Although women began to organize to fight politically for their rights beginning with the convention in Seneca Falls, New York, in 1840, they had been active in the antislavery movement and the spiritual revivals of the Second Great Awakening before that. Indeed, it was the experience gained in the abolitionist debates and the revival meetings that developed the leadership skills so needed in seeking women's rights in the latter part of the nineteenth century.[6]

The Depression of the 1930s and the world wars took attention away from women's cause and demanded that everyone be concerned with economic and military survival. The jobs gained by women during the wars did not automatically transfer to them after the wars, but after World War II, 8 million women remained in the work force and thereby increased the economic base of the women's movement, which was to begin again in the 1960s.[7] Not too surprisingly, the government that was willing to provide day care and public assistance for working women during the war withdrew these supports afterwards. Men returning from the wars feared competition from women in the job market, and there was general concern that the family would fall apart should women continue to work outside the home.

Although kinship has always been important in American society, there is no evidence that the extended family in which kin were involved in the daily life of the conjugal family (such as in the regular caring for children) has ever been common. The bilateral kinship system characteristic of our society, in which descent is reckoned through both sides of the family, has as a consequence that the only people who share the same kindred are some siblings. The isolation of the conjugal family in our society is pronounced in comparison to its embeddedness in a kinship network or lineage as is the case in primitive societies, but its present isolation is not particularly notable in comparison to our own historic past. For the most part, kin continue to play a role in the affairs of the conjugal family today, though this role, like all other aspects of our intimate environment, is changing.

A recent study of an American community, called "Middletown" by the Lynds who first studied it in the 1920s, suggests that things have not changed as much as we have imagined.[8] Indeed, some of the findings of this study seem to contradict what is taken for granted as commonplace changes in family life:

> Tracing the changes from the 1920's to the 1970's we discovered increasing family solidarity, a smaller generation gap, closer marital communication, more religion and less mobility.[9]

The modern researchers who made this study tend to focus on marital harmony and the positive, cohesive aspects of family life under the influence of a functional model of family interaction, rather than examining the darker, more conflict-ridden aspects of family life. They conclude that in contrast to the Lynds' fears of the early 1920s, Middletown marriages were now characterized by greater communication, greater equality, and greater sexual enjoyment. In contrast to the image of family disintegration, the new research concludes that parents spent more time with their children in the 1970s than they did fifty years before. They conclude that the changes that took place in Middletown between 1890 and 1920 were far more dramatic than those that took place in the following fifty years. When we consider that the sexual revolution, the generation gap, and the women's movement all supposedly occurred during the past fifty years, this is quite a statement.

LOOKING AHEAD

Since we have stressed the fact that our intimate partnerships are not merely a function of our personal choices but are shaped by socioeconomic factors as well, we will consider briefly a few such factors that seem to have bearing on how our life styles change. We will unabashedly look forward to the year 2025, the last year for which the Bureau of the Census is willing to predict changes in our population. What will our personal life styles look like in 2025? What will our society be like then?

Projecting the Population

Figure 18.1 represents the Bureau of the Census' best bet as to what the United States population will look like in the year 2025.[10] The Bureau anticipates that our population will have grown to slightly over 301 million from a 1985 population of 238.6 million—an increase of slightly over 62 million. But the Bureau also tells us that it could possibly go as high as 356.6 million or be as low as "only" 259.7 million. The upper and lower projections flare away from the most probable projection and graphically indicate the hazards of prediction even with reasonably good data. Notice that the curves are not the same from 1982 to 1985. We estimate our current population since the cost of counting it precisely each year is prohibitive—and the accuracy gained, if any, insignificant. When it is reasonable to anticipate such a different future in the case of demographic data we have been carefully studying for decades, one can understand the uncertainties in projecting qualitative trends only poorly understood in the present.

Nevertheless, a reasonable assumption would be that there will be more people in the United States in the year 2025 than there are today—the Census Bureau is not anticipating a nuclear holocaust. Under the most probable projection, that population will be considerably older. In 2025

FIGURE 18.1 Projections of the total U.S. population, 1982-2025. (Statistical Abstract of the United States: 1982-83, p. 8.)

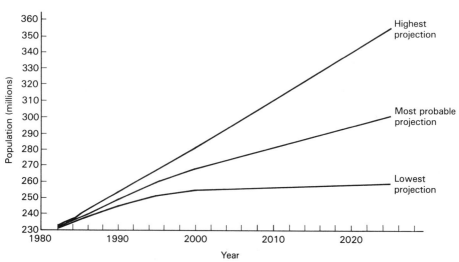

there will be 58.6 million people, or 19 percent of the total population over 65, compared to 28.7 million, or 12 percent in 1985. The proportion of the population under 18 or over 65 (who are very likely to be dependent in one way or another on wage earners between the ages of 18 and 65) will have increased to 41.5 percent from 39.4 percent in 1985. In other words, there will be fewer than two workers to support each dependent in 2025. The proportion of the population under the age of 5 years, however, will shrink from 7.74 percent in 1985 to 5.95 in 2025. The population in 2025 will have a slightly higher proportion of females (51.5 percent versus 51.3) and somewhat more blacks (15.3 percent versus 12.2).

Although it is impossible to specify much about the structure of such a society, it is probable that families and households will be smaller and the number of households in which there will be no children significantly increased, either because the couple decided not to have children in the first place, or because more couples will have passed their childbearing years and will be living without children. Overall, such a population mix would increase the likelihood of two wage-earner families and increasing divorce.

Projecting over the shorter period of time from 1975 to 1990, the Joint Center for Urban Studies discerns a number of trends.[11] In 1990, they contend, there will be:

> 20.2 million more total households
>
>   3.4 million more married couples
>
>   0.4 million without children at home
>
>   3.4 million with children at home
>
> 16.8 million more unattached individuals
>
>   7.0 million more single or previously married men living alone or with children
>
>   2.6 million more single or previously married women living alone or with children
>
>   7.2 million more single or previously married women living outside families
>
> An increase in two-worker husband-wife households from about 30 percent to 31 percent of all households.
>
> An increase in no-worker households from 25 percent to about 28 percent of all households.
>
> A decrease in one-worker households as a result of a drop of 9 percent (25 to 14 percent) in one-worker husband-wife households.
>
> An increase in other types of one-worker households from about 20 to 26 percent of all households.

Inferences about Life Styles

There are a number of trends that seem to be related to such a changing demographic picture. In the first place, the aging of the population increases the likelihood that while there will be fewer brothers and sisters and more grandparents and great-grandparents around, there is no guarantee that the generations will interact more or in significantly different ways than they do today, but they will have greater opportunity to do so. Since there will be increasing numbers of one- and two-person households in the future—if our projections hold—such intergenerational contact may help to compensate for what otherwise might be greater loneliness in interpersonal relationships. On the other hand, it may well be that such loneliness will be offset by increasing dependence on friendships of varying degrees of intimacy. In any case, it looks like more people will have living parents around until they are well into their forties. This is a dramatic change that cannot but have an effect.

A second trend seems to be toward greater percentages of two-worker families in the future. These families are likely to have more money and less time than single-worker families and will undoubtedly work out new patterns of work within the household as a result. One study found that working wives worked a total of 55 hours a week, compared to 57 hours a week for employed husbands and 45 for housewives in 1975.[12] Employed wives reduced the amount of time spent on house care (from 1965 to 1975) from 29 to 25 hours a week, but most of this reduction came as a result of their simply foregoing housework. Their husbands picked up only about 42 minutes a week of additional housework. This pattern is generally supported by other studies, although it is clear that men are becoming more involved in childcare, cooking, and housework in younger households.[13]

The Joint Center study speculates that two-worker families vary in their spending patterns and in their allocation of time to housework depending on the wife's attachment to the labor force, rather than her simple participation in it. That is to say, the more the wife works full time and the family feels it can depend upon her income—the more she becomes involved in a career—the more likely the spending patterns will reflect greater affluence and the more likely husband and wife spend equal time on housework. In relatively unattached cases, the family patterns do not differ significantly from nonworking wife households because the household cannot depend on the wife's income. Two-worker families are distinguished from other types of families in the extent to which they move within their own counties rather than around the country. Their higher income allows them to search for better housing or reduce the hassle for both to get to work, but the difficulty of finding jobs reduces their inclination to move to other parts of the country.

A third trend is toward an increase in single-parent families. Although it is true that most single mothers remarry quickly, those who do not are in most cases likely to experience a severe reduction in income and less time to devote to themselves in comparison to housewives. They also have greater mobility and, should the economy improve, may be able to improve their own standard of living. Most single-parent families move from the city rather than to it.

A fourth trend, less well established, is toward increasing cohabitation.[14] As noted in a previous chapter, however, this does not seem to be a permanent alternative to marriage, but rather a new step in approaching marriage. Nevertheless, cohabitation permits the partners more freedom to fashion the kind of partnership they personally prefer, since there are few social expectations as to what constitutes a good cohabitor as yet.

Virtually every study expects the divorce rate to continue to increase through 1990; it will probably remain high into the year 2025. Marriage, in all probability, will continue to be thought of as a personally satisfying contract that should be discontinued when it ceases to be so. The increasing equality between the genders should not only provide an economic base for women to live their own lives that has not been available to them in the past, but also familiarize both genders with the basic skills of living so that neither need be dependent on the other. Given the emphasis on personal satisfaction and the reduction in social constraints holding marriages together, increasing divorce seems inevitable. However, to the extent that the partners accept a new ethic of commitment to work out their partnerships even when the going gets tough, the rising divorce rate will not necessarily reflect quick decisions. Daniel Yankelovich, for one, believes that we are in the process of establishing such an ethic because of the general disillusionment with the notion that personal satisfaction means self-indulgence.[15] It should be remembered that we have had periods in the past when the proportion of the population that was married was lower than it is at present, but that this was because of higher death rates and later age at first marriage.

The demographic projections are not simply mathematically derived extensions of existing data. They are based on certain assumptions about how our society is going to change and what effects this change will have on our partnerships. Accordingly, we can step back a bit and look at some problems we now face. How we cope with these will affect the families of the future.

Negotiating an Energy Transition

The single most powerful factor affecting our economy at present seems to be the changing cost of energy.[16] Of all the factors that affect our life styles, the extent to which we enjoy material well-being seems to be the most significant. Life styles chosen under the conditions of poverty are not the same as those chosen under conditions of affluence, even though they may have the same structure, because if nothing else, the range of choice is greatly reduced for the impoverished.

We side with those analysts who contend that the era of cheap energy has ended and that it is questionable for the first time in American history whether or not new generations will enjoy the same standard of living as their parents.[17] In spite of current reports of an economic recovery and a world of abundance right around the corner for everyone, we believe it will be increasingly necessary for us to live with less—especially if we have any regard for the developing nations of the Third World and our own future generations. Rightly entered into, this era of relative material scarcity can produce a better way of life.

Our assessment of our current situation favors what Amory Lovins has called a "soft energy path"—a transition to renewable sources of energy, the elimination of the nuclear option, and a severe reduction in the use of fossil fuels by the year 2025.[18] The scarcity of fossil fuels, the problems of environmental pollution, the instability induced by the current "oil wars," and extreme worldwide poverty are some of the global issues we feel could be better negotiated through the use of diversified, and environmentally benign, energy technologies. However, should we decide to cope with our energy problems through a major commitment to the soft energy path, a number of social consequences are probable. Among them are these:

1. Residential patterns will become less dispersed.
2. There will be less personal choice in some areas, such as where to live and work, and less geographical mobility.
3. Industry will be more labor intensive.
4. Institutions will be more personal, and small groups will control the basic components of social life, such as food production and distribution and work environments.
5. The issue of the just distribution of social products will become more prominent, with the eventual equalization of distribution.
6. Values favoring material acquisitions will give way to values emphasizing the quality and durability of goods.
7. People's basic values will emphasize the role of humanity as part of a greater ecosystem to a greater extent as more and more of us become "ecoconscious."[19]

A number of observers believe that such an energy transition will be accompanied by an increased concern for the quality of interpersonal relationships and a deepened commitment to "inner growth."[20] Not only can inner growth compensate for—perhaps more than adequately—material well-being above a certain level of affluence, but increased sensitivity to oneself and other human beings becomes more important in a society less driven by its technology and more open to the democratic process.

There is certainly no necessity for such an ethos to become dominant as a result of an energy transition to renewable fuels, but it is quite compatible with such an approach, and to this extent it will further the search for alternatives in personal life styles and increase the opportunities for women to work outside the home. The soft energy path, should we take it, seems likely to further the trend toward accepting many kinds of partnerships as possible paths toward a better way of life.

Another scenario for the future—and one currently endorsed by the administration in Washington—draws on high technology to generate a new era of cheap energy from breeder or fusion reactors or from solar satellites.[21] The problems of pollution will be controlled, poverty throughout the world eliminated, and human beings freed from the drudgery of labor to develop space colonies and mine the asteroid fields or entertain themselves through even more elaborate gadgetry. In Gerard Oneil's version of this superindustrial model of the future, the political issues of the day would be more resolvable because of the unlimited wealth generated through extraordinarily cheap energy. After space colonies get underway, in a short time—perhaps no longer than twenty-five years—people could choose the type of community they would like to live in, from its geographic climate to its social ethos, by finding a satellite colony so constructed or building their own. Interestingly, Oneil seems to feel that homogeneous communities are generally preferable—though it would be possible to pick a heterogeneous one if desired.

In this extraordinarily optimistic view of the future, it is assumed that the good life—however defined—will be more readily available as a consequence of the abundance provided by technology. It extends our vision of progress, which we have always associated with the Industrial Revolution, well into the twenty-first century and assumes that there will be no major catastrophe in the short term, such as nuclear war or worldwide starvation (these are not assumed in the soft path model of the future either).[22]

One of the probable consequences of increasing reliance on high technology, however, is a reduction in democracy brought about by the opportunity available to a few to control the generation of energy from

After colonies get underway people could choose the type of community they would like to live in, from its geographic climate to its social ethos. (NASA.)

centralized locations and their perceived need to protect these extraordinarily expensive and technologically complex power plants from sabotage. It is perhaps possible that a worldwide abundance of energy would reduce the need to sabotage or participate in industrial espionage and that, with a larger pie, everyone would get a bigger—if not an equal—piece. Yet the potential for tyranny is great with this high tech path, especially in its more subtle form of rule by expertise. The technology necessary to generate such an abundant supply of energy is likely to be neither controlled nor understood by the people. We are just beginning to appreciate some of the implications of this today.

William Irving Thompson, cultural historian and founder of the Lindesfarne Association, contends we are exceeding the inner limits to growth because the factors that affect our everyday life are increasingly incomprehensible to us.[23] Not only are we extraordinarily dependent on one another—and in the case of energy on a very few others—for our daily needs, and greatly affected by what the powerful technology of a few does to our environment, but we are increasingly ignorant of how this technology works. Self-reliance is not rightly to be thought of today as the ability of an individual or a family to fashion its own way of life independent of others. Few are now able to do so. Rather, it is the ability of a small group or a local region to control the basic aspects of its economy and fashion the fundamental virtues of its life style. Appropriate technology is small scale and more understandable to the average person than high technology. Because it is more closely controlled by the local group, its consequences can be more readily assessed and corrected when necessary. This technology can be more adequately integrated into a meaningful symbolic world as well. At least so Thompson argues. He has been testing the idea in the Lindesfarne community near Aspen, Colorado, for the past several years. In general, high technology seems more intolerant of diversity of life styles and more inclined toward social control. The specter of 1984 hovers over this enterprise.

The Creation of an Ethos

What sets the dominant tone for an age? What "justifies" or "inspires" the behavior of a large number of people in that age? To what extent does this ethos really change the behavior of people who believe in it? Our discussion of negotiating an energy transition has begun to raise these most difficult questions in the concentration on two seemingly opposite perspectives—one that extols the virtues of a culturally homogeneous society focused around a single form of family as the only really acceptable family structure and another that advocates a culturally heterogeneous society in which many alternatives are acceptable because the character and quality of our loving is more important than the form or structure within which it is expressed, and because diversity promotes greater ecological adaptibility. This is a fundamental issue. Our sense of morality has been committed to the notion of a "one best way" through our religious and techno-economic training. The morality of multiple possibilities is not our common way of considering things.

In spite of the limitations of labels of any sort, and without implying any necessary relationships between the groups, it is interesting to notice the political alliance that seems to have significant power today and often does battle around "family issues." Those rallying around the notion of a one best way have at least the following convictions in common:

1. America is—or should be—the greatest nation on earth (economically, militarily, politically—and, with less agreement—spiritually).
2. The family is—or should be—strongest when the husband is head and is the primary (if not sole) breadwinner, and the wife and children obey him. The woman's place is clearly in the home.
3. Sexual intercourse is—or should be—for the purpose of making babies, and these babies, once conceived, have a right to life that takes precedent over the mother's right to control her own body.
4. America is threatened abroad by a godless communism that seeks to destroy her free enterprise system and subdue her people, and she is threatened at home by a godless humanism that seeks to destroy her by destroying the building block of her society—the family.

Such an ideology is commonly attributed to the "radical right"; nothing indicates that such convictions represent anything like the opinions of a moral majority. Nevertheless, such rhetoric justifies the alliance of a powerful minority that has already had considerable impact on American politics and has managed to contest much of the legislation pertaining to women's rights, family policy, and welfare rights. It is pro growth, pro high technology. It is patriarchical, and unabashedly authoritarian. In its rhetoric of a one best way, it offers answers in the face of uncertainty and remains attractive to many who have not as yet committed themselves to its cause. It would seem reasonable to expect that any number of crises could help to swell its ranks.

Although the image of the family championed by the radical right bears a number of similarities to the family of American nostalgia, it is also unlikely that such a family has ever been prominent in American life. As a vision of the good life for some it can be a helpful alternative, but as the basis for family policy it would bring great discomfort and distress to many. The issue really is choice. How much choice are we going to tolerate in the fashioning of our personal life styles in the future? Socioeconomic factors seem to be pushing us toward greater diversity of life styles. It is difficult to see how such widespread diversity could be thwarted by any ideology seeking to restrict choice, and yet is perfectly conceivable that as an ideology championed by the ruling class, it could declare all variation from its ideal unlawful and immoral. This has happened in the past, and there are ominous signs that it could happen again in the future. This would be, in our opinion, most unfortunate.

SUMMARY

The families and partnerships of the future, like those of the past, are not simply determined by sociological constraints. They are also products of human choice. There is a great deal of evidence that the family of American nostalgia will be less of a life style in the future than it has been in the past and that the trend toward greater acceptance of a wide variety of types of partnerships will continue.

Given an older population that is more dependent on the two-worker family for its standard of living, it is likely that three- and four-generational ties will supplement friendships and replace sibling relationships for increasing numbers of Americans. A smaller family and a greater commitment to the labor force by working women will increase the likelihood that the trend toward equality between women and men will continue. Increasing numbers of single-parent families, cohabiting adults on their way to marriage, and men and women who decide never to marry will continue to provide alternatives to the variation within husband-wife families. A small but continuing number of us will experiment in communal living, multilateral marriage, and other more radical departures from the family of our nostalgia.

The extent to which all this variety will be celebrated in social acceptance and supported by public policy is not determined by the simple prevalence of such diversity. We have suppressed much such diversity in the past. The ethos of the age must at least accept if not rejoice in human diversity, or find it extremely threatening. We are currently contending with these issues in the confrontation with the family politics of the radical right. We hope we have sketched enough of the benefits, as well as the costs, of other kinds of partnerships in this text so that the virtues—and vices—of any number of functional alternatives are more apparent. We can, indeed, invent the future—and we can do so more compassionately and more humanely than we have in the past.

NOTES

1. Andew Cherlin, *Marriage, Divorce, Remarriage* (Cambridge, Mass.: Harvard University Press, 1981).
2. William J. Goode, "Family Disorganization," in Robert K. Merton and Robert Nisbet (eds.), *Contemporary Social Problems* (New York: Harcourt Brace Jovanovich, 1976), pp. 511–54.
3. John Demos, "Myths and Realities in the History of American Family Life," in H. Birnbaum and J. Christ (eds.), *Contemporary Marriage: Structure, Dynamics and Therapy* (Boston: Little, Brown, 1976).
4. Carl N. Degler, *At Odds* (New York: Oxford University, Press, 1980).
5. Carl N. Degler, "What Ought To Be and What Was: Women's Sexuality in the 19th Century," *American Historical Review*, 79 (1974): 1467–90.
6. Alice Rossi (ed.), *The Feminist Papers* (New York: Bantam Books, 1973).

7. Carl N. Degler, "Revolution Without Ideology: The Changing Place of Women in America," *Daedalus*, 93 (1964).

8. Theodore Caplow, H. M. Bahr, Bruce A. Chadwick, Rubin Hill, and M. H. Williamson, *Middletown Families: Fifty Years of Change and Continuity* (St. Paul: University of Minnesota Press, 1982).

9. Ibid., p. 323.

10. U.S. Bureau of the Census, *Statistical Abstract of the United States: 1982-83* (Washington, D.C.: U.S. Government Printing Office, 1983), p. 8.

11. George Masnick and Mary Jo Bane, *The Nation's Families: 1960-1990* (Cambridge, Mass.: The Joint Center for Urban Studies of MIT and Harvard University, 1980), pp. 8,9.

12. John P. Robinson, *Changes in American's Use of Time: 1965-1975* (Cleveland: Communication Research Center, 1977), Table 4.

13. Betty Friedan, *The Second Stage* (New York: Simon and Schuster, 1981). Joseph Pleck, "Men's Family Work: Three Perspectives and Some New Data," *Family Coordinator*, 28 (1978): 481-88.

14. Masnick and Bane, p. 131.

15. Daniel Yankelovich, *New Rules: Searching For Self-Fulfillment in a World Turned Upside Down* (New York: Bantam Books, 1981).

16. An indicator of this effect is the extent to which the GNP is affected by energy prices. *Statistical Abstract: 1982-83*, p. xxiv.

17. Yankelovich, *New Rules*; E. F. Schumacher, *Small Is Beautiful* (New York: Harper & Row, 1965), and *Good Works* (New York: Harper & Row, 1979); William Irving Thompson, *Evil and World Order* (New York: Harper & Row, 1977); Theodore Roszak, *Person/Planet* (Garden City, N.Y.: Doubleday, 1978); and Amory Lovins, *Soft Energy Paths: Toward a Durable Peace* (New York: Harper & Row, 1977).

18. Lovins, p. 38.

19. Paul C. Stern and Gerald T. Gardner, "Psychological Research and Energy Policy" *American Psychologist* (April, 1981): 329-342.

20. Duane Elgin, *Voluntary Simplicity* (West Caldwell, N.J.: William Morrow, 1981).

21. Advocates of this position are Herman Kahn et al., *The Next Two Hundred Years: A Scenario for America and the World* (New York: William Morrow, 1976); Gerard Oneil, *The High Frontier* (New York: Bantam Books, 1979); Daniel Bell, *The Coming of the Post Industrial Society* (New York: Basic Books, 1976).

22. The catastrophists include Roberto Vacca, *The Coming Dark Age* (Garden City, N.Y.: Doubleday, 1979); Paul Ehrlich, *The Population Bomb* (New York: Ballentine, 1976). Robert Heilbroner, *An Inquiry Into the Human Prospect* (New York: Norton, 1977).

23. Thompson, *Evil and World Order*.

Glossary

abortion Abortion is the deliberate removal of the fetus from the womb and its destruction. This is properly called induced abortion to contrast it with spontaneous abortion, which, in some populations, occurs in as many as half of the cases of conception without outside interference.

abstinence Abstinence is the sexual code that prohbits sexual intercourse for both sexes outside of marriage. It is also obviously a means of birth control.

agape Agape is a Greek word for love used within the Christian tradition to mean the love of God for human beings. It is the altruistic love that can be commanded as in, "Thou shalt love the Lord thy God . . . and thy neighbor as thyself." We love because we were loved first by God. At minimum agape demands that everyone be treated as persons.

basic human needs Basic human needs are needs common to all human beings, which, if not met, will destroy the human being. Culture may prescribe the way in which these needs are met but not if they will be met or not.

belonging, love, acceptance needs This phrase defines the second level in Maslow's hierarchy of basic human needs. Love here is called deprivation love. We need this love in the same fashion that we need food and shelter. If we do not get enough of it we die from the lack of it, even if our other basic needs are met.

benefit Benefit in a partnership refers to the realization of something we desire, value, or need.

birth control Birth control is the general term applied to any method used to prevent the *birth* of children. Abstinence, contraception, sterilization, and abortion are common means of birth control. Infanticide, practiced among primitive peoples, is not, although it is a means of controlling population.

coalition A family interaction pattern in which two or more family members "take sides" against the remainder of the family. There may be several coalitions in a family at a particular time. Some coalitions may be short-lived, others quite persistent.

cohabitation Cohabitation is living together for an extended period of time without being married.

commitment Commitment is an acceptance of a mutual obligation to work together on the changing process of a partnership because that partnership is enriching the love between the partners and they wish it to grow.

commune A group of three or more adults who are living together and jointly attempting to redefine a life style.

companionate love A slow burning, long term love that is eventually extinguished by painful experiences.

conception Conception occurs when the sperm penetrates an egg and fuses with it. Conception normally occurs in the Fallopian tubes.

confirmation Confirmation is the capacity to "call forth" another person. It is the selective affirmation of the other's growth enhancing self-actualizing attributes.

conflict Conflict is the struggle resulting from the fact that partners are different in important ways. It is apparent in partnerships in which there are disagreements, arguments, and the sense of distance between partners.

congruence Congruence is the capacity of an individual to be aware of his or her inner feelings and accurately and appropriately communicate those feelings to others.

conjugal family The term coined by Lévi-Strauss to refer to the small family based on the marriage of a man and a woman whose primary social function is to unite different kinship groups in a socially acknowledged set of reciprocal rights and obligations.

contraception Contraception is the temporary prevention of the birth of children by use of various techniques.

cooperation Cooperation in a partnership is the agreement to work together toward growth enhancing objectives, despite acknowledged differences in other areas of the partnership.

cost Cost refers to what we have to pay in time, energy, and quality of the partnership in order to get what we desire, value, or need.

couvade The custom among some technologically primitive tribes of South America and Africa in which the husband is considered to have given birth to the child. He "lies in," complaining of his labor, while his wife delivers their child elsewhere.

date A date is a prearranged meeting to go somewhere or do something. In dating the couple is formed before the activity is experienced. The social activity of "hanging around" may provide the occasion for coupling.

dependability Dependability in a partnership occurs when the partners know in what ways their partners can be counted upon and includes the expectation that the partners will be there—open to conversation and ready to help—when needed.

developmental tasks Tasks that are thought of being crucial for a particular stage of the family life cycle. If these tasks are not adequately completed during the appropriate stage, the family's development will be slowed or conflict will occur.

disposable income Income often called "take home pay," which is available after taxes, pension plans, and other deductions are taken out.

division of labor The notion of a division of labor between the sexes acknowledges that in all societies men are commonly expected to perform different kinds of work than women. Some contend this is based on natural differences between the sexes. However what men and women are expected to do changes from one society to another, indicating strong cultural influences.

double standard The double standard is the sexual code in which it is OK for a man to experience sexual intercourse outside of marriage but not for a woman.

egalitarian marriage Egalitarian marriage is a marriage in which husband and wife have equal power and authority.

empty nest The stage in the family life cycle in which all of the children have left home and the parents are confronted with the task of readjusting their lives accordingly.

empty shell A partnership devoid of zest and vitality that has become largely meaningless to the partners yet persists because of inertia or because no other options are seen.

endogamy Endogamy is the norm or practice of marrying persons within one's own group, i.e., whites marry whites or Jews marry Jews more often than not.

eros Eros is the Greek word for the kind of love that is based on a strong affection for the particular characteristics thought to be possessed by the beloved. As a love style Lee suggests that the erotic lover's desire to jump into bed is a desire to determine by carnal knowledge if the beloved is as he/she seems.

erotophiles Erotophiles are persons who give evidence of their love for the erotic by their positive response to erotic materials.

erotophobes Erotophobes are persons who give evidence of their fear of the erotic by their negative response to erotic materials.

exogamy Exogamy refers to the norm or practice of marrying persons outside of one's own group—i.e., not marrying one's brother, sister, or first cousin.

feedback Feedback is the general term applied to the signals given off by our environment (personal or impersonal) in response to our behavior.

feedback, convergent Convergent feedback is information from our environment that our behavior is appropriate to our objectives.

feedback, divergent Divergent feedback is information from our environment that our behavior is not bringing us a result we desire.

fixed expenses Expenses, such as car payments, school tuition, and taxes that cannot easily be changed during a budget period.

flexible expenses Expenses over which you have some degree of control during a budget period, such as food, clothing, and entertainment.

friendship (philias) The love that is characterized by a shared set of values. Friends can be thought of as sitting side by side sharing a common view of the world.

generation gap A popular term to describe what seems to be basic value differences between parents and their children. These basic differences are more apparent between age groups—or generations—than between parents and their own children, and the generalization does not seem to be as useful as it was in the 1960s.

genitor Genitor is the term used by anthropologists to designate the biological father, who is sometimes distinct from the social father.

group marriage Group marriage is a rare form of marriage in which two or more men are married to two or more women and the children of any union are considered equally legitimate.

homogamy A homogamous mate choice was originally one in which the mate was similar to ego in terms of psychological characteristics. The definition has been expanded to include socioeconomic characteristics.

homologous organs Homologous organs are organs that have differentiated from the same basic tissues in the course of embryonic development.

infertility Infertility refers to the reduced ability to have children. It can be corrected by various techniques.

intimacy Intimacy is the characteristic of a partnership in which the partners can be open in revealing their feelings to each other and thereby feel close to one another.

labor Labor is the period of time during which the child is born. It begins with the *regular* contractions of the uterus and ends with the birth of the child.

leveling Leveling is the capacity to express any persistent feeling about a partnership to one's partner.

life style A standard of living achieved because of a particular command over resources given to an individual as a member of a particular socioeconomic class.

love The experience of love is fundamentally the awareness of being acceptable, worthy, and valuable as a person. At the level of relationship it is a feeling of being in touch with the rest of the universe. Harmony.

monogamous marriage   Monogamy means simply marriage between one woman and one man. Traditional expectations have added that such a union ought to be for life and include exclusive sexual rights with the spouse, common residence, economic independence from kin, children, and an understanding that he is the provider and she is the housewife. Many of these expectations are being abandoned.

multilateral marriage   A form of group marriage that is egalitarian—not based on either male or female dominance.

multiple marriage   A group of three or more adults who are living together and who consider themselves married to each other.

nuclear family   The nuclear family is the term George Peter Murdock gave to what he considered to be the basic unit of social structure. It is composed of a woman, her husband, and their children living together in common residence. In our middle-class model he works, she is a housewife and mother. They have an exclusive sexual relation in a lifelong, monogamous union.

open marriage   Open marriage is the term coined by George and Nena O'Neill to refer to a monogamous marriage in which the partners are encouraged to develop friendships of either sex outside of their marriage. Those relationships need not include sexual intercourse in order to be intimate. It is not necessary for such couples to maintain the couple-front, doing everything together.

partnership   Any human relationship in which there is a shared understanding of what is at stake.

passionate love   An intensely felt normally short term love that can be ignited by painful as well as pleasurable experience.

pater   Pater is the term anthropologists use to designate the social father, who is sometimes not the biological father.

patriarchy   Patriarchy is a social arrangement in which the father and his family are dominant over the wife and hers. Descent, succession, and inheritance commonly are traced through the father's line. In the household he is the chief authority.

permissiveness-with-affection   Permissiveness-with-affection is the sexual code in which it is OK to experience sexual intercourse outside marriage as long as the couple has a loving relationship.

polyandry   Polyandry is the form of marriage in which a woman has two or more husbands.

polygyny   Polygyny is the form of marriage in which the man has two or more wives.

postpartum   The period of recovery after childbirth during which the mother's body readjusts to life without the fetus in the womb.

psychosexual differentiation   The process by which we become male, female, or mixed.

power   The ability to impose one's will on another in spite of the other's opposition.

risk   Risk is involved in any growing partnership because the relationship between costs and benefits is not always clearly discernible.

scapegoating   A pathological pattern of family interaction in which the parents take the hostility they feel for each other and direct it toward one of their children because they cannot level with each other. The child becomes the scapegoat and is emotionally excluded from the family circle.

self-actualization   The process of growth beyond meeting deprivation needs in which a person begins to fully realize his or her unique potential.

self-disclosure   The process of revealing oneself to another person. A loving partnership is one in which each person feels free to "be themselves."

self-respect and self-esteem   Self-respect and self-esteem define the third level of Maslow's hierarchy of needs. A person can achieve a sense of being a unique individual only after he has been sufficiently accepted by a community.

separateness and togetherness Separateness and togetherness define the poles of the understanding in a partnership of how much of the activities are to be shared with the partner and how much are to be enjoyed alone.

sex roles Sex roles are the shared cultural expectations of what it means to be a woman or a man. Each culture has a somewhat different understanding of masculinity and femininity. The more precise term is gender role.

sex-role stereotypes Sex-role stereotypes are conventional definitions of what it means to be masculine or feminine; they are held onto in spite of evidence that women or men are not necessarily like that. The more precise term is gender role stereotype.

sexually transmitted disease Sexually transmitted disease refers to a number of diseases commonly transmitted through the contact of mucous membranes of the mouth, anus, and genitals during sexual contact. The most well-known of these are syphilis and gonorrhea; current problems include herpes and AIDS.

sterility Sterility is the permanent inability to have a child.

sterilization Sterilization is the normally permanent prevention of conception by various surgical techniques. Vasectomy in the male and tubal ligation in the female are two common procedures.

storge Storge is the Greek word for the basic kind of love we commonly call "affection." It is the basic relational love upon which all partnerships depend.

trial marriage Trial marriage, or "marriage in two stages," is a proposal to encourage couples to initially contract marriage with the intention of getting to know each other well *before* they decide to have children—a second contract. The first stage can be more easily terminated because no children are involved. Couples can also decide to remain childless. A decision to have children would require a more legally, morally, and socially binding contract.

trimester The period of pregnancy, commonly about nine months, is divided into three periods of about three months each called "trimesters."

violence Violence in a partnership is conflict that has gotten out of control. It is most commonly expressed as physical abuse, but can be any behavior that denies the partner the status of person.

vital partnership A vital partnership is one that is intrinsically rewarding and satisfying to the partners.

voluntary simplicity Voluntary simplicity is a term coined by Stanford Research Institute to describe a growing alternative to conspicuous consumption. Values, personal growth, and material sufficiency are stressed, not material abundance.

win-lose conflict Win-lose or "zero sum" conflict is conflict in which it is possible for one person to win only at the cost of another's loss. It is a very destructive conflict in intimate partnerships although common in the business world.

Selected
Bibliography

1 INTRODUCTION

Berger, Peter and **Hansfried Kellner**. "Marriage as a Socially Constructed Reality." in Ruth Coser (ed.). *The Function of the Family* 2nd ed. New York: St Martin's, 1981.

Hatfield, Elain and **G. William Walser**. *A New Look at Love*. Reading, Mass.: Addison Wesley, 1981.

Lasch, Christopher. *The Culture of Narcissism*. New York: Norton, 1979.

Lee, John Alan. *The Colors of Love*. Don Mills, Ontario: New Press, 1976.

Maslow, Abraham. *Toward a Psychology of Being*. 2nd. ed. New York: Van Nostrand Reinhold, 1968.

May, Rollo. *Love and Will*. New York: Dell, 1968.

Ramey, James. "Alternative Life Styles," *Society* (July/August, 1977).

2 ON PARTNERSHIPS

Fromm, Eric. *The Art of Loving*. New York: Bantam, 1970.

Maslow, Abraham. *Motivation and Personality*. New York: Harper and Row, 1970.

Laing, R. D. *The Politics of Experience*. New York: Ballentine, 1978.

Ornstein, Robert. *The Psychology of Consciousness* 2nd. ed. New York: Harcourt Brace Jovanovich, 1977.

Rimmer, Robert. *Adventures in Loving*. New York: New American Library, 1973.

Rodgers, Carl. *Becoming Partners*. New York: Delacorte Press, 1972.

Yankelovich, Daniel. *New Rules: Searching for Self Fulfillment in a World Turned Upside Down*. New York: Bantam, 1982.

3 CONFIRMATION AND COMMUNICATION

Boyd, Lenore Anglin and **Arthur J. Roach**. "Interpersonal Communication Skills Differentiating More Satisfying from Less Satisfying Marital Relationships," *Journal of Counseloring Psychology*, 24 (1977).

Buber, Martin. *To Hallow This Life*. New York: Harper and Row, 1951.

_____. *Between Man and Man*. Boston: Beacon Press, 1955.

_____. *I and Thou*. New Haven, Conn.: Yale University Press, 1956.

Campbell, Joseph. *Myths to Live By*. New York: Bantam, 1982.

Matteson, Roberta. "Adolescent Self Esteem, Family Communication, and Marital Satisfaction," *Journal of Psychology*, 86 (1974).

Peletier, Kenneth. *Toward a Science of Consciousness*. New York: Delta, 1978.

4 CONFLICT IN INTIMATE PARTNERSHIPS

Bach, George R. and Peter Wyden. *The Intimate Enemy: How to Fight Fair in Love and Marriage*. New York: William Morrow & Co., 1968.

Hary, Joseph. "Evolving Sources of Happiness for Men Over the Life Cycle," *Journal of Marriage and the Family* (May 1978).

Hillman, James. *The Myth of Analysis*. New York: Harper and Row, 1972.

Jorgensen, Stephen R. "Social Class Heterogamy, Status Striving and Perception of Marital Conflict," *Journal of Marriage and the Family* (Nov. 1977).

Miller, Sherod, Elam Nonnally, and Daniel B. Wackman. *Talking Together*. Minneapolis: Interpersonal Communication Program, 1979.

Steinmetz, Suzanne K. and Murray A. Strauss. *Violence in the Family*. New York: Dodd, Mead & Co., 1974.

Strauss, Murray. "Leveling, Civility and Violence in the Family," *Journal of Marriage and the Family* (Feb. 1974).

Tillich, Paul. *Love, Power and Justice*. New York: Oxford University Press, 1954.

5 DATING, HANGING OUT, AND HANGING AROUND

Bower, Donald W. and Victor A. Christopherson. "University Student Cohabitation: A Regional Comparison of Selected Attitudes and Behaviors," *Journal of Marriage and the Family* (Aug. 1977).

Bell, Robert R. and K. Coughey. "Premarital Sex Experience Among College Females, 1958, 1968, 1978," *Family Relations* 29 (July 1980): 155–357.

Caplow, Theodore et. al. *Middletown Families: Fifty Years of Change and Continuity*. St. Paul: University of Minnesota Press, 1982.

Clayton, Richard and Harwin L. Voss. "Shacking Up: Cohabitation in the 1970's," *Journal of Marriage and the Family* (May 1977).

Hill, Charles T., Zech Restum, and Letitia Anne Peplau." Breakups Before Marriage: The End of 103 Affairs," *Journal of Social Issues*, 32(1976).

Jurick, Arthur P. and Julie A. Jurick. "The Effects of Cognitive Moral Development Upon the Selection of Premarital Sexual Standards," *Journal of Marriage and the Family* (Nov. 1974).

Kirkendahl, Lester and Rodger W. Libby. "Interpersonal Relationships: Crux of the Sexual Revolution," *Journal of Social Issues* (April 1966).

Murstein, Bernard. "Stimulus-Value-Role: A Theory of Marital Choice," *Journal of Marriage and the Family*, 32(1970).

Trost, Jan. "Attitudes Toward and Occurance of Cohabitation Without Marriage," *Journal of Marriage and the Family* (May 1978).

6 ON THE NATURE AND EXPERIENCE OF LOVE

Hatfield, Elaine and **G. William Walser**. *A New Look at Love*. Reading, Mass.: Addison Wesley, 1981.

Hillman, James. *The Myth of Analysis*. New York: Harper and Row, 1970.

Kapleau, Phillip. *Three Pillars of Zen*. Boston: Beacon Press, 1965.

Lodge, David. How Far Can You Go? London: Penguin, 1982.

Tillich, Paul. *Love, Power and Justice*. New York: Oxford, 1954.

7 THE BIOLOGY OF SEX AND REPRODUCTION

Boston Women's Book Collective. *Our Bodies, Ourselves* 2nd. ed. New York: Simon & Schuster, 1978.

Ford, Clellan and **Frank H. Beach**. *Patterns of Sexual Behavior*. New York: Harper and Row, 1970.

Francouer, Robert. *Becoming a Sexual Person*. New York: Wiley, 1982.

Kaplan, Helen. *Disorders of Sexual Desire and Other Concepts and Techniques in Sex Therapy*. New York: Bruner Mazel, 1979.

Masters, William H. and **Virginia Johnson**. *Human Sexual Response*. Boston: Little Brown, 1966.

_____. *Human Sexual Inadequacy*. Boston: Little Brown, 1970.

_____. *The Pleasure Bond*. Boston: Little Brown, 1974.

Nass, Gilbert, Rodger Libby, and **Mary Pat Fisher**. *Sexual Choices*. Monterey, California: Wadsworth, 1981.

Schulz, David. *Human Sexuality* 2nd. ed. Englewood Cliffs, N.J.: Prentice-Hall Inc., 1984.

8 CONTRACEPTION AND ABORTION

Bawman, Karl E. *et. al.* "Legal Abortions and Trends in Age Specific Marriage Rates," *American Journal of Public Health* (Jan. 1977).

Center for Disease Control, Sexually Transmitted Diseases: Fact Sheet, ed. 34. Washington, D.C.: U.S.G.P.O., 1978.

_____. Sexually Transmitted Diseases: Abstract and Bibliography, 1979, Washington, D.C.: U.S.G.P.O., 1979.

Cherniak, Donna and **Allen Feingold**. *The Birth Control Handbook*. Montreal: Montreal Health Press Inc., 1975.

Guttmacher Institute. *Teenage Pregnancy: The Problem that Hasn't Gone Away*. New York: The Alan Guttmacher Institute, 1981.

Hatcher, Robert. *Contraceptive Technology, 1978–1979*, 9th ed. New York: Irvington Publications, Inc., 1978.

Reiss, Ira L. et al. "Premarital Contraceptive Usage: A Study and Some Theoretical Exploration," *Journal of Marriage and The Family* (Aug. 1975.)

Scanzoni, John. "Sex Roles Change and Influences on Birth Intentions," *Journal of Marriage and the Family* (Feb. 1978).

Thompson, Linda and **Graham Spanier**. "Influence of Parent, Peer and Partner on the Contraceptive Use of College Men and Women," *Journal of Marriage and the Family* (Feb. 1976).

Westcoff, Charles and **Norman B. Ryder**. *The Contraceptive Revolution*. Princeton, N.J.: Princeton University Press, 1977.

9   THE ART OF LOVEMAKING

Coult, Allen. "Yoga, Love and Orgasm," in *Modern Man in Search of Utopia*. San Fransicso: Alternatives Foundation, 1977.

Comfort, Alex. *More Joy*. New York: Crown, 1972.

_____. *A Good Age*. New York: Simon and Schuster, 1976.

Downing, George. *The Massage Book*. New York: Random House, Inc., 1972.

Hamilton, Eleanor. *Sex With Love*. Boston: Beacon Press, 1978.

Hariton, Barbara. "The Sexual Fantasies of Women," *Psychology Today* (Oct. 1977).

Masters, William H. and **Virginia E. Johnson**. *Human Sexual Inadequacy*. Boston: Little Brown, 1971.

Nefzawi, Shaykh. *The Perfumed Garden*. Suffolk: St. Edmondsbury Press, 1982.

Prescott, James W. "Body Pleasures and the Origins of Violence," *Bulletin of Atomic Scientists* (Nov. 1975).

Raley, Patricia E. *Making Love*. New York: The Dial Press, 1976.

10   GENDER ROLES AND SOCIAL INTERACTION

Constantinople, Anne. "Masculinity Feminity," *Psychological Bulletin* (Nov. 1973).

Fasteau, Marc Feigen. *The Male Machine*. New York: Delta Books, 1974.

Forisha, Barbara Lusk. *Sex Roles and Personal Awareness*. Morristown, N.J.: General Learning Press, 1978.

Green, Richard. *Sexual Identity Conflict in Children and Adults*. Baltimore: Pelican Books, 1974.

Hochchild, Arlee. "A Review of Sex Role Research," *American Journal of Sociology* (Jan. 1975.)

Maccoby, Eleanor. *Social Development*. New York: Harcourt Brace Jovanovich, 1980.

_____, and Carolyn Nagley Jacklin. *The Psychology of Sex Differences*. Stanford, Cal.: Stanford University Press, 1974.

Mead, Margaret. *Sex and Temperment*. New York: Mentor Books, 1952.

_____. *Male and Female*. New York: Mentor Books, 1955.

Money, John. *Love and Lovesickness: The Science of Sex, Gender Differences and Pair Bonding*. Baltimore: The Johns Hopkins University Press, 1980.

Sherfy, Mary Jane. *The Nature and Evolution of Female Sexuality*. New York: Random House, 1973.

Watts, Alan. *Nature, Man and Woman*. New York: Pantheon, 1969.

11 MARRIAGE IN HISTORICAL
AND CULTURAL PERSPECTIVE

Blanchard, Paul. "Christianity and Sex: An Indictment of Orthodox Theology," *The Humanist* (March/April 1974).

Berger, Brigitte and **Peter Berger**. *The War Over the Family*. London: Hutchinson, 1983.

Degler, Carl N. *At Odds*. New York: Oxford, 1980.

de Rougement, Dennis. *Love in the Western World*. New York: Harper, 1956.

Foucault, Michael. *The History of Sexuality*. Vol. 1. New York: Vintage Books, 1980.

Hunt, Morton. *The Natural History of Love*. New York: Alfred A. Knopf, 1957.

Lodge, David. *How Far Can You Go?* London: Penguin, 1980.

Stephens, William N., ed. *Reflections on Marriage*. New York: Thomas Y. Cowell Company, 1968.

Marcus, Stephen. *The Other Victorians*. New York: Basic Books, 1956.

Wynn, John Charles, ed. *Sexual Ethics and Christian Responsibility*. New York: Association Press, 1970.

Young, Wayland. *Eros Denied*. New York: Groves, 1964.

12 HUSBANDS AND WIVES

Allen, Gina and **Martin G. Clement**. *Intimacy: Sensitivity, Sex and Art of Love*. Chicago: Cowles Book Co., 1971.

Burke, Ronald J. and **Tamara Weir**. "Relationship of Wife Employment Status to Husband, Wife and Peer Satisfaction and Performance," *Journal of Marriage and the Family* (May 1976).

Hudis, Paula M. "Commitment to Work and to Family: Marital-Status Differences in Women's Earnings," *Journal of Marriage and the Family* (May, 1976).

Lopata, Helen Z. *Occupation Housewife*. New York: Oxford University Press, 1971.

Mazur, Ronald. *The New Intimacy: Open Ended Marriage and Alternative Life Styles*. Boston: Beacon Press, 1973.

Nilson, Linda. "The Social Standing of a Housewife," *Journal of Marriage and the Family* (August 1978).

Oneil, Nena. *The Marriage Premise*. New York: Evans, 1977.

13 PARENTS AND CHILDREN

Blood, Linda and **Rocco D. Angelo**. "A Progress Research Report on Value Issues in Conflict Between Runaways and their Parents," *Journal of Marriage and the Family* (August 1974).

Bronfenbrenner, Urie. *The Ecology of Human Development*. Cambridge, Mass.: Harvard University Press, 1980.

Cochrane, Susan and **Frank D. Bean**. "Husband-Wife Differences in the Demand for Children," *Journal of Marriage and the Family* (May 1976).

Gove, Walter and **Michael L. Geerken**. "The Effect of Children and Employment on the Mental Health of Married Men and Women," *Social Forces* (September 1977).

Hobbs, Daniel and **Jane Maynard Wimbech**. "Transition to Parenthood by Black Couples," *Journal of Marriage and the Family* (November 1977).

Humphrey, Michael. "Sex Differences in Attitudes to Parenthood," *Human Relations* (Nov. 1977).

Magolin, Gayla and **Gerald R. Patterson**. "Differentiated Consequences Provided by Mothers and Fathers for their Sons and Daughters," *Developmental Psychology* (July 1975).

Veevers, J. E. "The Social Meaning of Parenthood," *Psychiatry* (Aug. 1973).

Werner, Paul et al. "Having a Third Child: Predicting Behavioral Intentions," *Journal of Marriage and the Family* (May 1975).

14 THE DEVELOPING FAMILY

Gillespie, D. L. "Who Has the Power? The Marital Struggle," *Journal of Marriage and the Family*, 33 (Aug. 1971): 445–458.

Glenn, Norval. "The Contribution of Marriage to the Psychological Well-Being of Males and Females," *Journal of Marriage and the Family* (Feb. 1977).

Harking, Elizabeth Bates. "Effects of Empty Nest Transition on Self-Report of Psychological and Physical Well-Being," *Journal of Marriage and the Family* (Aug. 1978).

Harry, Joseph. "Evolving Sources of Happiness for Men Over the Life Cycle: A Structural Analysis," *Journal of Marriage and The Family* (May 1976).

Miller, Brent C. "A Multivariate Developmental Model of Marital Satisfaction," *Journal of Marriage and the Family* (Nov. 1976).

Nock, Stephen L. "The Family Life Cycle: Empirical or Conceptual Tool?" *Journal of Marriage and the Family* (Feb. 1979).

Rice, Philip F. *Contemporary Marriage*. Newton Mass.: Allyn & Bacon, 1983.

Rollins, Boyd C., and **Stephen J. Buhr**. "A Theory of Power Relationships in Marriage," *Journal of Marriage and the Family* (Nov. 1976).

_____, and **Kenneth L. Cannon**. "Marital Satisfaction Over the Life Cycle: A Reevaluation," *Journal of Marriage and the Family* (May 1974).

Scanzoni J. and **K. Polonko**, "A Conceptual Approach to Explicit Marital Negotiations," *Journal of Marriage and the Family* (Feb. 1980): 31–44.

15 FAMILY MONEY MANAGEMENT

Elgin, Duane. *Voluntary Simplicity*. W. Caldwell, N.J.: Morrow, 1981.

Hawkin, Paul. "I Don't Buy it: Commentaries on Prosperity Consciousness," *New Age* (January 1979).

Olson, Mancur and **Hans H. Landsberg** (eds.) *The No Growth Society*. New York: W.W. Norton, 1973.

Porter, Sylvia. *Sylvia Porter's Money Book*. New York: Avon, 1975.

16 DISORGANIZATION AND DIVORCE

Bane, Mary Jo. "Marital Disruption and the Lives of Children," *Journal of Social Issues* (Jan. 1975).

Beck, Dorothy Fahs. "Research Findings on the Outcome of Marital Counseloring," *Social Casework* (March 1975).

Burke, Ronald J. *et al.* "Husband-Wife Compatibility and the Management of Stress," *Journal of Social Psychology*, 94(1974).

Bohanan, Paul, *Divorce and After*. Garden City, N.Y.: Doubleday and Company, Inc., 1970.

Gersten, Joanne C. et al. "Life and Job Satisfaction," *American Journal of Epidemiology* (Jan. 1977).

Gunter, B. G. and **Boyle D. Johnson**. "Divorce Filing as Role Behavior: Effects of No-Fault Law on Divorce Filing Patterns," *Journal of Marriage and the Family* (Aug. 1978).

Pearlin, Leonard I. and **Joyce S. Johnson**. "Marital Status, Life Strain and Depression," *American Sociological Review* (Oct. 1977).

Wright, Gerald. "The Impact of No-Fault Divorce Law Reform on Divorce in American States," *Journal of Marriage and the Family* (Aug. 1978).

17 ALTERNATIVE LIFE STYLES

Bould, Sally. "Female-Headed Families: Personal Fate Control and the Provider Role," *Journal of Marriage and the Family* (May 1977).

Gerson, Menachem. *Family, Women and Socialization in the Kibbutz*. Lexington, Mass.: Heath, Lexington Books, 1978.

Glenn, Norval D. and **Charles N. Weaver**. "The Marital Happiness of Remarried Divorced Persons," *Journal of Marriage and the Family* (May 1977).

Jaffe, Dennis J. and **Rosabeth M. Kante**. "Couple Strain in Communal Households: A Four Factor Model of the Separation Process," *Journal of Social Issues* (Jan. 1976).

Jerome, Judson. *Families of Eden*. New York: Seabury Press, 1974.

Kephart, William M. *Extraordinary Groups: The Sociology of Uncoventional Life Styles*, 2nd. ed. New York: St. Martins Press, 1980.

Masnick, George and **Mary Jo Bane**. *The Nation's Families: 1960–1990*. Cambridge: The Joint Center, 1980.

Muncey, Raymond Lee. *Sex and Marriage in Utopina Communities*. Baltimore: Pelican Books, 1974.

Rimmer, Robert H. (ed.). *Adventures in Loving*. New York: New American Library, 1973.

Strong, Leslie D. "Alternative Marital and Family Forms," *Journal of Marriage and The Family* (Aug. 1978).

18 FANTASIES, FORECASTS, AND TRENDS

Blytheway, Bill. "Problems of Representativeness in 'The Three Family Study'," *Journal of Marriage and the Family* (May 1977).

Caplow, Theodore, et al. *Middletown Families.* St. Paul: University of Minnesota Press, 1982.

Forisha, Barbara Lusk. *Sex Roles and Personal Awareness.* Morristown, N.J.: General Learning Press, 1978.

Henderson, Hazel. *Creating Alternative Futures.* New York: Berkeley Publications, 1978.

Keller, Suzanne. "Does the Family Have a Future?" *Journal of Comparative Family Studies* (Spring 1971).

Lovins, Amory. *Soft Energy Paths.* New York: Harper & Row, 1977.

Oneil, Gerard K. *The High Frontier.* New York: Bantam, 1977.

Ramey, James, "Alternative Life Styles," *Society* (July/August, 1978).

Rimmer, Robert. *Love Me Tomorrow.* New York: New American Library, 1978.

Index

Psychosexual differentiation, 206–208
Pollution, 324

R

Radical right, 390, 391
Reinstein, Max, 355
Remarriage rates, 348
Resolution phase
    in female, 152
    in male, 149
Retirement, 311, 312, 334, 335
Rhythm, 174 (*See also* Contraception)
Risk, 36
Rogers, Carl, 18, 31, 44, 50, 59, 85, 264
Role
    discontinuity of conditioning, 67
    flexibility, 267–72
    lovemaking, 202
    mate selection, 107
    segregation of, 258 (*See also* Division of Labor;
        Gender role)
Routine, 308
Roy, Della, 221
Roy, Rustum, 221
Rubin's test, 164
Rumi, 250, 251

S

St. Augustine, 28, 227, 228, 247
St. Paul, 2, 4, 224, 225, 226
St. Thomas Acquinas, 228, 247
Scapegoating, 288
Scoring, 99
Second Great Awakening, 382
Self actualization, 5, 6, 20, 33, 45, 69
    criticism of, 11
    description of, 26–30
    in families, 287
Self awareness, 310
Self disclosure, 34
    engagement and, 103
    eros and, 132
    love and, 4, 5
    passionate love and, 127
Self image, 196
Self knowledge, 46
Self reliance, 389
Self worth, 319–21
Seneca Falls convention, 382
Separateness and togetherness, 33, 260, 263

Sex
    behavior, 96
    childbirth and, 162
    codes, 95, 96
    exclusive rights to in marriage, 254
    love and, 118, 129, 132
    touch and, 53, 54
    trouble and, 75–77
Sexual response
    figure, 153
    in female, 150–54
    in male, 147–50
    of older people, 154, 155
Sexually transmitted disease (STD), 184, 185
Shakespeare, William, 122, 211
Single-parent family, 367–70, 386
Singles lifestyle, 360
    housing and, 371
    never married, 371, 372
Skills, 58
Skinner, B. F., 374
Social sciences
    interpreting the past, 380
    natural sciences, 380
    prediction, 379, 380
Socrates, 116
Spermicides, 173
Spock, Benjamin, 276
Stereotypes, 312
Sterility, 163, 224
Sterilization, 180, 181
Storge (affection)
    defined, 6
    storgic lovestyle, 76, 129, 130
Storytelling, 14, 49
Surrogate mothers, 165
Swazi, 277
Symbols
    concepts and, 14
    language and, 50
    myths and, 12

T

Tchambuli, 217
Thomas, Dylan, 210
Thompson, William Irving, 389, 390
Tillich, Paul, 68, 69
Touch, 96
Tracer Company, 79
Trouble spots, 24–80
Tubal ligation, 180
Twain, Mark, 192

U

Udry, Richard, 220, 215
Uncertainty, 380
United States Bureau of the Census, 384

V

Value, 318–20
Van Eyck, Jan, 223
Veevers, J.E., 281
Victorian, gender roles, 232
Violence, 64
Vitality, 32
Voluntary simplicity, 321, 322
Von Hoffman, Nicholas, 342

W

Wages, 325
Wealthy, 329

Weddings, 305
White, Charles B., 154
Widow, 365–67
    friends, 366
    income, 367
    grief work, 366
Win-loose battles, 82
Withdrawal, 174
Working women, 244, 302, 303
Wyden, Peter, 84

Y

Yankelovich, Daniel, 246

Z

Zen, 122, 123, 218